BUILDING DEMOCRACY IN LATIN AMERICA

SECOND EDITION

BUILDING DEMOCRACY IN LATIN AMERICA

JOHN PEELER

LYNNE
RIENNER
PUBLISHERS

BOULDER
LONDON

Published in the United States of America in 2004 by
Lynne Rienner Publishers, Inc.
1800 30th Street, Boulder, Colorado 80301
www.rienner.com

and in the United Kingdom by
Lynne Rienner Publishers, Inc.
3 Henrietta Street, Covent Garden, London WC2E 8LU

Library of Congress Cataloging-in-Publication Data
Peeler, John A.
  Building democracy in Latin America / John Peeler.—2nd ed.
    p. cm.
  Includes bibliographical references (p.) and index.
  ISBN 1-58826-201-4 (pbk. : alk. paper)
  1. Democracy—Latin America.   2. Latin America—Politics and
government—20th century.   I. Title.
  JL966.P44 2004
  320.98—dc22

                          2004001838

British Cataloguing in Publication Data
A Cataloguing in Publication record for this book
is available from the British Library.

Printed and bound in the United States of America

The paper used in this publication meets the requirements
of the American National Standard for Permanence of
Paper for Printed Library Materials Z39.48-1992.

5 4 3 2 1

Contents

Illustrations

Preface

This is a book about the struggle to create a humane and democratic political order in a region, Latin America, where such a task has more often than not seemed impossible.[1] Yet, the last quarter of the twentieth century witnessed substantial movement toward that goal in virtually every country of the region. The thrust of my argument is that liberal democracy is both feasible and desirable in Latin America. It is feasible because the Latin American tradition includes ways of thinking and acting (e.g., elite settlements) that are adaptable to liberal democracy. Liberal democracy is desirable in Latin America because it works to protect individual freedom and to restrict the concentration of power.

This new edition of the book differs substantially from the first edition in content, organization, and tone. The first edition was organized historically and topically. This edition is organized analytically around three core chapters—on establishing, stabilizing, and destabilizing democratic regimes. And I develop more systematically here the argument that liberal democracy may not be able to survive in Latin America under conditions of globalization, unless democracy is substantially deepened within the region, and unless steps are taken to impose governance in the human interest on the global capitalist system.

The genealogy of the concept of democracy is explored in Chapter 1 of the book. Here, I simply note that although the term *democracy* literally means "rule by the people," it has come to be synonymous with "liberal democracy," an increasingly widespread type of polity. A liberal democracy is *democratic* insofar as it involves government by popular, competitive election, thereby providing democratic legitimation to the polity. But the people do not rule directly outside these periodic elections. A liberal democracy is *liberal* in that it limits governmental authority and protects individual rights, constructing dikes, as it were, against the supposedly sovereign people. Liberal democracy is the best and most durable system yet invented for protecting individuals against government oppression, but it is not fully democratic. A key issue is whether it is possible to move toward a more democratic polity without losing the benefits of liberal democracy.

What do I mean by "possible"? It can mean being consistent with prior and predetermining conditions. Some scholars argue that the history and culture of Latin America are such that democracy could never thrive there. Chapter 2 addresses this issue and concludes that democracy can indeed find indigenous roots in Latin America. Others argue that democracy requires a particular class structure, without which it will be fragile at best. Dietrich Rueschemeyer, Evelyne Huber Stephens, and John Stephens (1992) have developed such a structural argument with notable sophistication and meticulous research. Structures in general and class structure in particular clearly matter a great deal in determining what is possible. The cases examined here suggest that structures limit possibilities, but they do not determine outcomes.

Much research on regime transitions has emphasized the importance of statecraft, that is, purposeful action by political leaders to shape outcomes. Guillermo O'Donnell and Philippe Schmitter (1986), for example, in their *Tentative Conclusions About Uncertain Democracies,* sum up many cases in their multivolume study by emphasizing the indeterminacy of transitions from authoritarian rule. Outcomes are not determined by structures; they depend on the interaction of decisionmakers. This book tends to support this perspective, but it does not negate the importance of structure.

I propose that we consider structure and human action as mutually constituting each other. Any social structure, such as an economic system or a religion, sets boundaries on what any given individual can do without incurring costs (e.g., some would say that poverty results from refusal to do remunerative work under capitalism, or ostracism results from behavior considered immoral by the dominant religion). Social structures, in turn, are products of human actions that created them over time. For example, the comprehensive structure that is the capitalist system resulted in part from actions by landowners in seventeenth-century England to change traditional patterns of land tenure. That is, the landowners acted to change an existing structure, and in the process contributed to the creation of a new structure (capitalism). Action constitutes structure; structure limits action. Structures do not prevent actions, but rather affect the probability of their achieving their purposes. Weak structures are obviously more susceptible to change through human action than strong ones. By the same token, powerful actors (e.g., leaders who can mobilize large numbers of people or other resources) are more capable of changing structures.

From this perspective, neither structure nor action alone can explain social and political phenomena. It is essential to see them as interacting through time, mutually shaping each other. Therefore, in this book I eschew the argument about whether structure or action is the better explanation.

Any political system has a broad range of structures—called the regime—that determine which actors actually have governmental authority, how political conflict and cooperation take place, which actors receive or lose resources, and what role, if any, the vast majority of nonpowerful actors play in the political process. Like any other structure, the regime is the consequence of prior action and may be changed by action. But at any given time the regime constrains elites as well as other actors. Moreover, nonelite actors, though having less power than elite actors, nevertheless individually and collectively structure the environments of elites. And, of course, elites continue to be subject to global economic and political structures.

The political system of the United States may be used to illustrate the point. One of the features of the political regime is the two-party system, which was shaped by the actions of key leaders such as Franklin Roosevelt and Abraham Lincoln. Current leaders such as George W. Bush and John Kerry must work within the two-party system if they hope to accomplish anything, and voters must vote for Republicans or Democrats if they want to avoid wasting their votes. Thus, the structure binds both elites and nonelites. Yet, at the same time, party leaders by their actions, and the voters by their votes, are both reproducing and changing the party system. They reproduce it by continuing to act within it. They change it by redefining both the policy commitments and the social bases of the parties.

The termination of a regime is a matter of great interest in the study of comparative politics. Regime structures are more durable than lower-order structures, but they are nonetheless subject to change as a consequence of actions. Regime change will occur when some combination of elite and mass action disposes enough power to overcome regime structures. Often, the defection of regime supporters will help to shift the power balance and thereby create conditions appropriate to regime change.[2]

Again, let us turn to the political system of the United States for an example. The Civil War was a stupendous struggle for power at both mass and elite levels, which had the result of a sweeping transformation of the country's political, economic, and social structures. The war erupted when the antebellum political coalitions (structures) broke down and realigned as a result of the successful organization (action) of the Republican Party. After the war, an entirely new set of structures emerged that would take the country into the next century.

One additional set of factors in regime termination should be considered: international influences, including direct political or military intervention by a foreign power. The United States terminated several regimes in Central America and the Caribbean by this means between 1898 and 1933, as well as in the Dominican Republic in 1965, in Grenada in 1982, in Panama in 1990, and in Haiti in 1994. Such influences also include international economic actors such as the International Monetary Fund, which is often in a position to force politically destabilizing policies on Third World governments. Finally, international influences may include worldwide economic or political conditions, such as recession, that function as structural constraints on political regimes.[3] This book will show that such international influences have been very important in shaping the political and economic evolution of Latin America.

In the absence of an extant regime, elite and mass political actors confront a radically different set of conditions. A very important set of constraints on action has been removed—that is, the structures that most directly affect the political elites.[4] The scope for elite choice and action is abruptly increased. Those elites recently dislodged from political power will find their capabilities for action substantially reduced if not eliminated. Other elites will find their capabilities suddenly much stronger. However, this period of increased scope for choice is unlikely to persist for long, since actions inherently create new structures.

Further, the destruction of political regime structures still leaves structures intact in other levels and sectors. Sectors of the mass population may well be making demands that newly dominant elites cannot ignore. Aspects of the traditional social structure, such as ethnicity, are unlikely to have undergone fundamental change. The structure of the international economy will in all likelihood be unaffected by the end of the political regime in one country. The governments of powerful neighboring states may have strong preferences about the outcome of political struggles in the system in question.

Thus, in the wake of the termination of a regime, interaction among political elites constrained by surviving structures will create the structures of a new regime. If power in the interregnum is relatively concentrated in the hands of a single, relatively unified elite, it will be able to establish regime structures according to its preference and thereby dominate the regime. Good examples would include the victorious communist revolutionaries in China (1949) and Cuba (1959). More commonly, a winning coalition fragments after the destruction of the old regime. At the same time, elements of the losing elite may still have substantial power, as may other elites who did not participate on either side. The interregnum may therefore witness intense political conflict unconstrained by regime rules. The potential for violence is high, and the risks to both elite and mass actors are substantial. Conflict within the interregnum may produce a single dominant elite or coalition that triumphs over competitors in relatively short order (Russia, 1917). Alternatively, the interregnum may persist through a prolonged and possibly violent impasse (Mexico, 1910–1934; Vietnam, 1941–1975; Lebanon, 1975–1991).

Interregnum conflicts may lead competing elites to arrive at an explicit or tacit agreement about new regime structures that protect the vital interests of all participating elites.[5] John Higley and Michael Burton (1989) distinguish "elite settlements" (involving an explicit agreement among competing elites about regime rules) from "elite convergence" (reduction of conflict and increasing cooperation within a set of regime rules, without an explicit, comprehensive settlement). The type of political regime we know as liberal democracy, if stable, has usually been rooted in such settlements or convergence rather than in either unresolved conflict or clear dominance by one elite or coalition.[6] This is not an accident, since liberal democracy implies civil competition for political power within constitutional rules. If one elite is dominant, then competition will not be meaningful; if elites will not be bound by constitutional limits on their competition, they are essentially engaged in civil war, not civil competition.

In this book I will show how liberal democracy has in fact emerged in Latin America, consistent with my perspective on the interaction of structure and human action. Demonstrably, democracy was not and is not impossible in Latin America, but neither is it inevitable, as the cases of Paraguay and Cuba illustrate.

Having made the case that liberal democracy is both desirable and feasible in Latin America, I conclude the book with the argument that, ethically, liberal democracy embodies contradictions that lead toward a more equal distribution of resources and broadened opportunities for participation. Liberal democracy presupposes the equality of citizens, but it exists everywhere in a context of greater or lesser economic inequality, which inevitably produces political inequality. Liberal democracy depends for its legitimacy on popular participation, but it depends for its stability on controlling and channeling that participation. Liberal democracy may in fact achieve stability without enhancing equality and participation, but to the extent that it fails to do so, it will continue to embody these contradictions. This set of issues is addressed in Chapter 7, where a strategy for achieving a more profound democracy is laid out. In addition to reforms of liberal democracy at the level of national regimes, I emphasize political decentralization and civil society, democratization of the economy, and international cooperation to achieve increased political regulation of the global economy.

Thinking back to my work on the first edition of this book, completed in the late 1990s, I am now both more pessimistic about the future of liberal democracy in the region and more hopeful that Latin America may play an important role in the next stages of democratic development, deepening democracy at the national and subnational levels and imposing democratic governance on the global economy.

▦ Notes

1. This book deals with the conventional political region of Latin America, that is, the independent countries that were formerly colonies of Spain or Portugal, plus Haiti.

2. Przeworski (1991) has analyzed the logic of this process in great detail.

3. Note that these international influences result from actions of other governments, but they function as structures within the society at hand. The actions of X thus constitute structures for Y.

4. A change of political regime will not necessarily have affected lower-level structures controlling everyday life or even local political institutions, unless a popular uprising has taken place. Thus the majority of the population may be relatively unaffected by a regime change.

5. See Higley and Burton (1989); Higley and Gunther (1992); and Peeler (1985).

6. There are some major exceptions to this, perhaps most notably Third Republic France (1875–1940) and Chile (1932–1973), which both persisted for decades without either settlement or convergence.

1

Introduction: Basic Issues of Democratic Theory

The purpose of this chapter is to set the context for the study of democracy in Latin America by acquainting the reader with some of the seminal thinkers and fundamental issues in the study of democracy. We begin with the ancient Greeks and pass swiftly through some of the high points in the history of Western political thought.[1] Considerable attention is devoted to major controversies of the twentieth century, including the issue raised by this book's exclusive focus on Western thought: Is democracy appropriate only within the sphere of Western civilization, or is it in some measure a universally valid aspiration? In Chapter 2, I specifically address the question of whether democracy is culturally alien to Latin America.

The classic arguments about democracy usually turn in one way or another on whether to accord primacy to the achievement of genuine popular sovereignty, as the word *democracy* itself implies, or to emphasize limiting the authority of the government and protecting the rights and liberties of citizens. The two emphases are not in conflict if the government in question is not under popular control (e.g., an absolute monarchy), but by the late eighteenth and early nineteenth centuries liberals were as worried about popular abuses as monarchical abuses. As liberalism increasingly assumed a democratic guise during the nineteenth century, critics pointed out that the liberal version of democracy fell far short of the democratic ideal of rule by the people. But in practice, what could "rule by the people" mean?

Democracy in the Classical Experience

The modern practice of democracy has developed from a dialectic between the idea of absolute popular rule, with neither limits nor delegation of authority, on one side, and the idea of limited government respectful of popular rights on the other. Both concepts have their roots in ancient Greece. Plato (*Republic and Laws*) and Aristotle (*Politics* and *The Constitution of Athens*) offered typologies of regimes in which democracy was defined as a constitution in which the (poor) mass of the population (the demos) ruled. The ancient Greek concept of "the demos" was distinct from the modern idea of "the people": when the Greeks talked about the rule of the demos, they meant rule by the many over the few, by the poor over the rich.[2] Plato and later Aristotle distinguished democracy from a more desirable, balanced constitution in which neither the poor majority nor the rich minority dominated.

The Athenian democracy, with its restricted demos, was the historic high point of the radical concept of democracy, but the concept of the balanced constitution continued to be influential in subsequent centuries. The Roman republic was founded on just such a balance between a popular Assembly and an aristocratic Senate, and it sought—unsuccessfully in the end—to constitutionally restrict the concentration of power in any magistrate. Republican Rome was also the cradle of the concept of law as a rational code binding officials as well as subjects. The concept of "natural law" holds that the world is inherently rational, that correct reasoning enables humans to understand this natural rationality, and that they may then shape their own conduct and their own "positive" law accordingly. Imperial Rome, in five centuries, sucked the life from both the Republican constitution and the Roman concept of law, but without formally abolishing either.

The emergence of Christianity within the empire, and its adoption as the official religion after Constantine, radically recast these classical political ideas. Originally, of course, Christianity was a religion of the poor and the oppressed. Christian scriptures convey a positive view of the poor as especially deserving of God's love and of justice on earth. Even when Christianity became the established church of the empire and ceased to be a religion of the downtrodden, a succession of minority currents continued to raise issues of social justice.[3]

The church as a whole, however, evolved into a hierarchical institution closely allied to the secular rulers, which played the principal political role of legitimizing those rulers and the secular order in general. In return, the rulers protected and enriched the church. A central underpinning for this new political role of the church was a very negative view of life on earth, a view that resulted from the context of corruption and political decay of the late Roman Empire. If the world in general is a beastly place, if people in general are corrupt, and if the church must act in that world, then it must know the rules and to some extent follow them.

This negative perspective on the world was exemplified by St. Augustine, whose conception, in *The City of God,* of a corrupt "Earthly City" as a metaphor for life in this world inverted the classical idea of the polis as the highest form of human life. From Augustine's perspective, life on earth was inherently sinful; only salvation through Christ could give access to the virtuous "Heavenly City." This pessimistic view of human nature, so uncharacteristic of the classical Greeks and Romans, has since remained central to the political outlook of the Western world. Because human beings are seen as basically sinful, they—and the institutions they create—are not to be trusted.

■ The Rule of Law in the Middle Ages

After the final destruction of the Western Roman Empire in the seventh century, economic power and political authority were fragmented, while the church retained its unity. Political thought tended to reflect this situation. For the most part, secular rulers could not realistically expect to exercise absolute control over their subjects, whether they were peasants, merchants, or knights. Instead, the feudal system that evolved in western Europe was a complex network of rights and obligations. Monarchs had a right to obedience for certain purposes, if the ruler also fulfilled her or his duties to the subjects.

Moreover, rulers were held to be subject to the authority of the Pope and the bishops of the church as representatives of God and enforcers of God's law. Thus the medieval conception of kingship was emphatically limited. Royal authority was legitimate only if the monarch met his or her lawful obligations, respected the rights of subjects, and obeyed and protected the church.

The most systematic formulation of this medieval approach to political authority was that of St. Thomas Aquinas *(The Summa Theologica)*. Aquinas relied extensively on a long-neglected Aristotle to propose a revaluation of the political: denigrated by Augustine, the secular political order was seen by Aquinas as good. He departed from Aristotle in that he attributed the goodness of the secular political order to God's will. Similarly, Aquinas adopted the idea of natural law, so important to the early Romans, but changed it by equating it with God's will. Aquinas used these and other ideas from classical times to systematize the medieval worldview. He defended the idea of a limited and lawful kingship and even affirmed (as had Aristotle) the right to resist tyranny (i.e., unlawful rule). The church was at the peak of its power in Aquinas's day, and he strongly defended its right to instruct and even control secular rulers. Thus, with Aquinas, the medieval tradition of limited and lawful secular rulers reached its apotheosis under the overall dominance of a unified Roman Catholic Church.[4]

Even as Aquinas was writing, though, cracks were appearing in the monolith that was the church. The church's political standards were, of course, frequently defied even when it was at the peak of its power. But during the Renaissance, the church itself became increasingly corrupt and increasingly party to abuses of its own political principles. The Renaissance popes were secular princes who dominated the politics of a fragmented Italy and played a significant role on the larger stage of western Europe. Like other princes of the era, they tended to seek absolute power and to deal ruthlessly with their internal and external enemies. Machiavelli's famous treatise, *The Prince,* exemplifies the new viewpoint in its emphasis not on natural law, but on principles by which the prince may best safeguard his own interests. The medieval idea of limited and lawful authority was largely left behind. Increasingly, in Mediterranean Europe, obedience to church teachings was no longer taken for granted. People could choose to be practicing Catholics or to be secular. The politically active could choose to support the church's influence (i.e., to be proclerical) or to oppose it (i.e., to be anticlerical).[5]

At about the same time, the church's corruption led, especially in northern Europe, to the irrevocable religious schisms known as the Reformation. In contrast to the secularism of the southern European Renaissance, the driving motive of the Reformation was religious: to purify the church of its corruption and of centuries of doctrine and practice without scriptural foundation, or, failing that, to separate from the church entirely. The Reformation, like the Renaissance, had complex and somewhat inconsistent political effects. The destruction of the Catholic religious monopoly certainly increased the stature of the individual believer who, in most Protestant doctrines, was no longer seen as needing the intercession of priests for access to the grace of God. However, the erosion of the church's ability to constrain secular princes meant that the way was clear for the development of modern state sovereignty and absolute monarchy. Renaissance princes of such countries as England, Sweden, and the Netherlands harnessed the Reformation to serve their interests by breaking their subjection to Rome and establishing official Protestant churches.[6] In Protestant areas, then, without the unified church to enforce it, the old idea of natural law declined in importance and began a long transformation.

In parallel manner, the loyally Catholic monarchs of France, Austria, Spain, and Portugal actually used their new importance to a beleaguered Catholic Church to enhance their own powers at the expense of nobility and bourgeoisie and indeed at the expense of the church itself. Assuming the role of defenders of the Catholic faith, these kings and queens systematically undercut medieval rights and asserted effective control over the appointment of bishops in their realms. Thus, at the very time of the voyages of discovery, medieval traditions of limited government were being submerged in the Iberian mother countries. However, Catholic natural law doctrine never became as marginal in these Catholic bulwarks as it did in Protestant regions.

The Modern World Order: Capitalism and Contract

These changes in ideas were of course the counterparts of fundamental transformations taking place in European society, polity, and economy. Of all the complex changes that occurred in the early stages of the creation of modern European society, two are most relevant to the concerns of this book, and they are in some tension with one another: first, the emergence of the modern state and with it the modern idea of sovereignty; second, the emergence of capitalism as the dominant mode of economic practice. Instead of a territory and population regulated by a complex of overlapping rights and obligations in which the monarch was as much bound by law and custom as her or his subjects, Renaissance monarchs had increasing success in claiming absolute and exclusive control over territory and population. That is, they successfully claimed to be *sovereign*. Sovereignty entailed the claim of an absolute right to make laws governing the people in a certain territory, and it further entailed the claim to exclude any competing authority from that territory and population. The former claim was the essence of Renaissance absolutism; the latter was the foundation for the modern system of relations among sovereign states.[7]

Unlike the medieval world, with its overarching agreement on natural law and its respect for customary limits on authority, a world of sovereign states was potentially anarchic in that the sovereign ruler of each state was theoretically free to do anything. At the level of relations between states, this dilemma led to the emergence of international law, first systematically formulated by Hugo Grotius. At the level of relations between sovereign and subjects, there was a divergence between those countries where absolutism was not seriously challenged and those where it was. In the former cases (especially France, Spain, Portugal, and Austria) law and political theory tended to base royal authority on divine right, or the supposed will of God that the monarch rule and that subjects submit. However, this argument did not in the end prevail everywhere: especially in England and the Low Countries (Belgium, Luxembourg, and the Netherlands), the combination of traditions of limited government, powerful economic interests opposed to the monarchs, and strong dissenting religious sentiments permitted successful resistance to absolutism.[8]

England and the Low Countries successfully limited absolutism in part because of the second major change just mentioned: the emergence of capitalism. The economy of much of medieval western Europe was based on custom and legal regulation, with the market playing a secondary role. The absolutist monarchs of the Renaissance and early modern periods tended to continue this orientation in the form of mercantilism, or centrally licensed and regulated trade. But in England and the Low Countries, the class of merchants and craftspersons was strong and resistant to state control of its enterprises.

Since the efficacy of both natural law and custom as restraints on royal authority had eroded, some other justification was needed. For increasingly trade- and market-oriented societies, the idea of contract was intuitively sensible. Unlike natural law, contracts are acknowledged to be conventions agreed to and changeable by the parties. Unlike customary rules, contracts are relatively explicit in their terms. In a market setting, contracts are an everyday occurrence. It seemed natural, then, to think of the political order as also governed by contract.

The idea of a social contract was used in the seventeenth century both to justify limits on governmental authority and to justify absolute authority. All contractarian arguments posited an original, pregovernmental "state of nature," in which people existed free of governmental controls but also were exposed to risks of aggression from other people who were also free of governmental controls. The solution—and the origin of all legitimate government—was a social contract among the people to set up a government to protect them. All parties to the contract would agree to give up their "natural right" to take what they needed, in return for being assured that others would do the same.

The critical innovation of all contract thought was that authority was derived not from divine ordination or natural law or custom, but rather from the—at least implicit—consent of the governed. There were, however, wide differences concerning what this consent was supposed to have authorized. Thomas Hobbes *(Leviathan)* held that the original consent was irrevocable and the authority granted was absolute. In this he sought to support the claims of the English king Charles I to absolute authority, but his support was rejected by most royalists because they did not wish to grant that royal authority could be based on popular consent, even in the remote and metaphorical sense used by Hobbes. His argument was thus, however philosophically elegant, historically a blind alley.

John Locke *(Second Treatise on Government)* in England and Benedict de Spinoza in the Netherlands represented the main channel of social contract thought.[9] Each depicted the hypothetical social contract not as an irrevocable agreement to grant absolute authority to a sovereign, but rather as a revocable agreement to set up a limited government to serve the interests of the parties to the contract, by protecting their natural rights. If those holding authority derived from the contract violate its terms—and thus the rights of the parties—the latter may justly remove them.

It must be emphasized that neither Locke nor Spinoza was in practice a radical democrat, in that neither advocated direct rule by the people. Rather, they stood for rule by the representatives of the people, and they placed great emphasis on the obligation of government to protect the property of citizens. Both must thus be understood as defending the interest of the emerging capitalist class in limiting the right of government to interfere with individual liberty—particularly but not exclusively economic liberty. Nevertheless, their principle that legitimate authority derives from the consent of the governed and their rejection of hereditary rank laid the foundation for modern democratic thought. Since Locke, the mainstream of democratic theory has emphasized limited government and individual rights and, although accepting the principle of popular consent, has rejected direct popular rule in favor of representation.

Some predecessors and contemporaries of Locke and Spinoza, in the turbulent contexts of the Reformation, the Dutch struggle for independence from Spain, and the revolutionary struggle in seventeenth-century England, articulated a more radically democratic political vision. The Dutch Anabaptists, or Mennonites, can certainly be included here, as can some Protestant nonconformists in England. The best-known such group would be the English revolutionaries called the Diggers (see Walzer, 1965). Far from being contractarian, the Diggers, like the other religious democrats, reverted to the idea of a divinely ordained order in which all were equal in God's sight and therefore merited equal rights on earth.

The social contract approach also produced a radically democratic theory, that of Jean-Jacques Rousseau (*The Social Contract;* see Barker, 1947). Postulating the conventional state of nature, Rousseau differentiated himself from both Hobbes and Locke. He accepted Hobbes's argument that the insecurities of the state of nature can be corrected only if all parties to the social contract surrender all their natural rights, but he nevertheless held that it would be irrational for anyone in a state of nature to yield all natural rights to a sovereign, since the person would thereby continue to run all the risks of the state of nature relative to the sovereign. This was precisely Locke's key argument against Hobbes. Rousseau therefore agrees with Locke that the social contract must vest sovereignty in the people themselves, rather than in a magistrate set above the people by their consent. However, he holds that any scheme of representation must eviscerate popular sovereignty, which truly exists only at the moment of election of representatives; thereafter, effective sovereignty lies with the representatives, not with the people.

Rousseau thus poses the problem of how all of the people can be at the same time absolutely sovereign and absolutely subject to sovereignty. In brief, his answer is that this can occur only if all persons constituting the society surrender all their natural rights to a sovereign composed precisely of all persons constituting the society. Thus, each person would simultaneously be absolutely subject to the sovereign and would participate on an equal basis with all others in that absolute sovereignty. Rousseau's second and crucial stipulation is that all citizens participating in sovereign decisionmaking must have regard only for the common good, not for their own private interests. This is essential because once private interests shape choices, some citizens will prevail over others. This line of argument is summarized in Rousseau's concept of the general will, which amounts to the will of all the people if each were to think only of the common interest. Rousseau has thereby created an abstract model of the conditions for true democracy, a model far more systematic and rigorous than anything previously seen.

Of course, Rousseau is also sensitive to the criticism that his model has no connection with reality. Much of his treatise concerns itself with what is to be done in the event that citizens fail to put aside their private interests. The first contingency is honest disagreement among the truly public-spirited about what the general will requires; in this case, based on the premise of the equality of citizens, the minority will accept that they were in error and support the majority. The next contingency occurs when a minority (or even one person) does not accept the general will as articulated by a public-spirited majority. Here, the obdurate minority has put its private perspectives and interests above the general interest and may be overruled by the majority. But it is also conceivable that the majority of citizens would be so corrupted that they would act on their private interests rather than the interests of all, thus establishing a majority tyranny. In this instance, it is legitimate for a minority who understand the general will to impose that will on the ignorant majority. Following this logic to its conclusion, Rousseau comes to the final contingency, in which all citizens are ignorant of the general will and act tyrannically in pursuit of their particular interests. There is no answer within the terms of his argument; he is forced to fall back on the classical tradition of the quasi-divine legislator, not part of the community, who imposes the general will on an ignorant and corrupt society. Thus far has he brought us from his model of a perfect democracy. One might consider his argument a reductio ad absurdum for radical democracy.

Social contract thought thus produced a diversity of approaches. Hobbes and Rousseau were absolutists, the former defending an absolutely sovereign monarch separate from the people, the latter defending—at least in the abstract—an absolutely sovereign people. Spinoza and Locke (followed by the founders of the United States, notably Thomas Jefferson and James Madison) saw the social contract as, in effect, a constitution limiting and controlling governmental authority and protecting individual rights. The latter stream has been more influential, shaping the modern concept of democracy as necessarily constitutional and respectful of individual rights. The thrust against unlimited popular sovereignty was only implicit in Locke, since he was primarily concerned with guarding against monarchical tyranny, but became explicit among the political leadership of the nascent United States. Madison, for example, in *The Federalist Papers,* No. 10, defended the checks and balances of the new constitution as structurally retarding majority tyranny.[10]

The obviously artificial convention of the social contract was increasingly abandoned in the course of the eighteenth century. What replaced it was an acceptance that political organization was neither divinely ordained nor contractual but rather conventional, evolving gradually within a particular historical context.[11] The argument for limited government and individual rights was cast less in terms of contractarian rights and more in terms of prudence. Thus, Adam Smith's famous defense of laissez-faire economic policy *(An Inquiry into the Nature and Causes of the Wealth of Nations)* held simply that all of society would be better off if government refrained from controlling the economic decisions of individuals pursuing their own individual self-interests. In political discourse, the shift to prudential argument was slower, perhaps because the notion of inalienable natural rights was too useful to give up.[12] Earlier in the eighteenth century, Montesquieu *(The Spirit of the Laws)* studied the checks and balances of the English constitution without relying on the device of the contract, and David Hume systematically refuted contractarianism (Barker, 1947). By the 1790s, Jeremy Bentham (1988) and James Mill (1992) had developed the ideas of utilitarianism, which sought to evaluate good and bad in terms of whether a thing caused pleasure or pain, or more broadly, whether it was useful. The utilitarian calculus could be applied at the level of the individual or aggregated to the societal level, where the public interest was defined as "the greatest happiness of the greatest number."[13]

Many of these postcontractarians shared a paradoxical assumption that has become central to modern democratic theory: that human individuals, left alone to pursue their own interests, will serve not only themselves but the public interest better than if the best-intentioned government tried to control them. Prefigured by Hume, the archetype of the argument was provided by Adam Smith; it was echoed by the utilitarians and by Jefferson and Madison.

By the middle of the nineteenth century, the doctrine even had a name, "liberalism," and it received its fullest articulation in the work of John Stuart Mill.[14] Mill's classic, *On Liberty,* defended the proposition that the suppression of free speech was never justifiable because all society would benefit from the free exchange of ideas through which we progress toward truth.[15] Even in the hypothetical extreme case in which the whole truth were known, Mill argued that dissenting views should not be suppressed because the very need to defend truthful ideas would sharpen the faculties of those who hold them and thus help them achieve more of their potential as human beings.

Mill wrote in a context of the wrenching social, economic, and political change associated with the peak of the industrial revolution in England. Economic and political liberalism served the broad interests of the emerging industrialists. Both internally and internationally, English industrialists of the early nineteenth century were in a comparatively advantageous position to compete with craftspeople at home and abroad and thus generally advocated a reduction of government economic regulation. These same industrialists were often men of modest origins who lacked the franchise under the old patchwork of electoral laws of England. Thus their interest was served by the defense of the right of dissent, or freedom of speech. And initially, their interest was served by broadening and rationalizing the franchise, at least so as to include themselves. But democracy was no part of their intention. Liberalism evolved from its inception as a doctrine of limited government. Its rejection of hereditary privilege led it inexorably toward liberalization of the franchise, but that tendency made limited government all the more necessary, now as a hedge against majority tyranny as well as the more traditional monarchical tyranny that had preoccupied Locke. Alexis de Tocqueville's book *Democracy in America* exemplifies this deep liberal preoccupation with majority tyranny.[16]

John Stuart Mill confronted this preoccupation head-on in two of his later essays and in the process helped eliminate the last ideological barriers to democratization of the franchise. In *Representative Government* he extended the argument of *On Liberty,* holding that society would benefit by expanding the franchise because a broader range of ideas would be heard and that individuals would benefit as the exercise of citizenship developed their human capacities. In answer to the argument that workers were incapable of the responsible judgment required of voters, he answered that the very exercise of citizenship was what was necessary to develop that capacity. In *The Subjection of Women,* he applied the same argument to the question of women's suffrage, thereby becoming one of the first prominent male advocates of women's suffrage.

However, even though Mill provided an important philosophical underpinning for a democratized franchise, he still remained an advocate of limited government and of safeguards against majority tyranny. Thus in *Representative Government* he advocated giving the educated plural votes, as a means of balancing the weight of the ignorant majority while the latter are developing their citizenship capacities. As exemplified by Mill, liberalism by the late nineteenth century was increasingly committed to a democratic franchise but also to a continuation of the characteristically liberal restrictions on government power that would now serve to limit the power of the majority to truly rule. Even though the franchise would not approach universality until the 1920s and 1930s, the form of twentieth-century democracy was evident by the 1880s in Britain, the United States, and a few smaller countries: a liberal polity, democratically legitimated.[17] Democracy as we know it in the twenty-first century involves the limitation of government authority and the protection of rights, a fundamentally liberal orientation. Mechanisms of democratic consent centered on elections serve to legitimate the right of these liberal regimes to rule, but as Rousseau pointed out, the people are meaningfully sovereign only on election day.

The chief nineteenth-century dissenter against this emerging liberal political economy was Karl Marx.[18] His basic concern, of course, was the critique of the capitalist mode of production and not an analysis of democratic theory per se. But Marx saw the emerging theory and practice of democratic politics in his day as intimately related to—in the last analysis, determined by—the structure of power in the economy (i.e., control of the means of production by a capitalist ruling class in all the advanced, industrializing countries of Europe and North America). Thus, the basic determining reality of modern society was its capitalist economy. Other aspects of society, such as schooling, religion, and politics, would tend to serve the interests of the capitalist economy and the capitalist class who controlled it. This is not to say that all dissenting ideas and heterodox practices would be suppressed (obviously, Marx's were not) but rather that they would lack material support, be portrayed as irrational or inconsistent with (capitalist) reality, and only in extreme cases be directly repressed.

Capitalism, in Marx's view, produced liberalism as its central theory of economics and politics. With its emphasis on individualism, on free competition and discourse within a broad legal order, and on limited state authority, liberalism was well suited to the legitimation of capitalist practice. In the political realm, the principle of equality of citizens was combined with a limited state and toleration of economic inequality to produce a political system in which the majority of citizens could be co-opted into supporting an order in which capitalists remained dominant. Limitation of state authority would deprive a potentially hostile majority of a key instrument to regulate and control capitalism. In any case, Marx believed that the state was little more than "the form in which the individuals of a ruling class assert their common interests,"[19] having some autonomy relative to individual capitalists but serving the overall interests of capitalism. For example, key state functions would include enforcing capitalist property laws, guaranteeing the sanctity of contracts, and repressing working-class resistance.

In short, Marx believed that the democratic theory and practice emerging in his lifetime were mere illusions serving the interests of the capitalist ruling classes. As long as capitalism continued as the dominant mode of production, it could not be otherwise. Of course, Marx expected that capitalism would be driven by its own internal contradictions toward a final revolutionary confrontation in which the working class would finally seize control of economy and polity and impose (through a "dictatorship of the proletariat") a classless, communist society. Such a society would be without the internal contradiction between ruling class and exploited class; it would indeed be classless. Building on the immense productive capacity developed by capitalism, communism could establish a society of perfectly distributed plenty. The coercive function of the state as agent of the ruling class would be eliminated, and the state as such would, in Friedrich Engels's phrase, "die out."[20] The new society would presumably still have a politics concerned with decisions about collective action but would no longer need a state with coercive power to enforce class exploitation.

This vision, albeit not very thoroughly developed, contradicts the liberal approach to democracy on several points. First, Marx flatly denies that democracy can coexist at all with the inequality and exploitation essential to capitalism. For him, to apply the term to the elected, constitutional regimes emerging in his time was worse than a misnomer; it was a mystification. Second, like Rousseau, Marx rejects the notion that a true democracy could be characterized by limited authority. In the transitional stage of the dictatorship of the proletariat, that class (presumed to represent the overwhelming majority of the population at the time of the revolution) would simply impose its will on the defeated capitalists. In the projected classless, communist society, there would be no state whose authority must be limited and no reason to limit the scope of the (noncoercive) collective choices the people make.

Third, again like Rousseau, Marx makes a clear distinction between the "true," or "objective," interests of people and what they may believe their interests to be. Marx obviously knew that many—even most—proletarians of his day were not revolutionaries. They tended to accept to some degree the ideas and institutions of capitalism, including those of liberal democracy. This fact did not, for Marx, invalidate his thesis, since he expected that the historical development of capitalism would exacerbate its internal contradictions, leading the workers increasingly to see the need for proletarian revolution and the validity of a radically egalitarian vision of democracy in communist society. In contrast, political liberalism from Locke onward takes citizen beliefs as given and in principle vests ultimate sovereignty in the collective expression of those beliefs (i.e., in elections).

All his life, Marx struggled to bring about the revolutionary conditions that he thought were inherent in the capitalist system. Toward the end of his life, he and his followers had increasingly to confront serious anomalies. Capitalists and associated states proved far more intelligent and adaptable than he had earlier expected, continually ameliorating the worst contradictions of capitalism and co-opting the workers with concessions such as social services and expansion of the franchise. Correspondingly, the workers were not becoming more revolutionary. Thus, although the fundamental critique of capitalist political economy might continue to be valid, the specific historical expectations were increasingly cast into question. Marx, Engels, and the next generations of Marxists sought to deal with these problems. Marx, for example, came to accept the possibility that the working class might actually come to state power by electoral means in special cases such as Britain.[21]

The points to be explained break down into two categories: (1) Why hasn't the working class become revolutionary? and (2) What is to be done about that? On the first question, the key contribution is probably that of Antonio Gramsci (1971), who argued that capitalists had largely avoided the threat of revolution by establishing an ideological hegemony over the working class, such that workers come to accept and enact the fundamental values of capitalism and are thereby inoculated against revolutionary ideas. This is clearly an elaboration of Marx's ideas, but Marx had expected the hegemony to break down more easily than had in fact been the case.

"What Is to Be Done?" was the title of one of Lenin's most important writings, addressing precisely the question of how to proceed with a revolutionary agenda in the face of a nonrevolutionary proletariat. Lenin argued for, and succeeded in establishing, a "vanguard party" consisting of a small cadre who understood the true interests of the proletariat and would take the leadership of the revolutionary struggle. The revolutionary struggle, in short, would not wait upon the emergence of a revolutionary consciousness among the mass of workers. Rather, the party would undertake to shape that consciousness in the course of its struggle for revolution. Under the harsh, authoritarian conditions of imperial Russia, moreover, the party had to be not only small but secretive. It was operationally decentralized into local cells to frustrate police penetration but was nevertheless highly centralized in terms of doctrine and policy. Thus, Lenin's vanguard party, ruled by principles of "democratic centralism," became one major Marxist response to the conditions of twentieth-century capitalism. This approach conceded nothing to liberal conceptions of democracy; rather, democracy was to be found through adherence to the true or ultimate interest of the proletariat, to be realized in the fullness of time.[22]

The principal Marxist alternative to Lenin's approach was articulated by German revisionist social democrat Eduard Bernstein (1961). His argument, based principally on German circumstances, was that conditions in the late nineteenth century were so fundamentally different from what Marx had expected that an explicit revision of Marxist thinking was necessary. Specifically, he held that the emergence of modern liberal democracy and the welfare state rendered revolution both unnecessary and unlikely in advanced industrial society. Rather, socialists should devote their efforts to building a mass working-class base organized into labor unions and social democratic political parties, with the objectives of exerting political pressure for the humanization of capitalism in the short run, and in the long run gaining political power through electoral means and with it the capacity to bring about a peaceful transition to socialism.

Marx's radical critique of capitalism (and, incidentally, of liberal democracy) thus led, on one extreme, to the antiliberal democratic centralism of Lenin (and ultimately to Stalinism) and, on the other, to the fundamental acceptance of liberal premises embodied in Bernstein's revisionism. Many other currents of Marxist thought existed between these extremes, such as that of Gramsci. The problem for Marxists concerned with democracy has continued to be how to move toward Marx's vision of a true democracy while avoiding the contradictions of both liberalism and Stalinism.

▓ The Modern Democratic Republic

The advent of the twentieth century roughly coincided with the emergence in western Europe of political sociology as a distinct academic field, and in the United States we find the somewhat parallel evolution of political science. In each case, the development signified a heightened commitment to the accumulation of "scientific" knowledge about politics. Scholars on both continents tended to emphasize objective observation and theory building while making less explicit reference to questions of value. In Europe, in place of the old liberal faith in progress, we find newly skeptical analyses of the equivocal consequences of modernization[23] and several studies emphasizing the fundamentally elitist character of political parties and other institutions, even in ostensibly democratic settings.[24] A similar spirit was evident in the United States when Woodrow Wilson showed how the practice of government in the late nineteenth century corresponded only imperfectly with constitutional norms, or when Thorstein Veblen called attention to the existence of a powerful and prosperous upper class in a supposedly egalitarian society.[25]

In terms of the issue of democracy, the culmination of this pre–World War II trend in political studies was the wide-ranging *Capitalism, Socialism, and Democracy* by Joseph Schumpeter. In the context of a careful and jaundiced review of the prospects of both capitalism and socialism and their relationship to democracy, Schumpeter proposed a simple operational definition of democracy as a system in which the rulers are chosen by the people in periodic, competitive elections. He thereby hoped to obviate what he saw as useless philosophical speculation about the meaning of true democracy, choosing instead to define democracy as, in effect, the political system used by countries conventionally called democracies. This empirical and conventional approach would dominate postwar political science, particularly in the United States.

The wartime experience of fighting Germany, Italy, and Japan and the subsequent Cold War against the Soviet Union and international communism had the effect of focusing the attention of political scientists, in the United States and its allied countries, on democracy as an issue, as distinct from authoritarian and "totalitarian" regimes. This last category (exclusively exemplified by Nazi Germany, the Soviet Union, and other postwar communist countries) was said to be characterized by extreme concentration of power and the exertion of nearly complete control over almost the totality of life. Totalitarian regimes were thus held to be analytically distinct from authoritarian regimes, which exhibited less concentrated power and less complete control. In contrast, democratic regimes were seen as having relatively dispersed power and a relatively narrower scope of political control. Thus, under the pressure of military and political struggle, the liberal, limited-government approach to democracy that was already well institutionalized at the turn of the century was given new life, but the alternative radical vision was discredited by being linked to Nazism and communism.[26] The earlier arguments of Veblen, Robert Michels, Gaetano Mosca, and others, that power in democracies was less dispersed than it appeared, were problematic to the new paradigm and thus tended to be treated as merely quaint dissenting voices.[27]

The new democratic theory and related empirical studies displayed several general characteristics. First, they were preoccupied with stability as a goal and were thus essentially conservative. David Easton (1953, 1965) produced a pathbreaking adaptation of systems analysis to the study of politics, in which a stable system was taken as the norm. Gabriel Almond's use of structural-functional analysis (Almond and Powell, 1966) similarly assumed stability as a goal and treated political instability in the developing countries as pathological. Maurice Duverger's study of political parties and party systems (1962) is notable for its argument that two-party systems are preferable to multiparty systems because they better promote political stability.

A second general characteristic of studies of democracy of this period was that they emphasized "pluralism," or the relative dispersion of political power and participation in decisionmaking. David Truman (1951), following the earlier work of Alfred Bentley, developed a theory of politics as the interaction of organized interests, wherein the government's role was to provide the arena for the interaction and to register the outcome of power struggles among groups. Robert Dahl produced the concept of "polyarchy" to signify a political system in which participation was relatively high and power relatively dispersed among competing organized interests. He intended polyarchy to be roughly synonymous with the contemporary practice of democracy and to distinguish this practice from ideal democracy, which he held to be virtually unattainable.[28]

The pluralist model of democracy was essentially liberal in its emphasis on limited government and political competition. However, its preoccupation with stability gave its liberalism a conservative tone, a tone intensified by the pluralists' relative inattention to how economic and social inequalities might vitiate or eliminate the benefits of political equality. Various scholars emphasized these points in taking issue with the pluralist mainstream of the discipline. C. Wright Mills (1956) developed the thesis of "the Power Elite," a set of individuals who collectively held the reins of institutional power in government, the defense establishment, and private enterprise, thereby directly challenging the central proposition of pluralism, the broad dispersion of political power. Peter Bachrach (1967) criticized Dahl and other pluralists for their insensitivity to the effects of social and economic inequality on political power. Dahl himself, after about 1970, increasingly recognized the validity of some of these criticisms and devoted much of his attention to how polyarchy could become more democratic, how the premises of equality and popular rule could be brought closer to reality. Among his key proposals was a substantial decentralization, not only of political power but especially of economic power.[29]

▦ Renovating Democracy

Dahl thereby joined an extensive movement beginning in the late 1960s to think anew about democracy, to take seriously the goals of genuine equality and effective participation. The backdrop to this new theoretical direction included developments in the pluralist democracies and around the world. The 1960s saw the emergence of new movements in the United States and in Europe that posed radical challenges to the status quo. In the United States, the civil rights movement evolved toward a more militant black nationalism, and the Vietnam War provided an initial focus for an increasingly sweeping critique of American society by the New Left. The New Left had its counterparts in all the major countries of Western Europe. The thrust of these new critical movements was to question the authenticity of democracy in the context of social and economic inequality and exploitation, to question the premises of the Cold War and its emphasis on national security, and to demand fundamental democratization in the distribution of power and the practice of politics.[30]

Even as the New Left and black nationalism were on the march in the industrial democracies, Marxist revolutionary movements were posing parallel challenges to regimes in Latin America, Southeast Asia, and elsewhere, calling into question the capitalist world order on whose exploited periphery they found themselves. The movement against the Vietnam War in the United States and other industrial democracies increasingly assumed an anti-imperialist character that meshed with these challenges being posed from the periphery. From the standpoint of democratic theory, the key issue was how democratic a country could be if its government was the sponsor of oppressive regimes that repressed popular revolutionary movements.[31]

In this worldwide political context, an extended conversation about the renovation of democracy began in the 1960s and continued through the 1980s and into the 1990s. Out of a large and diverse literature, four outstanding examples will be cited here.[32] In the 1960s, C. B. Macpherson (1973, 1977) began a long-term project of retrieving core democratic values from a moribund liberalism. Arguing that liberalism as a political-economic doctrine had its roots in the "possessive individualism" of Hobbes and Locke and that even the humanistic, developmentally oriented liberalism of John Stuart Mill failed to resolve the fundamental tension between that possessive individualism and the ideal of democracy, Macpherson developed a model of "participatory democracy" that would actively encourage widespread participation in political decisionmaking for the principal purpose of fully developing the human capabilities of the citizens. His project was premised on "a view of man's essence not as a consumer of utilities but as a doer, a creator, an enjoyer of his human attributes."[33] He believed that a high level of participation was both necessary to and a consequence of a major reduction in the level of inequality in society. He did not believe that revolution was very likely in advanced industrial societies and thus thought that changes in both participation levels and inequality would have to come gradually, by effective use of points of weakness in the system.

Benjamin Barber (1984) developed a similar argument. Barber held that at a deep philosophical level, liberalism is hostile to democracy and that liberal democracy is consequently "thin democracy," dependent on limited participation and the exercise of control. He advocated "strong democracy," or "politics in the participatory mode where conflict is resolved in the absence of an independent ground through a participatory process of ongoing, proximate self-legislation and the creation of a political community capable of transforming dependent, private individuals into free citizens and partial and private interests into public goods."[34] Barber and Macpherson differed in some important respects. Barber was more cautious than Macpherson about the implications of capitalism for strong democracy, though he did call attention to ways in which modern monopoly capitalism may jeopardize strong democracy (p. 253). Most important, whereas Macpherson's developmental justification for participatory democracy contained at least the implication of a teleology, Barber sought to develop a model "without independent ground," that is, without presuppositions of what truly free and participatory citizens would decide (p. 129). Thus two renovators of liberalism came out on opposite sides of an old controversy: Should the beliefs and perceived interests of citizens be taken as given, or is there a standard by which it may be decided whether they are fully in possession of their human faculties and hence deserving of full citizenship?

Carol Gould (1988) made an argument for a comprehensive expansion of the scope of democracy. Holding that democracy is justified as the institutional form of decisionmaking that best provides equal rights to the conditions of self-development, she argued that the fullest possible participation should be extended in social and economic realms as well as in the political. By emphasizing the right to the conditions of self-development as the principal justification for democracy, Gould aligned herself with Macpherson's focus on the development of individual powers.

Further, in a treatment of "Democratic Personality" (chap. 11), she argued that two personality traits lend themselves to democracy: democratic agency and the disposition to reciprocity. By democratic agency, she meant a disposition to initiate joint action with others to some rational purpose determined by an understanding of common interests. Democratic agency is distinguished from passivity, or an absence of initiative. The disposition to reciprocity is an ability to understand another's perspective as equivalent to one's own—an expectation that the other will have the same ability and that actions with respect to one another will therefore be reciprocal. There is, in short, "a shared understanding by the participants that their actions are reciprocal" (p. 290). By arguing that these personality traits lend themselves to democracy and that democracy itself is principally justified by its ability to afford equal rights to the conditions of self-development, Gould implicitly affirmed these traits as both means to, and ends of, democracy. In short, personalities congruent with mutual reinforcement will be best served by democracy.

Macpherson, Barber, and Gould each criticized contemporary liberal democracy for its failure to provide for true equality of participatory opportunities. For each, the economic inequality associated with capitalism was central to the problem. Thus the contradictions between the twin progeny of liberalism, capitalism and democracy, have reached a crisis.

There are, moreover, other inequalities in modern societies that also obstruct the possibility of full democracy. Ann Ferguson (1991) explored, with particular reference to the United States, a feminist-socialist perspective on democracy. In addition to advocating "a feasible democratic socialism," Ferguson argued for six feminist values that would make for a *feminist* democratic socialism: (1) eliminating gender dualism; (2) setting up a nonracist and non-ethnicist society; (3) maximizing democratic parenting; (4) promoting sex for pleasure; (5) promoting committed sexual relationships; and (6) guaranteeing gay and lesbian rights (pp. 220–221). Ferguson's perspective reminds us that there is more to achieving full democracy than ending capitalism.

■ Revaluing Democracy

During much of the 1970s and 1980s, while Macpherson, Barber, Gould, and Ferguson were criticizing existing liberal democracy and calling for its renovation and full democratization, scholars and political leaders of the Latin American Left tended likewise to evaluate democracy negatively for the Latin American context. Emphasizing the meaninglessness of participation in the absence of real choice and the political implications of extreme economic inequalities, many critics judged liberal democracy to be fraudulent and called for socialist revolution as a prerequisite to the establishment of true democracy.[35]

Also in the 1970s, most countries of Latin America (except Venezuela, Costa Rica, and Colombia)[36] saw the establishment of military dictatorships, often overthrowing precarious elected governments. These military regimes were accepted and even encouraged by most U.S. administrations of the period (excepting only Carter—ambivalently) as serving U.S. national security interests by repressing potential communist insurgencies (Schoultz, 1981, 1987). This policy received its most explicit public articulation in a polemical article by Jeane Kirkpatrick (1982) that criticized Carter's preoccupation with human rights and argued that it was justifiable for the United States to support authoritarian regimes in the struggle against communist totalitarianism because the former could be democratized from within, whereas the latter could not.

However, by the mid-1980s widespread and severe economic crisis (associated with the massive growth of international debt in Latin America and the rest of the Third World) had combined with growing popular resistance to repression to bring an end to almost all military regimes across the continent. The opposition to military regimes in many Latin American countries focused attention on the task of restoring democracy and in the process built new ties of cooperation between previously antagonistic groups.[37] The driving conviction of this shift was that, whatever its shortcomings, liberal democracy could serve to protect human rights and provide a civil arena for political debate. In light of the success of the military regimes in repressing both violent and nonviolent opposition, those on the left increasingly forswore violence and pressed for democratization.

Impelled by, and to some extent impelling, these developments, the Reagan administration shifted its policy to open support for transitions to democracy, putting pressure on its principal clients in Latin America—military officers and economic elites—to facilitate transitions to democracy. This shift in Reagan's policy was furthered in the late 1980s by the rapid changes in Soviet society and foreign policy implemented by Mikhail Gorbachev after 1985, culminating in the end of Soviet hegemony in Eastern Europe and the end of the Cold War itself. A U.S. foreign policy premised on anticommunism was no longer relevant. Moreover, the effective end of Soviet competition with the United States in the Third World meant that the latter held most key economic cards (e.g., effective control over the World Bank and the International Monetary Fund [IMF]). Even Cuba, closely allied with the Soviet Union, found its Soviet subsidies steadily diminishing. With such economic leverage, the United States was able to promote democratization with some confidence that the resultant governments would not pursue economic policies inimical to U.S. interests.[38] Repeatedly during the 1980s, Latin American presidents elected on populist platforms abruptly reversed themselves and implemented orthodox neoliberal austerity policies in order to get help from the IMF with their economic problems.[39]

Thus, by the late 1980s, both the Latin American Left and the North American Right found themselves supporting democracy in Latin America, albeit for contradictory reasons and with conflicting objectives. These contradictions and conflicts would continue to drive developments during the 1990s.

■ Democratic Dynamics: Understanding Regime Change

Most of the theories discussed in this chapter deal with the question of what true democracy is. As one might expect of a body of theory emerging from stable liberal democracies, little attention has been paid to questions of political change: What conditions bring about change? How does change take place? With regard specifically to democracy, key issues of change obviously deal with the rise and fall of democratic regimes. It is also important to attend to the question of change within a democratic regime.

To the extent that North Atlantic political theory has dealt with these issues, it has tended to make a structural argument; that is, change will occur in a political regime only when, and to the extent that, overarching social, economic, and political conditions permit or encourage it. Marx's theory of proletarian revolution as a product of objective economic conditions was the archetype of this sort of argument, and Barrington Moore's classic book *The Social Origins of Dictatorship and Democracy* also adopted this strategy.[40] Non-Marxist political sociologists have usually pursued a similar but more static approach. For example, Seymour Martin Lipset was the first of many scholars to analyze aggregate social and economic data to find a pattern of correlations between overall levels of "economic development" or "modernization" and the presence of democratic political regimes.[41] The attempt on the part of the United States to understand and counter revolutionary insurgencies produced a spate of studies emphasizing the economic, social, and even psychological conditions for the emergence and survival of guerrilla movements.[42] Recently, David Easton (1990) attempted an analysis of "higher-order structures," or those relatively unchanging political patterns that condition and constrain political action and even other structures. However, the attempt is plagued by conceptual and logical problems and, though suggestive, remains inconclusive.

Mainstream North Atlantic social science has tended to view regime change as a problem best avoided. A variety of major studies in the 1960s treated political stability as a central goal of policy,[43] and Samuel Huntington's classic and highly influential work *Political Order in Changing Societies* (1968) argued that modernization and economic development would tend to lead to political instability, and that this was a serious problem. Gabriel Almond, Scott Flanagan, and Robert Mundt (1973) edited a volume that paid explicit attention to political crises, which they defined as periods when normal structural constraints on choice are weakened, permitting wider than usual political choice for elites and hence greater possibilities for change. But in paying attention to change, Almond and his collaborators nevertheless saw stability as the norm, only punctuated by crises, periods of significant change.

The most specific and substantial attention paid to the problem of change in general and of the rise and fall of democratic regimes in particular has come from students of the Third World in general and from Latin Americans and students of Latin America in particular. This should not surprise us, since political instability and change are far more characteristic of the region than stability. In the late 1970s and early 1980s, reflecting the resurgence of authoritarian regimes in the region, there was much preoccupation with the fall of democracies; this focus was exemplified in an influential multivolume collaborative work titled *The Breakdown of Democratic Regimes*.[44] During the early 1980s, only three Latin American countries—Venezuela, Costa Rica, and by some criteria Colombia—remained liberal democracies (these cases are compared in Peeler, 1985, and Peeler, 1992). However, even as the former book was being published, events in Latin America were transforming the political landscape, as country after country made the transition from authoritarian to democratic governance. Several large collaborative studies sought to focus attention on transitions to democracy and on the phenomenon of democracy in developing countries.[45]

Unlike previous structurally oriented analyses, the books discussed in the previous paragraph, although not denying the importance of structures in constraining behavior, emphasized the importance of political action, choice, and indeterminacy. The importance of elites was stressed both in regime breakdowns and in successful transitions. John Higley and Michael Burton (1989) developed the concept of the "elite settlement" as one of the principal means by which new democratic (or other) regimes could be established and stabilized. Higley and Richard Gunther later edited a comparative volume (1992) on this subject.

Karen Remmer, among others, criticized this emphasis on autonomous political action as a theoretical abdication, a failure to think rigorously about the causes of political behavior.[46] An important aspect of this structuralist perspective is a renewed emphasis on institution building, including the issue of parliamentary versus presidential constitutional structure.[47]

Another increasingly important current in comparative politics, rational choice theory, also emphasizes choices by autonomous actors, in this case on the basis of a deductive model of a self-interested actor, similar to that used in classical economic theory. Its advocates often see this approach as the key to a new science of politics (Bates, 2001; Ames, 2001; Przeworski, 1991), but it has been criticized as being unable to take account of the diversity of human motivations, and of the complexity of political processes in general and political change in particular (Weyland, 2001; Huber and Dion, 2001).

▪ Conclusion

In this chapter I have sought to provide the uninitiated reader with a brief survey and guide to the major theoretical issues in the study of democracy. A mode of governance that is clearly rooted in Western liberalism, liberal democracy nevertheless makes universal claims to its validity as a principle of political legitimacy and as a procedure or structure for public choice. The legitimacy principle of popular consent has historically been contested by alternative principles, but in the twentieth century all such alternatives faded away. However, liberal democracy has also been contested by those who accept the legitimacy of its principles but who see shortcomings in its implementation of those principles. At the dawn of the twenty-first century, though, it appears that no coherent, practical alternative to liberal democracy is on the horizon; what we can expect are a variety of continuing attempts to preserve it against relapses of authoritarianism and to renovate and improve it. Latin America will surely be one of the principal arenas of these struggles.

▣ Notes

1. This chapter will focus on the European, or Western, political tradition, with its roots in classical Greece and Rome. This is not to deny that other cultural regions have also produced ideas consistent with democracy. For example, consider the egalitarianism of classical Islam or Buddhism or the emphasis on decision by consultation and consensus in many African societies. Still, democracy as we have come to know it today is unequivocally linked to European roots.

2. Of course, women, slaves, and foreigners were entirely excluded from consideration. See Finley (1980, 1983, 1985).

3. See, for example, Hengel (1974); Gager (1975).

4. Aquinas benefited from the scholarship of the Muslim world, which had saved many classic texts, such as those of Plato and Aristotle, and had translated them into Arabic. After the fall of the Roman Empire, these same texts had been unknown in western Europe. Aquinas had access to translations of Aristotle from Arabic into Latin, and Aristotle had a major influence on his political argument.

5. Cf. Kristeller (1961).

6. Cf. Tonkin (1971).

7. See, for example, Miller (1990).

8. See Hill (1965, 1972, 1980); Walzer (1965).

9. Spinoza (1951). For Locke, Hume, and Rousseau on social contract, see Barker (1947).

10. See also Jefferson (1974); Pole (1987).

11. If U.S. leaders still used contractarian thought, it was because they were precisely faced with a situation that required overthrowing tyrannical rule and agreeing on a new political order. A generation later, the same situation would confront the leadership of Spanish America.

12. Note Jefferson's use of the contract concept in the Declaration of Independence and Thomas Paine's use of it in both *Common Sense* and *The Rights of Man*. Cf. Mary Wollstonecraft's counterpoint in *A Vindication of the Rights of Woman* (1929).

13. See also Goodin (1995).

14. John Stuart Mill (1975, 1994).

15. Cf. Adam Smith (1952). It is no accident that a key liberal slogan has advocated a "free market of ideas."

16. See also Tocqueville (1980).

17. This formulation is elaborated in Peeler (1985), chap. 1.

18. The best short collection of Marx's voluminous writings is Tucker (1978).

19. Marx, "The German Ideology," in Tucker (1978), p. 187.

20. Engels, "Socialism: Utopian and Scientific," in Tucker (1978), p. 713.

21. Marx, "The Possibility of Non-Violent Revolution," in Tucker (1978), pp. 522–524.

22. However, Gramsci believed that, in a liberal democracy, the vanguard party could potentially operate within the law to develop a counterhegemony that would lay the groundwork for a peaceful takeover of the state through elections.

23. Durkheim (1986); Tönnies (1971); Weber (1983).

24. Michels (1949); Pareto (1984); Mosca (1939); Ostrogorski (1974).

25. Wilson (1885); Veblen (1934).

26. See Friedrich and Brzezinski (1965); Arendt (1951); Kirkpatrick (1982, 1990).

27. Thus, among scholars of American politics, Floyd Hunter (1953) and C. Wright Mills (1956) were widely criticized for an alleged overemphasis on elite control in the United States.

28. Dahl (1956, 1961, 1971).

29. Dahl (1970, 1982, 1985, 1989).

30. Anderson (1995); Bracey, Meier, and Rudwick (1970).

31. Walton (1984); Small and Hoover (1992).

32. Also consult these recent works: Cohen and Arato (1992); Pangle (1992); Putnam (1993); Holmes (1995); Etzioni (1995); Beiner (1995); Van Parijs (1995).

33. Macpherson (1973), p. 4.

34. Barber (1984), p. 132.

35. For example, see Silva Michelena (1971).

36. See Peeler (1985, 1992).

37. Stallings and Kaufman (1989); O'Donnell, Schmitter, and Whitehead (1986); Munck (1989).

38. Hartlyn, Schoultz, and Varas (1992); Pastor (1989).

39. For example, Carlos Andrés Pérez in Venezuela, Fernando Collor de Mello in Brazil, Carlos Menem in Argentina, and Alberto Fujimori in Peru.

40. Moore (1966). See also Skocpol (1994); Rueschemeyer, Stephens, and Stephens (1992).

41. Lipset (1959); Lipset, Seong, and Torres (1993). See also Cnudde and Neubauer (1969).

42. Wickham-Crowley (1991, 1992) provides a good overview.

43. For example, Almond and Coleman (1960); Almond and Powell (1966).

44. Linz and Stepan (1978).

45. O'Donnell, Schmitter, and Whitehead (1986); Diamond, Linz, and Lipset (1989); Baloyra (1987); Malloy and Seligson (1987); Drake and Silva (1986); Perelli, Picado, and Zovatto (1995); Mayorga (1992b); Tulchin (1995).

46. Remmer (1991a).

47. See, for example, Linz and Valenzuela (1994); Mainwaring and Scully (1995).

2

Democracy and the Latin American Tradition

It is unequivocally true that the dominant political traditions of Latin America have been inhospitable to the development of democracy, even in its less than pure form, the "modern democratic republic," described in Chapter 1. This point has been forcefully and elegantly argued by several authors, Claudio Véliz among them.[1] Writing in the late 1970s, when military dictatorships dominated all of South America save Colombia and Venezuela, Véliz argued that Latin America's distinctive "centralist tradition" constituted a decisive barrier even to liberalism, much less to democracy. Both the political emphasis on centralization of authority in the Crown and the hierarchical yet flexible approach to Catholicism that he labeled "latitudinarian religious centralism" had, in his view, worked over five centuries to render Latin America unreceptive to democratic ideas and practices. He admitted that liberal and democratic ideas had considerable currency in the late nineteenth and twentieth centuries, but he interpreted that period as a "liberal pause" that gave way, in the 1970s, to a resurgence of the dominant centralist tradition. By this argument (and similar arguments of Howard Wiarda [1992] and Glen Dealy [1992]), democracy is a culturally alien hothouse flower that cannot long survive in the Latin American environment.

The notion that democracy is culturally alien to Latin America implicitly assumes that Iberian civilization has been largely insulated from currents that swept the rest of Europe. That is simply not the case, and it never was. In medieval times, Iberia was on the front lines of the fruitful confrontation between Christianity and Islam. In the Renaissance, Spain and Portugal were the leaders of Europe. Later, both countries were fully embroiled in the political conflicts of Europe, integrated—albeit unequally—into the economy of Europe, and conversant with the intellectual developments in the rest of the continent. Their American subjects were surely more isolated; however, educated people had communications not only with the mother countries but with other lands as well. Liberal economic and political ideas were well-known in

Latin American cities half a century before independence, and those ideas became just as much part of the Latin American tradition as Véliz's centralism.

Three other related features of Latin American society and politics must be considered major barriers to democracy: persistent and pervasive inequality, predatory relations between rulers and ruled, and clientelism. Since the colonial conquest, all Latin American societies have been characterized by huge gaps between rich and poor (among the largest in the world) with significant middle classes only emerging in some places in the course of the twentieth century. This pattern has persisted because those who rule have normally regarded the poor majority as objects for maximum exploitation: political and economic power tend to go together, and those who hold it are expected to enrich themselves further. The best way for the poor to cushion the impact of exploitation is to attach themselves to someone more powerful in a patron-client (or clientelistic) relationship whereby the subordinate (client) renders support to the superior (patron) in return for protection and perquisites (patronage). The patron is thus assured of supporters, and the client is assured of security in the face of deep inequality and exploitation. Clientelism, as well as the inequality and exploitation on which it grows, is profoundly subversive of democracy by undermining the premise of equality among citizens. While none of these features is unique to Latin America, they are particularly strong in the region.

Nevertheless, democracy does have numerous cultural roots in Latin American history and thought. Though not a dominant theme, democracy as a contemporary political project can and does draw on diverse elements of the Latin American experience. None of the elements cited hereafter is unambiguously democratic in any sense of the word; from the point of view of democracy, each is seriously flawed. Nevertheless, each lends itself to political action by those who would defy or limit authority (one key element of the modern democratic republic) or promote popular participation and political power (the other key element).

■ Elite Politics and the Roots of Democracy

In both Spain and Portugal, centralism as an ideology of royal absolutism became dominant only in the fifteenth century and was subject, in both kingdoms, to challenge and resistance. At the elite level, a principal focus of resistance to royal authority was the medieval tradition of *fueros,* special privileges and exemptions accorded to the church and its religious personnel, chartered towns, and the nobility.[2] *Fueros* commonly entailed exemption from taxation, as well as other special legal privileges such as ecclesiastical courts with exclusive jurisdiction over clergy. Obviously, a key objective of royal absolutists had to be to restrict and if possible eliminate *fueros;* just as obviously, their beneficiaries would do all they could to maintain them. The issue of such special rights and privileges became an important theme of political discourse throughout the colonial era and continues to have echoes even in twenty-first-century politics.[3]

Thus the practice of absolute royal authority actually carried with it a persistent and widespread assumption that one of the boons most to be desired from such authority was the grant of special privileges and exemptions that, in effect, committed the royal authority to refrain from exercising its full, absolute rights. There was, then, within the Iberian tradition, a concept of rights that limited state actions. In contrast to the Anglo-American, Lockean tradition, these rights were not conceived as prior to the state but rather were conceded by the state. But even though the rights were conceded by the monarchies, both the Spanish and Portuguese states found it quite difficult to withdraw or alter them unilaterally. Many political conflicts of the colonial era were over just such attempts by central authorities to change the rules.

Two examples illustrate this point. Francisco Pizarro, conqueror of Peru, was, like other conquistadores, initially vested with the duties of royal governor. The first viceroy, appointed by the Crown in the 1540s to discipline Pizarro, was instead overthrown and killed in battle by the conquistador.[4] Nearly a century later, during the period of Spanish control over Portugal (1560–1640), bands of Brazilian fortune-seekers *(bandeirantes)* raided Jesuit missions in what is now Paraguay, seeking Indian slaves in direct violation of royal policy. Yet the royal government did little to control the raids, except (after prolonged provocation) to authorize the Jesuits to arm the Indians.[5]

Thus, local elites and their followers were most jealous of their autonomy, sought to have it recognized by the Crown whenever possible, and resisted efforts by central authorities to reduce it. Flat rejection of royal authority was rare, but insubordination was common. Often enough, insubordinate elites got away with it, and by appeal to higher authority actually got decisions reversed. The formula *obedezco pero no cumplo* ("I obey but do not fulfill") was sometimes used by colonial officials to indicate that local conditions would not permit implementation of the order, notwithstanding the official's disposition to obey. Moreover, the Crown often neglected to enforce its own policies in marginal areas, effectively requiring autonomy of local elites. As late as the eighteenth century in one of the most isolated backwaters of the Spanish empire, Costa Rica, the governor complained bitterly that no labor was available to till his fields and that he had to do so himself if he wished to survive. There is no indication that the government in Guatemala, the colonial capital of Central America, cared very much about what happened in a place with neither minerals nor agricultural wealth.[6] Costa Ricans even in this century attribute their relatively democratic history to this early neglect and widely distributed poverty.[7]

There is nothing inherently democratic about this tradition of local elite autonomy. Indeed, the autonomy was typically used the more effectively to exploit Indians, Africans, and others not privileged with elite status. This was often true even of the church itself. For example, missions were normally accorded special exemptions from royal regulation of Indian labor, permitting them in some cases to exploit that labor more fully than secular landowners. On a broader scale, the church was often bequeathed land or other property, the income from which was essential to the subsistence of the clergy and the functioning of the institution. The clergy, in short, had an interest in effective exploitation of land and labor.

The church also produced the most eloquent defenders of humanitarian values. The best known is Bartolomé de Las Casas, bishop of Guatemala in the mid–sixteenth century and tireless defender of the native Americans against the depredations of conquerors and colonists. Las Casas's arguments ultimately convinced the Crown to impose new limits and regulations on exploitation of the Indians and to authorize the importation of African slaves as an alternative labor source. San Pedro Claver, active in Cartagena in the late sixteenth century, devoted his life to alleviating the misery of the Africans. In the late seventeenth and early eighteenth centuries, the Jesuits in Paraguay developed a very impressive chain of missions to the Guaraní peoples, devoted paternalistically to their settlement and material prosperity as well as their conversion. Each of these manifestations of ecclesiastical humanitarianism demanded recognition by the central authorities, protection from autonomous action of local settlers, and exemption from secular obligations such as taxation. At the level of policy, the demands were granted; at the level of practice, the results were less reliable.[8]

There was, then, a tradition of limits on and resistance to central authority, albeit not cast in terms of constitutionalism or natural rights. The power of the tradition was evident in more recent phenomena, such as most of the independence movements in Spanish America (with the principal exception of the popular movements of Father Miguel Hidalgo and Father José María Morelos in Mexico, on which more will be said later). Many creole elites (American-born whites) resented the perceived loss of power and privilege emerging from the Bourbon reforms of the mid–eighteenth century (designed precisely to enhance Crown control over the empire), and they frequently saw their economic interests directly threatened by a more efficient central control that might restrict contraband trading, even as they also depended on the Crown for protection against external attack and popular rebellion. This elite ambivalence about central authority was reflected in the political thought and practice of the independence period. Even when creole elites came to reject the legitimacy of royal authority and had to turn for legitimacy to popular consent, they opted universally for constitutionalism rather than pure democracy. In the unique case of Brazil, independence was brought about without eliminating the monarchy, but even there the new imperial regime was constitutional and, in principle, representative.[9] Even though in practice major regime changes were almost always made by force rather than through constitution-ally mandated procedures, no basis of legitimacy was ever devised that could replace a constitution grounded ostensibly in popular consent.

The same elite ambivalence toward central authority is evident in major developments in nineteenth-century Latin America. Caudillismo essentially involved the willingness of daring men to disregard utterly any claims of legit-imate authority, to seize the government and its benefits for themselves, for no better reason than that they had the power to do so.[10] A successful caudillo nec-essarily sought to centralize control in order to eliminate possible rivals, but caudillismo itself can never foreclose the possibility or probability of a new rival emerging.[11] Thus, with the definitive elimination of the royal claims to legitimate authority, the caudillos operated—for varying periods and to vary-ing degrees—autonomously as political entrepreneurs, in a competition remi-niscent of Hobbes's state of nature and the very antithesis of colonial central-ism. Indeed, those who were successful in imposing order often benefited from the support of the propertied classes and the imperial powers (Britain and the United States), whose interests were favored by order. Caudillos are a particu-larly vivid example of actors who relate in complex ways to their structural environment: they defy structures (e.g., authority claims), constitute new struc-tures (e.g., a new political regime), and are limited by structures (e.g., imperial power).

Caudillismo was also a precursor of democracy in a more direct sense. Caudillos were mostly of humble or, at best, middling origins. Their power lay in their capacity to mobilize and lead other common people. Caudillos and their movements thus embodied democracy in the literal sense that common people were coming to power. That is why some elites of the independence era were frightened of Tomás Boves (royalist) and José Antonio Páez (repub-lican), each a powerful leader of the formidable horsemen of the Venezuelan llanos (plains). Juan Manuel Rosas in Buenos Aires and Rafael Carrera in Guatemala, similarly, were caudillos with strong mass backing who were able to seize and hold power after independence.[12]

Liberalism was the major historical antagonist of caudillismo; the propo-nents of European and North American ideas of progress sought, like Domingo Faustino Sarmiento, to impose "civilization" on the "barbarous" caudillos.[13] Yet the practice of liberalism, and its offshoot, positivism, showed as much ambivalence toward authority as caudillismo itself. Liberal economic and political thought is deeply distrustful of the capacity of any state to serve the general interest through positive action. Thomas Jefferson's dictum, "That government is best which governs least," sums up the basic liberal orientation. Liberals in Latin America most particularly imbibed liberal economic doc-trine and consequently sought to promote economies based on free trade. They sought to eliminate government restraints on trade and economic subsi-dies to inefficient economic activities while encouraging those industries (export agriculture and mining) that could find external markets and attract external investments. Liberals often worked to eliminate forms of property that restricted the free market, such as land controlled by indigenous villages or the church; they thereby promoted a profound concentration of land in the hands of an emerging class of capitalist landowners or foreign corporations such as the United Fruit Company in Central America.

Most Latin American liberals were less deeply committed to the political side of liberalism, with its emphasis on constitutionalism, limited government, and freedom of expression. They usually did articulate such values but often honored them in the breach. Liberals were less liberal in politics for several reasons. First, they had to concentrate power in order to carry out their preferred economic policies. They were, after all, agents of change, actors, and the enforcement of change requires power. Second, the incorporation of positivism into liberal conventions in the late nineteenth century further reinforced pressures toward authoritarianism, since positivism saw progress as depending on a strong state led by people who understood the "scientific" laws of social progress. Thus the founders of the first Brazilian republic declared their intention to bring "order and progress" to a "New World in the Tropics."[14] Third, liberals and positivists were creatures of the same societies that produced the caudillos and had, perforce, to behave (in varying degrees) like caudillos in order to get and keep power. Fourth, liberalism was, for many, less a deeply held conviction than a flag of political convenience that would serve to identify them with a particular partisan coalition. Thus, for example, liberal parties in many countries evolved symbiotically with conservative parties, as competing clientelistic coalitions seeking control of the state but without clearly defined policy differences in practice. Finally, for those seeking respectability with the great powers or with large corporations, liberalism was a useful label.[15]

Here the liberals exemplify the interplay of action and structure that is the theoretical ground of this book. They were, on the one hand, actors who sought power in order to change society. They created new structures. On the other hand, they were deeply constrained by the informal rules of the game of caudillismo, the dominant political culture of nineteenth-century Latin America. Further, they had to operate within the structure imposed by a global liberal climate backed by the great powers. Finally, note the relativity of structure: Britain, as the leading great power, might change its policy at will, thereby taking action. But to a Latin American leader or government, any policy of a great power was an unchangeable part of the environment to which it was necessary to adapt; in short, it was a structure.

Several examples can provide a more detailed sense of the diversity and commonality of liberalism in nineteenth-century Latin America. Most observers would agree that the great Mexican statesman Benito Juárez represented the best of Latin American liberalism.[16] A full-blooded native American by birth, Juárez rose to prominence as a liberal leader in the era of the caudillo General Antonio López de Santa Anna and was instrumental in the overthrow of Santa Anna in 1855, after the disastrous war with the United States in which Mexico lost half its territory. Politically, Juárez was committed to constitutionalism and to the liberal ideal of a republic of equal citizens. Ironically, his commitment to economic liberalism led him to sponsor the destruction of indigenous communal landholdings in the name of progress. Ousted from power in 1861 by an alliance of Mexican conservatives with the French imperial regime of Napoleon III, Juárez led an insurgency that regained power in 1867 when the United States, freed of preoccupation with its own civil war, pressured the French to pull out.

Juárez's death only a few years later opened the way to the prolonged dictatorship of the other face of Mexican liberalism, Porfirio Díaz (1876–1910). Whereas Juárez was primarily a political liberal and constitutionalist, Díaz proved to be a positivist authoritarian who sought to enhance his personal power by making Mexico attractive to foreign investment and lucrative to those with capital. Concentration of property and income reached new heights, as did political corruption. The excesses of this liberal dictatorship in turn laid the foundation for what is arguably the defining epic of twentieth-century Latin America: the Mexican Revolution.

Similar stories can be told about liberalism elsewhere in Latin America. Many countries experienced an era, in the late nineteenth and early twentieth centuries, of highly elitist constitutional regimes in which substantial opposition freedoms were tolerated and a general tone of civility was maintained for more than one presidential term. These regimes often presided over periods of economic growth and rising standards of social well-being and tended to break down at times of economic crisis.

In Costa Rica, the retirement of military dictator Tomás Guardia in 1882 led to the inauguration of the "Liberal Republic," which would last almost unbroken until 1940. During this period there was only one abortive military regime (1917–1919), elections were regularly held and often were won by candidates opposed by the incumbents, and universal public education was given decisive impetus. The relatively strong and stable state was in a much better position than other Central American countries to actually extract benefits to the country from concessions granted to the United Fruit Company and other banana producers. For example, United Fruit agreed in both Honduras and Costa Rica to build a railroad from the coast to the capital; only in Costa Rica was the government able to insist that the job be finished. In Honduras, the rails extended no further than the company's plantations.[17]

Justo Rufino Barrios of Guatemala represents the more despotic face of liberalism.[18] Coming to power in 1873 after a civil war victory over the conservatives, Barrios sponsored a draconian destruction of indigenous communal landholdings as a means of making appropriate lands available for coffee cultivation, which then took off and became the foundation for the Guatemalan economy up to the present time. Politically, notwithstanding its liberal identity, the Barrios regime was a classic self-perpetuating personal dictatorship that lasted over a decade.[19]

The overall legacy of Latin American liberalism for democracy in the region has been ambiguous at best. Its predominantly economic thrust promoted the concentration of property and income and the destruction of indigenous communities. Its positivist variant was openly authoritarian. For the most part, the political commitments of Latin American liberals were weak and inconsistent, usually disregarded when they were inconvenient. Liberals were no more likely than conservatives to be sincere and consistent constitutionalists.[20] Thus, even though liberalism in theory stood for political equality and constitutional government, its inegalitarian economic practice and its inconsistent, often cynical political practice render its legacy suspect.

■ The Latin American Constitutional Tradition

The predominant interpretation of constitutionalism in Latin America sees the constitution as an inseparable aspect of political independence. The constitution, as a set of rules limiting the authority of the government, is seen as alien to the absolutism of the colonial era. It is my argument, however, that constitutionalism has much deeper Iberian and colonial roots and that those roots are quite distinct from the Anglo-American constitutional tradition.[21] Within the Western intellectual tradition, there are at least three distinct lines of constitutional thought: Roman, medieval, and contractarian/liberal.[22] These threads are woven together to form the Latin American constitutional tradition, a key structural element that shaped twentieth-century political practice.

The pronounced legalism of the Iberian tradition has its roots first in Rome. The Iberian peninsula was ruled by the Romans for several hundred years and received from the Romans more than just its languages. The Romans were the first to develop legal thought to a high level, particularly during the republican period, when the governance of the city was regulated by elaborate legal norms allocating powers to the Senate, the Assembly, and consuls and other officials. Even as the republic was breaking down under the weight of warfare and conquest, the expectation that actions of public officers would be clothed in law was maintained. Throughout the life of the Roman Empire and throughout its territory, the law was an essential instrument of rule. Even on the increasingly frequent occasions when emperors were forcibly overthrown and replaced, their successors were always careful to arrange the legal underpinning of their tenure. It was for this purpose that republican institutions such as the Senate were maintained long after they ceased to have an independent role. As much as any other indicator, the decline and fall of Rome may be marked by the decay of its rule of law. The ideal, nevertheless, survived in Iberia, as well as elsewhere.

While the church carried on and adapted the Roman legal tradition after the fall of the empire, a quite distinct political practice emerged in western Europe in medieval times. There were enormous variations, of course, but the general structure of the situation was marked by secular decentralization of authority matched with religious centralization in the hands of the papacy. The popes claimed supremacy over all secular authorities in Christendom, but church doctrine also allowed secular authorities substantial autonomy as long as they acknowledged papal authority and the governing principles of natural law as taught by the church.[23]

Secular decentralization and autonomy meant that in any given population and territory, a variety of entities (e.g., cities, guilds, knightly or priestly orders, estates) were recognized (by tradition, supplemented by written documents) as having rights to autonomy and the right to consent to measures, such as changes in taxes, that would affect them. Correspondingly, these recognized entities had obligations to their feudal lords and monarchs. The political rulers (lords and monarchs) also had obligations as well as rights. Their principal obligation, beyond keeping the peace, was to respect the traditional rights of their subjects. The political theory of Aquinas and others made clear that rulers who did not meet their obligations were tyrants (i.e., unlawful rulers) who might legitimately be resisted by their subjects.

In short, if the Roman tradition emphasized the importance of a comprehensive, written law that is applicable everywhere, medieval tradition emphasized the importance of traditional law that sets the boundaries of authority. Traditional law differs from place to place, though it must operate within the structure of natural law. For example, English common law and its constitutional tradition are rooted in medieval thought and practice.

Iberian societies had their forms of this medieval political pattern.[24] In particular, the regional nobility and the towns developed quite substantial autonomy, and corporate modes of consultation between monarch and subjects, such as the Castilian Cortes, did evolve. However, centuries of battles with the Moors gave a decisive advantage to the monarchs of Portugal, Castile, and Aragon, as Christian armies slowly and with great difficulty expelled the Muslims from the peninsula. Thus, medieval traditions limiting royal authority, which laid the foundation for the English constitution, had become marginal to political practice in Iberia by the fifteenth century. Still, the norm of legal autonomy for recognized collectivities was never totally lost and, indeed, became more relevant in the New World because of the distance and time involved in exercising central control.

The contractarian, or liberal, approach to constitutions is the most familiar to U.S. readers, but it is clearly the least important source of constitutionalism in the Iberian tradition. Reflecting the decay of medieval society and the emergence of the individualistic and competitive mentality that would be essential to capitalism, contractarianism had its strongest roots in England (Hobbes and Locke) and was part of commonsense discourse in the English colonies in the seventeenth and eighteenth centuries. The central idea was that political authority is based upon a contract among the people of a society; the very idea of a contract implies agreement of the parties to abide by its terms. Whereas the Romans founded political authority on law and worried not over-much about origins, and the Middle Ages founded authority on natural law and God's will, contractarians founded it on popular consent. This radical innovation was not completely absent from Iberian discourse (consult Spanish theologian and philosopher Francisco Suárez, for example), but it never became the dominant mode of political discourse as in British North America and was indeed actively repressed by the Bourbons in the eighteenth century in Spain and Spanish America (Brading, 1987, p. 116).

Contractarian thought did come to the fore in Latin America—and, indeed, in Iberia—in the early nineteenth century. Spain and Portugal absorbed it as part of the effects of the French Revolution and the Napoleonic conquests, which tended to emphasize a version of contractarianism adapted from the radically democratic but illiberal *Social Contract* of Rousseau. These effects were also felt in the New World, but in addition, the emerging Latin American countries had before them the obvious example of the United States. The idea of a political community establishing itself by mutual agreement in the form of a constitution was obviously the best—if not the only—available device for claiming political legitimacy after asserting independence. The earlier Roman and medieval traditions were of some utility in the struggle for independence, for example, in that they allowed municipal authorities to act autonomously in a situation in which central authorities were in no position to enforce the law or allowed an assertion of independence in response to allegedly illegal acts by central authorities. But precisely because these earlier traditions had been actively used by imperial authorities, they were not easily adaptable to an assertion of independence.[25]

The distinctive manner in which Latin Americans appropriated contractarian thought, however, was decisively shaped by the persistence of the older traditions. Colonial political organization, for example, had nothing to do with contractarianism, but it was deeply legalistic in a way reminiscent of the Roman Empire. Every measure taken had to be clothed in law to be valid. Real conditions (e.g., poor communications, diversity of local circumstances), however, often made it impossible to fully implement policies handed down from the center. This basic contradiction generated the widespread use of legal casuistry designed to stretch the interpretation of the law to include actions actually taken. Similarly, after independence, it has been deemed essential in all countries, almost all the time, to have a constitution as the ground of legitimacy, but these constitutions almost always have in their texts provisions for their emergency suspension, in whole or in part (Loveman, 1993).[26] The most arbitrary and repressive acts are typically rationalized casuistically as consistent with the constitution. Or, as was common in the recent transitions from authoritarian regimes in the 1980s, such acts are legally pardoned ex post facto.[27]

Another important feature of Latin American constitutionalism drawn from the earlier traditions is corporatism.[28] Contractarian thought is individualist in its essence, positing a society constituted by virtue of an agreement among egoistic individuals. By contrast, the medieval tradition is corporatist. Humans are construed to be inherently social, and the various collectivities to which they belong thus have a much more fundamental status than in contractarian thought. But these collectivities are only legitimate if they contribute to the overall collective good of the society. They must, in short, be recognized as legitimate by the supreme political authority if they are to be tolerated and participate in public affairs.[29] One of the principal functions of constitutions in nineteenth- and twentieth-century Latin America has been to ratify decisions made by rulers as to which groups or sectors shall be recognized as legitimate interlocutors in the political process. The twentieth-century expansion of political participation from the narrow elitism prevalent in 1900 to virtually universal citizenship as we begin the twenty-first century is seen much more in terms of incorporating identifiable collective actors than of extending rights to individuals.[30]

Within the contractarian tradition dominant in the United States, a constitution is supposed to define with some precision the limits on authority and the obligations enforceable on the various parties to the contract. But even though Latin American constitutions assume a conventionally contractarian form, their deeper significance is better understood in terms of Iberian/Roman legalism and medieval corporatism. In the legalistic tradition, all public actions must be within the law to be recognized as valid. Therefore, those who wish a course of action to take place will quite logically want to include it in the constitution as an obligation of the government. This is done not in the expectation that putting it in the constitution will make it happen, but rather to provide advocates with a powerful lever to use in their future struggle to make it happen. Royal laws for protection of the Indians did not prevent their abuse but did provide defenders such as Las Casas with a valid standpoint from which to challenge the abuse and gain some amelioration of conditions. The constitution, like the laws of the Indies, is not intended so much as a literal control on behavior as a definition of what behavior shall be considered legitimate.

The new constitutions of Brazil and Colombia both recognize indigenous peoples in a corporatist manner, giving them by name not only full rights of citizenship (which they had as individuals already) but also corporate rights to defend their own cultures and traditions. These provisions will not by themselves stop abuse of Amazonian tribes and other indigenous peoples, but by committing the state to respecting and defending them, the new constitutions strengthen the moral and legal resources of indigenous peoples and their defenders.

■ Popular Resistance and the Roots of Democracy

This section will focus on the Latin American tradition of popular resistance to oppressive authority. Since Latin America was built on the conquest and exploitation of native Americans and relied heavily on the labor of African slaves, revolts by either of these two groups would be the most obvious place to look for popular resistance. There are numerous examples of both. The indigenous rebellion led by Tupac Amaru in Peru in the 1780s nearly succeeded in taking Cuzco.[31] There were many other cases of indigenous uprisings, though none so close to success. On the margins of the empires, especially in southern Chile and Patagonia, northern Mexico, and the Amazon Basin, some indigenous peoples avoided subjugation, partially by flight and partially by armed resistance, well into the era of independence. Respect for such indigenous resistance became a tradition, institutionalized most fully by the indigenist mythology of the Mexican Revolution (see later discussion). The idea of a conquered people rising up against its exploiters is essentially democratic, in that such an uprising implicitly or explicitly entails a demand for self-determination. In addition to Mexico, several contemporary Latin American nation-states have appropriated such a tradition to bolster their own legitimacy.[32]

In Brazil and the Caribbean, where plantation agriculture employed large numbers of African slaves, rebellions were frequent, as were autonomous republics of escaped slaves. Of course, the most successful occurred in Haiti, where a slave revolt became a true social revolution, the first in the hemisphere. And the revolution in Haiti drew a strong, democratic inspiration from the French Revolution, whatever the subsequent failings of many of its leaders and whatever the long litany of betrayal and subversion of Haiti by outsiders. Some of the Brazilian escaped slave societies, or *quilombos,* survived for decades, and in the Guianas descendants of escaped slaves still maintain organized societies in the bush.[33]

All these instances of indigenous and African resistance represent something quite different from the types of elite resistance described in the previous section. These people were fighting for liberation from oppression at the hands of their conquerors and masters. To the extent that they succeeded, they established new social orders in which the old rulers were deprived of their privileges. They showed little or no interest either in the ancient Iberian tradition of *fueros* or in the more modern liberal emphasis on limitations on government authority. Rather, these instances of popular resistance demanded independence or self-determination for a particular people. In short, although aspects of elite resistance to authority have tended to provide underpinnings for constitutionalism, indigenous and African resistance movements have provided reference points for radically egalitarian democratic impulses.

Such resistance typically appealed little and posed considerable threat to the mass of Spanish- or Portuguese-speaking people (whether mestizos, mulattoes, or creoles) without property or office but with the status that came from being part of the dominant linguistic-ethnic community. The colonial social hierarchy (little changed by independence except at the top) typically had blacks at the bottom, then indigenous people (defined by their linguistic distinctiveness and semiautonomous social organization), then the mass of poor mestizos or mulattoes and propertyless whites. At the top were merchants, landowners, and, of course, royal officials. The poor mestizos, mulattoes, and whites would typically support the elites in the face of indigenous or slave rebellions, but they were themselves subject to intense exploitation, and there were many instances of popular resistance emerging from the poor masses. The best example from the colonial era was the Comunero revolt in Nueva Granada (now Colombia) in 1783.[34] The same Bourbon economic reforms that had touched off the contemporaneous Tupac Amaru revolt in Peru provoked mestizo resistance in Nueva Granada, where the indigenous presence was much weaker. In the latter case, craftspeople and small merchants who were disadvantaged by a combination of economic liberalization (loss of subsidies and protection from international competition) and tax increases rose against the viceroyal government and came very close to capturing Bogotá itself. The city was saved by a settlement negotiated between the rebel leadership and the authorities; once the rebel army was disbanded, the settlement was abrogated and the leaders were executed.

The Comunero revolt and others like it were characterized by professed devotion to the king even as the rebels resisted the authority of the king's officials. Almost universally, the allegation was made that the officials were exceeding their proper authority and trampling on rights previously granted by the Crown. Unlike the indigenous and black revolts, these rebellions did not directly challenge the legitimacy of the whole colonial order, but they were threatening enough to the creole elites that the latter stratum uniformly supported the royal authorities against the rebellions.

The struggles for independence in South America (Bethell, 1987c) were partially grounded in the same tradition of royalist legalism exemplified by the Comuneros, as local elites in Buenos Aires, Caracas, and Bogotá acted initially, in 1810, to defend legitimate royal authority in the face of Napoleonic usurpation of the Spanish throne. They also harbored grievances, however, against the officials of the king whose legitimacy they defended. Finally, the independence struggles came increasingly to draw on the radically democratic themes of the French Revolution itself.

In the struggle for independence in Mexico, a variation on this pattern blended popular and indigenous rebellions.[35] As the creole elites were taking control of the movement in northern and southern South America in 1810, in the old viceroyal capitals of Mexico and Peru equivalent elites clung to the Crown. In Mexico, however, a popular revolutionary movement emerged, calling not only for political independence but also for egalitarian social and economic reforms. The movement included both indigenous people and poor mestizos and whites. Under the leadership of Father Miguel Hidalgo and sub-sequently Father José María Morelos, the movement constituted a mortal threat to both the colonial regime and the Mexican class structure. Only after first Hidalgo and then Morelos were captured and executed was it possible to suppress the rebellion in 1814. Then, only after 1820, when liberals gained power in Spain and posed a new threat to the Mexican status quo, did the local elite support independence under the ephemeral imperial rule of Spanish general Agustín de Iturbide.

After independence, many caudillos arose out of similar popular rebel-lions, protests against injustices, and defiance of tyrannies. In such a context, a dynamic leader like Rafael Carrera, José Antonio Páez, or Juan Manuel Rosas would be precisely what a spontaneous popular insurgency would need in order to confront an entrenched regime successfully. Thus caudillismo, cen-tral to politics in the nineteenth century, is inextricably linked to popular revolt and resistance. Tragically, though, caudillos also transmuted the popu-lar impulse for justice into a clientelistic pursuit of office and favors.

Carrera illustrates the point.[36] He was a caudillo who came to prominence in opposing the Central American Federation, which broke up in 1838. By 1844, General Carrera was elected president with strong support from the church, conservative landowners, and the peasantry. A militant opponent of liberal secularization, he was able to hold the liberals at bay until his death in 1865, primarily because of his devoted popular support. He used this support to bolster conservative economic interests, which included promoting infra-structure development. He did not provide much in the way of real benefits to the majority of his devoted followers.

Robert Gilmore, in his study of caudillismo in Venezuela (1965), argued that Juan Vicente Gómez (in power from 1908 to 1935) was the last Venezue-lan caudillo, because he was uniquely successful in eliminating the social foun-dations for the emergence of rivals who might challenge him for power. Begin-ning as a general in the Andean army that seized power in 1899, Gómez shaped the perfect clientelist regime, effectively insulated against external opposition. What began as a movement against corruption and for renovation had deterio-rated (even before Gómez muscled aside his chief, Cipriano Castro, in 1908) into a government in the hands of a self-serving dictator and his clique.

The Mexican Revolution, which began in 1910 and occupied an entire generation in the world's most populous Spanish-speaking country, was the apotheosis of all these strands of democratic impulses in Latin America; as such, it embodied their contradictions.[37] The initial spark was the liberal reformist campaign led by Francisco Madero against the rickety dictatorship of Porfirio Díaz, under the slogan "Effective Suffrage, No Reelection" (which had been Díaz's own slogan when he was first elected in 1876). After fraud gave the election to Díaz, a popular insurrection forced him to leave the country, giving way to Madero. A conservative coup three years later resulted in the death of Madero and provoked insurrections by several independent groups, which were to struggle for supremacy over the next several years. All the insurrections shared a general sense of struggling against injustice and for the common people, but no systematic ideology ever became dominant. Each major insurgent group produced a revolutionary caudillo around whom military and political action centered. Most prominent among them were Emiliano Zapata, Venustiano Carranza, and Pancho Villa. By 1917, Carranza had achieved national dominance, and in short order both Zapata and Villa had been assassinated.

Under Carranza's leadership the constitution of 1917 was framed. It articulated the populist, reformist, and democratic aspirations of the revolution, mandating, for example, agrarian reform and state ownership of mineral resources. However, just as the Latin American tradition might lead one to expect, few of these reformist commitments were fully implemented. Similarly, reflecting the rallying cry of Madero, the president was prohibited from reelection. Again, the emerging revolutionary establishment acted as one would expect Latin American elites to act: they subscribed to the constitution while developing a political machine that would allow the top leaders to control elections and thus evade the substance of the prohibition. Two successors to Carranza, Generals Alvaro Obregón and Plutarco Elías Calles, set up an alternation in the presidency during the 1920s, but the plan was foiled when Obregón was assassinated just as he was to assume office for the second time. Calles, whose term was ending, sought to maintain his power without openly continuing in office; his means to that end was the official Institutional Revolutionary Party (PRI). Maintaining personal control over the party, Calles was able to rule through a series of client presidents for six years. But his last client, General Lázaro Cárdenas, turned on him and forced him to leave the country. During his term (1934–1940), Cárdenas furthered the development of the PRI in three ways. First, he cemented popular loyalty to the revolution by pushing through major reform measures such as an extensive agrarian reform, labor reforms, social welfare measures, and the nationalization of foreign-owned petroleum companies. Second, he organized the official party to incorporate its constituents into sectoral organizations based on occupation (i.e., peasant, labor, "popular," or state employee, and military groups; the last category was useful initially in absorbing revolutionary caudillos into the party but was subsequently abandoned). Third, by his own behavior after leaving office, he established the norm that past presidents do not continue to rule behind the scenes.

Cárdenas's decisive actions during his presidency reconstituted the most basic structures of Mexican politics. After he left office in 1940, the greatest popular uprising in the history of Latin America had been transformed into a near-perfect political machine. Most particularly, the old vice of caudillismo, the incessant and usually violent struggle for power, was transmuted into a ritual succession of constitutional dictators every six years without fail. The political action of peasants and workers was channeled into official organizations under party control. The political leadership takes care to maintain its rhetorical commitment to the goals of the revolution while in practice moving ever further from them.

The hegemony of the PRI has been eroding in recent years, but it still exemplifies the complex and equivocal place of democratic currents in Latin American politics. Rooted squarely in the traditions of the revolution, the PRI's historic role has been to mystify and mitigate the democratic impulses of that revolution.

Conclusion

While the Latin American political tradition is, on balance, not democratic, this chapter has sought to make the case that there are elements in that political tradition that are useful to those seeking to foster democracy in the region. This is to say, simply, that democracy is not wholly alien to the tradition. Democratic elements are regularly appropriated by political actors to legitimate their demands. In any country, those acting to resist abusive authority can draw upon instances of similar struggles from their own histories. Whether the struggle at hand is liberal and constitutionalist or radical and revolutionary, the tradition provides inspiration that is just as deeply rooted as authoritarianism itself.

Notes

1. On conflicting traditions in Latin America, see the interesting analysis of Knight (2001). See also Véliz (1980), and essays by Dealy, Véliz, and Wiarda, in Wiarda (1992). For analyses of clientelism, see Gay (1998); Hagopian (1996).

2. On this tradition, see Morse, in Wiarda (1992); Lockhart and Schwartz (1983), p. 361; Keen and Wasserman (1988), p. 126.

3. The tradition of *fueros* may be reflected in contemporary controversies over amnesty for military personnel accused of violating human rights during the dictatorships of the 1970s and 1980s in South and Central America.

4. Lockhart and Schwartz (1983), p. 103.

5. Ibid., pp. 267–268.

6. Monge Alfaro (1980), chaps. 4–7.

7. It would be a mistake to make too much of this rather self-serving national myth, but Costa Rica really was poor and isolated and seems to have suffered remarkably little interference even from Guatemala, much less points more distant. Costa Rica is discussed in detail in Chapters 3 and 4.

8. See Las Casas (1992). On the Jesuits, see Reiter (1995). On Claver, see Bushnell (1993), p. 20.

9. On the independence period, see Williamson (1992), chap. 6; Bethell (1987c). On the Brazilian empire, see Burns (1993).

10. Caudillismo is the pattern of political dominance asserted by self-made men on the principal basis of military prowess, in an era of political instability and decay during the decades immediately after independence. See Gilmore (1965).

11. Nevertheless, Gilmore (1965) argued that Juan Vicente Gómez did precisely that and consequently was Venezuela's last caudillo.

12. Boves was killed in battle during the War for Independence.

13. On Sarmiento and this theme generally, see Rock (1987), chaps. 3–4; Williamson (1992), chap. 8.

14. See Burns (1993).

15. See Halperín Donghi (1993), chap. 4; Burns (1980); Bushnell and Macaulay (1994), chaps. 9–11.

16. On Juárez, see Bushnell and Macaulay (1994), chap. 9; Meyer and Sherman (1991), pt. 6.

17. See Gudmundson and Lindo-Fuentes (1995).

18. On Barrios, see Torres Rivas (1993), chap. 2; Pérez Brignoli (1987), chap. 3.

19. Gudmundson and Lindo-Fuentes (1995) have argued that many of the developmentalist policies traditionally associated with late-nineteenth-century liberalism were in fact prefigured by earlier conservative governments in Central America.

20. In Argentina, Chile, and Colombia, for example, late-nineteenth-century elitist constitutionalism, generally comparable to the Costa Rican example cited previously, took place under conservative rule. See Rock (1987), chaps. 4–5; Blakemore (1993); Bushnell (1993), chap. 6.

21. Useful sources on constitutionalism in Latin American history include Loveman (1993); Baracho (1985); Wahl (1986); Pimenta (1989–1990); Bethell (1987a, 1987b, 1987c, 1987d, 1993); Vélez Rodríguez (1987).

22. I exclude here Aristotle's usage of "constitution" as a description of how a polis is *constituted* and how it works. See Aristotle (1892). The usage here implies explicit legal norms that, if followed, confer legitimacy on the acts of magistrates or rulers. See Finley (1983); Hill (1970); Wilkinson (1972); Balladares (1987).

23. In the late Middle Ages, the church taught that natural law comprises the universally valid dictates of reason as informed by divine revelation. See especially the works of Thomas Aquinas.

24. On Spanish and Portuguese history, see Payne (1973).

25. The Brazilian case is clearly distinct from Spanish America on this point. The Brazilian imperial regime was a less distinct break from the old regime; although it did use contractarian conventions in its constitutionalism, it relied heavily on the older traditions as well. See Burns (1993).

26. The ubiquity of constitutions is also partially attributable to changes on the international level, notably the rising power of Britain and the United States. Liberalism and constitutionalism were prevalent in those countries, so it was useful for Latin American elites to adopt those ideologies. The visible symbol of a constitution was a powerful tool in the search for international respectability.

27. See endnote 3 of this chapter for a comparison with the *fuero* tradition.

28. On this general cultural trait, see Williamson (1992), chaps. 4–5; Wiarda (1992), chaps. 1–5; Rouquié (1990), pts. 1–2; Davis (1972), chaps. 1–2; Jorrín and Martz (1970), chap. 1.

29. Contrast this pattern with Anglo-American pluralism, a version of liberalism that construes groups, rather than individuals, to be the primary political actors. Under the classic formulation of pluralism, central authority simply responds to pressure from groups; it does not decide which groups are legitimate participants. See Dahl (1989); Truman (1951).

30. Nothing in the preceding argument should be construed as setting up a black/white distinction between Anglo-American and Latin American constitutionalism. If there is one thing all political scientists can agree on, everywhere, it is that constitutions are never a perfect reflection of the realities of political power and political practice.

31. On Tupac Amaru, see Fisher (1966); Williamson (1992), pp. 200–202.

32. In addition to Mexico, these would certainly include Peru, Bolivia, Chile, and Paraguay.

33. On slavery, slave rebellions, and the Haitian Revolution, see Burns (1986); Williams (1984).

34. On the Comunero revolt of Nueva Granada and other revolts of the 1780s, see Phelan (1978); Williamson (1992), pp. 200–202.

35. On the Mexican independence struggle, see Meyer and Sherman (1991), pt. 4; Burns (1986), pp. 82–84.

36. On Rafael Carrera, see Woodward (1993); Gudmundson and Lindo-Fuentes (1995); Calvert (1985), pp. 64–65.

37. On Mexico, and the Mexican Revolution in particular, see Meyer and Sherman (1991), pts. 8–9; Knight (1986); Hellman (1983), chap. 1.

3

Establishing Democracy

There have been two broad waves of democratization in Latin America. The first, running from the 1920s through the 1960s, produced five stable liberal democracies (Chile, Uruguay, Costa Rica, Colombia, and Venezuela), and numerous democratic experiments that proved unstable in countries as diverse as Argentina, Brazil, Peru, and Guatemala. The second wave, beginning in the 1970s and still continuing, has seen the establishment of formally democratic regimes in most countries of the region.

▨ Early Democracies: Managing Participation

Five countries stand out in Latin America for the length and stability of their democratic experiences and because they started those experiences while democracy was still an exotic and fragile flower in the region. Chile and Uruguay began democratic regimes well before World War II, Costa Rica during and after the war, and Colombia (by some criteria) and Venezuela in the late 1950s. Each of the five countries built democracy on the structure created by its own history of political conflict and caudillismo, and each had failures and false starts. What distinguished these early liberal democracies from their neighbors was that competing elites in each case ultimately agreed on modes of absorbing the expansion of political participation while establishing and maintaining liberal, competitive political systems. In other cases, notably Argentina, Brazil, Peru, and Guatemala, such agreement was never achieved, and democracy was not successfully established. In each case, establishment of the regime reflected both internal conditions and the international conjuncture of the time. In Chile and Uruguay, the regimes broke down in 1973 and had to be reestablished in the 1980s. In Colombia, the achievement of a full liberal democracy has been slow in coming and beset by crises. In Venezuela, structural economic crisis in the 1980s and 1990s has brought the democratic regime to the edge of breakdown. Of the five cases, only Colombia has never met a reasonable standard of a consolidated democracy, but only Costa Rica has survived without a breakdown or a regime-threatening crisis.[1]

Even before the establishment of liberal democracy, elections were a regular part of the political process in all five countries, However, it is important to emphasize that elections were not the principal means of changing governments; rather, they typically served to legitimate an incumbent government or its chosen successor. Once individuals (in Venezuela or Costa Rica) or parties (in Colombia, Chile, or Uruguay) established hegemony, often by force of arms, they would utilize the government apparatus to control elections, thus perpetuating themselves in power. Opposition groups could normally capture the government either by force of arms or occasionally by coalescing with government dissidents to win an election in spite of the powers of incumbency.

The principal distinction of Chile in nineteenth-century Latin America was the relative political stability that prevailed from the early 1830s, precisely during the era when most other Latin American countries were suffering prolonged political turmoil.[2] By about 1860, the first clearly defined political parties (Conservatives and Liberals) emerged, quickly followed by the Radicals (Scully, 1992, chap. 2; Remmer, 1984, chap. 1; Collier, 1993). This tripartite pattern persisted through partisan realignments and even through the Augusto Pinochet dictatorship, reemerging with the opposition to Pinochet in the 1980s. In such a party system, the center party tended to play a moderating role, occupying the presidency the majority of the time. According to Timothy Scully (1992; see also Gil, 1966), the Liberal Party played that role until 1912 and the Radical Party from about 1920 to 1952; the Christian Democrats were the dominant center party from 1958 to 1973 (and resumed that position as the opposition to the dictatorship reemerged in the 1980s). After 1920, the traditional agroexport ruling class only regained hegemony by military force from 1973 until the early 1980s. During the long era of Chile's democracy (1920–1973) and especially after the consolidation of that democracy during the 1930s, the old ruling class protected its interests not by brute power but rather by maneuvering within the tripolar party system and by astutely using the checks and balances of Chile's democratic constitution of 1925.

The constitution provided for a strengthened presidency but also numerous checks and balances vested in the two houses of Congress (elected for staggered terms different from that of the president) and the courts (relatively insulated from political pressure). The new constitution was not actually implemented until 1932, after seven years of military intervention that included the dictatorship of Carlos Ibáñez and several other, short-lived military governments (Nunn, 1976; Ramírez Necochea, 1985; Drake, 1993). After 1932, the Chilean democracy was maintained unbroken until its overthrow in 1973. It was characterized by a multiparty system with a broad ideological range, durable and well-institutionalized parties and interest groups, and moderate levels of mass participation. Women were enfranchised in the late 1940s, but illiterates were permitted to vote only in 1970. The electorate was consistently divided into three roughly equal camps, Right, Center, and Left; none could capture a national majority alone, but each could win enough votes and congressional seats to protect its interests.

The Right, composed of the Liberal and Conservative Parties, was based largely in the countryside, where clientelistic control over peasants continued to provide a mass base to enable the upper-class leadership of these parties to compete in democratic electoral politics. Thus a core economic and political interest of the Right was to avoid policies that would erode control over the peasants, policies such as agrarian reform or peasant unionization. The Liberals and Conservatives, normally allies since 1912, formally merged to form the National Party in the 1960s. The Center, dominated before 1960 by the Radicals and subsequently by the Christian Democrats, was based on the urban middle class and working class. The interests of these two growing classes centered on the promotion of industrialization and a rising living standard, including expansion of government services. The Left, consisting largely of Communists and Socialists, had a mass base among urban and mining workers and some members of the middle class. The ultimate objective of the Left was the socialist transformation of society, but in a more immediate sense its core interests included maintaining and expanding space for labor organization and expanding government services.[3]

This tripartite balance shaped the policy characteristics of the democratic period in Chile. The center-left Popular Front governments of the late 1930s and early 1940s promoted labor union organization and worker rights and established an extensive social welfare system. But neither these governments nor those of the 1950s seriously attacked the vital interests of the Right. Specifically, no action was taken to enfranchise rural workers or to redistribute rural property. This moderation was a result of recurrent bargaining among political and economic forces, whereby the traditional landowners, backed by the Liberals and Conservatives, repeatedly demanded and got the cooperation of successive reformist governments in obstructing the organization of rural workers (Loveman, 1988, chap. 8). The resulting political order assured each of the major political forces enough power to block hostile initiatives while denying any sector the possibility of centralizing power. Presidential terms were six years, with no immediate reelection. The entire Chamber of Deputies was elected every four years. One-third of the Senate was elected every two years, for six-year terms. Congress was chosen on the basis of proportional representation, whereas presidential elections were by majority, with the proviso that Congress elect the president from the two leading candidates if no one received an absolute majority. Judges were effectively insulated from direct political control. Thus the formal constitutional structure served to stabilize the democratic regime by virtually blocking any actor from amassing enough power to push through major policy changes (Gil, 1966).

The political history of Uruguay during the nineteenth century was a notable contrast to the authoritarian stability of Chile, though the two polities did share a commitment to creating export economies.[4] The two traditional parties—Blancos and Colorados—that still dominate Uruguayan politics crystallized during the 1840s, the former basically conservative and based in the pastoral countryside, the latter liberal and rooted in Montevideo. In contrast with Chile (where clientelistic control was exercised most of the time without major civil strife), in Uruguay there were frequent civil wars, culminating in the war of 1903–1904, the last attempt by one of the traditional parties to seize power by force. The Uruguayans early on developed the practice of the elite pact as a means of putting an end to armed conflict. The winning side (usually the Colorados) would agree to share the perquisites of office with the losers (typically the Blancos) on both national and local levels. Whereas class conflict came to be directly reflected in the twentieth-century Chilean party system, in Uruguay the traditional parties maintained their dominance, concealing and transmuting class conflict.

The last of the great partisan civil wars in Uruguay ended in 1903 with a Colorado victory. This time, though, the Colorado caudillo who became president, José Batlle y Ordóñez (president 1903–1907, 1911–1915), refused to offer the Blancos participation in his government. Instead, he pushed through reforms that created a modern, activist state committed to providing material welfare to all citizens and to providing leadership and material support for the country's economic development. These policies built durable political support for the Colorados, which posed considerable danger for the Blancos. However, the Uruguayan outcome was not a slide into renewed civil war, because of the other set of changes brought about by Batlle, changes in the organization of the national government and the party system. In 1913, with his social and economic program in place, Batlle proposed to replace the president by a collegial executive. The eventual negotiation and adoption of this constitutional arrangement in 1917, supplemented by another pact of 1931 that provided for the distribution of public-sector jobs to both parties, effectively established a grand coalition style of government before partisan conflict reached the point of threatening stability.

Another distinctive aspect of Uruguayan democracy originated during this period: the electoral system of the "double simultaneous vote," also known as the Ley de Lemas, the law that regulates the participation of party factions in elections. From its origins each party has been an alliance of clientelistic factions; the electoral law not only recognizes but reinforces this feature. Any faction within a party may run its own list of candidates in a general election; representation in Congress and local government is allocated to factions on the basis of proportional representation. The votes for all lists within a party are counted toward the total of the party in both legislative and presidential races; the leading candidate of the party receiving the most votes wins the presidency. This occasionally (e.g., in 1971 and 1984) has had the effect of electing a president who did not personally receive the most votes, but it has also effectively maintained the electoral hegemony of the two factionalized parties.

If most of Batlle's institutional reforms were left intact in subsequent decades, their nationalistic, social democratic spirit and intellectual integrity were lost. A political system premised on shared power for all established interests and on patronage rather than policy coherence could discuss these issues at great length but was not equipped to resolve them. Instead, when the nation's problems periodically reached crisis proportions, the usual response was to release pressure by changing the organization of the government, from collegial to presidential and back. Thus in the context of the world economic crisis of the 1930s, President Gabriel Terra, a Colorado (indeed, a Batllista), collaborated with sectors of the Blancos to reestablish a presidential constitution. Terra was a dictator for ten years, but the presidential constitution persisted for another decade. In 1951, a resurgence of radical Batllismo led by Luis Batlle Berres (a nephew of the older Batlle) induced more conservative sectors of the Colorados (including the sons of Batlle y Ordóñez) to cooperate with the Blancos in pushing through a reestablishment of a form of plural executive, probably as a means of keeping Batlle Berres in check. In this form, the Uruguayan democracy gradually descended into crisis during the 1960s, culminating in the coup of 1973 (see Chapter 5).

Costa Rica presents an interesting historical comparison with the other four countries. In colonial times, Chile, Colombia, and Venezuela were rich and important; Costa Rica, like Uruguay, was poor and ignored.[5] Costa Rica did not suffer damage from the wars for independence; Colombia and Venezuela suffered severe destruction, and Chile and Uruguay saw considerable damage. After independence, Costa Rica was less subject to turmoil and civil war than Uruguay but slower to establish political stability than Chile. Costa Rica was among the first Latin American countries to commit itself to exporting coffee, and by 1850 that crop had become the mainstay of what had previously been the weakest economy in Central America, enabling a rather weak ruling class to consolidate its power and to stabilize the state well in advance of the other Central American countries (Stone, 1975; Gudmundson and Lindo-Fuentes, 1995, chap. 1).

Costa Rica was slower than the other four countries to develop clearly defined, durable political parties; the great liberal-conservative cleavage did affect Costa Rica, but those of liberal persuasion prevailed in the 1880s without ever needing to institutionalize a durable party. The church, linchpin of conservative thinking in the nineteenth century, was relatively weak in Costa Rica, and a self-conscious Conservative Party never formed. Instead, within the basic political economy of dominance by an agroexporting capitalist class, the political process consisted of a series of conflicts between identifiable factions within that class. These factions struggled for control of the state in a clearly defined cycle of personal hegemonies punctuated by unstable inter-regnums, a cycle that lasted until 1948 (Peeler, 1985, chap. 2). Politics gradually became less elitist in the first third of the twentieth century, with the implementation of direct elections, rising literacy, and the emergence of local *gamonales,* or political chiefs, who typically were not drawn from the national economic and social elite (Lehoucq and Molina 2002).

The elitist regime came under further challenge in the 1930s and 1940s. Communist organizing among banana workers mobilized workers on a large scale for the first time. President Rafael Angel Calderón Guardia, elected in 1940 as an establishment candidate, pushed through an advanced social security system and a new labor code, and forged a political alliance with the Communists. His chosen successor was elected in 1944. Strong opposition emerged from both Conservatives (led by León Cortés Castro and Otilio Ulate) and Social Democrats (led by José Figueres). A dispute over the outcome of the presidential election of 1948 (pitting Calderón against Ulate) led to a civil war in which Figueres's Army of National Liberation prevailed.

The negotiations that led to the establishment of liberal democracy are best seen as beginning in the crisis of 1948. As it became clear that Figueres had the upper hand in the civil war, several interests pushed for a settlement. The Calderonistas wanted to avoid the destruction of their reforms and their political position. The Communists wanted to retain legal status and their foothold in organized labor. Figueres's conservative and business allies, backers of Ulate, wanted the latter declared president without having to depend on the bayonets of Figueres. The Social Democrats wanted the way cleared for creation of the new social democratic order envisioned in their program. Figueres himself, in addition to these programmatic concerns, seemed intent on a total military victory that would leave him free to act.[6]

Setting up a governing junta, Figueres signed a pact with Otilio Ulate, providing that the latter would assume office within eighteen months and that the country would be ruled by a provisional junta in the meantime. Figueres, as president of the junta, used his extensive provisional powers to abolish the army, to nationalize banking, and to endow the state with the authority to guide the economy. These and other measures were intended to lay the groundwork for the social democratic program of restructuring society. This plan was frustrated when the Social Democrats' neglect of popular organization led to their defeat in elections for the Constituent Assembly, which instead had a strong majority for Ulate's conservative Unión Nacional. The innovative draft constitution proposed by the junta was rejected in favor of amendments to the existing document, including the enfranchisement of women. Most of the innovations decreed by the junta were ratified, but the Social Democrats nevertheless fell short of leading a thorough transformation of Costa Rica.

The Figueres-Ulate Pact of 1948 was an agreement between the two major sectors of the victorious opposition that served to regulate competition within a liberal democratic framework. From 1948 until the mid-1950s, Calderón and his supporters were outside the political process, twice trying to overthrow the government through invasions from Nicaragua. Only with the election of 1958 did Calderón reintegrate himself into the political process, joining the loose conservative coalition that was evolving to oppose the National Liberation Party (PLN), which had been built up by Figueres after the junta left office in 1949 and which led Figueres to victory in the 1953 elections. As of 1958, the transformation begun in 1948 was extended to include the principal loser of the civil war. There was no explicit pact defining the terms of Calderón's reintegration, but the commitments made during 1948–1949 facilitated the later incorporation of Calderón, in that his key institutional innovations (social security in particular) were left intact. Calderón was always able to gain political credit among potential voters for his establishment of social security. The decisions of 1948–1949 thus laid the foundation for civil political competition by minimally satisfying not only the victors but also the most important vanquished, Calderón.[7]

Costa Rica, smaller than the other countries studied in this section, is correspondingly more vulnerable to external pressure. Since 1949, the dominant Costa Rican elites have generally shown an understanding of how to maximize their scope for autonomous action relative to the United States. Costa Rican foreign policy is consistently pro-American, regardless of the party in power, and every Costa Rican government since 1948 has been anticommunist. The Costa Rican commitment to democracy is a prominent feature of the country's self-image and is stated in liberal terms that are congenial to U.S. ears. The relatively strong Costa Rican state has generally been administered with reasonable efficiency, and the economy has been managed to avoid the worst pitfalls, such as hyperinflation. This history of prudent competence has afforded the Costa Rican elites enough maneuvering room to maintain the welfare state and state control of banking and insurance, even though these features are in tension with U.S. conventional wisdom (Peeler, 2003b).

In Colombia, organized Liberal and Conservative Parties actually became the central organizing reality of the political process, as early as the 1840s: it remained possible for members of the colonial elite to bring together enough resources—using property and clientelistic ties—to control the government, without having to put themselves in the hands of rough caudillos of the type who came to dominate Venezuela. The political process became a struggle for hegemony, punctuated by periods of indeterminacy. However, the periods of hegemony in the Colombian case were more partisan than personal. As in Uruguay, a distinctive feature of Colombian politics emerged from this primitive party system: the practice of bipartisan coalitions as a means to end periods of turmoil or to facilitate change of party hegemony.[8]

The constitutional settlement presided over by Rafael Núñez after 1886 would govern the country through most of the twentieth century. Its major features were: (1) establishing a strong, centralized state (negating extreme liberalism); (2) establishing the Catholic Church while reaffirming religious liberty (protecting the basic Catholicism of society but negating doctrinaire conservatism); and (3) enshrining liberal concepts of enterprise and property (essential to promoting economic growth).

The conservative hegemony that started in 1886 collapsed in 1930, when a split in the party allowed the Liberals, in coalition with dissident Conservatives, to win national elections. Expansion of suffrage and the innovative social legislation the Liberals passed enabled them to gain a durable lock on power by attracting the loyalty of most of the new voters, especially with the emergence of the dynamic Liberal populist Jorge Eliecer Gaitán. Gaitán was not part of the old ruling class, and he indeed called for an end to the old elitist political and economic order (see Sharpless, 1978).

The Conservatives' defensive response was led by Laureano Gómez, who sought to mobilize a mass base for his party not only by appeals to traditional Catholic values but also by inflammatory condemnations of Liberals as subversive or even diabolical. When the Liberals split between Gaitanistas and regulars in 1946, the Conservatives won the presidential election with a minority in favor of Mariano Ospina Pérez. Conservative violence against Liberals, the assassination of Gaitán in 1948, and the Liberal response led to virtual civil war after Gómez was elected president in 1949 (with a Liberal boycott). Thereafter, the violence increasingly took on its own dynamic, as local and personal agendas such as revenge, plunder, and revolution made it steadily less possible for party leaders to control the violence for their own purposes.

By 1953, all factions of both parties, except the backers of the incumbent Laureano Gómez, supported the seizure of power by the commander in chief of the army, General Gustavo Rojas Pinilla, with the objective of enforcing an end to the violence. By 1957, however, Rojas had shown himself inclined to remain in power and build his own popularly based political movement in an effort to permanently supplant the traditional parties by taking away their mass support. The response of the traditional elites was to come together in 1956: a series of pacts among the major Liberal and Conservative leaders led to a popular referendum on constitutional amendments and the establishment of the National Front in 1957.

The National Front called for the two traditional parties to alternate in the presidency over four terms of four years each. The two parties would share equally all seats in the Chamber of Deputies, the Senate, and lower-level elective bodies. All appointive posts would also be equally shared. Thus the partisan balance was completely insulated from elections. Elections did matter, however, in determining the fate of individual leaders and factions within the parties. Moreover, other political parties were excluded from independent competition in elections: they could only compete by offering candidates and lists within the Liberal or Conservative Party.

The National Front was a direct response by the traditional political elites to the need to cooperate in the political demobilization of the populace, the better to maintain control through tested clientelistic mechanisms. This pact of political demobilization in fact lasted its allotted sixteen years, in spite of serious challenges. During the 1960s, chronic violence in many parts of the countryside gradually resolved itself into several durable revolutionary guerrilla movements, none of which could threaten the government's survival. Two major challenges to the National Front from within the constitutional system fell short. Under the National Front, voting turnout fell to very low levels (below even those of the United States) and has risen only slightly since the resumption of competitive elections in 1974. Other forms of political participation were also at low levels under the National Front. In short, the National Front accomplished the objectives set for it by the traditional party elites who negotiated it, but left a legacy of persistent political violence and widespread apathy.

The independence struggle destroyed the powerful ruling class of cacao planters of Venezuela.[9] After independence, Venezuelan politics evolved as a struggle for hegemony among caudillos, each with a clientelistic local power base that enabled him to raise an army and with ties to moneyed interests in Caracas that enabled him to buy arms and maintain his troops. Some caudillos were Liberals and others Conservatives, but party ceased being a factor at all after the definitive defeat of the Conservatives in the civil wars of the 1860s. Finally, under Juan Vicente Gómez (1908–1935), the logic of caudillismo was developed so fully, according to Robert Gilmore (1965), that Gómez was necessarily the last caudillo, for he systematically destroyed his rivals and used the windfall from petroleum sales to build up the state to the point that caudillismo was no longer possible after his death in 1935.

In the ten years after the death of Gómez, two successors (López Contreras and Medina Angarita) sought to bring about liberalization without loss of control. This effort failed in 1945 when Democratic Action (AD) collaborated with midranking army officers to overthrow the government of Medina Angarita. The ensuing reformist government lasted three years (hence its name, the Trienio). AD sought to bring about a rapid democratic revolution, including the full establishment of a liberal democracy, a major increase in the state's royalties on petroleum products, labor laws favorable to unions, secular educational reform, and important elements of a welfare state. AD was the only political organization with a popular base at that time, and thus in three elections during the period it completely dominated its competitors, in spite of the formal honesty and openness of the process. Venezuelan economic elites, foreign petroleum companies, and rival political party elites all supported AD's overthrow in a 1948 coup, which was followed by the dictatorship of Marcos Pérez Jiménez. But by 1957, most of those who had supported the coup were working actively to oust Pérez Jiménez, along with a large popular underground under the leadership of Communist and AD cadres.

Active consultations and cooperation took place among the various sectors opposed to the dictator. Many of the younger cadres of AD were working underground in close alliance with their counterparts in the Communist Party, seeking not only to oust the dictator but to create the conditions for a revolutionary transformation of Venezuela. The other major actors included: (1) top party elites: AD, center-left; the Independent Committee for Political and Electoral Organization (COPEI), social Christian, center-right; the Republican Democratic Union (URD), center-left; and the Communist Party of Venezuela (PCV), left; (2) the military elite not allied with Pérez Jiménez; (3) the business elite; and (4) the labor elite. Bitter rivals during the Trienio, AD, the URD, and the PCV collaborated against the Pérez Jiménez government after 1953. By 1956, COPEI, too, had been driven into opposition. These consultations bore fruit when the dictator was overthrown on 23 January 1958.

During 1958, several pacts laid the foundations of the new democratic order (López Maya and Gómez Calcaño, 1989, pp. 68–76; for texts of agreements, see pp. 109–123). The Pact of Punto Fijo was signed on 31 October 1958 by the top leadership of the URD, COPEI, and AD as the campaign for the first election was about to enter its last month. The party leaders agreed to defend constitutional government against any possible coup d'état, agreed to form a government of national unity (to guard against a systematic opposition that would weaken the democratic movement), and agreed to formulate a minimum common program to be enacted regardless of which party won the December elections.[10]

Margarita López Maya and Luis Gómez Calcaño point out (1989, pp. 74–75) that the centrist leaders devoted much effort in the early years of the regime to forging an understanding with the armed forces that would lead the latter to accept the apolitical, nondeliberative role assigned to them. The main thrust of these efforts concerned improving the socioeconomic conditions of military personnel and assuring them both full participation in decisionmaking and autonomy of action in all directly military affairs. These authors also consider the concordat with the Vatican (signed in 1964) as an additional pact important to the overall settlement in Venezuela. The hostile relations between the church and AD during the Trienio were thus transformed, and a major point of potential conflict between AD and COPEI was eliminated.

The Communists and leftist sectors of AD and the URD were largely left out of these complex negotiations and the resultant settlement. The centrist elites chose, in effect, to build a winning coalition around procedural democracy and mild reform and to risk the opposition of the Left. In reaction, and inspired by the recent success of Fidel Castro in Cuba, the Communists and the left wings of AD and the URD raised the banner of socialist revolution in 1961. By the late 1960s, the insurgency had been defeated, and many of the former guerrillas accepted amnesty and integrated themselves into political life as members of peaceful political parties of the Left (most notably the Movement Toward Socialism [MAS] and the Revolutionary Left Movement [MIR]). (See especially López Maya and Gómez Calcaño, 1989; Myers, 1986.)

Various other countries of South and Central America established democratic regimes during this period, though they were not as durable as those discussed to this point. Argentina poses an interesting contrast to Chile and Uruguay. The relatively stable elitist civilian regime in Argentina around 1900 was similar to regimes in power during the same period in Chile and Uruguay. But the Argentine elite could not adapt to the extension of universal male suffrage in 1912 and modest democratizing efforts of Ypólito Yrigoyen and his party, the Unión Cívica Radical, after his election in 1916. The Radical-dominated constitutional regime was overthrown by the army in 1930. Juan Perón's attempt to mobilize and incorporate the working class, after another military coup in 1943, was halted by a military coup in 1955; the armed forces subsequently intervened in 1962 and 1966 to prevent Peronist victories, and in 1976 to overthrow a Peronist government. Adaptation to mass political participation has come, with difficulty, only since the latest democratic restoration, in 1983 (Rock, 1987; Cavarozzi, 1983).

Brazil made a transition from its elitist republic (1888–1930) by way of a coup. Getulio Vargas ruled the country in an authoritarian manner from 1930 to 1945. Like Perón in Argentina, he fostered labor unions under his own leadership as a way of mobilizing and incorporating the working class. The liberal democratic regime established after World War II was built on competition between three forces: labor-based populism, rural landowners, and urban industrialists. When the populists gained the upper hand in the early 1960s, the armed forces overthrew the democratic regime and ruled from 1964 to 1985 (Schneider, 1996; Roett, 1992).

Peru witnessed the emergence of one of the earliest populist political parties, the American Popular Revolutionary Alliance (APRA), in the 1920s under the leadership of Víctor Raúl Haya de la Torre. After an early violent confrontation between APRA and the Peruvian armed forces, the latter consistently vetoed any electoral victory by the former, even though it became the country's largest party. A democratic regime (1963–1968) was overthrown by the military in 1968 to prevent such an APRA victory. Finally, ten years later, APRA was allowed to win elections to a constituent assembly, and a transition to a liberal democratic regime was undertaken (Klarén, 2000, chaps. 9–12; Rudolph, 1992; Palmer, 1980).

The Guatemalan dictatorship of Jorge Ubico was overthrown in 1944 by a reformist civil-military coalition very similar to those that came to power in Venezuela and Costa Rica in the same period. There was one crucial difference: the small Guatemalan Communist Party supported the coup, while its counterparts in Venezuela and Costa Rica had opposed the coups in those countries. With the Cold War gaining intensity, the United States was increasingly hostile toward the reformist government in Guatemala, even after a constitution was adopted and democratic elections were held. Finally, the Central Intelligence Agency (CIA) orchestrated a coup in 1954 that ended the democratic regime and led to three decades of military domination (Calvert, 1985; Handy, 1984; Jonas, 1991).

Conclusion: Early Democracies

Liberal democracy evolved in each of these cases out of a civil oligarchy in which political elites developed customs of political contestation, a political grammar, as it were. This is in accord with Robert Dahl's argument (1971, 1989) that democracy is more likely to be stable if methods of contestation are established before inclusion. Liberal democracies emerged when the regimes proved able to absorb and co-opt substantial expansions of suffrage and other forms of political participation without so altering the balance of political power as to provoke rebellion by major interests. This expansion of the polity took place only after a prolonged crisis in which conservative sectors resisted the expansion of participation. When parties and leaders emerged that were able to manage this expanded participation without threatening fundamental conservative interests, the crises were surmounted and liberal democracy was stabilized. Where it continued to be impossible to manage expanded participation while preserving stability, liberal democracy failed to take root.

All of these regimes represented decisive steps forward for their peoples, yet each was constituted to privilege order over justice. Had it been otherwise, they would not have lasted so long. All remained *politically* stable for decades because each was structured to maintain *social and economic stability*. These regulating structures varied according to the historical specificity of the cases, but all contrived to protect the basic distribution of resources under which the regime had arisen. Each system had a *centrist bias,* a proclivity to avoid radical departures. The Left was co-opted or marginalized in each case, part of mainstream politics but unable to implement its policy agenda without endangering the stability of the democratic regime. Conversely, the Right, although stronger than the Left in each case, had lost its political dominance with the establishment of liberal democracy and could only regain that dominance by terminating the democratic regime itself (as in Chile and Uruguay in 1973). The major elite protagonists and their constituencies had assurance of sufficient electoral success to be able to block assaults on their most basic interests, and none could expect to impose their will without compromise. Such compromises functioned to reduce to tolerable levels the uncertainty inherent in democracy (Przeworski, 1991, pp. 36–37).

The prominence of equilibrium and compromise in these cases was aided by the relative weakness of ideological cleavages, as distinct from conflicts of interest and competition for power and office. Even in the Chilean case, where a clear and broad ideological spectrum existed, prior to the Allende period the principal actors on both the right and the left showed themselves more concerned with the pursuit of office and the give-and-take of the political process than with ideological consistency.

From 1900 to 1975, most Latin American countries dealt with expanding political participation in one or more of three ways: (1) through populist authoritarianism and electoral manipulation (e.g., Getulio Vargas in Brazil or Juan Domingo Perón in Argentina); (2) through repression (e.g., overthrows of Perón and Vargas); (3) through revolution (e.g., Bolivia, Cuba, and Nicaragua). None of these routes led to stable democracy, though often they led through unstable democracy.

The five countries that are the subjects of this section, however, distinguished themselves by confronting the expansion of participation in ways that allowed the establishment and prolonged maintenance of liberal democratic regimes. All five could establish and maintain liberal democratic regimes for decades because of the evolution of highly institutionalized party systems.[11] The characteristics of these party systems varied enormously, but all showed a substantial centripetal tendency, that is, a tendency to encourage voters to support relatively moderate, rather than extreme, parties and candidates. The unavoidable winner-take-all character of presidential constitutions also encouraged moderation in candidates and voters for the purpose of maximizing votes in presidential elections, where there can be only one winner. The interaction of these two forces produced two-party, or bipolar, systems in every case but Chile, whose tripolar system orbited around a centrist party, thereby achieving moderation via a distinct mechanism.

A long history did not render any of these regimes immune from breakdown. Both the Chilean and the Uruguayan democracies broke down in 1973. In both cases, a breakdown of elite consensus was rendered acute by a relatively sudden political mobilization of the Left that was seen to threaten the basic interests of other elite sectors. Thus, these two oldest democracies, which arose to manage expanded participation, ultimately could not do so and fell. In contrast, Venezuela, Colombia, and Costa Rica confronted crises in the 1980s that had less to do with managing expanded participation and more with managing an increasingly complex, globalized economy. Although neither the Colombian nor the Venezuelan regime has broken down at this writing, both are clearly in crisis, while Costa Rica, also confronting serious challenges, is troubled but scarcely in crisis.

Why has the Costa Rican democratic regime been so much more successful than the other four countries in coping with regime-threatening crises? Part of the explanation certainly lies in the seriousness of the challenges.

Costa Rica has not had to deal with large-scale insurgencies and major drug cartels like Colombia has, nor has it had as far to fall economically as Venezuela has. As noted previously, Costa Rica received substantial external aid during the 1980s, far more on a per capita basis than Venezuela or Colombia. An additional explanation could be its intelligently formed political institutions, embodied in the constitution of 1949, such as the relatively even balance between president and legislature and the abolition of the army.[34] Finally, the Costa Rican political elite has long displayed an uncommon level of political wisdom and sophistication, as compared with its counterparts elsewhere in Central America (Peeler, 1999), or with those in Venezuela (Peeler, 1999). In confronting the challenges of the 1980s, then, these five older democracies had a great deal in common with the newer democracies around them.

▦ Later Democracies: Transitions from Authoritarianism

Between 1978 and the present writing, most of the countries of Latin America that were not already liberal democracies became so. The only exceptions are the continuing early democracies (Colombia, Costa Rica, and Venezuela), Haiti and Paraguay (which have had incomplete and rocky transitions), and Cuba (which has made no transition). These exceptions will be considered toward the end of this chapter. The rest made the transition to liberal democracy in an epoch of wrenching economic crisis and reorganization, as the old consensus of state-led development was everywhere replaced by a new orthodoxy, the "Washington consensus," in favor of global free trade and a reduced state role in economic and social matters.

Much of the literature on Latin American and comparative politics since 1985 has been concerned with this great transition.[12] Given that and the need to discuss fourteen countries in this section, there is no choice but to deal with this topic in a comparative and analytical manner rather than case by case, although major sources on each country are cited. Even proceeding comparatively, it is essential to keep in mind that notwithstanding the global and regional conditions that affected all of the countries and in spite of the similarities to be noted, each country has its own history, its own political and economic structures, and its own unique set of actors. To understand any case fully will require going beyond this comparative analysis and becoming familiar with the country on its own terms.

Authoritarian Regimes of the 1970s

Most of Latin America was under authoritarian rule during the 1970s, but the character of those regimes varied widely, which in turn profoundly affected the course of the transitions and the prospects for the emerging democratic regimes. *Personalist dictatorships* held sway in Nicaragua (until 1979),

Paraguay (until 1989), and Haiti (until 1987).[13] This is the most traditional form of dictatorship, in which one person monopolizes supreme political power, subordinates the armed forces and other institutions, and rules by force and fraud until overthrown. These societies are among the poorest and least developed of the region; one consequence is that the populations are relatively unorganized and inactive politically. Lack of mass political mobilization is both a condition for a personalist dictatorship and a consequence of it. Two of the three dictators in this set, Anastasio Somoza Debayle in Nicaragua and Jean-Claude Duvalier in Haiti, lost power precisely when an effective mass mobilization occurred. The third, Alfredo Stroessner in Paraguay, was simply removed in an elite coup when he became aged and infirm. Paraguay and Haiti have not yet completed transitions to liberal democracy, and will be further treated later in this chapter.

The authoritarian regimes of Hugo Banzer in Bolivia (1971–1979) and Joaquín Balaguer in the Dominican Republic were basically similar to the personalist type, but with variations.[14] Banzer did come to power as leader of the armed forces, but he exercised power as a personalist dictator and went on after his overthrow to become one of the principal power brokers of Bolivian politics in the 1980s and 1990s. Balaguer was not a military man but rather an old collaborator of the dictator General Rafael Leonidas Trujillo. After the U.S. invasion in 1965, Balaguer maintained himself in power by fixing elections from 1966 to 1978. However, his regime was not hard-line authoritarian: competitive elections were held, and most civil liberties were respected. It was clear, nevertheless, that the only acceptable outcome was Balaguer's continuation in power.

The remaining authoritarian regimes of the 1970s were products of the armed forces as institutions, though their characteristics varied greatly. In the most developed countries (i.e., the Southern Cone) and in Brazil, the regimes (labeled "bureaucratic authoritarian" by Guillermo O'Donnell, 1979) were committed to a sweeping purification and reorientation of society. This project entailed, as a matter of policy, extensive repression and violations of human rights, directed ostensibly against the political Left and justified as a necessary part of an unconventional war against subversion.[15] To varying degrees (most of all in Chile), these regimes adopted neoliberal economic policies that tended to reduce the state's dominance of the economy, but their primary emphasis was on national security, not economic reform. Because these regimes were totalitarian in aspiration (not, however, in practice), the task of building democracies to succeed them was more demanding than elsewhere, even though these countries remain among the most developed in the region.

In the three Central American cases of Guatemala, El Salvador, and Honduras, the armed forces as institutions ruled and displayed a rhetorical affinity to the authoritarian regimes of the Southern Cone.[16] But in Central America, at a lower level of development, the totalitarian aspiration was remote from reality. Instead, the rightist institutional Central American regimes tended toward a simple iron-fisted defense of the established social order, along with naked corruption much more extensive than what was found in the Southern Cone.

In the late 1960s and early 1970s, in the central Andes, the armed forces experimented with populist regimes, dedicated to challenging the economic elites and forcing through some economic redistribution.[17] The most sweeping attempt was made by General Juan Velasco Alvarado in Peru (1968–1975); similar but shorter-lived and less systematic efforts were made in Bolivia (1964–1971) and in Ecuador (1972–1976). In Ecuador and Peru, these populist regimes were ousted by more conservative military rulers, who then initiated the transition to democracy. In Bolivia, the rightist government of Hugo Banzer, after taking power in 1971, held power for eight years before initiating a transition in 1979.

Panama had a very similar military populist regime under General Omar Torrijos (1968–1981). Torrijos promoted various programs that had the effect of channeling more resources to the poor at the expense of the rich, but like other populists, he did little to change the basic economic and social structure. He did succeed—as Velasco Alvarado had not—in building a mass political constituency. His popularity was further enhanced by the successful negotiation of the new canal treaties with the Carter administration in 1979.[18]

Regional and Global Conditions

Beginning in the late 1970s, strong international pressures bore on all of Latin America to achieve (or to retain) formal liberal democracy,[19] with special emphasis on respect for human and political rights,[20] and to move away from state-centered models of development toward freer markets, freer international trade, and a major reduction in the size and power of the state. The new economic approach was called "neoliberalism," because it amounted to a reaffirmation of the classic economic liberalism of Adam Smith and the major British political economists of the early nineteenth century.

The United States, as the hegemonic power of the hemisphere, played a crucial role in placing both political and economic reform on the international agenda.[21] On the political front, U.S. policy under President Jimmy Carter (1977–1981) emphatically demanded respect for human rights on the part of allies as well as enemies, thereby putting pressure on the Latin American military regimes. Although conservative Republican Party members such as Jeane Kirkpatrick and Ronald Reagan were critical of Carter's human rights policy because it undermined friendly anticommunist authoritarian regimes, by late 1982 Reagan himself began to make the promotion of formal democracy a key component of U.S. policy, especially in Latin America. By the mid-

1980s, progress toward formal democracy came to be essential for a strong relationship with Washington.

The Reagan administration also promoted free market, laissez-faire, free trade economic reforms. This policy was rendered all the more effective because it coincided with the most profound and widespread economic crisis of the century in Latin America.[22] The large petroleum price increases imposed by the Organization of Petroleum-Exporting Countries (OPEC) in 1978–1979 seriously strained the economies of oil-importing countries, causing most to borrow heavily. Meanwhile, exporters such as Mexico and Venezuela borrowed heavily on optimistic projections of petroleum revenues. Thus both exporting and importing countries found themselves burdened with heavy debts. Starting in 1982 with Mexico, most Latin American countries, including both oil producers and oil consumers, found themselves either defaulting on their international debts or in grave danger of doing so. Unable to secure new credit, states across the region found that they could finance their bureaucracies and social services only by printing money, thereby provoking unprecedented levels of hyperinflation and thus deepening the economic crisis.

Although several governments tried a variety of economically heterodox approaches to solving the crisis, none were successful. The only way of getting additional credit was by conforming to the neoliberal strictures established by the major international lenders (the International Monetary Fund, the World Bank, the Inter-American Development Bank), which in turn are controlled by the United States and its advanced capitalist allies, which provide most of the capital of the lending institutions. Thus virtually everywhere by the late 1980s, economic policy was moving in a neoliberal direction. Government expenditures were cut, government workers laid off, state-owned companies privatized. Protective tariffs were lowered or eliminated and the national economies were reoriented from domestic consumption to exports.

These sweeping economic changes were, to say the least, unpopular. Because in most cases the onset of the economic crisis—and the early attempts to deal with it—took place under military rule, the wave of democratization clearly owes some of its impetus to the historical accident that compelled the military rulers to take the blame for the crisis. But by the same token, the longer the crisis continues without visible improvement in most people's lives, the more discredit will accrue to the new liberal democratic regimes. The course of development in each of these countries during the 1980s and 1990s had much to do with how successfully the various governments—whether authoritarian or democratic—dealt with the challenge of economic crisis.

Thus the authoritarian regime of Augusto Pinochet in Chile was able to last until 1989 in part because its neoliberal economic policy was successful in controlling inflation and promoting growth. Even though unemployment was high and income inequality was growing, it was difficult for the opposition to mobilize while the economy was relatively prosperous. At the other extreme, economic difficulties helped to bring an end to the military regimes in Peru and Bolivia by 1979, and to destabilize the democratic regimes in Venezuela, Ecuador, and Bolivia. Relative economic success by President Alberto Fujimori in Peru (1990–2000) and by President Carlos Menem in Argentina (1989–1999), following gross failures by their predecessors, permitted each to gain constitutional amendments allowing a second consecutive term and then actually to win reelection by comfortable margins.

How Authoritarian Regimes Ended

Adam Przeworski (1991, 1996) developed a useful model, called "extrication," of the negotiation processes by which authoritarian rulers may decide to end their regime and initiate a transition to democracy. He posited that in an authoritarian situation there are four relevant categories of actors. Within the regime are (1) hard-liners and (2) reformers. The former prefer maintenance of the regime to any change; the latter prefer change to the status quo but do not wish to go all the way to democracy. Outside the regime, in the opposition, are (3) moderates and (4) radicals. The moderates prefer full democracy but are willing to negotiate with regime reformers to secure extrication, even if some guarantees must be given that restrict democracy (see Figure 3.1). The radicals prefer full democracy and oppose any negotiation with the regime. A negotiated extrication requires that regime reformers and opposition moderates gain the upper hand and negotiate a transition (see Przeworski, 1991, chap. 2; cf. Casper and Taylor, 1996).

Many of the transitions of the late 1970s and early 1980s exhibited elements of this model, though each had its own unique character. In Peru (1975), Ecuador (1976), El Salvador (1979), Honduras (1981), and Guatemala (1984), military coups ousted hard-liners and installed reformers who were willing to negotiate a transition.[23] In the Dominican Republic (1978), Uruguay (1980), Brazil (1984), and Chile (1988), electoral defeat convinced incumbent rulers to move toward a more reformist position, accepting the electoral outcome and beginning negotiations with the opposition on the terms of transition.[24] In Bolivia, incumbent dictator Hugo Banzer decided on his own to terminate his regime and called elections (1979).[25] But the resultant electoral victory of a leftist coalition (1979, 1980) was resisted for two years by other factions of the armed forces and the business sector, who presided over a series of short-term military and civilian governments until acceptable terms for permitting Hernán Siles Zuazo to take office were agreed upon.

In four other cases, the model of a negotiated extrication was not applicable; hard-line regimes were simply overtaken, either by events beyond their control or by their own mistakes. They did not extricate themselves; they were overthrown. In Nicaragua, the transition was initiated after the revolutionary

Figure 3.1   Authoritarian Transitions: Interaction of Regime Reformers and Opposition Moderates

		Moderates ally with:	
		Radicals	Reformers
	Hard-liners	Authoritarian status quo 2, 1	Authoritarian liberalization 4, 2
Reformers ally with:	Moderates	Democracy without guarantees 1, 4	Democracy with guarantees 3, 3

Source: Przeworski, 1991, p. 69. Reprinted by permission of Cambridge University Press.
Note: The first numeral in each cell is the relative value of the outcome to reformers, and the second, the relative value to moderates, where 4 is the most desired outcome.

overthrow of Somoza in 1979. There was no effective negotiation between the authoritarian regime and the opposition.[26] In Argentina, the weakening military regime, in an effort to avoid having to negotiate extrication, staged the disastrous invasion of the Malvinas/Falkland Islands (1982). Defeat ensured that they had no choice but to initiate a transition to democracy. There was very little to negotiate, and they could not prevent the election and inauguration of Raúl Alfonsín, the candidate most outspoken in opposition to the regime.[27] In Haiti, the dictator Duvalier was ousted by his own army in 1986, in what may best be interpreted as a coup by hard-liners determined to renovate the regime in order to keep themselves in power, in the face of a growing popular movement for social justice and democracy (see discussion of this case later in the chapter).

Finally, in Panama, the populist Omar Torrijos was killed in a plane crash in 1981 and was succeeded by the gangster populism of Manuel Noriega. A Torrijos ally, he had come up through the military intelligence system and was commander of the Panama Defense Force in 1981. General Noriega, although less popular than Torrijos, took care to maintain his populist base as well as his military base. Noriega had long been a paid asset of the CIA, useful for his contacts in Cuba in particular. He was known to be corrupt and reputed to be involved in the drug trade, but as long as he kept a low profile, he was apparently considered too useful to be dispensed with, especially as the Central American crisis became more intense in the 1980s. However, more and more press reports appeared that documented his drug connections, his CIA connections, and his political corruption. In 1989 he was very heavy-handed in assuring victory for his designated presidential candidate, even though opposition candidate Guillermo Endara was widely reputed to have won. Also in 1989, a federal prosecutor persuaded a grand jury in Miami to indict Noriega on drug-trafficking charges. It is unlikely that the first Bush administration orchestrated or even authorized the prosecution of Noriega, since that could only be politically embarrassing in view of Noriega's past associations. Nevertheless, once he had been indicted, the administration had little choice but to abandon Noriega and demand his removal from power. By early 1990, after sanctions and intense political pressure had not moved him, Bush apparently believed that direct military action to remove and arrest Noriega was necessary for his own credibility and that of the United States. The ensuing invasion was a military success, and after eluding capture for a few days, Noriega was carted off to jail in Miami.[28]

The ending of every authoritarian regime here reviewed, whether brought about by negotiation (the majority) or by overthrow (four), left a legacy of significant structural limits or conditions on the successor regime. These might include amnesties for human rights abuses enacted by the outgoing regimes, or constitutional limits on the successors' freedom of action or control over the armed forces (as in Chile). Restrictions might also be more informal, as in the continuing political power of the armed forces to resist policies not to their liking or the economic and political power of the United States, as regional hegemon, to have its wishes respected by governments dependent on it, such as those in Haiti, Panama, or Central America.

Only in the case of Argentina might it be argued that the end of authoritarianism left the successor regime completely free of restrictions. Yet even in this case it is clear that, at most, this was true for a few weeks at the beginning of the Alfonsín government. Alfonsín might have been able, at the beginning, to impose radical reform on the armed forces, but he showed no interest in doing so. Within months, the military had recovered sufficient power to actively resist his efforts to control them and to exact important concessions from him.

Transitions to Democracy

The establishment of democratic regimes necessarily overlapped the processes by which authoritarian regimes were terminated. Nevertheless, it is analytically useful to distinguish the two processes. Authoritarian regimes can be ended without necessarily resulting in the constitution of a democratic regime. The Mexican and Cuban Revolutions are clear examples of this, as are coups d'état that replace one set of authoritarian rulers with another. Negotiated extrication need not lead to democracy either, though in the late twentieth century most extrication processes were at least clothed in democratic symbols and rhetoric.

What, then, have been the routes and methods by which so many Latin American countries have made the transition to democracy in the past twenty years? How can we explain the rarity, thus far, of authoritarian relapses, even in the less developed countries whose democracies appear quite fragile?[29] Liberal democracy came to be accepted, by the mid-1980s, as inherently desirable by virtually the entire political spectrum of elites and activists, except die-hard right-wing supporters of the military regimes.[30]

This was an especially significant change for the Far Left, which had long held to the Marxist-Leninist view that liberal democracy was a sham that served only to mask bourgeois domination. But it was the Far Left that suffered the most under military repression, and it increasingly adopted the view that the protection of individual rights that is entailed in liberal democracy, far from being a sham, was vitally important. Moreover, while the goal of a socialist revolution was receding ever further into the future, liberal democracy would at least give those of the left an arena in which they could articulate their critiques of capitalism. Some considered that, at least in the short term, they had little choice but to pursue neoliberal economic policies if they gained control of the government. Finally, those on the left were no more immune than others to the lure of patronage and other perquisites of office. Politicians and scholars of the Center and Center-Right also often had their commitment to democracy strengthened by the experience of authoritarianism. Particularly in Central America, the Central Andes, and the Caribbean, in countries with no history of stable democracy, the last period of authoritarianism seems to have enhanced appreciation for democracy among centrists who might, in the past, have seen political conflict as a struggle for durable hegemony, not for transitory advantage within a constitutional order.

A key implication of this new valuation of democracy was that political conflicts—whether over ideology, policy, or patronage—needed to be dealt with in a civil manner designed to avoid the outbreak of political violence. Civil competition cannot be sustained if the stakes are so high that losing is unacceptable or if the rules are so biased that victory is unattainable. A key tool in most transitions to democracy has long been a pact among rival elites that guaranteed both fair regulation of competition and policy moderation (Peeler, 1985; Higley and Gunther, 1992). In half of the fourteen cases considered in this section, the transition was facilitated by some sort of pact or pacts that served to regulate competition and conflict. The broadest type, called an "elite settlement" by Michael Burton, Richard Gunther, and John Higley (1992), would include all or almost all significant elites and would address all major issues among the elites, either by resolving them or by agreeing to suspend conflict over them. If the outgoing authoritarian elite remained politically significant, it would be included in an elite settlement.

Elite settlements and other pacts. Uruguay and El Salvador may be construed as having approached this ideal type, the elite settlement. In Uruguay, two of the three principal parties negotiated the Naval Club Agreement with the military regime after the latter was defeated in a constitutional referendum in 1980.[31] The agreement carefully specified and controlled the transition process, so that, for example, the parties were able to reestablish the former electoral law, and the armed forces received guarantees against prosecution for human rights violations. When the Blancos, who had boycotted the negotiations, finally accepted the terms of the agreement, it became the foundation for the Uruguayan transition to a renewed democracy.

In El Salvador, more than a decade of civil war followed the initial overthrow of the authoritarian government of Carlos Humberto Romero in 1979.[32] With strong aid from the United States, an attempt was made during that period to complement the war against the Marxist insurgency by establishing a minimally democratic regime based on the center-right Christian Democrats and the far-right National Renewal Alliance (ARENA). Leftist parties were either in rebellion or were repressed. However, the interest of all Central American governments in pacification led to the signing of the peace plan brokered by Costa Rican president Oscar Arias in 1987. After 1989, with the Cold War waning and the Reagan administration out of office, the United States (and the Cuban and Nicaraguan patrons of the insurgent Farabundo Martí National Liberation Front [FMLN]) began to look for an exit from Central America. A Salvadoran peace settlement was achieved in 1992 and has been implemented. The FMLN has gained access to the political process, where it is increasingly successful, but few of the substantive social reforms it advocated have begun. The armed forces and ARENA have had to give up their goal of annihilating the Left and to accept a broadening and deepening of political participation. Essentially all significant elites were parties to this settlement tolerated by the hegemonic power, the United States.

The transitions in Brazil and Peru show some affinity with elite settlements but cannot properly be so regarded. In each case, the new regime was shaped not by the sorts of closed-door, small-group negotiations that produced the Uruguayan and Salvadoran pacts but instead by highly public, massive constituent assemblies (in 1979 in Peru and 1987 in Brazil).[33] The assemblies were certainly broadly representative of all significant sectors of the respective societies, and they did lay down the definitive constitutional parameters of the emerging democratic regime. In these ways they were similar to elite settlements, but they really were a different phenomenon entirely. Whereas the elite settlements were quite detailed documents intended to be implemented, the constitutions were to a considerable extent symbolic statements of aspirations, part of a long Latin American tradition of laws as statements of values rather than as governing rules (see Chapter 2).

Three other countries, Chile, Bolivia, and Nicaragua, have made significant use of elite pacts but not of true elite settlements or of definitive constituent assemblies.[34] In Chile, the authoritarian constitution of 1980 mandated that General Pinochet, as president, submit to a plebiscite in 1988, without opponents, on the question of his continuing in office for another eight years. The opposition leaders of the Center and Center-Left (principally Christian Democrats and Socialists) formed the "Concertación por el No" to fight for rejection of Pinochet. Although right-wing parties remained committed to Pinochet, and left-wing parties (mainly the Communists, still outlawed) were excluded from the Concertación, Pinochet was in fact defeated, 55 percent to 43 percent. This obliged Pinochet to activate the provision of his own constitution that provided for competitive elections a year later, in 1989. The Concertación reconstituted itself as the Concertación por la Democracia to fight the competitive election, bringing victory to their candidate, Patricio Aylwin, with 55 percent of the vote. Two rightist candidates obtained a total of 34 percent. The Concertación has remained together through three presidential elections (1989, 1993, and 1999) and has controlled the government since the transition.

The Concertación is not an elite settlement.[35] Much of the Right remains devoted to Pinochet and largely unreconstructed in its preference for a right-wing authoritarian regime. The Right participates as the principal opposition in the post-Pinochet constitutional regime primarily to defend the authoritarian features of that regime that limit the maneuvering room of the elected governments.[36] Although the Left tacitly cooperated with the Concertación in the 1988 campaign, important leftist sectors continue to reject the legitimacy of the post-Pinochet regime. The Concertación is simply a center-left coalition for both electoral and governmental purposes. The Concertación has been essential to the political defeat of the Right in elections and to whatever grudging and partial retreats the Right has made in policy since 1989. The fact that Christian Democrats and Socialists have been able to work constructively together since then has laid to rest the ghost of sectarian polarization that contributed so much to the demise of democracy in 1973. But precisely because the Concertación is not an elite settlement, a future victory by either Left or Right could endanger the stability of the already diluted Chilean democracy.[37]

In Bolivia, too, pacts among elites have been vital to the transition to and practice of democracy, especially since 1985, but they have not been elite settlements. At the end of the Banzer regime in 1979, the elites were so deeply fragmented by competing ambitions, interests, and ideologies that no elected government could be produced until 1982. Moreover, the government of Siles Zuazo (1982–1985), with its fragile unity and narrow base in parliament, could not complete its term and had to agree to early elections. As of 1985, then, there was little reason to expect that, after six years, the transition in Bolivia would lead to a stable democracy. Since the election of 1985, a consistent pattern has emerged whereby a fragmented party system has repeatedly required the formation of coalitions to elect a president in Congress after no candidate receives a popular majority. These coalition pacts usually continue for a time as the basis of the new president's working majority in Congress (Gamarra and Malloy, 1995; Mayorga, 1994b, 1995a). René Mayorga (1995a, 1995b) has studied this pattern of shifting presidential coalitions in Congress, in which any party or movement might find itself in partnership with any other for largely pragmatic reasons, and has labeled it "parliamentarized presidentialism." Mayorga has argued that the recurrent necessity of negotiation among rival elites is the most important key to the stability—albeit minimal— of Bolivian democracy.

Nicaragua's transition has also been substantially affected by a key pact that was conceived as an elite settlement but failed to become one. As the earlier discussion of the end of the Somoza regime makes clear, I regard the transition to democracy in Nicaragua as beginning in 1979, when the Sandinistas came to power.[38] A tumultuous decade of revolution and counterrevolution, of foreign intervention and economic destabilization and decay, led finally to Nicaragua's adherence to the Arias Peace Plan in 1987, and in 1990 to an agreement between the Sandinista government and the National Opposition Union (UNO),[39] which permitted the elections of 1990 to take place in relatively peaceful conditions. The electoral victory of Violeta Barrios de Chamorro as the UNO candidate came as a surprise to virtually everyone. The Sandinistas had assumed they still retained overwhelming popular support as the embodiment of the revolution. Their opponents, including the U.S. government, assumed that the Sandinistas would cheat. Both sides were wrong. Most of the leaders of both UNO and the contras clearly expected that Chamorro's victory would lead to the definitive expulsion of the Sandinistas from power and the reversal of all major revolutionary policies and programs. The dominant expectation was literally counterrevolutionary. But the newly elected Chamorro confronted the reality that the Sandinistas remained the largest, best-organized political force in the country, and also controlled the army and police.

Her solution, engineered by her closest adviser (and son-in-law), Antonio Lacayo, was a pact with the Sandinistas that provided for command of the armed forces and police to remain with the Sandinista incumbents (the commander of the armed forces was Humberto Ortega, brother of the retiring president, Daniel Ortega). The commanders in turn committed themselves to loyally serving the new president. The military and police commitment also implicitly promised that the Sandinistas' mass followers would be reined in, discouraged from pushing agitation to the point of destabilizing the new government. Chamorro's pact with the Sandinistas could have been the base for an elite settlement, but its achievement would have required that she hold her own coalition together. That proved impossible, though; the majority of UNO deputies in the Assembly defected and became, in effect, her principal opposition, whereas the Sandinistas in the Assembly teamed with the pro-Chamorro minority to give her a small majority at the beginning of her term. Defections would erase even that fragile majority by 1995. The U.S. government was of course quite unsympathetic to Chamorro's gambit and used its influence to bolster the opposition.

The abortive elite settlement remains very important in the Nicaraguan transition. Had UNO remained united and carried out a thorough counterrevolution, this might easily have led to a renewal of civil war and would certainly have pushed even more Nicaraguans to the edge of desperation. With the end of the Cold War, the end of the Sandinista government, and the manifest weakness of the isolated Cuban regime, extensive U.S. aid (widely expected by UNO leaders) was unlikely to make it through the hazards of the policy process in Washington. The real choice was between a truly counterrevolutionary government that could not govern and a compromise government that could govern at least minimally. Chamorro did not accomplish a great deal in her term, but she did finish it and hand power to an elected successor. That would have been much less likely without the Sandinista pact.

Interestingly, the Sandinistas were not particularly helped by the pact. They have suffered a severe split, and have consistently fallen short of an electoral majority. Nor has Chamorro been helped. Her heir apparent, Lacayo, was blocked from running by a constitutional amendment prohibiting presidential candidacies of close relatives of the sitting president. Thus, even though the pact was important to a peaceful transition in Nicaragua, it was deeply illegitimate in the eyes of most UNO leaders. It was ironic, therefore, that after right-wing Liberal Arnoldo Alemán defeated Daniel Ortega in the presidential runoff in 1996, a split in Alemán's coalition gave control of the Assembly to a tacit alliance between the Sandinista National Liberation Front (FSLN) and dissident Liberals. Subsequently, and even more ironically, Alemán and Ortega forged and implemented a pact whereby their two parties would share most elective offices, to the disadvantage of other parties such as the Conservatives (Walker, 2003).

Transitions without pacts: hegemonic influence. The other seven of fourteen countries discussed in this section made transitions to democracy without major reliance on pacts. However, five of the seven made the transition under the decisive sponsorship and guidance of the United States as regional hegemon. These five small countries of Central America and the Caribbean are Guatemala, Honduras, Panama, Haiti, and the Dominican Republic.[40]

The shape of the transition in these five countries can only be understood in the context of U.S. policy, although within that context each country has its own internal conditions that also must be understood. Within a structure/action framework, this is a situation in which action by the United States constitutes structure for the small states involved, in that U.S. policy is a condition they must adapt to, without having much control over it. The moderating role played in some other countries by pacts among elites has in these cases been played by the hegemon.

The course of Guatemalan history for half a century was in substantial part determined by the CIA-sponsored overthrow in 1954 of the reformist government of Jacobo Arbenz, second reformist president after the overthrow of the dictator Jorge Ubico in 1944 (Schlesinger and Kinzer, 1982; Immerman, 1982). Until 1985 the country was under the direct control of a series of reactionary military governments (including one civilian president from 1966 to 1970, under effective military control) closely allied with the agroindustrial elite and tacitly supported by the United States. Since that time, under pressure from the United States, Guatemala has had a constitutional democracy with a series of civilian presidents drawn from the center-right and right of the political spectrum. Guatemala was a signatory to the Central American Peace Plan promoted by Costa Rican president Oscar Arias in 1989. Under that plan, the government negotiated at length with the main insurgent party (the National Revolutionary Union of Guatemala [URNG]), concluding in late 1996 an agreement that terminated the insurgency and permitted its incorporation into the legal political process. A movement associated with retired general Efraín Ríos Montt (who held power under a military government in 1982–1983, and who was responsible for intense repression in rural indigenous areas of the western highlands) has been in the ascendant in the late 1990s and early in the twenty-first century, and seems likely to continue to control the presidency, drawing votes especially from rural areas, including the western highlands, which suffered so much repression under Ríos Montt.

Ríos Montt, however, is not the candidate of the armed forces, most of whose officers are thought to distrust him. The resurrection of Ríos Montt suggests that the armed forces may be losing some control over the political process. Although the armed forces did intervene in 1993 to force out a president who attempted a Fujimori-style coup, the military currently shows little interest in governing (as long as its prerogatives remain untouched). To stop Ríos Montt, the armed forces might have to intervene again, this time in defiance of a popular mandate. Democracy in Guatemala remains an illusion kept in place by an international structure centered on U.S. foreign policy.

Honduras also found itself caught up in the international politics of counterinsurgency during the 1980s, and it is to that involvement, in large part, that it owes its transition to a precarious democracy. Until the 1980s, Honduras was without question Central America's poorest country, distinguished by a relatively weak landed class, minimal industrialization, and the economic and political dominance of the great banana companies, particularly United Fruit. A long series of alternating hegemonies between the traditional Liberal and National Parties marked the country's political history; the ruling party normally operated in alliance with the army. The mass of the population, poor, dependent, and mostly illiterate, had little to do with politics, except for a few thousand banana workers organized in unions. The United States traditionally showed little interest in Honduras as long as it treated United Fruit well.

This pattern came under strain in the early 1980s as the Sandinista revolution focused the minds of U.S. policymakers on Central America. Honduras, as Nicaragua's northern neighbor, had obvious geopolitical significance. In 1981 the United States successfully discouraged General Policarpo Paz García from perpetuating himself in office and induced the military to begin a transition to an elected civilian regime. The United States channeled quantities of aid into Honduras second only to the aid sent to neighboring El Salvador—and the latter country was fighting a major guerrilla war, whereas Honduras was not. The price of the aid for Honduras was that the United States was lent several bases, and Honduras turned a blind eye to operations of the Nicaraguan contras from Honduran territory. A succession of reasonably honest elections produced four successive civilian, constitutional presidents drawn from both traditional parties, after 1981. These presidents, though, never succeeded in controlling the military or stopping human rights abuses, though such abuses were much less frequent than in neighboring El Salvador and Guatemala. Although the economic elite was much weaker than in Guatemala or El Salvador and the political elite less predatory, it remained clear that democracy in Honduras was likely to persist only as long as international support endured.[41]

The transition to democracy in Panama was of course profoundly conditioned by the U.S. invasion that ousted Manuel Noriega. Opposition presidential candidate Guillermo Endara arrived by U.S. transport and was duly sworn in as constitutional president. Thus was Panama's transition to democracy begun. However, Endara's government was weighed down by economic crisis and received relatively little aid from the United States. Given its levels of education and economic development, one would expect democracy to have been more successful in Panama than it has in fact been. Since the overthrow of Noriega there has been a series of competitive and reasonably honest national elections, with opposition candidates usually winning, but democracy in Panama continues to be fragile. It seems likely that the constant presence of the United States as a political actor in Panama has retarded democratic development in at least two ways. First, it has provided economic elites with a crutch that allows them to neglect the political learning that is necessary to operate a democracy successfully. Second, it has provided a ready-made foil for populists and nationalists that allows many Panamanians to persist in an oversimplified analysis of national problems. Thus, after nearly a century of national independence, democracy in Panama remains, at best, in its infancy.

During the same epoch (the first third of the twentieth century) when the United States acted to secure Panamanian independence (and the canal), the United States also intervened militarily in several other Caribbean and Central American countries, including the Dominican Republic.[42] The stated purpose in each case was the preservation and enhancement of political stability, governmental efficiency, and sound probusiness economic policy. The political effect was baleful without exception, leading in every case but Puerto Rico to prolonged dictatorships and the complete failure to establish stable democracies.

In the Dominican case, the U.S. occupation was followed, in 1930, by the seizure of power by General Rafael Leonidas Trujillo, U.S.-trained commander of the U.S.-trained army. Trujillo would rule with tacit U.S. support until his assassination in 1961. What began as a transition to democracy was truncated by a military coup that overthrew recently elected president Juan Bosch in 1963. A popular uprising in 1965 led by military supporters of Bosch was put down by a massive U.S. occupation. The following year, with U.S. blessings, elections were held, which were won by Joaquín Balaguer, a longtime collaborator of Trujillo. Balaguer had a constituency among business elites, the military, and public functionaries inherited from Trujillo, and he did not hesitate to use the usual range of manipulation and intimidation in order to magnify that constituency and twice gain reelection (1970, 1974). He enjoyed strong support from the Johnson and Nixon administrations, but when it became apparent that he had failed to control the 1978 election, initial efforts to annul it or to falsify results were actively discouraged by the Carter administration. As a result, the opposition Dominican Revolutionary Party (PRD) gained control of the government and held it for two presidential terms, until 1986, when the aged Balaguer was returned to office. After being reelected in 1990, his victory in the disputed elections of 1994 was accepted by the PRD only on the condition that his term end with new elections in 1996, in which he would not be a candidate. Electoral fraud is less widespread than it used to be, and there have been several reasonably honest elections. With electoral politics being refereed by the United States, there was no necessity for the competing political forces to agree among themselves. The pact of 1994, recognizing Balaguer's victory but curtailing his term, is the first instance of elite pact-making in the Dominican Republic, and the United States was, at a minimum, a very interested observer. In 1996, PRD candidate Francisco Peña Gómez led in the first round but confronted a surprising alliance of the two patriarchs, Balaguer and Juan Bosch, in support of the runoff opponent, Leonel Fernández, the candidate of Bosch's party. The result in the 30 June runoff was a 51 percent victory for Fernández and the likelihood of continued behind-the-scenes influence for Balaguer. Since 1996, Balaguer, Bosch, and Peña Gómez have all died, and the Dominican democratic regime has entered an era without its founding patriarchs. Dominican democracy, however, must still be accounted fragile and externally sponsored. It is, in all its fragility and contradiction, the best example of the United States having successfully promoted democracy.

The cases reviewed in this section show clearly that the evolution of political regimes can be decisively affected, particularly in small and weak countries, by external structural influences, both intentional and unintentional. In several cases, U.S. intervention helped to end dictatorships, and recent U.S. policy has certainly promoted free and fair elections and respect for human rights, but such influence has limits. By definition, democracy as rule by the people cannot be externally imposed because then it would not be the people ruling but the outside power. However, liberal democratic formal institutions, with their emphasis on limited government, individual rights, and political competition, clearly can be insisted upon by an outside hegemonic power. Political elites acting within such an externally structured context may in time learn to operate the system with less and less supervision and may indeed learn to appreciate its virtues.

Transitions without pacts: relative autonomy. The other two countries that made transitions without pacts were much less subject to outside intervention, and thus these cases are more fully explicable in terms of internal conditions. Beyond their relative autonomy and the relative unimportance of pacts in their transitions, however, Argentina and Ecuador share very little.

In Argentina, the military government, having confronted severe economic crisis and military defeat in the Malvinas/Falklands War, was unable to negotiate terms of the transition.[43] It made some attempts to do so, but the Radical Party and other elements of the opposition refused to agree to the military conditions. In the end, the transition occurred on the terms demanded by Alfonsín and the Radicals. There was also no pact with the principal opposition party, the Peronists. Indeed, the scope of the unprecedented Radical Party electoral victory of 1983 led some Radical leaders to entertain thoughts of a new epoch of Radical political hegemony, like that before 1930. From this perspective, the Peronists were not a legitimate opposition force but rather a historical aberration that could finally be eliminated. Similar sentiments of what one may call a hegemonic vocation were of course widespread among Peronists, but their very defeat caused them to begin reevaluating their long-standing assumption that they were the natural tribunes of the people. The attitudinal basis for a civil relationship between a governing party and a loyal opposition began to evolve only after the Radicals suffered electoral reverses in provincial and congressional elections. By the late 1980s, it became clear to both Radicals and Peronists that an Argentine democracy would necessarily be a multiparty democracy.

The Peronist victory in the 1989 elections led to the first transition in Argentine history from a democratically elected president to a democratically elected successor from the opposition. As such, it marked the success of the Argentine transition to democracy. Yet the particular conduct of Carlos Menem as president, and tumultuous times after Menem left office, raise important issues for the future of democracy in Argentina, issues that will be discussed in subsequent chapters.

The Ecuadoran military extricated itself from the government by 1978, arriving at only minimal procedural agreements with the various civilian political leaders. The latter, for their part, embarked on the electoral competition for political power without an explicit or implicit pact regulating that competition. Ecuador has never had institutionalized political parties; rather, individual leaders formed personalist movements around themselves, relying on some combination of patronage, economic interest, regional loyalty, class conflict, and charisma to maintain the loyalty of their followers. The most durable cleavage continued to be between Guayaquil and Quito, but in each region many leaders competed with each other for elite and popular support. The new democratic era simply meant that this kaleidoscopic political competition would take place, for a time indeterminate, within liberal democratic procedures. Most Ecuadoran presidents reach office with a Congress controlled by multifarious and fluid opposition parties, and thus have grave difficulty governing.[44]

The democratic regime has survived in Ecuador, in spite of the failure of every elected president since 1978. Although the evolution of democracy there seems to owe little to external influence, its persistence is probably due to military reluctance to seize power in light of predictable unhappiness in Washington at such an eventuality. Political elites show little sign of commitment to the principles and practice of liberal democracy. Their continued acceptance of it is a matter of political convenience: in the present domestic and international environment, none of them can establish hegemony.

The Argentine and Ecuadoran cases show much less influence of external structures on the transition, but that influence is by no means negligible, at least in raising the probable cost of any reversion to open authoritarianism. Internal structures, such as Argentina's highly institutionalized parties and Ecuador's inchoate party system (see Chapter 5), were important in shaping the contours of the transition in each country, contours within which political action occurred.

The ambiguous transition in Mexico. The political order under which Mexico's Institutional Revolutionary Party (PRI) and its direct predecessors ruled uninterruptedly for nearly seventy years deserves recognition from political scientists as one of the most ingenious and successful in modern history.[45] After the last of Mexico's nineteenth-century caudillos, Porfirio Díaz, was

overthrown in 1910, and after more than twenty years of civil war and authoritarian rule by a succession of revolutionary generals, the last of those generals, Lázaro Cárdenas, took office in 1934. He pushed through several popular
measures such as agrarian reform, labor law reform, and nationalization of
petroleum. He also rebuilt the revolutionary party along corporatist lines, with
organized sectors representing the major interests of peasants, workers, military, and the "popular" (the last being predominantly state employees). The
party was to be the mechanism by which these diverse interests could be rec-
onciled. The military sector was eventually eliminated, once the last major
regional caudillos were domesticated or suppressed. The business interests
were notable by their absence. Officially, the Mexican Revolution continued
to be nationalistic and even a bit socialistic: it would not do for business to
appear within the revolutionary tent. Indeed, Cárdenas's relations with business were tense, and understandably so, given his major policy initiatives.
Also absent from the party was the church, for the regime remained officially
anticlerical. Nevertheless, Cárdenas achieved a certain modus vivendi with
the Catholic hierarchy, choosing not to go out of his way to persecute the
church when he had trouble enough on other fronts.[46]

If Cárdenas's economic and social policies were radical, constituting the
high-water mark of revolutionary change in Mexico, his crafting of the revolutionary party was profoundly conservative and virtually ensured that there
would never again be a president as radical as Cárdenas himself. The party's
structure not only represented all major constituencies of the revolutionary
coalition, but also organized them for patronage, thereby domesticating them
and ensuring that they could be controlled by the top leadership. Further, Cárdenas definitively established the principle that presidents would serve for one
six-year term and no more. The constitution and the official party enabled them
to be virtual dictators while in office and to designate their successors, but they
would not continue to rule from behind the scenes after leaving office. Cárdenas himself stuck firmly to this principle, and so did his successors.

The significance of this practice was that by depersonalizing caudillismo,
the fundamental cause of instability was removed. The ambitious no longer
needed to conspire against the incumbent government if they were denied a
seat at the table; they only needed to wait six years, tend their political connections, and hope for better placement in the next government. The essence
of the Mexican regime under Cárdenas and thereafter remained caudillismo,
but it was liberated from the life cycle of any single incumbent (unlike
Stroessner and Castro) and freed from endemic turmoil. It is among the most
stable regimes in modern history and, by the same token, among the most
resistant to change.

After Cárdenas, the Mexican political system entered a prolonged era of
political stability. Presidents followed presidents (five in all), each designat-
ing his successor, each retiring to the background. The PRI retained over-

whelming electoral dominance and captured virtually all elective offices. The party's sectoral organizations, in tacit alliance with big business and foreign investors, moderated popular demands while ensuring that everyone who played the game got at least small rewards. The only serious opposition was from the rightist National Action Party (PAN), which, notwithstanding its strength in the north, was rarely an electoral victor. One reason was that the PRI machine was quite capable of controlling electoral outcomes whenever necessary. Nevertheless, Mexico during this period was by no means a harsh dictatorship. Indeed, to the superficial observer, Mexico might have appeared a democracy, but it was really what Guillermo O'Donnell and Philippe Schmitter (1986) called a *dictablanda,* or soft dictatorship (as distinguished from a *dictadura,* or hard dictatorship).

The prolonged crisis of the Mexican regime began with a clearly defined event, the massacre of students in the Plaza of Tlatelolco, Mexico City, in 1968. Students animated by the example of the Cuban Revolution and encouraged by a widespread climate of revolutionary agitation in Latin America at the time sought to take advantage of international attention focused on the Olympic Games in Mexico to highlight the gross injustices in Mexican society. Rising tensions culminated in the bloody repression of a massive demonstration in Tlatelolco. The repression was ordered by President Gustavo Díaz Ordaz and carried out under the command of Interior Minister Luis Echeverría. Echeverría was rewarded with the presidency for the 1970–1976 term. Tlatelolco showed the regime reduced to the use of massive force to control the public arena and using such force against demands that were central to the legitimacy of the revolutionary heritage. The emperor had no clothes. President Echeverría sought to cover himself with the tried and true tactics of "populist philanthropy" (Williamson, 1992, p. 403), spending heavily on agrarian reform, food, education, housing, and health while also promoting economic expansion. As a result of these heavy commitments to agrarian reform and social programs, the Mexican state found itself severely overextended when Echeverría's successor, José López Portillo, took office. However, López Portillo was saved from having to impose an unpopular austerity program by the very timely confirmation of massive petroleum deposits along the coast of the Gulf of Mexico. López Portillo then had a ticket for even more extravagant social spending; in fact, his government borrowed heavily on projections of growing oil production and rising prices. Prosperity continued into the early 1980s. Then, as petroleum prices unexpectedly entered a severe slump, Mexico found itself unable to service its international debt. The strategy of overextending economically to confront the crisis of political legitimacy had reached its limit, and the Mexican crisis ripped the cover off what came to be known as the Third World debt crisis.[47]

In response to this economic crisis, from 1982 onward a line of sober economic technocrats would hold the presidency through the end of the century, each nominated by his predecessor and imposed upon the increasingly skeptical politicians of the ruling party. Mexican economic policy was increasingly reoriented from the politically driven populism of the 1970s toward an increasing commitment to neoliberal orthodoxy. The economic crisis and the neoliberal response were the progenitors of a renewed political crisis that emerged in 1988.

Dissidence within the PRI led finally to one of the party's most serious splits.[48] A sector associated with Porfirio Muñoz Ledo and Cuauhtémoc Cárdenas (son of Lázaro Cárdenas), frustrated in their attempt to prevent the nomination of another economic technocrat in 1988, split off and ultimately formed the National Democratic Front (FDN; it was transformed after the election into the Democratic Revolutionary Party [PRD]) as a vehicle for Cárdenas's presidential candidacy. Disillusionment with poor economic conditions, social injustice, and political corruption reinforced Cárdenas's appeal and that of Manuel Clouthier, nominee of the PAN. The PRI nominated Carlos Salinas de Gortari, another economist trained in the United States and the principal architect of Miguel de la Madrid's economic policy. The PRI's electoral machine, unenthusiastic about the nominee but needful of winning the election to guarantee continued patronage, was caught by surprise by an apparent Cárdenas victory and had to resort to naked manipulation under cover of a highly suspicious computer failure in order to achieve a bare majority for Salinas (50.7 percent), as against official totals of 31 percent for Cárdenas and 17 percent for Clouthier (see Table 3.1). Salinas thus entered office with less political legitimacy than the PRI had had at any time since 1970, but without the economic means to spend his way out of the hole, as Echeverría had done.

Salinas had little choice but to stay the neoliberal course, and he staked Mexico's economic future—and the PRI's political future—on negotiation of the North American Free Trade Agreement (NAFTA) with the United States (and Canada, which had already signed such a pact with the United States). He found in the first Bush administration (1989–1993) and its successor, the Clinton administration, willing partners committed to the basic principles of

Table 3.1   Mexico: Presidential Election Results, 1940–2000 (percentage)

	PRI	PAN	FDN/PRD	Other	Turnout
1940–1976 (mean)	86.0	10.6[a]	—	7.0	55.0
1982	71.0	15.7	—	9.4	66.1
1988	50.7	16.8	31.1	1.4	49.4
1994	50.2	26.9	17.1	5.8	74.0
2000	36.1	42.5	16.6	4.8	64.0

Sources: Craig and Cornelius, 1995, p. 258; Klesner, 1995, pp. 138, 145; Pérez Herrero, 2001, 283.

Note: a. Mean for 1952–1970. PAN did not contest the other elections.

neoliberal economics. Although there were many skeptics in all three countries and many interests that would be threatened, ultimately in 1993, Clinton was able to push through the ratification of the treaty as negotiated by the Bush administration. Salinas, still with a PRI congressional majority, was then able to do the same in Mexico. But the promised benefits of free trade were slow to appear, and Mexican economic conditions continued to be poor, while the social fabric was shredding.

Under these conditions of chronic crisis and endemic corruption, the regime sustained a series of new blows to its economic and political health, though it continued to have the means to survive. An indigenous-based rebellion of the Zapatista Army of National Liberation (EZLN) began in Chiapas at the beginning of 1994.[49] The Zapatistas sought, through armed negotiation, to call attention to unjust conditions in Chiapas and elsewhere in Mexico and to the lack of true democracy, and to oblige the government to address these issues. Negotiations did begin, but the Zapatistas resisted government attempts to either co-opt or intimidate them, and the government refused to make meaningful concessions.

Meanwhile, politics on the national scale grew more byzantine and more deadly. In the space of a few months, assassination claimed the lives of an archbishop; the PRI's presidential candidate, Luis Donaldo Colosio; and a former PRI party chairman. The alleged triggermen were apprehended in each case, but efforts to trace down the real authors went nowhere. There was possible drug cartel involvement in each case, but even more troubling was the possibility that some or all of the killings amounted to the settling of political accounts (Paternostro, 1995).

Salinas chose to replace the slain Colosio with yet another economic technocrat, Ernesto Zedillo, who faced strong opposition from the PAN (Diego Fernández) and the PRD (Cárdenas). With a weak candidate and widespread disillusionment and disaffection, the PRI faced the same dilemma in 1994 as in 1988: to avoid losing even more legitimacy, the regime needed a credibly honest election but would thereby run a serious risk of losing. The results were similar to those of 1988 in that Zedillo officially received just over 50 percent of the votes, but this time the PAN came in second and the PRD third (see Table 3.1). There were allegations of fraud, but few maintained that Zedillo was not the true winner.

The PRI hegemony continued to decline at the local and regional levels. Proportional representation was adopted in 1977, for some seats in Congress, to increase the representation of opposition parties, while the majority of seats remained under the single-member district, plurality rule (Craig and Cornelius, 1995, p. 284). In 1997 the PRI finally lost its majority in the Chamber of Deputies. In the 2000 election the PRI remained short of a majority, but had the largest number of seats in both chambers. While the PAN and the PRI both got the majority of their seats in single-member districts, the PRD got about half its seats under proportional representation. The party system has become more differentiated regionally (with the PAN especially strong in the north, and the PRD especially strong in the Federal District and the south).

Zedillo was no sooner inaugurated in 1994 than a massive sell-off hit the Mexican peso in December 1994. Weighed down by economic distortions and policy errors of more than a decade, the peso lost more than half its value against the dollar in the course of a month. The Clinton administration realized that a continuing uncontrolled crisis could have serious effects on the U.S. economy, along with potential devastation of the Mexican economy. Therefore, after committing funds already at his disposal, he worked hard to get an aid package through Congress but confronted deep skepticism from both parties. With final approval of the plan, featuring loan guarantees of $40 billion, the battered Mexican economy began to stabilize, but with lasting damage to the population's standard of living and to the government's credibility. Corruption, deception, and incompetence seemed to be the trademarks of the PRI regime. Zedillo's initiation to office, in short, was nothing short of disastrous.

In addition to coping with the peso crisis and its political fallout and continuing inconclusive negotiations with the Zapatistas, the Zedillo government sought and secured, in January 1995, a pact with the principal opposition parties to guarantee the credibility of future elections. Although the pact was nothing more than a mechanism for consultation and negotiation among the parties concerning alleged electoral irregularities, it represented a major step toward political accommodation for Mexico and brought to mind similar pacts that were turning points in the establishment of democratic regimes in Venezuela in 1958 and in Uruguay in 1984. Notwithstanding mutual mistrust between the PRI and the opposition, the elections of 2000 were reasonably honest and resulted in the triumph of PAN candidate Vicente Fox. Neither the PAN nor any other party held a majority in either chamber of Congress, so the first non-PRI president in seventy years had very limited room to maneuver in governing the country. Mexico's transition to democracy has been accomplished, but its future stability is uncertain.

There was no elite settlement in the Mexican transition, though there were pacts. Mexico is neither a clear case of a transition under hegemonic pressure, as in much of Central America, nor a clear case of autonomous transition, as in Argentina or Uruguay. On one hand, because of its proximity to the United States and its economic dependence on that country, nothing that happens in Mexican politics can be viewed in isolation from the great neighbor to the north. On the other hand, it is by no means clear that U.S. influence was decisive in this case.

Elites and transitions to democracy: an overview. Adam Przeworski (1991, p. 80) argued that all transitions to democracy are negotiated, some with representatives of the old regime and some only among the pro-democratic forces seeking to form a new system. Negotiations are not always needed to extricate the society from the authoritarian regime, but they are necessary to constitute democratic institutions. Democracy cannot be dictated; it emerges from bargaining.

The preceding discussion tends to confirm the truth of this assertion, though it should be added that in the cases of the smaller countries of the Caribbean Basin, a key negotiator has been the U.S. government, whose policy has favored, at the least, competitive and honest elections (except for the early Reagan years). Even such a powerful actor cannot always impose liberal democracy, but it can raise the costs of resisting democratization, and thereby obtain, most of the time, formal compliance from the internal elites. Still, it is common to find that human rights continue to be violated, usually by the armed forces or semiofficial death squads. Electoral fraud may be less widespread, but is still commonly alleged, and often with reason. The political culture of tolerance has, as yet, only shallow roots.

The remaining cases, mostly South American, confirm that democracies have emerged from elite bargaining of various sorts, ranging from something close to a comprehensive elite settlement to agreements taking in only part of the relevant universe of elites or addressing only some of the outstanding issues. Because liberal democracy requires elites to forswear force and fraud and to accept control of the government by their opponents, they need to have confidence that their opponents will stand by the same commitments. In the absence of such mutual assurance, democratic institutions will inevitably be fragile, as in the cases of Ecuador, Nicaragua, and Haiti, for example.

At a more general level, these cases tend to support the centrality of elites to any political processes. This is not to say that the rest of the population (i.e., nonelites) does not matter (see below), but only that political action by nonelites has an impact on the society as a whole to the extent that it is either mobilized or channeled by elites. I am using "elite" here as a synonym for "leadership," which obviously may emerge from nonelite sectors. Even spontaneous popular riots acquire an "elite" in this sense, a person who is at least momentarily able to guide or focus the attention of the rioters on one object rather than another. Not a few riots or public manifestations have in fact been systematically promoted by leaders opposed to the dominant elites of society, who may be seen, effectively, as counterelites.

Political success or failure for all these elites and counterelites depends heavily on whether they can really demonstrate mass support. To be able to do that, they must somehow relate themselves effectively to the felt needs and preoccupations of some sector of the society and then induce that sector to support them as they bargain with other elites.

Nonelites: the people and transitions to democracy. Roles played by the middle-class minorities (professionals, successful merchants, and bureaucrats, whether public or private) and by the poor majorities (workers, peasants, small merchants, and the marginal poor) constitute a variable and highly significant element in the several transitions treated in this chapter. Nonelite actions with national impact on the transitions to democracy may be divided into several categories: (1) popular riots and rebellions, (2) social movements, (3) political mobilization, and (4) abstention.

By popular riots and rebellions, I mean relatively spontaneous violent protest or resistance against public authorities or policies. Established opposition elites do not promote or control such riots or rebellions, though counterelites may emerge from them. Several countries have experienced such episodes, commonly in response to the economic strains imposed by neoliberal adjustment policies. In general, if directed against authoritarian regimes (e.g., in Nicaragua in 1978), these actions might strengthen hard-line elements but could also provide popular support to insurgencies like the FSLN. If directed against democratic regimes (as in Venezuela in 1989), the actions tended to put in doubt the legitimacy of those regimes.

Social movements are collective actions of people beyond the level of the family but not part of any existing party or other political institution.[50] Social movements emerge to meet felt needs of the people involved and may become institutionalized over time. One type of social movement that was highly relevant to democratic transitions was organizations of relatives of the disappeared or of other victims of authoritarian violations of human rights. The classic example was the movement called the Madres de Plaza de Mayo in Argentina, who began in the late 1970s to appear in the principal plaza of Buenos Aires in front of the presidential palace (La Casa Rosada), marching silently every week with signs demanding that the government provide information as to the whereabouts of missing sons, daughters, spouses, or grandchildren (Guzmán Bouvard, 1994; Jelin, 1994; Quiroga, 1993). By forcing the issue of the disappearances onto the public agenda, these women publicly cast doubt on the legitimacy of the military regime and provided a vivid example of courage in the face of repression. Their very status as mothers made it extremely difficult and politically costly for the regime to repress their protests or to retaliate against them, though several were in fact killed. Similar social movements developed in other countries, most notably Chile and Guatemala.

In the transition processes, competing elites repeatedly attempted the political mobilization of nonelites. A key choice for nonelites, then, was how to respond to these appeals. If authoritarian regimes could count on enough popular support (as in Chile in the 1980 constitutional referendum), they could perpetuate themselves in power. Even when they lost elections (as in Uruguay's 1980 constitutional referendum or the 1988 presidential plebiscite in Chile), a substantial popular vote would strengthen their hand in negotiating the transition. Conversely, opposition elites needed highly visible popular support to be effective in making demands on the military authorities. Popular demonstrations against the military regime in Argentina after its defeat in the Malvinas War helped to push it toward the exit, and the strength of Alfonsín's electoral victory in 1983 helped him avoid making concessions before his inauguration. A key question, in short, concerns the causes for which people were willing to mobilize themselves (Casper and Taylor, 1996).

The other side of that coin was abstention, the decision on the part of citizens to abstain from voting or other political action, to take what Albert Hirschman (1970) called the "exit" option. Clearly, one reason so many transitions to democracy were successful during this period was that large numbers of citizens did mobilize to support the cause of democracy: they did not abstain, withdraw, or exit. However, as we shall see in Chapter 5, a key problem of the resulting liberal democracies has been to maintain levels of participation adequate for purposes of legitimacy but not so intense as to threaten stability.

Finally, it is important to remember that nonelites may respond to and engage in politics in ways that may profoundly affect their own lives and their immediate communities, without breaking the surface of national politics. Every time people within a community or neighborhood organize to address a common problem, such as the water supply or crime, they are engaged in politics in the very direct sense that they are making collective decisions and taking collective action to address common issues. The national arena is not the only place for politics. Indeed, politics at the base, grassroots politics, may be, can be, the most authentically democratic of all. Grassroots politics also can be deeply undemocratic, when a small elite dominates everyone else. For example, shantytowns in Rio de Janeiro and elsewhere are commonly controlled by criminal gangs (Hellman, 1994).

Conclusion: Later Democracies

The complex and diverse transitions from authoritarian to liberal democratic regimes over the last two decades in Latin America cannot be convincingly understood within any one theoretical framework. For every meaningful generalization, there are exceptions and caveats. If we emphasize elite choices and negotiations (as do Juan Linz and Alfred Stepan [1978], Guillermo O'Donnell and Philippe Schmitter [1986], and John Higley and Richard Gunther [1992]), we must nevertheless acknowledge the weight of economic and social structure, the global conjuncture of political and economic forces, and, of course, tradition and culture. If we try to make economic and social structure primary (like Dietrich Rueschemeyer, Evelyne Huber Stephens, and John Stephens [1992]), we will still run afoul of contingencies of human choice and policy. Explanations based on global pressures for democratization cannot deal with the immense variation in timing and result. If, like Claudio Véliz (1980) and Howard Wiarda (1992), we make culture and tradition determinative, we will find it hard to account for real cases of democratization. If we emphasize mass political action and social movements, we confront the inevitable emergence of elites.

Human societies are inherently complex, and causation in society is necessarily multiple and recursive. That is, any social phenomenon is both cause and effect. Human beings take actions that affect their environment; the environment at the same time affects them and limits the range of actions they can take. Action is neither an illusion nor an inconvenient anomaly: it is fundamental to being human. Thus it must be part of our understanding that people take actions that are not predetermined and that have real effects. At the same time, we should be foolish to think that such actions are unaffected by the actors' environment. It remains a key task of analysis to sort out the interplay of various environmental influences in distinct cases.

For the problem at hand, it is clear that we must acknowledge central roles for distinct sectors of the political elites, in making choices about how they interact with each other, how they confront economic and political challenges and crises, and how they respond to popular demands. We will not be able to understand the transitions without taking account of these choices. But the structural context of the choices is just as important: international political and economic pressure, the severity and timing of economic crises in each country, the character and intensity of popular political mobilization. All these and other structural factors will shape and limit elite choices. A society's history, as processed through its culture, structures how both elites and nonelites define their situation and respond to it. Thus the pervasiveness of clientelistic behavior among elites and nonelites (in Brazil or Ecuador, for example) has deep historical and cultural roots that make it hard for people to behave in any other way in the political arena; they thus in turn shape the character of the emerging regime in their country. Choices may change the structural context, but they cannot transcend it.

▇ Stragglers: Persistent Failure to Democratize

Most Latin American countries made the transition to liberal democracy in the 1980s and 1990s. Three countries (Paraguay, Haiti, and Cuba) have not made such a transition, but each authoritarian regime is nevertheless undergoing significant political change that could lead to democratization.[51] These three countries have been swimming against the current of the international structural conjuncture that has favored transitions to democracy over the past two decades. Advocates of democratization in these countries carry the heavy weight of traditions and institutions hostile to their goal. Still, the combination of external and internal pressures has brought change in each case. It is possible that democracy will flow from this change, but this is by no means inevitable.

These three cases, as disparate as they are, have in common the fact that they have been characterized by self-perpetuating monopolies on political authority. Such political monopolies, of course, have been the rule throughout Latin America until recently, and in that sense, Paraguay, Haiti, and Cuba are closer to the regional tradition than their neighbors that have made the democratic transition. Caudillismo and its adaptations are very much alive in these cases. Paraguay and Haiti have overthrown long-standing authoritarian regimes, but have yet to establish functioning liberal democracies. The Paraguayan dictatorship of Alfredo Stroessner (1954–1989) was the closest of the three to pure, personalistic caudillismo; although Stroessner ruled through the institutions of the armed forces and the Colorado Party, he exercised thorough personal control over both and used that control to perpetuate himself in power. Subsequent political struggles in Paraguay have largely been among rival factions of the Colorados, with opposition elements such as the Radical Liberal Party playing peripheral roles. Paraguay has, with some difficulty, maintained formal, constitutional democracy since the early 1990s, but the threat of coups or insurrections remains significant.[52]

In Haiti, the Duvalier dynasty, father and son, ruled from 1957 to 1986, and the country has yet to emerge from its shadow. A succession of unstable military and civilian governments after Duvalier finally gave way to the popularly elected government of Jean-Bertrand Aristide (a radical priest with a strong following among the poor, and a program of redistribution and democratization) in 1990.[53] The military overthrew him less than a year later. After President Aristide was restored to office by the U.S.-led intervention of 1994, he was able to effectively dismantle the old army and police and to begin training a new police force. However, neither Aristide's forces nor the international troops succeeded in disarming the large number of supporters of the old regime who participated in unofficial terrorist squads. The public peace and the security of the new democratic regime thus remained in check. Aristide's ability to provide concrete benefits to the poor majority of the population was limited by the small amount of external aid and by the continued power of his opponents in the Congress. General elections were held under international observation in late 1995, which led to victory for Aristide's Lavalas Party and for its presidential candidate, René Préval.

Aristide was returned to office in elections in 1999, but he has faced an irreconcilable opposition that has rejected the results of a parliamentary election and increasingly demanded Aristide's removal. Aristide has resisted domestic and international pressure to come to terms with the opposition, and has faced an indefinite suspension of aid until he does so. Thus the United States and the international community remain the moderators of Haitian politics.[54]

The Cuban revolutionary regime has evolved a single ruling party with a legal monopoly. However, the personal leadership of Fidel Castro remains, after over forty years, the central feature of the revolutionary regime. Cuba came under intense stress in the wake of the collapse of the Soviet Union and the end of the extensive aid that had permitted the regime to both transform the social structure and maintain its autonomy from the United States. A succession of U.S. administrations have continued to pursue a basically hostile policy toward the Cuban regime, but have been unable to force it to change. Notwithstanding some economic liberalization, the hard-line revolutionaries continue in control, resisting any significant political liberalization. Cuba assuredly faces a transition after the departure of Castro, but its destiny remains uncertain.[55]

The three regimes are different not only because of very distinct social structures and political traditions; they also differ in their levels of popular social and political mobilization and in their levels of state capability and performance.[56] Paraguay is characterized by the least-mobilized populace; correspondingly, the Stroessner regime remained stable over decades without ever developing high levels of state capability. Haiti is very similar in this respect to Paraguay. Cuba's revolution has explicitly depended on organizing and mobilizing the populace in support of the revolutionary project, and the regime has successfully developed the capability to guide and control the people thus mobilized. All three regimes have thus enjoyed prolonged political stability because of a balance between political mobilization and state capabilities.

Each has nevertheless been destabilized in recent years, and each is undergoing extensive political change whose outcome remains uncertain. Destabilization occurs when the structural balance between political mobilization and state capabilities is upset due to a relative loss of state capabilities, either because the state itself becomes weaker or because political mobilization increases. Destabilization has both endogenous and exogenous causes. Endogenous, or internal, causes may include the inevitable effects of aging on the effectiveness of a personalist leader like Stroessner or Castro. Finally, even if the state does not lose capability, the populace may become more politically mobilized as a result of development of economic and social structures (e.g., rising incomes, improved education, better communications). Political mobilization may be particularly stimulated when expectations have been raised and then dashed. In Haiti, the regime of Jean-Claude Duvalier suffered considerable rigidification even as it confronted an increasingly effective mobilization of the poor majority by Jean-Bertrand Aristide. Duvalier was overthrown by elements in his own armed forces, hoping to block the radical threat from Aristide.

Exogenous, or external, structural causes of destabilization include global economic conditions such as the great debt crisis of the early 1980s, which undermined the capability of all regimes, authoritarian and democratic, to meet the expectations of their populations. The foreign policy emphasis of the United States on human rights and democratization constituted an important exogenous cause of destabilization. In Cuba, indeed, U.S. policy since the early 1960s has been explicitly intended to destabilize the revolutionary regime and, in conjunction with endogenous factors, seems finally to be having some such effect.

Most authoritarian regimes found it necessary to respond to these structural pressures (internal and external) by carrying through full transitions to democracy. The three regimes considered here, however, were more resistant. However, they have each undergone substantial liberalization short of full democratization. Here again the insights of Adam Przeworski (1991, chap. 2; see Figure 3.1 above) prove quite useful, because he focuses our attention on the probable interest calculations of distinct sectors of both the authoritarian regime and its opposition. Recall that he distinguishes between hard-liners and reformers within the regime and between moderates and radicals in the opposition. Once endogenous and exogenous causes have increased instability in the authoritarian regime and the corresponding opportunities for change, actors in the distinct sectors of state and opposition have choices to make. Regime hard-liners are assumed to prefer the authoritarian status quo over any other outcome and to reject a democracy without guarantees for themselves and their supporters. Conversely, the opposition radicals are assumed to prefer democracy without guarantees and to reject the authoritarian status quo. In view of these diametrically opposed extremes, much depends on the relative strength of regime reformers and opposition moderates and upon their orders of preferences. If both reformers and moderates choose to negotiate with each other, democracy with guarantees is a reachable outcome.

The present cases of authoritarian regimes in transition, however, cannot be assumed to be headed toward democracy (although they may be). In Paraguay, we find liberalization and a continuing struggle for control between regime reformers and hard-liners. Opposition moderates have shown themselves willing to collaborate with the regime reformers, but a definitive settlement appears far off. In Haiti, Aristide represents the opposition radicals who prefer democracy without guarantees. He has returned to power with significant international pressure, but has neither consolidated his position nor come to terms with more moderate elements of the former opposition, nor with elements of the old Duvalier regime. Instead, he has governed in an increasingly arbitrary, ineffective manner. His position is thus highly precarious, as is the democratic regime.

In Cuba, the Castro regime retains considerable institutional strength and popular support that allows regime hard-liners to resist liberalization, but endogenous and exogenous pressure for change may be expected to increase with the death or retirement of Castro. The fundamental dilemma is that while the regime's goal is the development of a revolutionary consciousness in the people that will permit the building of authentic socialism, the means is a continuing centralization of effective power in the hands of a tiny revolutionary elite and, ultimately, in the hands of Castro. The people cannot be trusted until they have achieved true revolutionary consciousness, and they cannot do that as long as they are without the power to shape their own society and their own lives. The revolutionary purists thus appear trapped in a cycle in which they must repeatedly act to cut off excessive pragmatism in order to preserve the hope of a revolutionary future, although they can never actually achieve that future because of the contradictions of their own situation.

The pragmatists, or reformers, are those who would adapt Cuba to global structural "realities." In the 1970s, pragmatism meant accommodating the Soviet Union. Now, it means insertion into the global marketplace. Either way, if they succeed, the radical promise of the Cuban Revolution will be betrayed. Presently, there are enormous pressures and incentives for Cuba to forsake its revolutionary project and make its peace with global capitalism and liberal democracy. The reformers may not intend to go all the way, but they risk reaching a point of no return where the opposition can no longer be suppressed. At that point Adam Przeworski's analysis (1991) will become relevant to Cuba. That is, reformers, having gained the upper hand, might find that they need to collaborate with opposition moderates to avoid being purged by the hardliners.

Castro himself seems quite genuinely to have sympathies with both hardliners and reformers. His periodic shifts of emphasis probably reflect his own analysis of the immediate requirements of the revolutionary project. Finally, however, his commitment is to an uncompromising vision of the revolution. He is willing to make tactical shifts to ensure the survival of the revolution, but he will not accept reforms that he thinks will undermine the essence of the revolution. And he is the one who defines that essence.

Cuba will change fundamentally; we know this because Castro is mortal, and this revolutionary caudillo continues to be the very core of the revolution. His authority is far more extensive and transcendent than that of Stroessner, and there has been no effective institutionalization of his authority or routinization of his charisma. There is a constitutional successor (Raúl Castro) who will have effective control of party, army, and state; that control may suffice to entrench a new "revolutionary" autocracy. If so, it will be nothing like Fidel Castro's revolution. Finally, there is the grim possibility that the United States, in collaboration with Cuban exiles, will attempt, covertly or overtly, to impose a post-Castro regime. That would almost certainly mean a devastating war in Cuba.

Przeworski rightly points out that as liberalizing reforms proceed, regime reformers have declining incentives to remain allied with the hard-liners and more incentives to negotiate with the opposition moderates, especially if the reformers believe they have sufficient popular support to survive in a democracy with guarantees.[57] Thus the eventual outcome in these cases could well be a democracy with guarantees, even though the immediate outcome is a liberalized authoritarianism.

Conclusion: Stragglers

Not one of these three surviving authoritarian regimes is on a sure course for a democratic transition. All three are in transition, but toward what we cannot know. Paraguay may be the most likely to make a successful democratic transition. It is certainly the furthest along at this point. Its advantages include a relatively unmobilized population. Its weaknesses include a tradition of unvarnished caudillismo and a ruling elite whose commitment to democracy is not very deep. But as long as the international structure of incentives favors democracy, the Paraguayan elite may be expected to play the game, including a progressive easing up on the opposition parties. Given some time, the habits of liberal democracy might take deeper root. Haiti appears far more polarized and institutionally weak than Paraguay, and it is difficult to reach any sort of optimistic prognosis.

The autumn of Cuba's revolutionary patriarch poses perhaps the most intriguing possibilities, because the Cuban regime combines high levels of organizational development and popular mobilization with a completely personalistic, charismatic supreme leader.[58] The Cuban population certainly has the cultural sophistication to operate within a liberal democracy, should they want to do so, but many citizens and the majority of the ruling elite reject liberal democracy as a poor substitute for the aspirations of the revolution. A transition to liberal democracy is possible after Castro, given the right set of circumstances. More likely is a continuation of a progressively depersonalized revolutionary regime, along the lines of China after Mao Zedong or Vietnam after Ho Chi Minh.

■ Conclusion

At this writing, liberal democratic regimes have been successfully established in most of Latin America; indeed, only Cuba has entirely resisted the second wave of democratization beginning in the late 1970s. While popular mobilization and organization were in every case important in placing democratization on the political agenda, the actual establishment of liberal democracy always depended on some mixture of elite negotiations and outside pressure. In the early cases, managing the expansion of popular participation was the central objective, while in the second wave, popular mobilization helped to open the way for transitions from authoritarian rule. However, such transitions were almost always negotiated with the authoritarian regimes, since the latter retained substantial political and coercive resources. All of the democracies of Latin America bore the birthmark of efforts to contain and control the people. In this sense they were not full democracies, but at best polyarchies. Most were imperfect even as polyarchies, meeting only minimal standards of formal democracy such as periodic competitive elections. But in view of the region's dismal political history, even minimal democracy was an improvement for most. We now turn to issues of stability, instability, and consolidation of these democratic regimes.

■ Notes

1. Useful comparative analyses are provided by Collier and Collier (1991); Rueschemeyer, Stephens, and Stephens (1992); Mahoney (2001); and Korzeniewicz (2000).

2. Principal sources on Chilean political history and political economy include Bethell (1993); Loveman (1988); Remmer (1984); Petras (1969); Gil (1966); Kinsbruner (1973); Scully (1992, 1995); Zeitlin (1984); Zeitlin and Ratcliff (1988); Osorio (1990); Ramírez Necochea (1985); Nunn (1976); Valenzuela (1978, 1989); Oppenheim (1993); Nef and Galleguillos (1995).

3. Collier and Collier (1991), in their massive comparative study, have argued that Chile dealt with the problem of incorporating labor into the political system by depoliticization and control of the labor movement, while in Uruguay that movement was mobilized by one of the traditional ruling parties, the Colorados.

4. Principal sources on Uruguayan political history and political economy include Weinstein (1988, 1995); Gillespie (1991); Gillespie and González (1989); González (1991, 1995); Kaufman (1979); Vanger (1980); Finch (1981); Rottenberg (1993); Panizza (1990).

5. Principal sources on Costa Rican political history and political economy include Monge Alfaro (1980); Ameringer (1982); Yashar (1995, 1997); Longley (1997); Chalker (1995); Stone (1975); Cerdas Cruz (1985); Vega Carballo (1982); Muñoz Guillén (1990); Rovira Mas (1988); Oconitrillo (1982); Gudmundson and Lindo-Fuentes (1995); Peeler (1985, 1992). It is a commonplace of Costa Rica's national mythology that its historic poverty and equality laid the foundation for the country's later development of democracy. However, contemporary historians now see this as overstated.

6. See Aguilar Bulgarelli (1980); Oconitrillo (1982); Rovira Mas (1988). The church and the U.S. embassy worked actively to promote a settlement. Archbishop Sanabria's basic position was that a way must be found to stop the bloodshed. The U.S. position was more complex and profoundly ambivalent (see Schifter [1986]; Longley [1997]; Yashar [1997]). The United States was increasingly concerned about the Communist presence in the Picado and Calderón governments, but Calderón had been a highly reliable ally in World War II and was furthermore a close friend of Nicaraguan president Anastasio Somoza, another faithful U.S. ally. However, Somoza was temporarily at odds with the United States over the Nicaraguan presidential succession. The United States also distrusted Figueres's close alliance with President Juan José Arévalo of Guatemala, a reformer viewed with suspicion in U.S. government circles. Figueres's strong anticommunism recommended him, but his advocacy of extensive reforms elicited uneasiness. He was not well-known to U.S. policymakers. Thus the United States was dealing with conflicting cues (indeed, the State Department and the ambassador were not always of the same persuasion) in a situation that was not per-

ceived as central to U.S. interests. It is thus not surprising that as the crisis heated up in the late 1940s, the United States did not play an active role. But with the advent of civil war, and the reduction of the alternatives to Calderón (and the Communists) or Figueres, U.S. policy crystallized in favor of a negotiated departure of Calderón. The U.S. ambassador, along with the papal nuncio, was critical in arranging such an agreement in the final days of the war, thus averting an assault on San José itself.

7. See Bowman (2002), chap. 4, for a carefully researched argument that the advent of democracy in Costa Rica owed almost nothing to pacts. In contrast to the early incorporation of the Calderonistas, the Communists and other leftist parties, constitutionally outlawed in 1949, were not permitted unrestricted electoral participation until 1970. The constitutional proscription of Communist parties was finally officially lifted in 1975. However, unlike Calderón, the Left received no policy satisfaction: all they got was the privilege of participating. See Oconitrillo (1982); Salom (1987).

8. On Colombian history, see Bushnell (1993); Guillén Martínez (1979); Dix (1987); Hartlyn (1988); Archer (1995); Martz (1997).

9. On Venezuela, see Salcedo-Bastardo (1979); Lombardi (1982); Kornblith and Levine (1995).

10. On the elite settlement in Venezuela, see Arroyo Talavera (1988); López Maya and Gómez Calcaño (1989); Levine (1989); Karl (1987); Blank (1984); Hillman (1994).

11. In Mainwaring and Scully (1995), see the chapters by Kornblith and Levine on Venezuela, Yashar on Costa Rica, Scully on Chile, González on Uruguay, and Archer on Colombia. On Costa Rica, see also Rovira Mas (1994); Fernández (1994).

12. Major comparative studies include O'Donnell, Schmitter, and Whitehead (1986); Diamond, Linz, and Lipset (1989, 1995); Baloyra (1987); Higley and Gunther (1992); Przeworski (1991); Huntington (1991). Major comparative studies focused on Latin America include Malloy and Seligson (1987); Drake and Silva (1986); Wiarda (1990); Mainwaring and Scully (1995); Camp (1996a); Conaghan and Malloy (1994); Jonas and Stein (1990); Needler (1987); Tulchin (1995).

13. On Nicaragua, see Booth (1985); Walker (1986, 1991). On Haiti, see Mintz (1995); NACLA (1987). On Paraguay, see Abente (1995); Lewis (1993a).

14. On the Banzer period, see Malloy and Gamarra (1987, 1988); Dunkerley (1984); Kelley and Klein (1981); Klein (1992). On the Balaguer period, see NACLA (1982); Black (1986); Espinal (1987); Conaghan and Espinal (1990); Kryzanek (1996).

15. See especially O'Donnell (1979); Collier (1979). On Argentina, see also Rouquié (1994); Cavarozzi (1983, 1986). On Brazil, see also Stepan (1988, 1989); Martins (1986). On Chile, see also Valenzuela (1978, 1989); Valenzuela and Valenzuela (1986); Arriagada (1988); Garretón (1989). On Uruguay, see Gillespie (1986); Rial (1986); Dutrénit Bielous (1994); González (1995).

16. On Central America, see Torres Rivas (1993); Pérez Brignoli (1987); Weaver (1994); O'Shaughnessy and Dodson (1999). On Guatemala, see Calvert (1985); Handy (1984); Jonas (1991). On El Salvador, see Baloyra-Herp (1985); Montgomery (1995). On Honduras, see Morris (1984); Peckenham and Street (1985).

17. On Peru, see Stepan (1978); Palmer (1980); Rudolph (1992). On Bolivia, see Malloy and Gamarra (1987, 1988); Ladman (1982). On Ecuador, see Isaacs (1993); Martz (1987).

18. During the same period, the military regime of Osvaldo López Arellano in Honduras showed substantial affinities with this type.

19. A useful survey on international dimensions of democratization is Whitehead (1996).

20. Human rights, as codified in international law and treaties, would include, for example, the right not to be tortured, arbitrarily imprisoned, or caused to disappear. Political rights would include freedom of speech and the press, and honest, competitive elections.

21. See Schoultz (1981, 1987); Stallings and Kaufman (1989); Hartlyn, Schoultz, and Varas (1992); Smith, Acuña, and Gamarra (1994a, 1994b); Remmer (1991b); Haggard and Kaufman (1995); Bresser Pereira, Maravall, and Przeworski (1993).

22. The causes of the crisis are beyond the scope of this book. See Stallings and Kaufman (1989).

23. On Peru, see Rudolph (1992); McClintock and Lowenthal (1983). On Ecuador, see Isaacs (1993). On El Salvador, see Montgomery (1995). On Honduras, see Morris (1984). On Guatemala, see Calvert (1985); Jonas (1991). For a comparison of Ecuador and the Dominican Republic, see Conaghan and Espinal (1990). Note that especially in El Salvador, Honduras, and Guatemala, pressure was intense from the United States for a transition to democracy. This pressure developed because the United States was preoccupied with the revolution in Nicaragua from 1979 onward and wished to avoid the embarrassment of propping up authoritarian allies in the isthmian region. Cf. Allison and Beschel (1992).

24. On the Dominican Republic, see NACLA (1982); Black (1986). On Uruguay, see Rial (1986). On Brazil, see Martins (1986); Fleischer (1986); Soares (1986). On Chile, see Caviedes (1991); Garretón (1995). The Dominican case was marked by direct and public pressure from the Carter administration for President Balaguer to recognize his defeat.

25. On Bolivia, see Malloy and Gamarra (1987, 1988); Mayorga (1991).

26. On Nicaragua, see Booth (1985); Walker (1986, 1991); Torres and Coraggio (1987). Anti-Sandinista elements of the opposition, with the help and encouragement of the United States, did attempt to negotiate an extrication that would leave in place some checks on Sandinista power, but these efforts came too late to affect the outcome of the insurrection.

27. On Argentina, see Cavarozzi (1986); Vacs (1987); Wynia (1986).

28. On Panama, see Ropp (1982, 1996); Priestley (1986); Pérez (1995).

29. Major analyses of the transition in Latin America include O'Donnell, Schmitter, and Whitehead (1986); Higley and Gunther (1992); Przeworski (1991); Haggard and Kaufman (1995); Malloy and Seligson (1987); Baloyra (1987).

30. Public opinion was also typically favorable toward democracy in the abstract, but important sectors in most countries also showed sympathy for authoritarian rule. Often, the same individual might simultaneously articulate both attitudes. See, for example, Leslie Anderson (1995); Basañez (1994); Booth and Richard (1996).

31. On the transition in Uruguay, see Gillespie (1986, 1992); Rial (1986); Dutrénit Bielous (1994); González (1995); Caetano and Rilla (1995); Caetano, Rilla, and Pérez (1987).

32. On the peace settlement in El Salvador, see Montgomery (1995).

33. On the Brazilian constituent assembly, see Bruneau (1992); Crespo Martínez (1991); Lamounier (1994a); Rizzo de Oliveira (1988); Stepan (1989). On the Peruvian constituent assembly of 1979, see McClintock and Lowenthal (1983).

34. On the development and political role of the Concertación in Chile, see Cavarozzi (1992); Garretón (1993a, 1995); Drake and Jaksic (1991); Angell (1993); Oppenheim (1993); Petras and Leiva (1994); Puryear (1994); Scully (1995). On the role of pacts in the Bolivian transition, see Gamarra and Malloy (1995); Gamarra (1994); Mayorga (1992b, 1994a, 1994b, 1995b). On the Chamorro/FSLN pact in Nicaragua, see Vargas (1995); LaRamée (1995). For a comparison with Guatemala, see Jonas (1989).

35. But cf. Cavarozzi's argument in Higley and Gunther (1992). Patricio Silva, in a private communication, argues that "although the Concertación as such is not an elite settlement, it represents a political project (democracy with free market economy) which is, in itself, the basis of a general agreement between the Concertación sector and right-wing elite sectors."

36. Such as nine unelected senators, an extremely difficult amendment process, a military budget independent of the elected president, and an electoral system that systematically overrepresents the rightist minority.

37. The Concertación is thus in a position similar to the democratic center in the German Weimar Republic of the 1920s: continuation of the democratic regime depends on the continuing electoral strength and cooperation of the center parties. As is well-known, when the Center failed in Germany, the result was Nazism.

38. This is a controversial judgment. Huntington (1991) represents the more customary position of U.S. policymakers and allied scholars, that the FSLN revolutionary government was itself authoritarian or even totalitarian. Thus it would follow that the transition began in 1990 with the electoral defeat of the Sandinistas. Nevertheless, along with most Nicaragua specialists, I hold that a careful review of the record of the Sandinista decade shows that there was indeed a serious project of democratization that sought to incorporate the essential elements of liberal democracy and to go beyond them. Consult Coraggio (1985); CIERA (1984); Ruchwarger (1987); Coraggio and Deere (1987); Tirado López (1986). The Sandinista model was neither purely liberal nor totally Marxist-Leninist; rather, reflecting the amalgam that was the FSLN, it displayed features of both in an uneasy and contradictory mix. The "popular organizations" were arms of the FSLN and were patterned directly on Cuban paradigms. However, there was never an attempt to create a Marxist-Leninist single party like the Communist parties of Cuba or the Soviet Union. Rather, the party system and electoral system were intended to be competitive and were so. Many Sandinistas expected that the Front would achieve a durable electoral dominance as the natural leaders of "the people." Some may have secretly aspired to a Mexican-style party hegemony. But in any case they held two general elections (1984, 1990) under intense scrutiny from international observers. Both were widely judged free and fair. They lost the second, and they surrendered power. See Walker (1991).

39. UNO was a loose and fractious alliance of most of the elites opposed to the Sandinistas. It had been pieced together with strong leadership and financial support by the United States as a means of presenting a united civil opposition, even while both the U.S. government and UNO maintained a tacit alliance with the various armed counterrevolutionary groups (contras), which were also largely created and financed by the U.S. government.

40. On the transition in Guatemala, see Rosada Granados (1992); Jonas (1989, 1991). On the transition in Honduras, see Rosenberg (1989); Paz Aguilar (1992). On the crisis and transition in Panama, see Smith (1992); Ropp (1996). On the transition in the Dominican Republic, see Black (1986); Conaghan and Espinal (1990). On the post-Duvalier transition in Haiti, see Mintz (1995); NACLA (1994). The Haitian case is considered later in this chapter.

41. See Bowman (2002) for a detailed analysis of the impact of militarization on the prospects of democracy in Honduras.

42. Other countries included Haiti, Cuba, Puerto Rico, and Nicaragua. See Bradford (1993); Cerdas Cruz (1992); Pastor (1992); Schoultz (1998). Puerto Rico is not treated in this book. After the Spanish-American War (1898), the island was made a U.S. dependency and denied the opportunity for independence. Since World War II, it

has been self-governing, theoretically entitled to independence, but economically quite closely tied to the United States.

43. On the Argentine transition, see Cavarozzi (1986); Vacs (1987); Wynia (1986); Halperín Donghi (1994).

44. On the Ecuadoran transition, see Isaacs (1993); Conaghan and Espinal (1990); Conaghan and Malloy (1994); Conaghan (1995).

45. Major sources on Mexican politics include Craig and Cornelius (1995); Cornelius (1996); Camp (2003); Hellman (1983, 1994); NACLA (1997); González Casanova (1970); Schmidt (1986); Morris (1995); LaBotz (1995); Roett (1995); Woldenburg (1995); Cordera and Sánchez Rebolledo (1995); Cansino (1995); Knight (1994); Acosta Silva et al. (1995); Carrigan (1995); Muñoz Patraca (1994); Fox (1994); Coppedge (1993); Knight (1986, 1992); Hellman (1983).

46. The principal opposition party of modern Mexico, the National Action Party, was founded in 1939 and sought to draw in these various strands of conservative opposition to the revolutionary regime: religious people and the clergy, businesspeople, and in general anyone disillusioned with the regime. See Craig and Cornelius (1995), pp. 269ff.

47. See Stallings and Kaufman (1989); Haggard and Kaufman (1995).

48. Additional sources on Mexican politics since the mid-1980s include Muñoz Patraca (1994); Cansino (1995); Schulz and Williams (1995); Cornelius (1996) Bruhn (1997); Gutmann (2002); Levy (2001).

49. Writing on the Zapatista rebellion has been voluminous. Useful sources include Carrigan (1995); Harvey (1998); Womack (1999); Zermeño (1995); Stephen (1995); Nash (1995); Dietz (1995).

50. On social movements and politics in Latin America, see Eckstein (1989); Escobar and Alvarez (1992); Jaquette (1994); McManus and Schlabach (1991); Corradi, Fagen, and Garretón (1992). For an important general analysis, see Tarrow (1994).

51. I use "authoritarian regime" to mean a persistent system of rule in which rulers gain and retain political power by coercion rather than consent and are not effectively checked by laws. The distinction between authoritarian and totalitarian regimes, commonly used from the 1940s until the 1980s, is no longer relevant, because it depended on the supposedly total control exercised by the latter. If control were total, then totalitarian regimes could not be overthrown from within, whereas authoritarian regimes could be ousted from within because they exercised less extensive control. Since the breakdown of communist rule in Eastern Europe and the Soviet Union, we know that supposedly totalitarian regimes were susceptible to overthrow from within. They thus cannot be differentiated on principle from authoritarian regimes. Cf. Linz (1975); Kirkpatrick (1982, 1990).

52. On Paraguayan politics and parties in general, see Abente (1995); Roett and Sacks (1991); Mora Mérida (1981); Lewis (1982, 1993a, 1993b); Miranda (1990); Lambert (2000); Fournier and Burges (2000).

53. On Haiti, see Mintz (1995); NACLA (1994); Fatton (2002).

54. The Reagan and George H. W. Bush administrations rhetorically supported democratization in Haiti while doing a great deal behind the scenes to undermine Aristide and to prevent him from returning once he had been overthrown. The Clinton administration was more positive toward Aristide and finally did bring about his return. Important sectors of the Clinton administration were nevertheless very suspicious of Aristide and sought to bolster potential opponents once Aristide had returned. The George W. Bush administration has been extremely skeptical of Aristide but has refrained from overtly advocating his removal. See Fatton (2002).

55. Major sources on Cuban history include Pérez-Stable (1999); del Aguila (1994); Simons (1996); Pérez (1995).

56. Huntington (1968) emphasized that political stability depends on a relative balance between levels of mobilization and institutionalization. Almond (1973) similarly argued that stability depends on the political system's capability to produce outcomes that respond to demands coming from the society.

57. Of course, they may miscalculate, as Gorbachev did in the Soviet Union in 1991.

58. I refer to Gabriel García Márquez, *The Autumn of the Patriarch* (1976).

4

Stabilizing and Consolidating Democracies

Once democratic regimes have been established, their stabilization depends on the development of key political institutions (particularly the state itself, and parties and party systems), social organization and social capital, and cooperation among elites. The concept of stability implies the persistence of a pattern over a substantial period. Operationally, I will consider a democratic regime stable if it has passed through three electoral cycles without the breakdown of its key rules and procedures. That is, any changes in rules and procedures are to have been adopted through the rules and procedures provided for that purpose in the constitution or law.

There are relatively few Latin American countries where democratic regimes have moved beyond stability to consolidation. Juan Linz and Alfred Stepan (1996a, p. 15) define the consolidation of democracy as the evolution of the democratic system to the point where it is "the only game in town," that is, where the only way to achieve a change of government is by means of democratic election under rules adopted by democratic decisionmaking. Neither military coups nor other types of insurrection are considered realistic ways of gaining power. Larry Diamond (1999, p. 65) treats consolidation as the process of gaining broad and deep legitimation, such that both elites and masses come to believe that a democratic regime is better for their society than any alternative regime, notwithstanding poor performance at any particular moment. Note that while Linz and Stepan treat consolidation as a state, Diamond treats it as a process. Moreover, while Diamond considers legitimation as the nucleus of consolidation, Linz and Stepan consider the mere acceptance of democracy as the only game in town as a sufficient base for consolidation.

If we consider consolidation as a concept applicable to any regime, not just democracies, then clearly Diamond's emphasis on legitimation poses too high a barrier. A regime such as the French monarchy before the revolution was certainly consolidated in the sense of being the only game in town, though surely not legitimate to the degree posited by Diamond. Indeed, if we consider the consolidation of that regime as a process, as Diamond so wisely advocates, then it appears that the monarchy's claim to legitimacy on the basis of hereditary authority progressively eroded in the eighteenth century as the alternative principle of popular consent took root in people's thinking. But it was only toward the end of that century that the monarchy ceased being the only game in town, and the regime became thus deconsolidated and ultimately fell.

Democratic consolidation will here be considered as a process of progressively eliminating threats of insurrection and foreign or military intervention in the political process, to the point that political action is only possible by means of elections and constitutional government. A regime will not be considered to have eliminated these threats until it has passed through the criteria of stabilization, and in addition has experienced at least two transitions of government from a governing party to an opposition party without being destabilized by insurrection or by foreign or military intervention.[1] Thus the criteria for consolidation are somewhat higher than for stabilization. Stabilization requires simply that the system not break down, while consolidation implies that alternatives to the democratic system cease to be realistic. Both operational definitions stipulate a duration of three electoral cycles, but consolidation requires in addition that there be at least one transfer of power to the opposition.

◼ The State and Governmental Institutions

Any political regime, whether democratic or not, can achieve stability only on the basis of a strong state.[2] To the extent that the state is in fact incapable of exercising effective control over its territory and population, the rules of any regime will be unenforceable, essentially fictional. In Chapter 2 we reviewed the historical importance of legalism and constitutionalism as bases for democracy in Latin America, and in the era of democratization they are more important than ever. Historically, however, Latin American states have been weak, and constitutions have not been literally enforced. If democracy is to be stabilized in the early twenty-first century, Latin American states will have to be stronger. In this section we consider the main elements of debates about such institutions as presidential versus parliamentary governments, the political role of the military, electoral systems, staggered versus coinciding terms for president and legislature, centralism versus federalism, presidential reelection, and the survival of authoritarian features in democratic constitutions.

A principal focus of constitutional debate across much of the region in recent years has been the relative merits of presidential versus parliamentary systems of government.[3] Since independence, of course, Latin America has almost universally hewed to variations on the presidential system of the United States, with its independent, separately elected president and Congress that relate to each other through a variety of constitutional checks and balances tending to ensure that neither branch can acquire absolute power. Many scholars (but few politicians or generals) have argued that the presidential system works against political stability in the Latin American context. For example, it is typical that congresses are elected by some variation on proportional representation (leading to representation of many small parties), whereas presidents are either elected with a plurality well below an absolute majority or by means of a runoff second round. In either case, the newly elected president will be inaugurated without assurance of a working majority in Congress.

In contrast, advocates of a parliamentary system point out that the chief executive holds office only so long as he or she has a majority in parliament, either through a single majority party or a negotiated governing coalition. Governmental gridlock common in presidential systems is thus avoided by vesting unambiguous authority in a government that depends on parliament for its tenure.

Advocates of presidentialism typically emphasize its consistency with Latin American culture and tradition and point to the high levels of party fragmentation present in most Latin American parliaments. The likely result of parliamentary government, they argue, would be short-lived governments and frequent crises during which caretaker cabinets would have to administer public affairs in the absence of a majority mandate. It is far better, they say, to stay with the presidential system in which one person with extensive powers and discretion has a mandate to govern for a fixed term, independent of the vagaries of legislative politics. Mark Jones (1995) argued that presidential regimes can be stable and effective if electoral systems generate majority or near-majority legislative support.

In recent years, democratically elected presidents (e.g., Alberto Fujimori in Peru, Víctor Paz Estenssoro in Bolivia, and Carlos Menem in Argentina) have fed the arguments of both sides as, acting by both constitutional and extraconstitutional means, they have implemented sweeping programs of economic reform without either congressional action or popular consent. Presidentialists often point out that such bold initiatives would be far less likely in a parliamentary system because of the need to consult the members and hold the majority together. Parliamentarists see such arbitrary actions as inherently contrary to democratic principles and hold that a parliamentary system would tend to restrict such initiatives. In any case, most of the presidents who have tried this gambit have come to grief. Carlos Andrés Pérez of Venezuela, Fernando Collor de Melo of Brazil, and Abdalá Bucaram of Ecuador were constitutionally impeached and removed from office. Menem and Fujimori, after achieving constitutional amendments to permit reelection, were each reelected. But Menem was finally forced to retire (and his 2003 comeback was frustrated by lack of popular support), while Fujimori fled the country in the face of a major corruption scandal.[4]

The only Latin American country to have recently given formal consideration to parliamentarism is Brazil. Under its new constitution, a referendum was mandated to allow the voters to make two choices: (1) between monarchy and republic and (2) between presidential and parliamentary governmental systems. The referendum took place in 1993, and the electorate decisively opted for the status quo: a presidential republic (Lamounier, 1994a, 1994b; Schneider, 1996). The issue of presidential versus parliamentary government is of considerable theoretical interest, but it seems clear that no major Latin American country is on the verge of a shift to a parliamentary system.[5]

René Antonio Mayorga (1995b) argued that Bolivia's newfound stability is in considerable measure attributable to "parliamentarized presidentialism," a practice whereby presidents are normally elected by Congress but only after they are able to negotiate majority coalitions. Such coalitions, moreover, are then renegotiated periodically for purposes of governing. Mayorga argued that without forswearing its presidential system, Bolivia has gained most of the benefits of a parliamentary system. But should the country adopt a runoff system for presidential elections in place of the congressional election when no candidate gains an absolute majority, then stability will be adversely affected because the need for such coalitions would diminish (see also Gamarra, 1997). The contrast with Ecuador is instructive here: Ecuadoran presidents are elected by runoff, typically lack congressional majorities, and are usually confronted by gridlock, whereas Bolivian presidents since 1985 have usually had governing majorities based on negotiated coalitions (cf. Gamarra and Malloy, 1995; Conaghan, 1995). However, in 2003, Bolivia suffered a crisis very reminiscent of Ecuador, as President Gonzalo Sánchez de Lozada was confronted with massive popular demonstrations against his economic policies. After scores of demonstrators (largely indigenous people and coca producers) were killed by police, Sánchez de Lozada resigned and was replaced by his vice president.

Most Latin American countries now provide for a runoff popular election in the event that no candidate receives an absolute majority (or sometimes, a specified plurality such as 40 percent). And except where one or two parties are overwhelmingly dominant, a runoff is commonly needed. The Ecuadoran pattern described in the previous paragraph is thus not uncommon in the region. In recent years, presidents have lacked a reliable congressional majority in Brazil, the Dominican Republic, Nicaragua, and Guatemala.

Other countries, notably Colombia, Costa Rica, and Venezuela, provide for no runoff, simply electing the candidate receiving the most votes. This has worked satisfactorily in these countries because of their highly institutionalized bipolar party systems. However, as the Venezuelan party system decayed, the election of 1993 saw the victory of Rafael Caldera with under 30 percent of the vote. His coalition gained an even smaller proportion of seats in Congress, and as a result he lacked a reliable majority. The Bolivarian constitution of 1999 continues to provide for election of the president by plurality.

Systems for electing the legislature are the other component of this great dilemma of presidential governance. The majority of Latin American legislatures are elected through proportional representation (PR), which in most cases has led to representation of several small parties (certainly good in itself) but has also often meant seating a legislature without a clear majority. The few cases of stable and strongly bipolar party systems have generally produced majorities in spite of PR, but any decay in party dominance is likely to release the fragmenting tendencies of PR. In the heyday of Venezuelan democracy in the 1970s, Democratic Action (AD) was able to gain a majority even under PR, but in the crisis-ridden elections of 1993 and 1998, no party was even close to a majority.

Even as PR is criticized for impeding effective governance by obstructing the formation of legislative majorities, other reformers have criticized it for vesting too much power in national party elites and thereby weakening the link between representatives and their constituents. Consequently, a principal initiative of Venezuelan state reformers since the late 1980s was the implementation of single-member districts for one-half the members of Congress. The goal was to counteract excessive party dominance by reducing leadership control over party lists, but the change might well have promoted two-party dominance (a well-known effect in the United States and the United Kingdom, where single-member, plurality election is used exclusively). However, its implementation coincided so closely with the meltdown of the Venezuelan party system in the 1990s that it is difficult to say whether or not this particular reform contributed to that breakdown (Coppedge, 1994b). In any case, the new constitution of 1999 further reduced proportional representation (from 50 percent to 40 percent of seats), a change that redounded to the benefit of the governing Fifth Republic Movement (MVR) of President Hugo Chávez (Martínez Barahona, 2002).

In Mexico, the ruling Institutional Revolutionary Party (PRI) sought as early as the 1970s to respond to critics by diluting the single-member, plurality system for electing members of Congress. The argument was that the PRI could elect almost all members under the plurality system, thereby underrepresenting other parties. The implementation of proportional representation for 40 percent of congressional seats did in fact increase the representation of other parties, so that by 1994, opposition parties had 40 percent of deputies and half of senators (Camp, 2003, chap. 4; Pérez Herrero, 2001).

There have been similar arguments across the region on several other issues of how formal governmental structure may affect democracy. Proposals to separate presidential from congressional and local elections are motivated by a desire to reduce the concentration of power but inevitably would also have the effect of further reducing the possibility of cooperation between president and Congress.

Also notable are proposals in several countries to make government more responsive by enhancing the autonomy and authority of state, provincial, and local governments. In view of long-standing patterns of clientelism in many local and regional governments, it may be that the main beneficiaries of such a reform would be local political elites—if the reforms really were to give them control of significant new resources.

Most of these proposed reforms in state institutions are inspired by a fundamentally liberal spirit of restricting the concentration of power. Within this perspective, the efficacy of the government would be distinctly secondary because, in Thomas Jefferson's words, "That government is best which governs least." It might be argued that adopting a parliamentary system would serve both efficacy and liberty by restricting presidential power and giving more power to the people's representatives; most of the other reforms would primarily restrict the concentration of power.

Two other types of institutional reform, however, are emphatically oriented toward increasing governmental efficacy by means of concentrating power. Although prohibitions on presidential reelection are traditionally widespread in the region, several presidents at the peak of their popularity have succeeded in pushing through constitutional reforms permitting their reelection. The major cases are Carlos Menem in Argentina, Alberto Fujimori in Peru, and Fernando Henrique Cardoso in Brazil. The new Venezuelan constitution of 1999 both lengthens the presidential term by one year and allows for immediate reelection.

Last, but very important, many ostensibly democratic constitutions contain major authoritarian features, sometimes dating from the nineteenth century (e.g., giving the president the authority to declare a state of siege or emergency and thereby rule by decree) and sometimes having been mandated by the outgoing authoritarian regime (as in Chile's appointed senators, or Brazil's continuing recognition of the tutelary role of the armed forces in its new constitution; cf. Loveman, 1993).

All these issues of formal governmental structure are important for the fate of democracy. They define the rules of the political game, the boundaries within which actors do politics. That is precisely why one of the main preoccupations of political actors is the shaping of those formal structures. Again we come to our central theme: structures matter because they constrain action, but structures are also constituted and changed by action.

■ The Military and Democratic Politics

With the third wave of democratization since the late 1970s, the political roles of the armed forces have been profoundly transformed all over Latin America

(Diamint, 2003; Stepan, 1988; Fitch, 1998). Whereas through the mid-1970s the majority of countries were under direct military rule, by 1990 there were few military regimes. Yet the armed forces have not ceased to be politically powerful. It is thus necessary to analyze the many roles that the military plays in democratic regimes.

Table 4.1 summarizes the main roles played by the armed forces in Latin America in the 1990s. Note that they frequently play more than one role, and that at times their roles may conflict.

The only Latin American country that has achieved anything like the civilian control of the military characteristic of consolidated democracies is Costa Rica, which abolished its army in 1949 and replaced it with the lightly armed Civil and Rural Guards. These forces have minimal military training, and the officer corps are directly controlled by the major political parties. The other major case of effective civilian control was that of Venezuela prior to 1988, where the armed forces were prohibited from political participation, while at the same time higher-level military promotions had to be approved

Table 4.1   Roles of the Armed Forces in the 1990s

Democratic Actors	Political Actors	Economic Actors
Civilian Control	*Moderator*	*State Capitalists*
Costa Rica	Brazil	Brazil
	Ecuador	Ecuador
External Defense	Bolivia	Guatemala
Peru	Honduras	Peru
Ecuador		
Institutional Pressure Group	*Roadblock*	*Organized Crime*
Mexico	Guatemala	Colombia
Dominican Republic	Colombia	Guatemala
Panama	Nicaragua	Paraguay
		Haiti
Counterinsurgency	*Revolutionary Agent*	
Colombia	Venezuela	
Peru	Ecuador	
Mexico	Bolivia	
Counternarcotic	*Impunity*	
Colombia	Colombia	
Peru	Peru	
Mexico	Mexico	
Bolivia	Brazil	
	Chile	
	Argentina	
	El Salvador	
	Guatemala	

by Congress, thereby giving the major parties important leverage over military careers. Both Panama and Haiti initiated the abolition of their armies in the 1990s, but the fall of President Aristide of Haiti in early 2004 will probably lead to reestablishing the army.

There are other military roles consistent with democracy in that the armed forces do not question their obligation to obey constitutional authority, even though they may wield very substantial power. Such is the case when the military constitutes an "institutional pressure group." In Mexico after the defeat of the PRI in 2000, for example, the armed forces are no longer part of the ruling-party establishment, nor have they gone into the opposition with the PRI. Rather, they seem to be using their leverage to promote their institutional interests in policy and budget matters. Much the same appears to be happening lately in the Dominican Republic.

Although armed conflict between Latin American states is rare, most maintain military establishments in part to confront external threats. This is the quintessential legitimate role for armed forces. In 1995, Ecuador and Peru fought a significant battle over a disputed tract on the eastern slopes of the Andes in southeastern Ecuador. Peru fared better in the conflict, and Presidents Alberto Fujimori and Jamil Mahuad negotiated a territorial settlement reflecting that fact in 1999. Ironically, both men would be forced out of power less than a year later, but the settlement was respected by successor governments in both countries.

Counterinsurgency was a principal justification for many of the military regimes of the 1970s, but it also continues as a mission assigned by democratic governments in several countries. Colombia has persistently failed to defeat the guerrilla insurgencies of the Revolutionary Armed Forces of Colombia (FARC) and the National Liberation Army (ELN), and the Colombian Armed Forces still have battling with those insurgencies as their principal mission. In Peru, the Shining Path and Tupac Amaru guerrillas posed serious security threats through the early 1990s, and the armed forces were correspondingly assigned the mission of confronting those threats. Mexico has also confronted significant regional insurgencies, most notably that of the Zapatista Army of National Liberation (EZLN) in Chiapas, but these movements do not seriously threaten the national government, posing more of a political than military challenge.

Another common mission assigned by democratic governments in the 1990s was counternarcotics. This has been a major preoccupation of the armed forces in Colombia, Peru, Bolivia, and Mexico, while in many other countries the military is often ordered to carry out counternarcotics operations. Both counterinsurgency and counternarcotic operations have frequently led to credible charges of human rights violations, especially in Colombia and Peru. In Colombia, fighting the drug trade has provided many military and police officers with an irresistible temptation for corruption. Indeed there is good evidence that the drug trade has corrupted elements of the guerrilla forces, as well as the government.

Without actually controlling the government, many Latin American militaries wield more power than would be proper under fully democratic control. For example, in Brazil and Ecuador the armed forces still act as moderators of civilian politics, taking upon themselves the prerogative of setting the boundaries of the permissible in civilian politics. It was not taken for granted that the Brazilian armed forces would accept the election of Lula da Silva in 2002, and he made a point of cultivating the high command. In Ecuador, the high command took control after lower-ranking officers had worked with the indigenous movement to bring down Jamil Mahuad in 2000, enforcing the constitutional succession of Mahuad's vice president.

Another extrademocratic political role is as an agent of political change. This is most notable in Venezuela after the election of Hugo Chávez in 1998. Chávez enjoyed considerable support in the military ranks, and took every opportunity to purge the officer corps of his enemies. At this writing, the Venezuelan armed forces appear fully in support of Chávez's populist agenda. The Sandinista army played a similar role under the elected government of Daniel Ortega in the late 1980s, but unlike the Venezuelan army, the Sandinista force was an arm of the Sandinista National Liberation Front (FSLN) from the beginning of the regime. When the Sandinistas seized power in 1979, the old national guard was disbanded and replaced by the Sandinista army.

Conversely, some armed forces continue to act as roadblocks, impeding access to power by former guerrillas in Guatemala or Colombia, for example. The roadblock role is sometimes played by extraofficial, shadowy vigilante or death squads that cooperate with the armed forces and police, even using off-duty personnel, but that can be plausibly denied by the military commanders. Such death squads first became prominent under the military regimes of the 1970s, but have continued to be active in many countries under democratic regimes.

As a widespread consequence of negotiated transitions to democracy, many countries enacted amnesty laws that prohibited the punishment of accused violators of human rights under the former dictatorships. Such amnesties were either adopted by the outgoing dictatorship and imposed on the incoming elected regime (e.g., Chile) or adopted by the elected government under military pressure (e.g., Argentina). Either way, these laws protected most officers accused of human rights violations. With the passage of time, the efficacy of that protection has begun to erode. Thus in Chile, former president Augusto Pinochet and several other high-ranking officers were declared subject to prosecution, while in Argentina newly elected president Nestor Kirchner gained the repeal of that country's amnesty law, and the prosecution of several prominent military officers. Impunity thus remains an important political issue throughout the region, and there are signs that many violators may ultimately be held to account.

The armed forces in many countries are important economic actors. Most notably in Brazil, but also in several other countries, the armed forces own important corporations. In Brazil the military controls aircraft, missile, and armored-car manufacturers that are among the world leaders in arms exports. Elsewhere, military-controlled companies are not internationally prominent, but in Guatemala and Ecuador, for example, they provide the armed forces with a resource base independent of the national defense budget. Moreover, these business activities provide officers with innumerable opportunities for corruption, a problem that is particularly serious in Guatemala, Colombia, and Paraguay, where elements of the armed forces may literally be seen as part of organized crime.

In short, while the armed forces have retreated from direct political control, yielding the stage to democratically elected leaders, they continue to be important to the stability of democratic regimes. Most often, the roles of the military pose significant challenges to democratic stability.

■ Parties and Party Systems

Political parties and party systems were unquestionably central to Latin America's previous democracies of long standing (see Chapter 3) and in their various forms continue to be central to an understanding of democratic politics in contemporary Latin America. Parties and competition among them are essential to the practice of liberal democracy because they process and structure the options to be made available to the electorate, thereby converting millions of votes into a collective decision about who will govern. Still, after two decades or more of democratic practice in most of the region, parties have come under attack and have undergone decay, as social movements and populist politicians have portrayed them as antidemocratic instruments of political elites. The new constitutional order of Venezuela since 1999 is perhaps the clearest attempt to date to transcend what was called *partidocracia* (partyarchy; cf. Coppedge, 1994b; Hillman, 1994; Marta Sosa, 2002), and to implant a more direct and participatory democracy. But it remains unclear how a continuing, durable, or stable democratic regime on the scale of a modern state can do without a strong system of competing parties.[6]

Scott Mainwaring and Timothy Scully (1995) used several criteria for classifying party systems as either institutionalized or inchoate. The first is regularity of party competition as measured by Mogens N. Pedersen's index of electoral volatility, which measures the net change in the seat or vote shares of all parties from one election to the next (Mainwaring and Scully, 1995, pp. 6–9). A second criterion is the development by parties of stable roots in soci-

ety, as indicated by similarity of voting patterns between concurrent legislative and presidential elections, survey and electoral data, party penetration of
major social organizations, and party longevity (pp. 9–15). The third criterion
is that "citizens and organized interests must perceive that parties and elections are the means of determining who governs, and that the electoral process
and parties are accorded legitimacy" (p. 14). This would be best measured by
cross-national survey data; lacking that, the authors made informed estimates
based on the case studies. The final criterion is that party organizations must
be relatively solid. Again, hard data are not systematically available, and the
authors resorted to estimates (pp. 15–16; for an update, see Mainwaring,
1999). Their measurements and estimates are summarized in Table 4.2.

Two points must be noted about this scheme. First, only the first criterion
is based on reliable, quantifiable, and comparable data. The others, to varying
degrees, depend on informed estimates. We would thus be ill-advised to impute
undue rigor to the classification. Second, the scores represent an average char-
acterization of each party system for the period of the 1980s and 1990s. The
scheme thus takes little or no account of the longer history of the party systems.
At the same time, it also does not attempt to measure changes in party systems.
These matching long-term and short-term blind spots mean that the classification, already of debatable rigor in general, may come to quite questionable conclusions about individual cases. For example, long-term patterns in Argentina,
combined with developments under President Menem and his successors, indi-

Table 4.2　Party System Institutionalization in Latin America

Country	Criterion 1	Criterion 2	Criterion 3	Criterion 4	Aggregate
Costa Rica	2.5	3.0	3.0	3.0	11.5
Chile	2.5	3.0	3.0	3.0	11.5
Uruguay	3.0	3.0	3.0	2.5	11.5
Venezuela	2.5	2.5	2.5	3.0	10.5
Colombia	3.0	3.0	2.5	2.0	10.5
Argentina	2.0	2.5	2.5	2.0	9.0
Mexico	1.5	2.5	1.5	3.0	8.5
Paraguay	1.0	2.5	1.0	3.0	7.5
Bolivia	1.0	1.0	2.0	1.0	5.0
Ecuador	1.0	1.0	2.0	1.0	5.0
Brazil	1.0	1.0	2.0	1.0	5.0
Peru	1.0	1.0	1.0	1.5	4.5

Source: Mainwaring and Scully, 1995, p. 17. Reprinted from *Building Democratic Institutions: Party Systems in Latin America,* edited by Scott Mainwaring and Timothy R. Scully, with
the permission of the publishers, Stanford University Press. © 1995 by the Board of Trustees of
Leland Stanford Junior University.

Note: Criteria are scored as 3.0 = high, 1.0 = low. Criterion 1 is regularity of party competition. Criterion 2 is development of stable roots in society. Criterion 3 is legitimacy of parties and
elections. Criterion 4 is solidity of party organizations.

cate that the Argentine party system is less institutionalized than Mainwaring and Scully suggest. Indeed, as of 2003, only the Peronists appeared to retain substantial electoral strength, and that party was so deeply split as to be unable to function as a unit. Developments in Venezuela since 1989 also point to a complete collapse of what was a highly institutionalized party system, and to severe declines in the two major parties that dominated that system. Conversely, Bolivia may be experiencing a significant increase in party system institutionalization. All these caveats notwithstanding, the Mainwaring-Scully classification is an excellent place to start, with the proviso that we need to be alert to party system changes. Parties and the party system continue to be strongly institutionalized in Chile, Colombia, Costa Rica, and Uruguay. Most other countries, including most of those not considered by Mainwaring and Scully, display prominent features of inchoate systems.

In Chile, the formerly tripolar party system (right/center/left) has reemerged in the 1980s in the form of a center-left bloc and a right bloc, marginalizing those of the extreme left.[7] The successful Concertación that fought the plebiscite of 1988 went on to win the presidency in 1989 (with 55 percent), 1993 (with 58 percent), and 1999–2000 (with 51 percent) and to capture and hold the majority in the Chamber of Deputies after 1989. Surviving authoritarian provisions of the constitution of 1980 (e.g., the provision for eight appointed senators) have prevented the Concertación from achieving all its desired constitutional amendments and policy initiatives, but the transition in Chile must still be judged relatively successful, and that success must be attributed in large part to the old parties (i.e., the Christian Democratic Party [DC] and the Socialist Party [PS]), a new party (the Party for Democracy [PPD], a socialist splinter), and the new party system. Since 1988, these three parties, with several smaller associates, have maintained the only coalition capable of capturing an absolute majority of the vote. Substantively, this coalition is committed to establishing a liberal democracy within the framework of the authoritarian constitution of 1980 and to moving gradually within that constitution to make such changes as may be possible for further democratization. They have been opposed by a right-wing coalition basically committed to maintaining the 1980 constitution with as few changes as possible and by a left-wing coalition that refuses to accept the legitimacy of the constitution as an institutional framework within which to work.

The key point here is that a reorganized party system has been critical to the reestablishment of stable democracy in Chile. However, the new party system also poses long-term challenges to democratic stability. Both Right and Left are not only outside the governing coalition but outside the liberal democratic consensus. There are no important elements of the Right or the Left that are outside the Concertación but unequivocally supportive of liberal democracy. Were the Right to come to power, it would implement what Guillermo O'Donnell and Philippe Schmitter (1986) have called a *democradura,* or hard democracy, stepping back from the moderate democratization espoused by the Concertación. Should the Left come to power, it would insist on a much more rapid and profound democratization, even at the risk of rupture with the Right and its military allies such as General Pinochet. Thus the new Chilean party system permits a stable democracy within the gradually receding limits of the 1980 constitution, but only by maintaining the Concertación intact and in power. Alternation in power, a normal feature of liberal democracy, cannot happen in Chile without risking the regime itself.

Chile faces three possible scenarios. First, the political dominance of the Concertación could continue, with the Right and Left continuing to be marginalized. In this model, the Right would probably suffer a gradual loss of strength, particularly after the demise of Pinochet. The Left, already much weakened by the defection of the Socialists and by the discriminatory effects of the electoral system, would also continue to be marginalized. Chile would evolve toward a dominant party system in which many parties could run for office, but the Concertación would always win national elections.

A second scenario would see part of the Right (most likely National Renewal [RN]) accepting the legitimacy of the Concertación's approach to liberal democracy and becoming a possible coalition partner for the DC. The party system then would offer two alternative governing coalitions, the center-left Concertación and a center-right DC-RN coalition.

A third scenario would have most of the Left (including the Communists) agreeing to work within the Concertación's model of liberal democracy and becoming thereby an alternative coalition partner for the Socialists. Here again, two alternative coalitions would be possible, Concertación and center-left (socialist-communist). If both the second and third scenarios happened, then virtually the entire political spectrum would be committed to a liberal democratic institutional framework, as has happened in Uruguay. If neither occurred, and if the Concertación could not maintain its electoral dominance, Chile would risk developing a party system in which the only possible governing coalitions were formed by parties disloyal to the democratic regime itself.[8]

In Uruguay, the parties and party system have shown even more continuity with patterns from before the dictatorship.[9] Silvia Dutrénit Bielous (1994) used the metaphor of an archipelago (the parties) reemerging after a tidal wave (the dictatorship). However, changes already under way before 1973 have continued, so that by the 1990s it was clear that the long-standing dominance of the two traditional parties (Colorados and Blancos) was at an end. The leftist Broad Front (FA) already had surpassed 20 percent of the vote in 1971 and reemerged at about that level during the transition in 1985. Subsequently the FA split, and the center-left New Space (NE) emerged. In the 1994 general elections, national results showed a virtual tie among the Colorados (31 percent), the Blancos (29.9 percent), and the FA (29.3 percent), and NE received 4.9 percent (Caetano, 1995, p. 8). Moreover, FA candidate Tabaré Vázquez won the mayoralty of Montevideo with more than 42 percent. Jeffrey Cason (2002) showed that the traditional parties responded to the rise of the FA by pushing through a change in the electoral law to provide for a runoff if no presidential candidate receives over 50 percent of the vote. They then used that provision in 1999 to coalesce against the FA candidate, denying him a victory. Cason suggested that this result may be a harbinger of the evolution of the party system from the old two-party rivalry, through the three-party system, to a pattern of competition between the FA (center-left) and a coalition of the Colorados and Blancos (center-right).

The Uruguayan party system is distinguished from that of Chile in several ways. The Left in Uruguay has become much stronger than its Chilean counterpart, whereas the Uruguayan Right has become weaker. Both traditional parties are now dominated by centrist factions, with minority rightist factions. There are now three parties capable of electing a president in Uruguay, but it is not an ideologically defined tripolar system like that in pre-1973 Chile. Rather, we have a Left (including even the former Tupamaro guerrillas) that is committed to operating within the institutions of Uruguayan liberal democracy, competing against two centrist traditional parties, each with its semiloyal right wing. This in turn means that electoral alternation is possible without threatening the democratic regime itself, unless the right wing of either major party regains dominance. In such an eventuality, the situation would be similar to that in Chile at the present time, where democratic stability depends on the Concertación remaining united and in control of the government. Though the structure of the two-party systems is thus markedly different, both confront a Right that is at best semiloyal to democracy but unable at present to win a national majority. With the advent of a powerful Left in the new Uruguayan party system, it is unlikely that any president could escape the need to negotiate a majority coalition in Congress, but the fragmentation of the major parties under the Ley de Lemas (the "double simultaneous vote") always made such negotiation necessary anyway. The adoption of a runoff election for the presidency has not changed the system for parliamentary elections, and thus does not obviate the need for a negotiated congressional majority.

Colombia, Costa Rica, and Venezuela have not had to make transitions to democracy in the past decade, but economic and political problems have subjected them to many of the same strains as those confronting the reestablished democracies of Chile and Uruguay.[10] Each of these countries entered the 1980s with a stable democratic regime based on two-party, or bipolar, systems and strongly institutionalized parties. Each has faced serious economic dislocations that have challenged the dominant parties. Costa Rica was on the front lines of the Central American political crisis of the 1980s and was subjected to strong external political pressures as a result. Colombia had to deal with chronic guerrilla insurgencies and the burgeoning international drug trade that established important centers in Colombia. Venezuela was also affected by the drug trade, but its crisis was principally economic. Only Costa Rica can still be considered politically stable (and it is not without severe challenges), whereas Colombia's and Venezuela's futures as liberal democracies are more in doubt.

Of the three surviving older democracies, the oldest, Costa Rica, has weathered the storms of the 1980s and 1990s with the least damage. Whereas the party systems of Colombia and especially Venezuela were showing significant signs of change or even breakdown in the 1990s, that of Costa Rica has, if anything, become more institutionalized since the beginning of the 1980s. What was previously a bipolar system, with one strong party (the National Liberation Party [PLN]) and a shifting series of ad hoc opposition coalitions (cf. Peeler, 1985, tab. 5, p. 100), has become a stable two-party system, with some continuing parliamentary representation for leftist and regional parties. The two major parties, the PLN and the Social Christian Unity Party (PUSC), regularly receive over 95 percent of the presidential vote, over 85 percent of the legislative vote, fifty-five of fifty-seven legislative seats, and a great majority of local elected positions (Yashar, 1995; Chalker, 1995). The PUSC held the presidency and a congressional majority from 1990 to 1994, and a general tendency toward alternation of the PLN and the PUSC in power appears firmly entrenched. In spite of popular protests, resistance from organized labor, and the emergence of locally based social movements, the regime remains basically quite capable of responding to demands in a manner sufficient to keep political pressures manageable. Abstention rates in national elections continue to be in the range of 15–20 percent, the same level that has been consistently present since compulsory voting was implemented in the late 1950s.[11]

The ancient two-party system of Colombia (Hartlyn, 1988; Bushnell, 1993; Martz, 1997) has been under severe strain more or less continuously since the late 1930s, though reports of its demise, to paraphrase Mark Twain, were frequently exaggerated (Peeler, 1976, 1985, 1992). Every president from 1982 onward has made a serious attempt to negotiate an end to the insurgencies, and some groups (most notably the April 19 Movement [M-19]) have laid down their arms and have been incorporated into the legal political process. However, M-19 and other former guerrillas have been subjected to assassination of their leaders and militants by right-wing death squads that function with impunity. Other guerrilla groups have refused to give up the armed struggle, and the Colombian armed forces have been unable to defeat them.[12]

Another challenge to the Colombian system evolved with the rise of the international drug trade (especially in cocaine but also including marijuana and, increasingly, heroin) during the 1980s, for which Colombia became a major center (Thoumi, 1995). For present purposes, the drug trade posed two problems and a dilemma. The first problem was that the drug trade rendered the preexisting problem of violence all the more severe and complex. This was especially true because of the second problem: corruption. The drug cartels sought systematically to penetrate and corrupt every center of power in Colombian society, including business, the police, the armed forces, the political elite, and the guerrillas; they had substantial success in all arenas. Among major institutions, only the church proved largely immune. By the mid-1990s, the political system was convulsed by credible accusations that President Ernesto Samper himself had knowingly accepted political contributions from the Cali cartel.

The dilemma posed by the drug trade was that it evidently provided a subsidy of unknown magnitude for the Colombian economy. It was not by chance that Colombia avoided the worst dislocations of the economic crisis of the 1980s and was under less pressure to conform to neoliberal policy strictures (Pizarro and Bejarano, 1994). Thus Colombian policymakers had to know that any success in bringing the drug trade under control would likely have negative macroeconomic consequences. Yet they had no choice but to try to control it, given the threat the drug trade posed to their control of the country and the intense pressure imposed on Colombia by the United States.

The Colombian political elite responded to this array of challenges in a characteristic manner, with moderate political reforms that made it substantially easier for new parties to win elections and that devolved considerable authority to elected local officials. The election of mayors was an innovation of the mid-1980s, for example. President Virgilio Barco's attempt to push significant constitutional changes through Congress failed in late 1989. A popular mobilization in early 1990, led by university students, gathered petitions to place the question of a constituent assembly on the ballot of the 1990 legislative elections. An overwhelmingly positive vote (but with low turnout) led to a second positive vote coinciding with the presidential elections later that year. By decree of newly elected president César Gaviria Trujillo, the special Constituent Assembly was elected in December 1990 (with the astonishingly low turnout of 16 percent) and met for five months in early 1991. The election rules guaranteed representation to insurgent groups such as M-19 that had laid down their arms, and to indigenous and black ethnic minorities. In fact, M-19 had over one-fourth of the delegates, second only to the Liberals, whereas the fragmented Conservatives were well behind. The composition of the Assembly appeared to foreshadow a new party system, but the low turnout must be kept in mind.

The debates of the Constituent Assembly were the object of close national attention and organized pressure, and public political discourse was dominated by constitutional issues for over a year. The prominence of the unexpectedly large M-19 delegation was especially notable as representing a potential break with the power monopoly of the traditional parties. There was widespread expectation that adoption of a new constitution could mark a major turning point in the development of Colombian democracy.

The new constitution contains several initiatives designed to enhance political democracy, including ballot and electoral reform, approval of referenda and plebiscites as valid channels of lawmaking and constitutional amendment, restriction of presidential emergency powers, prohibition of presidential reelection, congressional power to force the resignation of ministers by a vote of censure in both chambers, and the establishment of a Constitutional Court separate from the Supreme Court. The armed forces retain their autonomy but are restricted from trying civilians in military courts. Social policies oriented to protecting the poorest parts of the population are also enshrined in the constitution.[13]

In spite of the hints of change in the Constituent Assembly and the new constitution, the electoral dominance of the liberals, in particular, was reasserted in the 1994 elections and in subsequent local and congressional elections (Boudon, 2001). However, the 1998 and 2002 elections displayed fragmentation of both Liberal and Conservative Parties, and seemed to augur instability in the party system. The candidate elected in 1998, Andrés Pastrana, formerly a Conservative, ran as an independent. Similarly, the victor in 2002, Alvaro Uribe Vélez, is a former Liberal who ran as an independent. Uribe has achieved substantial popularity with a hard-nosed policy toward left-wing guerrillas and drug traffickers, as well as less cooperation with, and increased pressure on, rightist paramilitaries. Paradoxically, the Colombian party system is both unstable and resistant to change, even as the state's capacity to control the territory and population is under severe challenge.

From 1973 to the late 1980s, Venezuela must be considered one of the most fully developed democratic party systems outside the advanced industrial democracies. The two major parties, Democratic Action and the social Christian Independent Committee for Political and Electoral Organization (COPEI), received 85 to 90 percent of the vote in presidential elections and about 75 percent in congressional elections, alternated in the presidency (AD having five presidents and COPEI two during the period), and predominated in local and state electoral office. The two parties also extensively penetrated and controlled organizations of civil society, turning them to the purpose of supporting the national power of the party and maintaining control through extensive patronage that was ultimately financed by the country's oil wealth and channeled through the state. The center-left Movement Toward Socialism (MAS), led by former guerrillas, became increasingly integrated into the party system, though it never rivaled the two major parties in electoral strength.

It may be argued (see Peeler, 1999) that this party system was so efficient in mobilizing votes and concentrating them to produce democratically elected governments that worked that it provoked the very backlash that undermined it. The system became so centralized, so resistant to initiatives from the base or to the rise of alternative political leadership—in a word, *institutionalized*—that it came to be called a *partidocracia,* or "partyarchy."[14] In response to widespread demands for reforms that would revitalize democracy by weakening partyarchy, various changes were made during the 1980s to decentralize the state and weaken the grip of the party organizations (see the next section). A new political movement, the center-left, labor-based Causa R, was able to use these new institutional openings to achieve substantial electoral success in the early to mid-1990s (López Maya, 1994).

Although the 1988 presidential and parliamentary elections continued the pattern of AD-COPEI dominance, change was already well advanced below the surface. The winning presidential candidate, former president Carlos Andrés Pérez of AD, was not the choice of the party organization; he won the internal party election on the basis of his personal popularity, having presided over the oil boom of the mid-1970s. At the same time, COPEI turned its back on its founder, former president Rafael Caldera. When Pérez, acting independently of his party organization, implemented a sweeping neoliberal adjustment plan shortly after his inauguration, the shock waves shredded the party system. Massive urban riots in Caracas and elsewhere led to many deaths and much destruction. Condemnation of the president was almost universal, coming even from AD members of Congress. Demands for Pérez's resignation became a steady drumbeat as he continued to use his presidential powers to impose his reform program. Two military rebellions in 1992 further shook the confidence of Venezuelans in their democracy, but public opinion polls continued to show a preference for democracy even as people expressed rejection of the Pérez government (Myers, 1995). Caldera took the leadership of the opposition to Pérez with an eloquent speech in the Senate after the first military rebellion, in which he flatly condemned government policy and rejected COPEI's qualified support for Pérez in the name of preserving democratic stability.

After Pérez was finally impeached and forced from office in mid-1993, the elections of December 1993 brought Caldera back to the presidency, but this time at the head of a loose ad hoc coalition in opposition to both AD and COPEI. Caldera's winning share of the vote was only 30 percent, whereas candidates for AD, COPEI, and Causa R were virtually tied at 22 to 23 percent. Moreover, abstention hit a record high of 40 percent, a precipitous decline from 18 percent in 1988 and 13 percent in 1983. AD and COPEI together received only 45 percent of the vote, less than half their 1988 total. The party system was in crisis, and since it was the keystone of the democratic regime, it follows that the regime was in crisis too.

The general failure of the Caldera government to address the country's economic problems prolonged the political crisis. Public disillusionment with the parties and with elections further depressed turnout (already low by historic standards) in state and local elections. Ironically, this permitted AD and COPEI, with their superior organizations, to make a partial comeback in governorships and local governments, but popular support for the regime remained weak. Into this context emerged the movement led by Hugo Chávez Frías, leader of the attempted coup of February 1992, who successfully ran for president in 1998 on a populist platform of sweeping aside the old parties and the corrupt political elite. In the course of several elections from December 1998 through 1999, Chávez and his Fifth Republic Movement completed the demolition of the old party system and established a new constitutional order. In a context of ongoing, profound economic, social, and political crisis, the shape of a new Venezuelan party system will necessarily wait upon reequilibration of the regime. As Juan Linz (1978) suggested, that will apparently involve an actual change of regime within the democratic genus.[15]

Having now considered the party systems that Mainwaring classified as strongly institutionalized (Chile, Uruguay, Colombia, Venezuela, and Costa Rica), we turn to the category that Mainwaring and Scully (1995) called "inchoate" party systems. Included here are virtually all of the other Latin American countries (save Cuba), and it will become obvious that the category is residual (i.e., noninstitutionalized party systems) and that our understanding will be better served by asking additional questions, such as how close they come to institutionalization, how they are changing, and whether the party systems facilitate or retard democratization.

We begin with the special case of Argentina.[16] Mainwaring and Scully (1995) included Argentina among institutionalized party systems, but I have not. Although the Peronists and the Radicals have long been central to the Argentine party system, it has not been a true two-party system but instead a series of unsuccessful attempts to impose a single-party hegemony. James McGuire (1995) made this clear in his contribution to the Mainwaring-Scully volume. In Argentina the two major parties were highly institutionalized, but the party system was not. That is, the relationship between the major parties was subject to major changes with each shift in party control of the presidency. It is by no means clear that the party system is stable, or institutionalized; indeed, the two principal parties are less well institutionalized in the early twenty-first century than they were a decade earlier.

The Radicals successfully displaced the Conservative hegemony after 1916 but were themselves displaced from their hegemony by the Conservative coup of 1930. Juan Perón established the hegemony of his own Peronist movement after 1946 but was displaced by the coup of 1955. Successive military and civilian governments from 1955 to 1973 failed to disperse the popular base of Peronism, and the party won control of the government again in 1973. The Peronists were ousted again in 1976 by the last and most savage of the military regimes. To the surprise of almost everyone, the post-Malvinas elections of 1983 brought a Radical victory over the Peronists; for a while, among Radicals, there was talk of a new era of Radical hegemony, but that ended with the economic meltdown of 1988–1989. Carlos Menem came to office in 1989 on the basis of a classic Peronist campaign in favor of social justice for workers and then by 1991 gravitated to a neoliberal policy that would mean a severe increase in unemployment as the principal price for achieving low inflation. His successful imposition of a sweeping program of neoliberal reforms (Corrales, 2002; Weyland, 2002) put great stress on the Peronist political coalition, with its strong base among the industrial working class and the poor. Yet Menem's victory in 1989 reawakened Peronist dreams of hegemony as well, dreams that were fed by Menem's political success in getting the constitution amended to permit reelection and then getting himself reelected by an overwhelming margin in 1995. Large numbers of Peronist voters continued to support Menem through the constitutional referendum of 1994 and the presidential elections of 1995 (Fraga, 1995, p. 34). Guillermo O'Donnell (1994) used Menem as one of the principal examples of what he called "delegative democracy," a regime in which a popularly elected leader assumes the right to pursue any policies, regardless of electoral promises, as delegate of the people.[17]

A major attempt to break the mold of two-party dominance came in the early 1990s from the National Solidarity Front (FREPASO), which achieved substantial success in the federal capital and Buenos Aires province with a centrist, anticorruption program and posed a significant threat in particular to the Radicals in the federal capital. FREPASO allied with the Radicals to block Menem's bid to run for a third term in 1999, and elected the Radical Fernando de la Rua as president in that year. De la Rua, however, presided over a deep economic crisis that led to his premature resignation in 2001, followed by a series of Peronist provisional presidents. After de la Rua's debacle, both the Radicals and FREPASO were discredited, and the 2003 presidential contest came down to a runoff between two Peronists, Menem and Nestor Kirchner. When Menem could see that he would lose the runoff, he withdrew and Kirchner was elected. Although it would be foolhardy to write off the Radicals (and other non-Peronists) entirely, for the moment the Argentine party system consists for all practical purposes of Peronists, even as the party (Partido Justicialista) has ceased to function as an organization.

A basic obstacle to the institutionalization of a competitive party system in Argentina is that leaders and activists in both parties (especially the Peronists) have tended to regard themselves as *movements* rather than *parties;* that is, they have implicitly or explicitly assumed that they speak, potentially, for the whole nation. The very idea of a party is that it represents *part of the nation,* whereas a movement may purport to represent everyone. If one movement represents the whole people, then there is no necessary or legitimate role for other parties. Competition becomes no more than a tactical necessity. It remains to be seen whether the two major Argentine parties have moved definitively away from this perspective (cf. McGuire, 1995).

Brazil is as puzzling a case as Argentina.[18] By far the largest and most populous Latin American country, it has also long been a regional leader in industrial development and stands relatively high on most measures of economic development. Most of Brazil's republican history has been marked by elected governments, though a true liberal democracy prior to its current incarnation, since 1985, existed only from 1945 to 1964. Whereas Argentina's parties have persisted through many regime changes (even if the party *system* is judged not to be institutionalized), in Brazil both the parties and the party system have been transformed with each regime change. The party system of the Empire did not last into the Old Republic. The party system fostered by Getulio Vargas did not survive the coup of 1964. The party system promoted by the military regime transformed itself in the course of the transition and continues to be in flux. In the 1990s, there was only one party, the Workers Party (PT), that moved considerably beyond personalism, institutionalized its organization, and developed a national capability for mass political mobilization (Keck, 1992). As such, the PT posed a major challenge to other parties; the national campaigns of 1989, 1994, and 1998 all placed PT leader Lula da Silva in the presidential runoff against opponents backed by ad hoc coalitions of centrist and rightist parties. In all cases, Lula lost to the center-right candidate (Collor in 1989, Cardoso in 1994 and 1998), but he finally won the presidency in 2002. The party system remains characterized by high volatility and low institutionalization, again with the exception of the PT. Even the latter party suffered the internal strains one might expect as Lula took the reins of government and pursued policies less radical than many of his supporters wanted and expected.

Mexico, having just elected its first non-PRI president in 2000, is still in the early stages of transition, and its party system is necessarily in flux. Nevertheless, it appears that both the PAN (a presidential winner for the first time in 2000) and the PRI will continue to compete nationally, while the PRD has established itself as a viable party on the left, with particular strength in the Federal District and the south. Thus, while the party system is not yet institutionalized, its likely course of development is clear.[19]

None of the other countries to be considered here have parties as thoroughly institutionalized as Argentina's, and of course none have institutionalized party systems. A key question involves levels of mass political mobilization by parties. In many countries with inchoate party systems, there is nevertheless a significant history of mass political mobilization by at least one party. This would certainly be true of Bolivia, Peru, and perhaps Ecuador, Panama, and the Dominican Republic.[20] In each of the first two cases, at least one party has not only been institutionalized but has developed a true mass base that goes beyond a mere clientelistic search for jobs and favors. In Bolivia, that party is the National Revolutionary Movement (MNR), principal party of the 1952 revolution and still a principal player in national politics. In

Peru, it is the American Popular Revolutionary Alliance (APRA) and, to a much lesser extent, Popular Action (AP). Yet as in Argentina, the presence of institutionalized parties with mass bases has not meant an institutionalized party system. A principal cause has been personal ambition of competing leaders who can gain more (e.g., congressional seats for themselves and their supporters) by splitting off than by remaining with a party they do not control. The MNR failed in its initial project of a Mexican-style single-party hegemony and proved highly prone to fragmentation. President Siles Zuazo (1982–1985), for example, was a founding leader of the MNR who broke away in the 1960s. The Bolivian party system as it has evolved since 1978 includes, in addition to the MNR and its splinters, the conservative National Democratic Alliance (ADN), founded and led by General Banzer and various leftist or formerly leftist parties such as the Revolutionary Left Movement (MIR) and the Free Bolivia Movement (MBL). There is some sign that Bolivia may be moving toward a more institutionalized party system whose most distinguishing mark is the negotiation of electoral and governing coalitions among competing party leaders, with the MNR, the MIR, and the ADN as the principal players. However, the system continues to generate important new "outsiders" as well, such as beer magnate Max Fernández, radio and television personality Carlos Palenque, and coca farmer Evo Morales (of the Movement Toward Socialism), who nearly was elected president in 2002.

In Peru, an institutionalized party system built around APRA and AP might have emerged after 1980 but was nullified by the successive economic failures of the presidencies of Fernando Belaúnde (AP, 1980–1985) and Alan García (APRA, 1985–1990). As a consequence, by the 1990 election there was no doubt that "outsiders" would prevail over the established parties. Though it first appeared that well-known novelist Mario Vargas Llosa would win, he was ultimately overtaken by the virtually unknown Alberto Fujimori. Both were antiparty candidates. In 1992, Fujimori staged a coup, suspending the constitution and dissolving Congress and the Supreme Court. He presided over the adoption of a new constitution, arranged to be reelected in 1995 and 2000, but was forced out shortly after his second reelection by a massive popular uprising occasioned by a corruption scandal. A principal leader of that uprising, Alejandro Toledo, was then elected to replace Fujimori, defeating former president Alan García. In light of the weakness of the old parties, the emergence of a wholly new party system seems to be in process, though perhaps with APRA remaining a significant force.

In several other countries there have been popularly supported parties or movements of some durability, but always highly personalistic rather than institutionalized. Ecuadoran politics long orbited around populist leaders such as José María Velasco Ibarra and later, Abdalá Bucaram; today, in the absence of any such overpowering personalist leader, Ecuadoran parties continue to be highly personalist and prone to fragmentation, though the indigenous population organized itself quite strongly in the 1990s and became a force to be reckoned with. Indigenous support was a major force behind the election of former colonel Lucio Gutiérrez as president in 2002. The Ecuadoran party system thus continues to be highly personalist and inchoate, but with an increasingly powerful and organized indigenous movement that is not particularly personalist.

Personalist politics is also prevalent in Panama, where populist caudillo Arnulfo Arias was succeeded by strongmen Omar Torrijos and Manuel Noriega. After the U.S. arrest of Noriega in 1990, Panamanian politics have orbited less around dominant personalities, but the party system remains distinctly inchoate. The continuing power of personality is attested to by the 1999 presidential election, in which Mireya Moscoso de Arias (widow of Arnulfo Arias, who was overthrown by General Omar Torrijos in 1968) defeated Martín Torrijos (son of Omar).

Dominican politics from the assassination of Trujillo in 1961 to the late 1990s revolved around two caudillos, the conservative Trujillo collaborator Joaquín Balaguer and the nationalist reformer Juan Bosch. Bosch founded the Dominican Revolutionary Party (PRD), but later defected to form the Dominican Liberation Party (PLD). Balaguer founded and led the Reformist Party (PR). Balaguer, the dominant figure until the late 1990s, president from 1966 to 1978 and from 1986 to 1996, was forced to shorten his last term in order to gain acceptance of his election. He then engineered a coalition with the PLD to elect Leonel Fernández over PRD candidate Francisco Peña Gómez in 1996. In 2000, Hipólito Mejía of the PRD defeated Balaguer and Danilo Medina of the PLD. The Dominican party system appears to be moving toward institutionalization as a three-party system, with each of the parties moving beyond its founding generation and tending to lose whatever ideological definition it once had.

Most of the other countries classified as having inchoate party systems (El Salvador, Nicaragua, Guatemala, Haiti, Honduras) have little history of popular mobilization by parties. In some of these cases, formerly stable elitist party systems are being rendered inchoate by the emergence for the first time of genuinely popular parties or movements.[21] This is most clearly the case in Nicaragua and Haiti, where the Sandinista National Liberation Front and the Lavalas movement, respectively, mobilized majorities of the national populations for the first time in their countries' history. Preexisting elitist parties were not equipped to confront such a challenge save by use of force and fraud. In this they were aided by U.S. administrations deeply mistrustful of the popular movements.

The stories of the two countries differ in many ways. In Nicaragua, the Sandinistas took power by force in 1979 and attempted a revolutionary transformation of society. By 1980, the United States was openly supporting their opponents; under Ronald Reagan (1981–1989) the United States was in a state of undeclared war with the Sandinista regime. Nevertheless, the Sandinistas probably expected that their organization and popular support would keep them in power indefinitely, but they lost the elections of 1990 in an environment of economic crisis and externally supported civil war. Subsequently, under President Violeta de Chamorro, the party system and political system remained in flux through the 1996 elections (Vargas, 1995). There is some tendency toward a bipolar party system pitting the Sandinistas (who can count on about 40 percent of the vote) against all opponents: an overwhelming majority of anti-Sandinista voters in 1990, 1996, and 2001 coalesced around one candidate (Chamorro, Arnoldo Alemán, and Enrique Bolaños, respectively). The Constitutionalist Liberal Party (PLC) of Presidents Alemán and Bolaños has emerged as the principal rival of the FSLN, but split into pro- and anti-Alemán factions with the decision of Bolaños to prosecute Alemán for corruption.

In Haiti, Lavalas leader Jean-Bertrand Aristide led a nonviolent popular movement that was critical in forcing Jean-Claude Duvalier from power in 1986 and that finally brought about Aristide's election to the presidency in 1990. Overthrown nine months later by a military coup, Aristide was finally reinstated by the U.S.-led, UN-sponsored intervention of 1994. In late 1995 the Lavalas movement won the presidency with René Préval and control of Congress with an overwhelming majority in the first truly honest elections in the country's history. Aristide was returned to power in the elections of 2000, but the opposition refused to recognize the legitimacy of either that election or the parliamentary elections. The Lavalas movement broke into pro- and anti-Aristide sectors, and the opposition continued to be deeply fragmented. Haitian politics thus entered a prolonged stalemate, ending with the removal of President Aristide in early 2004.

In both of these cases, the emergence of movements that could effectively mobilize mass support threw the old, elitist party systems into terminal chaos. However, as during the post-Trujillo crisis in the Dominican Republic in the 1960s, the hegemonic presence of the United States provided the old elites in Nicaragua with the opportunity and the resources with which to attempt a reconstitution and reorganization of their vested interests as the opposition to the newly dominant popular movements. With massive U.S. support, the anti-Sandinista elites developed enough electoral mobilization capability to compete successfully with the Sandinistas. In Haiti, in contrast, U.S. policy was consistently ambivalent: the first Bush administration said it opposed the overthrow of Aristide, but did nothing to effect his return. The Clinton administration said it favored his return, but dragged its feet until 1994, then hamstrung him once he did return. The second Bush administration refused to support Aristide but opposed his overthrow. In short, while the United States was, to say the least, unenthusiastic about Aristide, it did little to marshal an effective opposition.

The remaining Central American cases (Honduras, El Salvador, and Guatemala) have not seen such a clear-cut emergence of movements with a new capability for mass mobilization. The Farabundo Martí National Liberation Front (FMLN) in El Salvador certainly aspired to be such a movement, and it did develop the capacity to occupy and govern a substantial part of Salvadoran territory during the 1980s. It posed a genuinely revolutionary threat to the old order in which the armed forces ruled in alliance with the economic elite; it might have won power if the United States, after the fall of Anastasio Somoza in Nicaragua, had not intervened to prop up and reform the old regime. But in fact the Salvadoran regime was renovated and did negotiate a peaceful settlement with the FMLN in 1990. The latter, competing in elections for the first time, was at first much weaker than the ruling National Renewal Alliance (ARENA), but the FMLN did emerge as the country's second political force, and steadily gained strength. The very emergence of ARENA as a mass-based right-wing party must be seen as a direct response to the threat of the FMLN. El Salvador, like Nicaragua, now appears to be developing a bipolar party system with the former guerrillas at one pole and opponents at the other.

Guatemala was also subjected to the rule of a succession of reactionary military governments (after the U.S.-sponsored coup in 1954) and also fought a serious insurgency, the National Revolutionary Union of Guatemala (URNG), during the 1980s. But the insurgency never seriously threatened to take power, U.S. aid and intervention was much less prominent than in El Salvador, and no new conservative party emerged with a strong mass-mobilization capability. Instead, several small center-right parties emerged, most importantly the Guatemalan Republican Front (FRG), built around former dictator Efraín Ríos Montt (1982–1983), which did indeed show substantial popular support, particularly in rural areas. However, Ríos Montt was decisively defeated in the presidential election of 2003. The Christian Democratic Party was deeply discredited by the corrupt Cerezo government (1985–1990). The former URNG and other sectors of the Left have also formed parties for electoral competition, but have not achieved the political weight of the FSLN in Nicaragua or the FMLN in El Salvador. The Guatemalan party system, in short, remains inchoate.

Finally, the Honduran party system was less affected by the Central American turmoil of the 1980s than any other country in the region save Costa Rica. It is perhaps the last country in Latin America that could be construed as having a traditional party system dating from before mass mobilization. The Liberal and National Parties have their roots in the nineteenth century, like their counterparts elsewhere, and have long taken the form of rival elite coalitions with relatively minor ideological differences, weak organizational structures, and minimal capacity for mass mobilization beyond a very simple clientelism.

For decades up to the 1980s, Honduran politics consisted of successive party hegemonies achieved by alliances with the army, which permitted one of the two parties to perpetuate itself in power until the other party could wean the army away. Some mass political mobilization by labor unions, but not by parties, has occasionally occurred. The pattern has changed since the early 1980s, as the United States, anxious to legitimize its Central American allies in the struggle with the Sandinistas, pushed the army to end its most recent dictatorship and to permit honest political competition. In this new environment, some new parties emerged, but no party or movement developed the mass mobilization capability to challenge the traditional parties. The Liberal and National Parties continue to dominate elections. Now, however, elections are relatively free, and both parties have held the presidency. There has been some success in imposing civilian control over the army. Honduras, in short, retains an institutionalized party system, but only because it has not yet confronted the challenge of mass political mobilization. In the absence of such a challenge, we may expect the traditional two-party system to persist. However, because of low levels of mass mobilization, Honduras clearly does not fit into the same category as the other institutionalized party systems.

Samuel Huntington (1968) distinguished between "civic" and "praetorian" polities primarily on the basis of whether political institutions (especially parties) were strong enough (i.e., institutionalized) to organize and channel the level of political participation existing in the society. Civic polities are stable because their parties and other institutions are adequate to the political participation they confront. If participation is low, institutions do not have to be as strong in order to achieve stability. Instability is characteristic of periods when participation is on the increase and institutions are adapting, periods that are also likely to display strong economic change. The case of the Honduran party system brings us back to Huntington, reminding us that institutionalization does not simply rise with political development; rather, inchoate systems are a consequence of political change. Thus, Uruguay, Chile, and Costa Rica have highly institutionalized party systems at high levels of mass mobilization, and their party systems are either stable or moving toward a higher level of institutionalization. These countries have the best prospects for continued stable democracy. Conversely, Guatemala, Ecuador, Panama, and Peru have poorly institutionalized party systems at low levels of mass political mobilization, and institutionalization is either stable or deteriorating. The basis for stable democracy in these cases is very weak. In Venezuela and Colombia, party systems that were highly institutionalized have deteriorated; in Venezuela, indeed, the party system has essentially collapsed. Consequently, prospects for stable democracy have diminished. In Brazil and the Dominican Republic, party systems appear to be becoming more institutionalized, so that prospects for stable democracy have improved. The remaining cases, each with its own characteristics, are intermediate.[22]

■ Social Structure, Civil Society, and Democracy

The structure of a society, including especially its system of classes, is both shaped by and shapes the political structure. This section will review that relationship, with particular attention to what theorists call "civil society," the organizations and movements through which individuals act to shape their social world.

As was made clear in Chapter 1, there is a long-standing body of theory about the relations between social structure and democracy. As far back as Aristotle, it was thought that a strong middle class, neither rich nor poor, was essential for democracy. Rousseau was similarly persuaded of the need to avoid extremes of wealth and poverty. Tocqueville's book *Democracy in America* placed great emphasis on the strength of the smallholding agrarian and trading middle class in the United States as an explanation for the strength of democracy. Marx believed that liberal democracy as it was taking shape in Europe was directly linked to the interests and predispositions of the bourgeoisie, or middle class, and that authentic democracy would have to wait on the economic and political dominance of the working class.

In the twentieth century and into the twenty-first, similarly, there has continued to be an emphasis on the kind of society that is conducive to democracy. The classic study by Seymour Martin Lipset (1959) again focused attention on the importance of a strong middle class. Barrington Moore (1966) argued that democracy had historically been consolidated in countries with a bourgeoisie that was strong relative to the landed aristocracy. In contrast, Dietrich Rueschemeyer, Evelyne Huber Stephens, and John Stephens (1992) argued that democracy has been strongest in those societies where the working class is strongest and best organized. They held that democracy has been weaker and less stable in Latin America than in Europe precisely because the working class is consistently weaker in Latin American societies and thus less able to compel the bourgeoisie to accept democratization.

The primary mechanism by which social structure affects the political regime is through organization, or civil society. Larry Diamond (1994, p. 5) defines civil society as

> the *realm of organized social life that is voluntary, self-generating, (largely) self-supporting, autonomous from the state, and bound by a legal order or set of shared rules.* . . . Civil society is an intermediary entity, standing between the private sphere and the state. Thus it excludes individual and family life, inward-looking group activity (e.g., for recreation, entertainment, or spirituality), the profit-making enterprise of individual business firms, and political efforts to take control of the state. (emphasis in original)

An active and pluralistic civil society is essential to the functioning of a healthy liberal democracy, and the question of civil society has thus received considerable attention from students of the transition to democracy. Tocqueville recognized this quality of American democracy, and the most influential shapers of twentieth-century pluralist democratic theory, from Bentley to Truman and Dahl, worked from the premise that democracy is built on the foundation of widespread political participation through diverse, autonomous organizations that represent the diverse interests and demands of the society.

One of the most systematic and influential recent analyses of civil society is by Sidney Tarrow (1994), who analyzed the phenomenon of national social movements in the West. He argued that such movements have only emerged since the eighteenth century as a result of enhanced communications and the consequently increased capacity to assemble large numbers of people for sustained collective action. Such movements will take shape in response to political opportunities that permit large-scale political mobilization. The modes of action of social movements may initially be "outside the system," but will tend, like strikes, to be absorbed into normal politics. Tarrow raised the question of whether the social movements involved in contemporary democratization processes will similarly be absorbed into politics as usual. His conclusion, in brief, was "not necessarily."

Robert Putnam (1993) analyzed the distinct political patterns in northern and southern Italy: in the former region democracy appears firmly established on the basis of what he called "social capital," or habits and skills of active participation in organizational life, whereas in the latter region such social capital is deficient and democracy, correspondingly, less well established.

Within Latin America, corporatism has been an important alternative to pluralism as an approach to civil society. Recall that whereas pluralism posits autonomous organization of civil society, corporatism treats the state as convening, recognizing, and even organizing the entities or corporations that represent society's distinct interests. Whereas pluralism relies on the free interplay of conflicting interests to serve the public good, corporatism vests the protection of the public good in the state. To the extent that the authoritarian regimes of the 1970s and early 1980s sought to do anything other than repress civil society, they largely sought to impose a corporatist structure on it. For example, Paul Drake (1996) analyzed how labor movements in the Southern Cone (Argentina, Chile, and Uruguay) survived authoritarian attempts to either destroy or control them, reemerging with substantial strength in the struggle for a transition to democracy. Taking a longer perspective, Ruth Collier and David Collier (1991) showed how distinct modes of incorporating the working class into politics in major Latin American countries shaped the political arena and hence the prospects of stable democracy. Collier and Collier used a theoretical approach, "critical junctures," quite consistent with that of the present book. They postulated that cleavage or crisis in a society may produce a critical juncture wherein fundamental political changes occur. It is the cleavage or crisis that makes change possible by loosening the bonds of preexisting structures (cf. Almond, Flanagan, and Mundt, 1973). They distinguished four major patterns of incorporation, each of which produced a heritage with major problems. In Brazil and Chile, workers were incorporated using depoliticization and control, and the result has been a polarizing multiparty politics. In Mexico and Venezuela, incorporation took place through radical populism, with the result of integrative party systems that absorbed the workers and limited social conflict. In Uruguay and Colombia, a traditional party mobilized the workers, resulting in a combination of electoral stability and social conflict. Peru and Argentina incorporated the workers through labor populism and produced political stalemate.[23]

Civil society was particularly important during the authoritarian regimes of the 1970s and early 1980s, when political parties opposed to the government were restricted or outlawed. It was during this period in many countries that groups emerged in neighborhoods to organize sectors of the populace in pursuit of common goals such as setting up community kitchens, providing childcare, or pressing the authorities for local improvements. These neighborhood associations were often tolerated because they were not overtly political, but they nevertheless provided crucial experience and opportunities for communication.[24]

Perhaps the most spectacular type of civil society organization was that which emerged to provide aid to victims of human rights violations. Although not avowedly political, these groups were frequently subject to repression because they necessarily attacked and questioned the authorities responsible for the torture, disappearance, and possible death of their loved ones. Certainly the most well-known were the Madres de Plaza de Mayo in Argentina, a group of women whose children had disappeared under the dictatorship. Beginning in the late 1970s, these women met weekly in the Plaza de Mayo facing the presidential palace (La Casa Rosada) to march silently with placards demanding that the government tell them where their loved ones were. At a time when murder, torture, and disappearances were still happening, their courage helped to inspire other Argentines to dare to oppose the regime and thereby shaped the climate that led to the transition of 1982–1983. Similar stories can be told of civil society opposition of authoritarian regimes elsewhere.

In addition to these social movements specifically oriented to resisting authoritarian repression, the importance of civil society, in the more traditional sense defined by Diamond previously, was enhanced during the dictatorships. Organized labor was one of the most important sectors. Drake (1996) found that the labor movements in Argentina, Chile, and Uruguay were certainly adversely affected by authoritarian rule, but they were not wiped out. On the contrary, however weakened and chastened, they nevertheless proved able to mobilize workers against the regimes, thereby providing important nuclei for resistance by other sectors of the population.

Religious organizations also continued to operate under authoritarianism. The progressive wing of the Roman Catholic Church reached the height of its power during the 1970s, in the wake of the Bishops' Conference in Medellín in 1968. That conference, following on the Second Ecumenical Conference in Rome in the early 1960s, committed the Latin American church to the struggle for social justice, the "preferential option for the poor" (Berryman, 1987). From this orientation sprang liberation theology, an interpretation of the Bible as emphatically placing Christ and God the Father on the side of the poor and oppressed. A parallel development at the grassroots was the basic church communities *(comunidades eclesiales de base)*, relatively small groupings of the faithful within parishes devoted to reading the scriptures and interpreting them in terms of everyday social injustices and struggles. Similar tendencies were evident in the mainline Protestant denominations such as the Methodists and within traditionally peace-oriented churches such as that of the Mennonites.

Some religious organizations provided support for authoritarian rule. Many of the more conservative, fundamentalist Protestants tended toward a strong anticommunism that made them sympathetic to the declared agendas of the authoritarian regimes. Simultaneously, more traditionalist forces within the Catholic Church resisted the implications of liberation theology and struggled, with support from Rome, to reassert control over the hierarchy and the parishes. Traditionalist and conservative bishops and clergy tended to be less politically active and more willing to accept and work with incumbent authoritarian regimes.[25]

If civil society was generally a force for democratization of authoritarian regimes, after the transition to liberal democracy the political role of elements of civil society became more complex and problematic.[26] The politics of religion has generally become less polarized under the new democratic regimes, but liberation theology is by no means finished, and there are still struggles within the Catholic Church to define its orientation. Again, much the same may be said of the mainline Protestants. The more conservative Protestants are gaining steadily in the number of their adherents but are perhaps a bit less aggressive in their anticommunism since the self-destruction of the Soviet Union. In general, churches and religious people have been less politically prominent since the restoration of democracy, a conclusion that is scarcely surprising given the much wider range of avenues for political expression that are now available.

Most sectors of civil society did survive the dictatorships: labor, for example, was largely able to resume legal activity in support of worker demands, including protection of the right to strike. But labor often lacked the power and leverage to achieve its objectives in the context of the global resurgence of neoliberal free trade policy. In general, labor and peasant organizations were able to protest prejudicial economic policies and might occasionally contribute to the defeat of governments but could not normally bring about a basic change in neoliberal economic policies.[27]

The indigenous sector of civil society was not prominent under the dictatorships but has become much more active under democracy. Indigenous people naturally have more power in countries where they constitute a large part of the population. For example, in Ecuador, the diverse indigenous groups have formed a very powerful joint organization that has staged several popular protests and strikes and has won important concessions from a succession of democratically elected governments. In Bolivia and Guatemala, indigenous peoples long submerged politically have begun to emerge and to assert themselves in national politics. In Peru and Mexico, as well, indigenous peoples are asserting themselves more strongly and showing surprising capacity for operating in the modern global communications system.[28]

Not surprisingly, civil society tends to be more active and inclusive in societies like Argentina, Uruguay, and Costa Rica, which have more literate populations. It is striking, however, that even in poorer societies with less education, such as Bolivia and Ecuador, civil society showed significant development in the 1980s and 1990s. As Tarrow pointed out, with modern communications, it is possible even for the poor and humble to organize to defend their interests.

Civil society under democratic rule faces several dilemmas. In many cases, such as Chile and Uruguay, the reemergence of parties has tended to push civil society organizations away from the center of action and to deprive them of some of their ablest activists. Moreover, the mission of such organizations as the Madres de Plaza de Mayo has become more ambiguous as they make demands on popularly elected governments rather than on the authoritarian perpetrators of abuses. A further problem has been that civil society organizations are often susceptible to co-optation by parties or the state: either the rank and file demand that the organization deliver material benefits (e.g., neighborhood improvements, jobs) from the state, or the leaders seek to use their capability for popular mobilization as a ticket to personal political advancement. Either way, such organizations can easily move from being part of the solution to part of the problem, from being a force for authentic democracy to being one more component of the clientelist political machinery. Finally, because of its very diversity, civil society cannot in the best of cases be a substitute for a viable, institutionalized party system. Parties are the mechanism by which a national electoral mandate is generated and carried out, however well or badly. The organization of civil society is essential to empower people to deal with their own problems and defend their own interests, but without a strong party system civil society cannot approximate a common national purpose.

▨ Elites

All the elements of stability discussed in this chapter—state institutions, party systems, civil society—necessarily operate through elites, "persons who are able, by virtue of their strategic positions in powerful organizations, to affect national political outcomes regularly and substantially" (Burton, Gunther, and Higley, 1992, p. 8). Classes and other large collectives act only through the individuals who emerge from mobilization of sectors of the class, and who purport to speak for the class. Social movements may begin spontaneously, but inevitably produce elites who lead their action. At the same time, the theoretical framework of this book reminds us that elites necessarily operate with parameters established by their own constituents and the structures of the larger political order.[29]

Elites and masses in a democratizing Latin America face a significant dilemma. The region's tradition leads all too often to the replication of clientelistic relations between leaders and followers. That is, even in an ostensibly democratic context where all citizens are equal, habit will lead people to expect their leaders to behave like patrons, dispensing favors in return for support, and habit will press leaders to act in just such a way, and to expect their followers to behave as clients, offering support in return for favors. Clientelism is a language everyone understands; democracy is not.

Examples abound. President Menem in Argentina and President Fujimori in Peru sought to impose sweeping economic reforms, and had significant success, but a good case can be made that they owed that success in good part to their willingness to play the game by rewarding their supporters. Conversely, President Pérez lost out in Venezuela when he refused to play the game (Weyland, 2002). After almost losing the election of 1994, President Ernesto Zedillo of Mexico sought to respond to the demand for social justice by establishing a National Solidarity Program (PRONASOL) to channel resources to the poor, but in practice the program became a means of rewarding supporters and depriving opponents. The Sandinista National Liberation Front in Nicaragua and the Lavalas movement in Haiti began as movements authentically committed to social transformation, but in the practice of day-to-day politics in the 1990s, each assumed an ever more clientelistic character. The same appears to be happening to Chávez's MVR in Venezuela.

For elites to make a positive contribution to the stabilization of democracy, they need to use their relative autonomy to resist this cultural pressure, and to remain committed to a more democratic style of leadership, bringing people together for larger goals rather than simply distributing individual or parochial benefits. Correspondingly, those who are not leaders will best promote democratic stability by not expecting their leaders to be primarily dispensers of favors. In general, the countries with the most stable democracies (Uruguay, Chile, Costa Rica) are precisely those that have made the most progress away from clientelism, though none has entirely left the pattern behind. Indeed, even advanced industrial democracies continue to suffer from the effects of clientelism in politics.

Most elites in Latin America have historically not been friends of democracy. The most recent wave of military governments, in the 1960s and 1970s, was led by military elites profoundly skeptical of democracy. Social and economic elites, the business and professional sectors, were organized under the dictatorships for collaboration and lobbying. Still, transitions from authoritarian rule were never successful without support and leadership from some elite sectors, whose defection from the regime often marked the beginning of the end. In Brazil, for example, as President João Batista Figueiredo fought to keep control of the election of his successor by blocking the campaign for direct presidential elections, an important faction of the ruling party with strong business connections defected to the opposition, the Party of the Brazilian Democratic Movement (PMDB). The defectors were rewarded with the PMDB vice presidential nomination for José Sarney (who then became the first civilian president after the death of President-elect Tancredo Neves). In Chile, the Concertación that campaigned against Pinochet in 1988 and 1989 drew on significant business support, although perhaps the majority of the business community continued to support the Pinochet regime. In Nicaragua, the ouster of Somoza in 1979 was substantially aided in the final weeks by the emergence of an independent elite coalition ("The Eight"), who demanded Somoza's resignation while maintaining their independence from the Sandinistas.

However, business and professional organizations were well situated to thrive under the new democratic regimes, since those regimes were urgently in need of economic growth, for which they needed collaboration from those with capital to invest. Even more urgently, the new democratic governments needed external credit, and to get it they had little choice but to pursue neoliberal policies likely to be popular with the more globally oriented business sectors. In 2003 the new leftist government of Lula da Silva drastically tempered its agenda of reforms in order to keep these economic elites onboard.

Like Lula, reformist elites, those seeking to transform structural conditions that, for example, lock the majority of Latin Americans in poverty, are most often severely constrained in their actions, both by internal structures of economic, political, and military power and by external forces such as the United States or the International Monetary Fund. A very clear example is provided by the series of Concertación governments in Chile since 1989, which have been constrained in the scope of reforms they can pursue by a range of institutional, economic, and political barriers.[30]

The operational definition of democratic stability used in this chapter is the survival of the regime through three electoral cycles without the breakdown of key rules and procedures. By that minimal criterion, Costa Rica certainly is the most stable democratic regime in the region. Chile and Uruguay, since the restoration of democracy, have achieved stability. Venezuela, stable for so long, cannot be so considered at present. Colombia technically meets the criterion, but few who know the country well would be entirely comfortable in calling it a stable democracy. Brazil appears to have achieved stable democracy. Mexico and Argentina, as large and relatively developed countries, might be expected to have achieved more stability than they have. In the case of Mexico, its authoritarian PRI-dominated regime was extremely stable for decades, but the recent victory by Vicente Fox, presidential candidate of PAN, means that Mexico has just embarked on a democratic regime; it is too soon to call it stable. Argentina has suffered repeated economic crises that have destabilized the polity. The system actually broke down in 2001, when the elected president was forced to resign by popular protests, and two acting presidents could not stay in control. Thus, even though President Kirchner seems to have made a good start at restoring stability, it is too soon to call Argentina a stable democracy.

Many other countries are flirting with stability, but are still quite vulnerable to disruption of the democratic regime. El Salvador, Nicaragua, Panama, Guatemala, and Honduras all meet the minimal criteria of democratic stability (no system breakdowns, three successive competitive elections), though none is even close to a democracy of high quality. Paraguay, Ecuador, and Peru cannot by any stretch be considered stable democracies, though each displays the formal features of democracy. Haiti's formal democracy was overthrown in early 2004. Table 4.3 summarizes these findings regarding stabilization, and goes further to summarize findings on consolidation, discussed below.

Following Huntington (1968), I suggest that stability is largely a function of relatively strong institutions (i.e., states and party systems) and of political participation or mobilization that is powerful enough to make democracy meaningful, but not so powerful as to overwhelm the political institutions. Costa Rica has maintained this balance for more than half a century. Venezuela has lost it since 1989. The Dominican Republic may be close to achieving it. Brazil has, perhaps, achieved it, but precariously. In most other countries, popular mobilization and demands on the system threaten stability.

This is not to say that popular participation or mobilization is a bad thing. On the contrary, it is of course the essence of democracy. However, when democratic regimes fail to develop strong enough institutions to handle popular participation in an ordered manner, stability will be threatened.

In the next section we raise the bar, asking what are the conditions for actual consolidation of democratic regimes.

Conclusion

Consolidation implies stabilization: it cannot occur until stabilization has occurred. As suggested in Table 4.3, all but one of the early democracies

Table 4.3   Democratic Stabilization and Consolidation

	Stabilization Criteria		Consolidation Criteria	
	No Breakdown	Three Elections	Eliminate Threats	Two Transitions to Opposition
Early Democracies				
Costa Rica (1952–)	X	X	X	X
Venezuela (1958–1968)	X	X		
(1968–1988)	X	X	X	X
(1988–)				
Chile (1932–1973)	X	X	X	X
(1988–)	X	X	X	
Uruguay (1946–1973)	X	X	X	X
(1985–)	X	X	X	X
Colombia (1958–)	X	X		X
Third-Wave Democracies				
Brazil (1985–)	X	X	X	X
Dominican Rep. (1966–)		X	X	X
El Salvador (1990–)	X	X	X	
Nicaragua (1984–)	X	X	X	
Panama (1990–)	X	X		X
Guatemala (1985–)	X	X		X
Honduras (1985–)	X	X		X
Bolivia (1982–)	X	X		X
Mexico (2000–)	X		X	
Argentina (1983–)				X
Paraguay (1989–)		X		
Ecuador (1978–)				
Peru (1980–)				
Haiti (1990–)				

achieved consolidation, but Chile and Uruguay suffered the destruction of their consolidated democratic regimes in 1973. Uruguay has since regained consolidated status, while Chile, lacking any transitions to an opposition party, cannot yet be considered consolidated as a democratic regime. Venezuela's consolidated regime has decayed badly since 1989, and although it has not been destroyed, it can no longer be considered consolidated. Colombia, having consistently failed to solve its chronic security problems, must be considered short of consolidation, notwithstanding its relative stability.

Among the third-wave democracies, only Brazil seems to have satisfied the minimal criteria for democratic consolidation. Notwithstanding a party system among the most inchoate in the region, repeated economic crises, and the persistence of social injustices among the worst in the world, Brazil's democratic regime has maintained its continuity even through the impeachment of President Collor in 1992 and the election of leftist Lula da Silva in

2002. Every presidential election since 1985 (except the reelection of Fernando Henrique Cardozo in 1998) has been won by an opposition candidate. There is now almost no likelihood of a military coup or insurrection that could threaten the government. The Brazilian democracy, in short, may not be of very high quality, but it appears consolidated. It is the only game in town.

None of the other countries that have achieved democratic stability have moved beyond that to reach consolidation. The Dominican Republic is perhaps on its way to consolidation, but there has not been enough time since the system broke down in 1996, when President Balaguer had to foreshorten his term before the opposition permitted him to take office. The passage of the great patriarchs from the scene probably bodes well for the future consolidation of Dominican democracy. In the postinsurrectionary cases of Nicaragua and El Salvador, negotiated settlements laid the basis for stability, but until the former guerrillas are permitted to actually win elections and take office, it cannot be said that these countries are consolidated. In Panama, Guatemala, Honduras, and Bolivia, both popular insurrection and military coups remain realistic possibilities even though these countries have been minimally stable in recent years.

Consolidation as defined here does not entail any statement about the quality of the democratic regime; rather, it connotes that the regime, whatever its merits, is "the only game in town." At this writing, only Costa Rica and Uruguay might be construed as having democracies qualitatively comparable to those of Western Europe. The others meet a less demanding standard. We turn in the next chapter to what happens when democratic regimes are destabilized, deconsolidated, or destroyed.

▨ Notes

1. This definition is based on the argument in Peeler (2003c, pp. 1–2).

2. A state is a relatively permanent administrative apparatus that purports to exercise compulsory and exclusive control over a particular territory and population. A state may govern its territory and population through a variety of regimes (such as democracy or military dictatorship), and each regime may produce a series of distinct governments, or sets of people who actually operate the state apparatus at any given time.

3. See Mainwaring and Shugart (1997); Linz and Valenzuela (1994); Linz and Stepan (1996a, 1996b); Lijphart (1994); Lijphart and Waisman (1996); Lijphart (1992); von Mettenheim (1997); Domínguez (1997); O'Donnell (1996); Huntington (1996); Horowitz (1990); Lipset (1990); Stepan and Skach (1993); Mainwaring and Shugart (1994); Mainwaring (1993); Thibaut (1993); Gamarra (1992); Mayorga (1992b); Andrade (1992); dos Santos (1992); Cintra (1992); Lehoucq (1996); Ensalaco (1994); Carey (2003). For a theoretical overview of broader questions of institutionalism, see Polity Forum (1995).

4. This pattern has been analyzed in detail by O'Donnell (1994) under the term "delegative democracy." He argued that popular election is construed to provide a mandate to the leader, as delegate of the people, to take whatever action he deems

appropriate in the interests of the people, whether or not it accords with campaign promises or indeed falls within the law. For alternative perspectives on this phenomenon, see Corrales (2002); Weyland (2002).

5. The new Haitian constitution does have a prime minister responsible to the legislature, but that body is so much weaker than the president that the prime minister remains effectively responsible to the president. Similarly, Peru has long had a prime minister, but there too this official is fully responsible to the president.

6. See especially Mainwaring and Scully (1995). See also Seligson and Booth (1995); Goodman, LeoGrande, and Forman (1992); Perelli, Picado, and Zovatto (1995); Chalmers, Campello de Souza, and Borón (1992); Torres Rivas (1993); McDonald and Ruhl (1989); Roberts (2002).

7. See Scully (1995); Baño (1995); Garretón (1993a, 1995); Munck (1994); Saffirio (1994); Barrett (1999); Angell and Pollack (2000); Agüero (2003).

8. For the concept of a semiloyal opposition, see Linz (1978), pp. 27ff.

9. See González (1995); Dutrénit Bielous (1994); Mieres (1994a, 1994b); De Riz and Smulovitz (1992); Cason (2002).

10. See Peeler (1985, 1992). On Colombia, see Archer (1995); Martz (1992); Murillo Castaño (1999); Boudon (2001); Cepeda Ulloa (2003). On Costa Rica, see Yashar (1995); Rojas Bolaños and Sojo (1995); Vega Carballo (1992); Fernández (1994); Rovira Mas (2001b); Cortés Ramos (2001); Hernández Naranjo (2001); Booth (1998). On Venezuela, see Kornblith and Levine (1995); Goodman et al. (1995); McCoy et al. (1995); Hillman (1994); Coppedge (1993, 1994; 2003); Crisp (1994); Ellner (2003); McCoy (1999); Hellinger (2003).

11. On the contemporary Costa Rican party system, see Rovira Mas (2001a), pt. 3.

12. On the Colombian party system, see Martz (1997); Archer (1995); Archer and Shugart (1997); Cepeda Ulloa (2003).

13. On the new constitution, see Restrepo (1992); Hartlyn (1994b); Archer and Shugart (1997); Murillo Castaño (1999).

14. See Coppedge (1993, 1994a, 1994b); Brewer-Carías (1988); Martz (1994); Hillman (1994).

15. On the Chávez period, see Ramos Rollón (2002); Ellner and Hellinger (2003); Ellner (2003). Coppedge (2003) explores the conflict between Chávez's vision of democracy as popular sovereignty and the classic vision of liberal democracy that characterized the pre-Chávez period. Many observers, including Coppedge (1994) and Hillman (1994), questioned the authenticity of Venezuela's liberal democracy.

16. See McGuire (1995); Cavarozzi (1986, 1992); Fraga (1995); Borón et al. (1995); Remmer (1984); Peruzzotti (2001); Godio (2003); Levitzky (2003).

17. For a critical view of the delegative democracy argument regarding Menem, see Peruzzotti (2001).

18. On the Brazilian party system, see Hagopian (1996); Mainwaring (1995, 1999); Schneider (1996); Roett (1997); Lamounier (2003).

19. On recent developments in the Mexican party system, see Cornelius (1996); Bruhn (1997); Guttmann (2002); Levy (2001); Pérez Herrero (2001); Langston (2002); Dresser (2003); Camp (2003).

20. On party systems in Bolivia, see Gamarra and Malloy (1995); Mayorga (1995a); Archondo (1999); Toranzo Roca (2002); Seligson (2003). On party systems in Peru, see Cotler (1995a, 1995b); Mauceri (1995); Schmidt (1996); Adrianzén (1998); Klarén (2000); Degregori (2003). On party systems in Ecuador, see Conaghan (1995); Cabezas Castillo (1995); Conaghan and Espinal (1990); Selverston-Scher (2001); Saint-Upéry (2002); Seligson (2002). For comparison of party systems in the

Central Andes, see Conaghan and Malloy (1994); Ramos Jiménez (2001); Peeler (2003a). On party systems in Panama, see Ropp (1997); O. Pérez (1995); Smith (1992). On party systems in the Dominican Republic, see Hartlyn (1998); Conaghan and Espinal (1990).

21. On party systems in Honduras, see Ruhl (1997); Rosenberg (1995); Paz Aguilar (1992); Torres Calderón (2003). On party systems in El Salvador, see Montgomery (1997, 1995); Baloyra-Herp (1995); Eguizábal (1995); Ramos (1998). On party systems in Guatemala, see Jonas (1995); Rosada Granados (1992); Martínez Cortez (2003). On party systems in Nicaragua, see McCoy and McConnell (1997); Anderson (1995); Richard and Booth (1995); Godoy Reyes (1992); LeoGrande (1992); Williams (1994); Prevost (1991); Weaver and Barnes (1991); Walker (1997, 2003). On party systems in Central America in general, see Booth and Richard (1996); Rovira Mas (1992, 1994); Rojas Bolaños and Sojo (1995); Domínguez and Lindenberg (1997); Seligson (2000). On party systems in Haiti, see Mintz (1995); Fatton 2002.

22. Institutionalization, as Huntington was well aware, is a dynamic concept. The Venezuelan experience makes clear that a highly institutionalized party system may be vulnerable to destabilization precisely because it is so highly institutionalized as to block change.

23. See Tarrow (1994); Levine (1993); Diamond (1994); Keane (1988); Oxhorn (1995); Cohen and Arato (1992); Hall (1995).

24. The strong role of civil society organizations in resisting authoritarian rule constitutes an implicit critique of the argument (see Chapter 2) that Latin American political culture is incompatible with democracy. For an explicit analysis of this question in light of public opinion data, see Booth and Richard (1996); Seligson (2000). A good collection is Albala-Bertrand (1992). See also Corradi, Fagen, and Garretón (1992); Hipsher (1996); Guzmán Bouvard (1994); McManus and Schlabach (1991); Jaquette (1994); Escobar and Alvarez (1992); Silva (1996); Drake (1996).

25. On religion and politics in Latin America, see Cleary and Stewart-Gambino (1992); Mainwaring and Wilde (1989); Pottenger (1989); Berryman (1987).

26. On civil society and democracy, see Levine (1993); Calderón and dos Santos (1995); García Delgado (1994); Keck (1995); Markoff (1996). For a relevant analysis of civil society in postcommunist transitions, see Bernhard (1996).

27. See Murillo (2003) for a survey. For examples of labor and peasant action, see Avritzer (1995) on Brazil; Vunderink (1991) and Edelman (2000) on Costa Rica; Espinal (1995) on the Dominican Republic. A comparative historical perspective is provided by Cooper et al. (1993).

28. On indigenous organizations and movements, see Yashar (1998); Warren (1998); Peeler (2003d).

29. The argument of this section is more fully developed in Peeler (2001).

30. On the political role of socioeconomic elites, see Evans (1979); Gil Yepes (1981); Borner, Brunetti, and Weder (1996); de Soto (1989); Grinspun and Cameron (1993); Naim and Francés (1995); Vilas (1995b); Peeler (2001); Winson (1989) on Costa Rica; Acosta Silva (1996) on Ecuador; Kornblith (1995) on Venezuela; Castillo Ochoa (1996) on Peru; Hagopian (1996) on Brazil.

5

Destabilization, Deconsolidation, and Decay

The story of democracy in Latin America in the past two decades has been as much about destabilization, deconsolidation, and decay as about stabilization and consolidation. While most countries retain formally democratic regimes, the panorama is not encouraging. This chapter will consider a variety of challenges to democratic regimes.

■ Destabilization and Destruction of Early Democracies

Each of the early democracies discussed in Chapter 3 underwent significant stress in the 1970s and 1980s. The two oldest, Chile and Uruguay, were actually overthrown in 1973, while Costa Rica, Venezuela, and Colombia underwent significant stresses while surviving as democratic regimes.

Chile and Uruguay

The balance of the Chilean and Uruguayan regimes began to break down in the 1960s. In Chile, the Christian Democratic Party (DC) government of Eduardo Frei, elected in 1964 with the support of the Right, and of a U.S. government preoccupied with preventing another victory for the Left in the wake of the Cuban Revolution, was more narrowly and exclusively partisan than its predecessors, making little attempt to negotiate with its rivals on the right and left. Christian Democratic self-assurance was reinforced by Frei's unprecedented absolute majority, which was followed by a capture of a majority of the Chamber of Deputies in 1965. The Christian Democrats tended to ignore the importance of the Right's support in these two victories, using the power base thus obtained to push through their program aimed at taking electoral support from the Left while undermining the electoral base of the Right. The program included an extensive agrarian reform law (encouraged by the U.S. Alliance for Progress); moreover, the Christian Democrats and the parties of

131

the Left began for the first time to actively organize the rural work force. These two initiatives directly challenged the interests of the Right to an unprecedented extent, even as the Christian Democrats aimed directly at weakening the Left. Not surprisingly, both Left and Right responded with hostility to this Christian Democratic attempt to establish a lasting electoral dominance (Remmer, 1984; Scully, 1992, 1995; Loveman, 1988).

By 1969 the Christian Democratic gambit had failed. Without rightist support, the DC lost its majority in the Chamber. In spite of growing support for Salvador Allende and his Popular Unity (UP) coalition on the left, another center-right alliance proved impossible to achieve. In 1970, Allende won the presidency in a narrow victory in a three-way contest. His government, like Frei's, was committed to the constitution but it was also committed to bringing about major changes in the social and economic structure. Pressed for radical action by his more leftist supporters, and consistently obstructed by centrist and right-wing forces occupying positions of power in Congress and the courts, Allende had an ever-narrower constitutional ground on which to stand. However, when Popular Unity actually increased its share of the vote in the congressional elections of 1973, his opponents realized that they had no hope of removing him constitutionally. It was then that key Christian Democrats joined the Right in supporting a military coup. The procedural democracy that had for so long preserved a policy impasse could not survive the breakdown of that impasse.

In Uruguay, economic stresses made themselves unmistakably evident by the mid-1960s. Export production was stagnating, the state was growing but without adequate means to finance that growth, and standards of living were declining. In the face of these difficulties, both the Right and the Left gained strength, creating a steadily increasing likelihood of political crisis. A presidential constitution was reestablished in 1966. The two-party system was not working particularly well. A right-wing Colorado vice president (Jorge Pacheco Areco) succeeded to the presidency in 1967, and the fragmentation of the two major parties combined with the electoral system to produce, in 1971, a right-wing Colorado successor (Juan María Bordaberry), who represented a small minority of the electorate. With strong commitments to impose order and discipline on the society, both Pacheco and Bordaberry tended to compensate for their lack of a popular mandate by an increasingly authoritarian exercise of their powers. At the same time, in addition to serious economic stagnation and a fiscal crisis of the state, there was a paucity of new ideas and a surplus of temporizing and buck-passing. Popular frustration at the evident inability of the government to confront these problems was manifested generally in an increase in strikes and agitation and in the emergence of two major political movements (Weinstein, 1995; Gillespie, 1991).

The Tupamaro urban guerrilla movement of the late 1960s and early 1970s sought to adapt the experience of the successful Cuban Revolution to the unique urban setting of Uruguay, where there is no Sierra Maestra in which to take refuge and oppressed peasants and rural workers are a small part of the population (Guillén, 1973). The thinking was that the city itself and its workers would shield and support the guerrillas. The Tupamaros rejected the legitimacy of Uruguay's liberal democracy, following the Marxist revolutionary analysis that it was a fraud and a distraction for the working class and that only a violent seizure of power could permit a true revolution and hence the ultimate establishment of a genuinely democratic regime. The Tupamaros proved uncommonly adept at covert organization and at carrying out propagandistic attacks embarrassing to the regime. But the Tupamaros alone never came close to the mass support that the Left had during the same period in Chile. They are more similar to the Chilean Revolutionary Left Movement (MIR); that is, they are primarily a cadre of underground combatants with a network of covert supporters.

Alongside the Tupamaros emerged a mass-based leftist movement, the Broad Front (FA), challenging the traditional parties in the electoral arena. The FA grouped together diverse social democratic, socialist, and communist parties and factions around a very general program of criticism of the status quo and a commitment to move toward socialism. It was thus quite similar to the Chilean Popular Unity in its basic orientation and composition. But whereas in Chile the communists and socialists were mass-based parties with long histories that had coalesced often for electoral purposes, their counterparts in Uruguay had never before attracted a mass base. Thus, when the FA gained 18 percent of the vote in the 1971 elections, this was utterly without precedent.[1] The stability of the two-party system in Uruguay was severely threatened.

Under these conditions of a paralytic regime confronted by increasingly insistent demands for radical change, the armed forces were drawn ever more into the political arena. Influenced by the new doctrine of national security that had become current in Latin America since the Cuban Revolution, many officers were losing patience with the seeming inability of the democratic regime to cope with what they saw as serious threats to national security. In February 1973, faced with a series of military mutinies demanding economic and social reforms as well as the suppression of the Tupamaro insurgency, and finding himself unable to mobilize civilian support for the democratic regime, Bordaberry accepted the establishment of a military National Security Council that would, in effect, supervise his exercise of the presidency. The slow-motion coup culminated five months later when Bordaberry closed Congress after it refused to lift the immunity of a member accused by the armed forces of complicity with the Tupamaros.

One of the great issues of democratic theory is how to combine political equality with economic equality in order to approach true equality of power. And if democracy is indeed to be liberal, it must do this without sacrificing individual liberty. During its first democratic era, Uruguay came closer than any other Latin American country to achieving all three ends: political equality, economic equality, and liberty. Yet Uruguay never really left behind the clientelist politics of the nineteenth century, and clientelism came to permeate the liberal and democratic structure of the modern polity. José Batlle y Ordóñez's nationalist vision became a ritual and the nation a cow to be milked.

The pathology of democracy in Uruguay was thus markedly different than in Chile. While democracy in Chile was an arena for open class struggle, the traditional parties in Uruguay blurred class conflict by establishing clientelistic political ties. They were unable to adapt to liberal democracy by opening themselves and the system to new ideas and visions. The parties and the polity they created became so fragmented and immobilized that an effective response to crisis was impossible. Yet it was ironic that these same ties of clientelism and habitual loyalty enabled the traditional parties to reemerge as dominant political actors in the transition of the 1980s.

Costa Rica

For Costa Rica, the 1960s and early 1970s were not a time of crises like those that led to regime breakdown in Chile and Uruguay. However, the twin crises of the 1980s (the Third World debt crisis and the Central American revolutions), though different in character, were similar in intensity to the crises that destroyed democracies in Chile and Uruguay. That Costa Rica's democracy survived is thus worthy of attention in this comparative analysis. The debt crisis increased Costa Rica's dependence on U.S. aid and vulnerability to U.S. pressure, as the country, like many others, found itself unable to service its debt.[2] At the same time, the escalation of the U.S. confrontation with the Sandinistas made Washington pay more attention to the region and rendered Costa Rica, as Nicaragua's southern neighbor, strategically important. The result was that Costa Rica received more aid than it might otherwise have obtained, cushioning the effects of the debt crisis. However, successive governments were under much more U.S. pressure on several issues than was customary, with demands for covert contra bases in Costa Rica and the expansion and militarization of the Civil and Rural Guards (the lightly armed forces Costa Rica maintains in lieu of an army). The government of Luis Alberto Monge (of the National Liberation Party [PLN], 1982–1986) proved highly amenable to these pressures, but Monge's successor, Oscar Arias Sánchez (PLN, 1986–1990) was more resistant (Longley, 1997; Yashar, 1997).[3]

Costa Rica also found itself under substantial pressure regarding its economic and fiscal policies as a result of its inability to pay its foreign debts. The major source of credit in such emergencies is the International Monetary Fund (IMF), which, as always, insisted upon steps to increase government revenues, reduce expenditures, and lower barriers to trade. The implications for Costa Rica's welfare state and government-directed economy were serious.

The pressure was intense to privatize banking and insurance; open the medical system further to private practice; and reduce budgets for health, social security, and education. In general, Costa Rican elites had to accept a substantial reduction in social services and a significant shrinkage of the government role in the economy because the state simply lacked the necessary resources and could not borrow what it needed abroad to maintain them. Nevertheless, it is striking that the social democratic state still exists in recognizable form in spite of over a decade of neoliberal pressure. In economic policy, as in strategic policy, the Costa Rican elites have had substantial success with a strategy of bending to pressure in order to avoid being broken.

Costa Rica continues to display a propensity to political pacts and negotiation between the major parties. In June 1995, President José María Figueres (PLN, son of former president José Figueres) signed a political pact with his predecessor, Rafael Angel Calderón Fournier (of the Social Christian Unity Party [PUSC], son of former president Rafael Angel Calderón Guardia), to ensure parliamentary support for an array of economic policy initiatives, which would in general continue the neoliberal policy direction of the Calderón government (1990–1994). The pact was advantageous to Figueres because the PLN was one vote short of an absolute majority in the Legislative Assembly. Nevertheless, he was widely criticized by his own partisans for accepting the neoliberal approach of the PUSC.

Venezuela

The major challenges confronting Venezuela in the past decade have been centered on the consequences of the worldwide stagnation and decline of petroleum prices (Karl, 1997). Successive governments since Juan Vicente Gómez have used petroleum revenues to enhance the capabilities of the state to deal with problems of Venezuelan society. The government's share of oil profits expanded gradually over the years as new contracts were negotiated. Careful management of this resource meant that the Venezuelan government was traditionally one of the most solvent in the Third World (Crisp, 2000; Karl, 1987, 1997; Hillman, 1994; Ellner and Hellinger, 2003).

When the world oil crisis of 1973–1974 sent prices skyrocketing, it was thus natural that newly elected president Carlos Andrés Pérez should react in a highly self-confident manner. First iron and steel and later petroleum itself were nationalized, and government social programs were rapidly expanded. Rising government expenditures were financed with international loans based on the assumption of continuing increases in oil prices. But when prices in fact leveled off, the government failed to adjust, and the external debt began to be a major problem. The difficulties were compounded by the inability of the succeeding administration of Luis Herrera Campins to carry out an austerity program. By 1983, Venezuela found itself alongside Mexico and Nigeria as an oil-rich country in deep economic trouble. Little progress was made during the administration of Jaime Lusinchi, so that when Pérez returned to the presidency in early 1989, he had little alternative but to impose an orthodox austerity program, even though he had campaigned as a populist. The resultant riots and repression profoundly undermined the confidence of the people. In 1992, two abortive military coups further shook the country. Pérez was forced out of office by impeachment in 1993, and Rafael Caldera was elected president later that year on a vaguely populist program opposed to neoliberal reforms. However, Caldera was consistently unable to right the economy. With disillusionment and anger widespread, former colonel and coup leader Hugo Chávez won the 1998 elections and initiated a period of extensive institutional change and ever deeper political polarization.

Colombia

The evolution of Colombia since the establishment of a liberal democracy after the end of the National Front in 1974 cannot be characterized as a consolidation of the regime. If anything, we are witnessing a process of slow-motion breakdown. The major problems were an inability to either defeat or reach a settlement with several major guerrilla groups, the growing power and impact of drug trafficking, and the persistence and growth of social violence on all levels. Despite these formidable problems, the formal aspects of the political order have remained remarkably stable. Full electoral competition has been unbroken since 1974, with the opposition winning the presidency in 1982 and 1986. Parties and coalitions of the Left have competed in elections throughout the period, generally receiving less than 5 percent of the vote. Voter turnout and other forms of political participation have increased since the end of the National Front but remain at rather low levels compared with those in Venezuela and Costa Rica. There has been some fragmentation of the party system; parties of the Left (notably the April 19 Movement [M-19]) have gained, while the Conservative Party has been weakened by serious defections, including that of senior statesman Alvaro Gómez (Archer, 1995; Cepeda Ulloa, 2003; Pizarro Leongómez, 2003).

Elections held in 1990 may have indicated the early stages of fundamental shifts. The first of the guerrilla groups to reintegrate itself into civil political life, M-19, after a poor performance in congressional elections, finished third in the presidential race (12.5 percent, more than the official candidate of the conservatives). The Conservative Party split, with Alvaro Gómez leading his National Salvation Movement to a second-place showing. The Liberal Party easily led both congressional and presidential votes, and César Gaviria Trujillo was elected president. The voters also approved a referendum to call a constitutional convention, elections for which were held in December 1990. The meteoric rise of M-19 continued, as it received about 35 percent of the vote, against 26 percent for Gómez's National Salvation Movement. The governing Liberals were in third place, the official Conservatives fourth. However, the national elections of 1994 showed the Liberals and Conservatives still very much in control: together, they received 90 percent of the presidential vote. The decentralization institutionalized with the new constitution, however, began to undermine the parties' control, such that the 2002 elections left them with less than a majority of the Chamber of Deputies (Sabatini, 2003). The 1998 and 2002 presidential elections were each won by a dissident from one of the traditional parties (Andrés Pastrana, a former Conservative, and Alvaro Uribe, a former Liberal). The old party system is clearly in flux.

It is at less formal levels that the crisis of the regime becomes more apparent. The effort to deal with the guerrilla movements that have been active since the 1960s has been schizophrenic, alternately emphasizing repression and the search for a negotiated political settlement that would permit the integration of these movements into national political life. The only clear success has been the integration of M-19 into political life after it agreed to forswear violence. Even so, M-19 and other groups on the left have suffered severely from political assassinations at the hand of right-wing death squads. The other major guerrilla movements remain in the field, although negotiations continue. The government has been progressively less able to concentrate its attention on the insurgencies because of the growing size and power of the underground drug economy. Colombia has for many years been a major supplier of marijuana to North America, but in the past twenty years it has also become the nerve center of the rapidly growing cocaine industry. From a Colombian point of view, the positive side of this phenomenon is the uncounted dollars that the drug trade pumps into Colombia.[4] But this is heavily outweighed by the negative consequences, notably for the Colombian political elite and political system. The Colombian state lacks control over the country's largest industry and the most general threat to social order.

Confronting these threats, the political elites and the state have shown themselves remarkably incapable of meaningful innovation. Both the major parties and the military have been unreceptive and often hostile toward efforts to promote new approaches that might cause significant changes in Colombian social structure. Their response has basically been a reaffirmation of two strategies that have worked in the past: repression and negotiation. But because the elite capacity for action is weak and dispersed, the two strategies have frequently canceled each other out, as happened with Belisario Betancur's attempt to open the political system to the leftist insurgencies, which was frustrated in November 1985 by the seizure of the Palace of Justice by the M-19 and the assault on the palace by the army (Carrigan, 1993). More fundamentally, in twenty-five years of counterinsurgency and ten years of a war on drugs, the Colombian state has shown itself incapable of prevailing in either struggle by repressive means, and the strategy of negotiation has not worked because the established elites have been unwilling to make the concessions that a new settlement would involve. Instead, they resorted to tinkering with institutions, most notably in the new constitution of 1991, which contains numerous provisions that further democratization in theory but do little in practice to change the basic power structure of society.

President Ernesto Samper (Liberal Party), elected in 1994 under a cloud of allegations of having received campaign contributions from the Cali drug cartel, clung to power in spite of mounting evidence against him, including the conviction and imprisonment of key campaign officials. Nevertheless, Samper's solid liberal majority in Congress refused, in June 1996, to accept the prosecutor's recommendation that he be impeached, voting instead to exonerate the president on the grounds that any violations occurred without his knowledge. There was also much speculation that drug money had already so penetrated the political class as to render a majority of members of Congress unwilling to expose themselves to similar investigations, which might follow if Samper were convicted.

Samper was succeeded in 1998 by Andrés Pastrana, who undertook a major attempt to negotiate a peace settlement, including granting safe zones to the two major guerrilla groups. By the end of his term in 2002 this effort had come to naught, and the next elections were won by Alvaro Uribe, a hardliner who implemented an opposite strategy of attacking not only the leftist guerrillas, but also the paramilitaries, in an effort to force them to negotiate a peace settlement.

The rest of the chapter will be devoted to the major factors contributing to destabilization of democracies since 1990.

■ Economic and Social Pressures

The effects of economic crisis and economic reform were generally quite negative for the majority of Latin American populations. Income distributions became less equal, real incomes declined, and unemployment rose. Yet democratic regimes dealt with adversity just as well as authoritarian regimes did, and the stability of democratic regimes was not significantly undermined by coping with economic crises.

The great debt crisis of the 1980s and the roughly simultaneous emergence of the "Washington consensus" among international lenders and aid donors, favoring not only fiscal austerity and reduction of trade barriers but also extensive privatization of state enterprises and a general reduction of the state's role in economy and society, undoubtedly helped to push many of the authoritarian regimes out of power and thus facilitated the transitions analyzed in Chapter 3. However, the new liberal democratic regimes have themselves confronted many of the same stresses, for recovery has been slow, income and property have become measurably more concentrated, middle-class jobs in the state sector have been eliminated, and the quality and coverage of social programs have declined. These stresses are justified in neoliberal theory as necessary to a fundamental economic readjustment, which will in the long run lead to higher growth rates that will benefit the whole society.[5]

In the context of this analysis of democracy, it is not necessary to involve ourselves in the argument among economists as to the merits of the neoliberal model and its predictions. However, we must take account of neoliberalism and the Washington consensus as political facts, as demands placed upon all governments in Latin America (indeed, all developing countries). How have responses varied between countries or between governments? What political characteristics or structural features help to explain this diversity? What have been the results of neoliberal policy reform? And finally, for our purposes, the central question: How have neoliberal economic reforms affected democratic regimes?

How Have Responses Varied?

Responses to neoliberal pressures for reform have varied, both between countries and between governments in the same country.[6] Policies of both authoritarian and democratic governments have ranged from defiant populism (e.g., Velasco Alvarado and Alan García in Peru) to highly orthodox neoliberalism (e.g., Augusto Pinochet and Patricio Aylwin in Chile). The populist approach was characterized by the maintenance and expansion of subsidies ensuring the popular standard of living (e.g., price controls, social services, public employment). Populist policies tended to produce fiscal deficits because tax collections could not keep up with program costs, and severe inflation usually emerged. Exports tended to be discouraged by support for high wages and artificially high currency values. Imports were typically blocked by high tariffs in order to promote import substitution industrialization, on the theory that protection of internal markets was the only way for local industry to establish itself. Severe deficits in the balance of payments commonly emerged in the wake of the global petroleum crisis of the late 1970s. The populist approach was sustainable only so long as there was either international lending support for the fiscal and balance of payments deficits or an ability to raise revenue internally to pay off those deficits. Few governments proved capable of doing the latter, and when international lending dried up in the early 1980s, the debt crisis ensued (see Stallings and Kaufman, 1989; Dornbusch and Edwards, 1991). It was the debt crisis that rendered most governments susceptible to pressures for neoliberal reforms.

Most governments avoided the spectacular defiance of the conventional wisdom that characterized Siles Zuazo in Bolivia (1982–1985), Alan García in Peru (1985–1990), or Daniel Ortega in Nicaragua (1985–1990), but most did pursue some variant of populist policy and did resist pressures for neoliberal reforms. Confronted with deficits and hyperinflation and unable to service debts, several governments attempted so-called heterodox shock treatments intended to stop inflation and promote economic growth without all the highly unpopular deflationary measures advocated by the IMF. Good examples are the Austral Plan of Raúl Alfonsín in Argentina and a succession of plans adopted by José Sarney and Fernando Collor de Melo in Brazil. In each case, initial success was followed in a few months by a disastrous descent into economic crises even worse than before.

A less radical defense of populist policy—effectively, a policy of strategic retreat—was mounted by countries wherein the crisis was less acute and wherein there was considerable investment in welfare state programs and state-owned enterprises. Uruguay and Costa Rica best exemplify this category. In these cases a succession of governments from both major parties have avoided direct confrontation with the IMF and international lenders while implementing only the minimum of neoliberal reforms absolutely necessary to keep international finance flowing. In well-established democracies such as these, unpopular neoliberal measures frequently elicited popular protests, but governments generally stuck to their guns and implemented those policies to which they had committed themselves.

Most governments in the region, confronted with debt and fiscal crises and with hyperinflation, and politically unable either to finance social programs or to cut them, responded to neoliberal pressures ad hoc, resisting them as long as possible, agreeing to unpopular reforms when absolutely necessary, and failing to implement reforms when internal political pressures grew too intense. Honduras, the Dominican Republic, and Ecuador are typical. In the Dominican case, both the Dominican Revolutionary Party (PRD) governments (1978–1986) and Balaguer (1986–1996) maneuvered uncertainly between the extremes of neoliberalism and populism, perhaps cushioned by close economic ties with the United States. Honduras also benefited from U.S. aid during the Reagan administration (1981–1989) and its obsession with Central America, but has been increasingly on its own since 1989. The governments of Rafael Leonardo Callejas and Carlos Roberto Reina agreed to reforms when necessary, but implemented them without enthusiasm. In Ecuador, a succession of weak governments, confronting a highly fragmented Congress and an increasingly mobilized public, have needed help from the IMF on a regular basis but have been consistently inconsistent in their economic policies. This pattern culminated in the 1996 election of populist Abdalá Bucaram, who promptly reversed himself and adopted stringent neoliberal reforms, only to face massive popular protests and his removal from power by a congressional vote in February 1997. Bucaram, with a poorly institutionalized party system, held office only six months before a combination of popular rage and political rivalries swept him away. The next elected president, Jamil Mahuad, was ousted in a coup by the major indigenous confederation in alliance with junior military officers, but international pressure led the armed forces high command to promptly hand power to the elected vice president. The military leader of the coup, former colonel Lucio Gutiérrez, was elected president (with indigenous support) in 2002 (Acosta Silva, 1996; Schemo, 1997; Lucero, 2001).

In several cases, incoming presidents have used political blitzkrieg to implement draconian neoliberal shock plans. Major examples include Víctor Paz Estenssoro in Bolivia (1985), Carlos Salinas de Gortari in Mexico (1988), Carlos Andrés Pérez in Venezuela (1989), Carlos Menem in Argentina (1990), Alberto Fujimori in Peru (1992), and Abdalá Bucaram in Ecuador (1996). In each of these cases, presidents made extensive use of discretionary powers and the element of surprise to impose a neoliberal transformation of the national economy. Price controls, tariffs, and subsidies were severely cut, state-owned firms were privatized, state employment was pruned, and major emphasis was placed on controlling inflation by controlling wages. The predictable result was a rise in unemployment and underemployment, an increase in the poverty rate, and a general decline in the standard of living. Pérez's presidency did not survive the shock: bloody popular riots in 1989 and military revolts in 1992 set the context for his impeachment and removal from office in 1993.[7] The successor government of Rafael Caldera reverted to ad hoc policymaking, and in 1998 the former leader of the first attempted coup of 1992, Hugo Chávez, was elected president with promises of radical reform of the corrupt political system (Ellner and Hellinger, 2003).

Salinas rode out the political crisis and achieved enough economic success to ensure the election of his successor, Ernesto Zedillo, in 1994. However, between the election and the inauguration, the Mexican economy came unglued in a major financial panic, a hemorrhage of capital stopped only by a U.S.-backed rescue plan. Unlike Caldera, however, Zedillo sustained Salinas's commitment to neoliberalism in spite of widespread opposition within Mexico. In the historic election of 2000, Vicente Fox of the opposition National Action Party (PAN) won election as president, ending seventy years of domination by the Institutional Revolutionary Party (PRI). Fox continued to favor neoliberal policies, and was especially committed to the North American Free Trade Agreement (NAFTA).

Both Menem and Fujimori proved so popular with their control of inflation that each was able to secure a constitutional amendment permitting immediate reelection and to gain overwhelming reelection victories in 1995 (Halperín Donghi, 1994; Stokes, 1997). Their political success certainly owes something to an authoritarian propensity in Latin American political culture, but is also based on sustained economic stability, even when it has come at the cost of increased poverty and unemployment. By 1999, both Fujimori and Menem were forced from power amid uncertain economic conditions and corruption scandals.

In Bolivia, Paz Estenssoro was the first democratically elected president in Latin America to successfully carry out comprehensive neoliberal reforms. His success was facilitated by the strategic defeat of the major labor federation, the Bolivian Workers Central (COB), and particularly the tin miners' union. Strikes protesting the closure and privatization of the tin mines were forcefully repressed, and the major labor leaders were arrested and exiled. After 1986, organized labor ceased to be a threat to the neoliberal agenda of the government. Paz Estenssoro's alliance with the conservative National Democratic Alliance (ADN) of Hugo Banzer permitted the enactment and implementation of a comprehensive package of neoliberal reforms that, in addition to dismantling the tin industry, privatized other state-owned firms, reduced the state bureaucracy, and cut back on social programs. Hyperinflation was quickly ended. The policies of Paz Estenssoro and his minister of economy, Gonzalo Sánchez de Lozada, were so popular that not only Sánchez de Lozada but also his two principal opponents in the elections of 1989 thought it prudent to pledge a continuation of the basic elements of Paz Estenssoro's policy. Although Sánchez de Lozada finished first, he was short of a majority, and Congress ultimately elected the third-place candidate, Jaime Paz Zamora, who had struck a deal with Banzer. Paz Zamora's economic policy did in fact continue the broad outlines of the Paz Estenssoro policy in the period 1989–1993. Sánchez de Lozada was elected president in 1993 and continued with the neoliberal agenda. In short, three successive governments, over more than a decade, have maintained neoliberal economic policies in Bolivia (Gamarra, 1994). Subsequently, Hugo Banzer and Sánchez de Lozada continued the basic neoliberal posture into the twenty-first century, but the latter was forced to resign in 2003 by popular protests and shootings of protesters by police.

The government of Fernando Henrique Cardoso (1994–2002) in Brazil exemplifies a more moderate version of this blitzkrieg neoliberalism. As economy minister under his predecessor, Itamar Franco, Cardoso had fostered a successful neoliberal program, the Real Plan. On the strength of that success, he was elected president and continued the plan. He was successful in getting Congress to approve a constitutional amendment to allow him to run for a second four-year term (Ellison, 1997), and he was in fact reelected.

The only country with a consistent record of neoliberalism since the mid-1970s has been Chile.[8] After more than a year of policy incoherence, the Pinochet government became thoroughly committed to neoliberal reform of the Chilean economy after about 1975. The so-called Chicago boys, economists trained by Milton Friedman at the University of Chicago, came to dominate Chilean economic policy. Unchecked by political opposition or popular mobilization, the neoliberal model was systematically implemented. Long-protected industries were gutted by sudden exposure to international competition. Unemployment rose. Real wages fell. State-owned firms were privatized (with the major exception of the copper-mining industry, nationalized under Allende in 1971). Public employment was slashed. The result was that Chile experienced two prolonged periods of macroeconomic growth (roughly 1976–1981 and 1985–1996), punctuated by a serious recession (1982–1985).

Although the recession was auspicious for the first serious campaign of public opposition to Pinochet, the authoritarian regime weathered the crisis. By 1988, Pinochet seemed very securely in power. Most observers were surprised when the Concertación actually defeated him in the referendum of that year and went on to win the general elections of 1989 (see Chapter 4). But the center-left Concertación was at pains to assure voters and business interests that it proposed no substantive change in Pinochet's economic policies. It simply proposed to do more to cushion the negative effects of those policies on the poorest people. In fact, the successive Concertación governments of Patricio Aylwin (1990–1994) and Eduardo Frei (1994–1998) have hewed closely to the neoliberal economic policies set by Pinochet, even as they have taken important steps toward departing from the authoritarian legacy in other respects.[9]

Even Cuba, the only Latin American country that has consistently confronted neoliberalism with a serious alternative model (state-led, centrally planned socialist development), has had to accept and adapt to a degree of economic opening that would have been unimaginable before the crisis of European Marxism-Leninism removed its principal external support (Halebsky and Kirk, 1992). The Cuban regime has sought, since the mid-1980s, to correct many of the rigidities and weaknesses of the Soviet model, to mobilize internal capital and initiative, to attract external capital and tourism, all the while avoiding a fundamental weakening of the political leadership of the revolution. Whether Cuba can succeed is a big question.

How May This Diversity Be Explained?

Potential explanations fall into two broad categories: structural and political. The existence of a global concentration of power in the hands of institutions and governments with strong interests in promoting neoliberal policy reforms is, of course, a structural explanation of why no countries and few individual governments have systematically refused to implement such reforms. The diversity of responses to these pressures, however, can itself be explained structurally by referring to the distribution of power within each of the societies. Stephan Haggard and Robert Kaufman (1995), for example, argued that when transitions to democracy have occurred without an economic crisis, the economic policy of the new democratic government will be more constrained by organized parties and interests aligned with the outgoing authoritarian regime. Most clearly in the case of Chile, this pattern helped to guarantee the continuity of neoliberal economic policy. However, there are several cases in which the economic policy of the authoritarian regime was not so consistently neoliberal but still limited the maneuverability of the incoming democratic government if the transition occurred without a severe economic crisis. An example would be Guatemala, where the military regime was distinguished by corruption and repression but lacked a coherent economic strategy. The transition was driven more by U.S. political interests than by economic crisis, but the armed forces and their allies retained strong positions and vested interests in the Guatemalan economy and were capable of frustrating the efforts of successor governments to devise and implement a more coherent economic policy (Jonas, 1991; Handy, 1984).

Conversely, Haggard and Kaufman argued, when transitions have occurred in a context of economic crisis, the outgoing authoritarian regime and its partisans will be less able to constrain economic policies of the newly elected government. Perhaps the clearest example of this is Argentina, where the regime was pushed into the 1982 Malvinas adventure precisely by its weak economic position; the cost of the war and its loss then exacerbated the economic crisis. The newly elected Alfonsín government was under no pressure to adopt an economic policy congruent with that of the military government and indeed adopted the heterodox Austral Plan.

The Haggard-Kaufman analysis may be extended to include the broader question of whether or not the transition was negotiated with the authoritarian government. As we saw in Chapter 4, in the vast majority of cases the transition was negotiated, and economic policy was usually part of the negotiation. In Uruguay, for example, the adhesion of the Broad Front (FA) to the Naval Club Pact with the military government in 1984 committed the principal party of the Left to an indefinite postponement of radical social and economic reform. That agreement was indispensable to the transition. Even though subsequent negotiations for a social pact failed to bring the major unions on-board, the continuing commitment of the FA to democratic stability as a first priority meant that the basic lines of economic policy would continue within the broad neoliberal framework established by the military regime (Gillespie, 1992).

Haggard and Kaufman (1995, pp. 14–15) also suggested that the character of party systems shaped the possibility of effective economic policy:

> Fragmented and polarized party systems heighten party rivalries, magnify conflicts among organized interests, and weaken the capacity of the executive to initiate reform. These very failings can increase the incentives for reformist executives to bypass representative institutions and the constitutional process altogether. Even if they succeed in initiating reform, however, the continuity and credibility of policy in such systems is jeopardized by the difficulty of forging stable electoral, legislative, and bureaucratic majorities, by ideological polarization between government and opposition, and by the resulting exacerbation of political business cycles.

In contrast, they argue, effective policy is more likely in cohesive party systems with limited fragmentation and muted polarization. A good example of the former pattern would be Ecuador, whereas the latter would be exemplified by Bolivia. In Ecuador, a succession of weak governments of varying ideological stripe have consistently faced obstructive parliaments and have been consistently inconsistent in economic policy. In Bolivia, the fragmentation and chaos of 1978–1985 has given way to negotiated coalitions bridging ideological gulfs and capable of formulating and carrying out consistent policies (Conaghan and Malloy, 1994). But Bolivian president Sánchez de Lozada was forced to resign by popular protests in 2003.

This Bolivian example illustrates yet again that the distinction between "structural" and "political" explanations is not black and white. To this point we have been discussing structure, that is, distributions of power that fundamentally shape what is possible. A political explanation, in contrast, concerns choices made by political actors, such as elite settlements. Such choices are in principle undetermined by structure, though structure may set boundaries for choice. The Uruguayan and Bolivian examples we have just considered as illustrating structural effects may as well be used to show the effects of political choices. The decision of the Broad Front to adhere to the Naval Club Pact helped to set the fundamental characteristics of the posttransition party system, a decisive political structure that facilitated the success of the Uruguayan transition. But the Broad Front decision was in no way structurally determined. It was, if anything, a result of political learning, which implies a capacity to transcend and to change structures. Much the same point can be made about the Bolivian example: the historically rooted structures of Bolivian politics could not have produced the transformation of the party system that took place after 1985.

Clearly, then, much of the variation in responses to global neoliberal pressures for reform must be attributed to particular choices made by particular leaders and groups, including mass publics. Why did Paz Estenssoro, Pérez, Fujimori, and Menem all choose to adopt wholly unexpected neoliberal policy departures? It is surely true that they were responding to the structural characteristics of their respective countries, but it is also true that there might have been other responses, as illustrated by Brazil, where neoliberal orthodoxy was consistently evaded until the advent of Fernando Henrique Cardoso as economy minister (1993) and then president (1995).

What Have Been the Results of Neoliberal Policy Reform?

Haggard and Kaufman (1995) summarized the macroeconomic trends for major new democracies in Latin America and Asia (see Table 5.1). The table compares macroeconomic performance (annual averages) of major Latin American and Asian countries that made the transition to democracy during

Table 5.1 Macroeconomic Performance in New Democracies

Indexes	Five Years Before Transition		Transition Year		First Democratic Government		Second Democratic Government	
	Crisis[a]	Noncrisis[b]	Crisis	Noncrisis	Crisis	Noncrisis	Crisis	Noncrisis
GDP Growth	0.6	6.3	0.2	6.2	0.5	7.1	1.5	7.9
Inflation	68.9	17.5	166.8	16.0	896.2	22.3	1,062.3	35.4
Fiscal Deficit/ GDP	−3.7	−2.2	−7.3	−1.1	−7.7	−2.1	−1.8	−0.6
Investment/ GDP	19.4	23.0	17.9	23.8	17.8	26.6	16.0	26.1

Source: Haggard and Kaufman, 1995, pp. 175–177.

Notes: a. Countries that made the transition in a context of economic crisis include Argentina, Bolivia, Brazil, Peru, Uruguay, and the Philippines.

b. Countries that made the transition without a crisis include Chile, Korea, Thailand, and Turkey.

the 1980s, on four dimensions: growth in gross domestic product (GDP), inflation rate, fiscal deficit as a percentage of GDP, and investment as a percentage of GDP. The cases are divided into two categories, those that made the transition during an economic crisis (mostly Latin American) and those that made it without such a crisis (mostly Asian).[10] Data are provided for the five years before the transition, for the year of the transition, for the first democratically elected government, and for the second such government.

These data illustrate several points. First, the noncrisis countries performed consistently better on each of the four indexes than the crisis countries. Second, neither crisis nor noncrisis countries showed consistent improvement in all indexes over the period of the study, though the noncrisis countries did relatively better over time. Third, countries that were in economic crisis at the time of the transition tended to remain in crisis, whereas a noncrisis transition would predict continued avoidance of crisis. Overall, it is obviously better not to have an economic crisis, but the absence of crisis at the time of transition is no guarantee of consistent economic improvement. Neoliberal theory promises such improvement in the long run, but evidently the run used by Haggard and Kaufman is not long enough.

There is ample critical literature concerning the impact and accomplishments of neoliberalism in Latin America and globally. Peter Evans has long been committed to the view that—neoliberal antistatism notwithstanding—development has historically required leadership from a strong and effective state (Evans, 1979, 1995; Evans, Rueschemeyer, and Skocpol, 1987). Recent edited volumes brought a critical perspective to the analysis of the neoliberal challenge.[11] Numerous studies of individual countries also addressed the effect of neoliberal reforms.[12] Luiz Carlos Bresser Pereira, José María Maravall, and Adam Przeworski (1993) offered a very influential social democratic approach to economic reform.

Hard evidence remains inconclusive, but the most common criticisms of neoliberalism center on an alleged increase in inequality, poverty, and unemployment growing from unfettered capitalism and the loss of sovereignty implied in the subordination of state policy to the control of international lenders and transnational and national capital. Carlos Vilas (1995a, pp. 154–155), for example, provided data on income distribution trends during the 1980s in four Latin American countries (see Table 5.2). These data showed that income did indeed become more concentrated in Brazil and especially Guatemala, but somewhat less concentrated in Costa Rica and Mexico. James Petras and Fernando Ignacio Leiva (1994, pp. 128–129) showed data for Chile that indicated that income distribution did indeed become more unequal in the years before the transition to democracy but may have become slightly less unequal since 1988 (see Table 5.3).

Table 5.4 carries the trends into the late 1990s, analyzing the ratio of income of the lowest to the highest 20 percent in each of five countries. While Costa Rica displays a consistently moderate ratio and Brazil shows a consistently high one, clear trends toward more or less concentration cannot be discerned.

John Weeks (1995, p. 121) showed that GDP growth per capita became negative during the 1980s for virtually all of Latin America after being positive everywhere but Nicaragua during the 1970s. At the same time, exports, which supposedly would be promoted by neoliberal policies, in fact grew

Table 5.2 Changes in Household Income Polarization, 1980s

	Year	Share of National Income, Household Income Category				Share of the Highest 20% Divided by Lowest 20%
		Lowest 20%	Middle 60%	Top 20%	Top 10%	
Brazil	1983	2.4	35.0	62.6	46.2	26.1
	1989	2.1	30.4	67.5	51.3	32.1
Costa Rica	1986	3.3	42.2	54.5	38.8	16.5
	1989	4.0	45.2	50.8	34.1	12.7
Guatemala	1981	5.5	39.5	55.0	40.8	10.0
	1989	2.1	34.9	63.0	46.6	30.0
Mexico	1984	4.1	40.1	55.9	39.5	13.6
	1989	4.4	42.1	53.5	—	12.1
	1992	5.0	40.8	54.2	38.2	10.8

Source: Vilas, 1995a, p. 155. Copyright © 1995 by Westview Press. Reprinted by permission of Westview Press.

Table 5.3   Chile: Changes in Income Distribution, 1978–1990

Quintile	1978[a]	1988	1989	1990
1 (poorest)	4.6	4.2	4.6	4.9
2	9.5	7.5	7.9	8.4
3	14.1	10.9	11.3	11.5
4	19.9	16.9	16.6	17.2
5 (richest)	51.9	60.4	59.6	58.0

Source: Petras and Leiva, 1994, p. 129. Copyright © 1994 by Westview Press. Reprinted by permission of Westview Press.

Note: a. May not add to 100 due to rounding.

more slowly in the 1980s than in the 1970s in all cases save Argentina, Costa Rica, and Venezuela. Although performance may have improved in some cases in the 1990s, living standards certainly have a way to go even to regain 1980 levels, and export growth has been disappointing (Haggard and Kaufman, 1995; Calderón and dos Santos, 1995). For the 1990s, annual growth rates in GDP per capita are provided in Table 5.5. Note that low and negative growth rates are concentrated among the poorer countries (they are listed in descending order of the United Nations Development Programme's Human Development Index), with the exception of Colombia (which underwent a prolonged political and military crisis) and Mexico (which suffered a severe financial crisis).

We may, at a minimum, conclude from these data that neoliberal economic reforms have been associated with a worsening of economic conditions for the majority, which may or may not prove temporary. The transition to democracy has clearly not shielded people from these consequences, but there

Table 5.4   Trends in Income Share, 1980–1998 (ratio of highest 20% to lowest 20%)

	1980–1987	1981–1993	1997–1998
Brazil	26.1	32.1	29.7
Gini Index	0.57		0.61
Chile		18.3	18.6
Gini Index	0.46		0.57
Costa Rica	16.5	12.7	11.5
Gini Index	0.42		0.46
Guatemala	10.0	30.0	15.8
Gini Index			0.56
Mexico		13.6	16.5
Gini Index			0.53

Sources: United Nations Development Programme, 1991, pp. 152–153; 1996, pp. 170–171; 2002, pp. 194–197.

Table 5.5   Annual Growth Rates, GDP per Capita, 1990–2000

Argentina	3.0
Bolivia	1.6
Brazil	1.5
Chile	5.2
Colombia	–0.6
Costa Rica	3.0
Cuba	3.7
Ecuador	–0.3
El Salvador	2.6
Guatemala	1.4
Haiti	–2.7
Honduras	0.4
Mexico	1.4
Nicaragua	0.6
Panama	2.3
Paraguay	–0.4
Peru	2.9
Uruguay	2.6
Venezuela	3.3

Source: United Nations Development Programme, 2002, pp. 190–193.

is some evidence that democratic governments have at least been able to mitigate the worst effects of neoliberalism. Macroeconomic performance has generally improved, particularly as regards inflation, but improvements have been slow to manifest themselves in daily lives. The "long run" so dear to neoliberal theorists has yet to come (Przeworski et al., 1996).

The issue of the alleged loss of sovereignty is even less susceptible to measurement but is no less significant as a political controversy.[13] Every stabilization plan negotiated with the IMF occasioned embittered criticism from nationalists and leftists upset at the apparent loss of national control over economic policy and indeed over the economy itself. Proposals for privatization of state-owned enterprises (e.g., banks, insurance companies, mines, petroleum) proved particularly neuralgic: even in Chile, paragon of neoliberal virtue, the major copper mines, nationalized by Allende, were kept in state hands by Pinochet and his democratically elected successors. There has been some privatization, notably in Argentina under Menem, and some opening of state-owned firms for private investment (e.g., in Bolivia), but on the whole, this has not turned out to be a central feature of the neoliberal reform process. More broadly, the IMF (and indeed, the Washington consensus) has been widely condemned as allowing the poorest to pay the costs of an adjustment that will primarily benefit the rich and the multinational corporations. By the early 1990s, in fact, the IMF and the World Bank were showing signs of sensitivity to these criticisms, as they promoted programs to soften the impact of structural adjustment programs on the poorest sectors (e.g., World Bank, 1991).

The neoliberal demand that state employment and social services be reduced is quite fundamental and has elicited strong resistance. The people affected naturally protested in any way they could. Relatively progressive states such as Costa Rica and Uruguay had achieved enviable levels of human development on such dimensions as life expectancy and literacy, largely on the basis of heavy state investment in social services over many decades. These benefits understandably came to be seen as rights or entitlements, and any state efforts to control their costs elicited resistance. Even in less progressive states, such as Peru, the minimal and miserable social services provided by the state were often vital to the very survival of the poorest and to some semblance of decency for the poor. At the same time, the bureaucracies of the state and state-owned enterprises were everywhere a principal source of employment for the middle class, emerging in growing numbers from secondary schools and universities. The prospect that good, secure jobs and a respectable living standard might not continue to be available provoked bitter resistance in most countries from both public employees and students. One result of this resistance is that in most countries, public employment has not been reduced nearly as much as neoliberal reformers would like.

Neoliberalism, in short, has had decidedly mixed results so far. The Latin American economies are now quite different than they were twenty or even ten years ago, but it is not yet demonstrable that they are better off, even at the macroeconomic level. At the microeconomic level of individual citizens, workers, and consumers, the costs of the "lost decade" of the 1980s weigh heavily and have yet to be paid.

How Have Neoliberal Reforms Affected Democracy?

It has been repeatedly shown, with steadily increasing statistical sophistication, that there is a positive association worldwide between economic development and democracy.[14] However, it is quite clear that in the specific context of Latin America in the 1980s and 1990s, this global correlation does not suffice. One problem is that countries across a wide range of economic development have crossed the threshold to democracy more or less simultaneously. A second problem is that democracy in the more developed countries is not necessarily more stable than in less developed Latin American countries (e.g., Bolivian democracy was arguably more stable in the 1990s than Argentine or Brazilian democracy). A third problem (on which this section will focus) is that economic change (e.g., neoliberal reform), even if it promotes economic development, may destabilize political democracy.[15]

Karen Remmer (1990, 1991b, 1993) systematically investigated the political impact of economic crisis in Latin America. She found that democracies on the whole have coped at least as well with economic crises as authoritarian regimes. She concluded that economic crises during the 1980s did undermine support for incumbents and did promote higher levels of electoral volatility, but without fostering political extremism, the exhaustion of elite consensus, or democratic breakdown. Conversely, she found that elections during the 1980s enhanced rather than undermined the capacity of leaders to address macroeconomic problems. In short, Remmer argued that on the whole, democratic regimes are more capable and less fragile than the conventional wisdom allows for. Indeed, the very durability of democratic regimes in contexts of economic crisis and radical neoliberal reform is testimony to the adaptability of this type of regime. Liberal democracy in the Latin America of the 1980s and 1990s is clearly not a hothouse flower.

Kurt Weyland (2002) and Javier Corrales (2002) each carried out comparative analyses of the politics of neoliberal reform, with Weyland comparing the experiences of Argentina, Brazil, Peru, and Venezuela, while Corrales compared Argentina and Venezuela. Their approaches differed substantially. Weyland explained the distinct patterns he found on the basis of prospect theory, based on social psychological research, while Corrales argued that Menem succeeded in Argentina while Pérez failed in Venezuela because the former had a cooperative relationship with his ruling Peronist party, while the latter confronted increasingly strong opposition from his party, Democratic Action (AD). Both authors appeared untroubled by the "delegative democracy" syndrome, wherein an elected president completely reverses electoral promises on the grounds that the people, in electing him, delegated policy discretion to him.

Nevertheless there is ample cause for concern. These concerns relate on the one hand to the issue of inequality and on the other to the issue of the meaningfulness of popular participation. As we saw in Chapter 1, the liberal theory of democracy assumes the equality of all citizens. Clearly, this is a goal that is never fully achieved, but the advent of neoliberal free market reforms poses a particular challenge to the assumption of equality because the unfettered market tends to produce inequality as a result of multiple levels of competition: some win, some lose. And, obviously, economic power enhances political power. Latin America as a region has been characterized by extreme inequalities since the conquest; neoliberal reforms certainly have not diminished that inequality and in most cases have probably made it a bit worse.

Liberal democracy entails a mechanism by which the people, the citizens, can choose those who will govern (Schumpeter, 1950) or choose desired policies (Downs, 1957). The claim of liberal democracy to be democratic rests on the ability of the people to choose their governors or affirm preferred policies, with reasonable assurance that the authorities thus chosen will implement the policies thus approved. However, in the neoliberal era, it has been quite common for newly elected presidents not only to fail to carry out their promises but indeed to carry out policies diametrically opposed to what they promised (O'Donnell, 1994). This was clearly the case with Paz Estenssoro in Bolivia (1985–1989), Menem in Argentina (1989–1998), and Pérez in Venezuela (1989–1993). Interestingly, only in the last case was the president called to account.

One of the most prominent features of neoliberal policymaking poses serious challenges to democracy. Because neoliberal reforms typically damage the immediate well-being of many, it is usually considered necessary to insulate economic policymaking from the democratic political process (Corrales, 2003). This has been particularly evident in Bolivia, Argentina, and Peru, but there is a widespread tendency to put economic technocrats in control of economic policy, on the assumption that the long-term public interest will thereby be better served than by making policy responsive to the will of an allegedly ill-informed public (Corrales, 2003). Now, it is certainly true that the public may be ill-informed, and liberal democratic theory since Madison and Tocqueville has been concerned to provide checks on popular sovereignty for that reason. Still, what is left of democracy when candidates gain election by telling direct falsehoods and then vest policymaking power in officials beyond the reach of the people?

We have seen that liberalism embodies a contradiction between the liberal democratic presupposition of equality and the tendency of economic liberalism to promote inequality. "The real world of democracy" (Macpherson, 1972) is one in which economic power distorts political equality, in which citizens have only minimum and episodic control over government, and in which citizen participation in politics is largely restricted to voting (and may well not even include that). This pathology is characteristic of all liberal democracies, not merely those of Latin America. In Latin America, indeed, the principal political agenda of the 1980s and 1990s has been to secure, to institutionalize liberal democracy; the issue of how to improve it has had a lower priority.

State Weakness and Militarism

Since colonial times, Latin America has been plagued by states that claimed extensive authority but lacked the real capability to exercise it. The contemporary liberal democracies continue to display this feature, and as a result have great difficulty mounting any coherent program. Militarism has long been a response to state weakness, as those who control military force and organization come to see themselves as uniquely qualified to lead their countries, and militarism in new and old forms continues to be important in liberal democratic regimes today.

State weakness has many aspects. Weak states lack the resources to control their own territory and population. They can neither tax their own population nor attract or extract resources from the exterior. This incapacity in turn means that the government will be administratively incapable of carrying out any policy for the distribution or redistribution of resources, because it does not control those resources. Those with military power have historically moved into the vacuum of a weak state to take it over, but with rare exceptions such military regimes have done little to strengthen state institutions and capabilities. On the contrary, most military rulers have sucked the society dry for their own benefit and left the state poorer and weaker.

Haiti provides the most extreme example of this pattern. From its beginning after the world's only successful social revolution by slaves broke French domination in the early nineteenth century, Haiti was governed by an almost unbroken series of corrupt dictators, often manipulated by the United States and European powers to serve their interests. The country had almost no capacity to fulfill any of the normal functions of a state. The United States sent in the marines from 1916 to 1934 with the ostensible goal of building up the country's institutions and infrastructure. While the physical infrastructure was undoubtedly improved, the postoccupation state was just as weak, and came under the immediate domination of the constabulary force trained by the marines, the Garde d'Haiti. The military regime of Paul Magloire was succeeded by the civilian dictatorship of François Duvalier and his son Jean-Claude Duvalier, which lasted until the latter was overthrown by the military in 1986. Throughout this period the authoritarian state did essentially nothing for the vast majority of Haitians, though it did have the coercive capability to intimidate opponents. With the overthrow of Duvalier, Haiti entered a transitional period, but whether it will be a transition to democracy remains uncertain. Father Jean-Bertrand Aristide built on his support among the urban poor to win the first honest popular election in Haitian history in 1990, but was overthrown within a year. Finally restored to office in 1994, replaced by his ally René Préval in 1995, elected for a new term in 1999, Aristide was consistently unable to overcome state weakness, a disloyal opposition, skepticism among aid donors, and his own corruptibility. Aristide was overthrown in early 2004. The mass of Haitians remain as miserable as ever, and Haiti's prospects for establishing a stable democracy are quite low (Mintz, 1995; Fatton, 2002).

The Colombian state is far stronger that the Haitian state, but it also confronts challenges far greater and more complex than those of Haiti. The country has suffered from persistent rural insurgency since the late 1940s, which by the 1960s evolved into several leftist guerrilla movements. Two of those movements, the Revolutionary Armed Forces of Colombia (FARC) and the National Liberation Army (ELN), are still active. By the 1980s, drug cartels trafficking in marijuana, cocaine, and ultimately heroin were well established. By the late 1980s, rightist paramilitary forces emerged, at first tacitly collaborating with the Colombian armed forces to carry out dirty work such as assassinations and terrorism that the military did not want to be associated with. By the late 1990s, however, the paramilitaries appeared increasingly autonomous. The drug trade increasingly penetrated all parts of Colombian society, so that the guerrillas, the paramilitaries, the police, the military, and the political leadership were all to some degree compromised by involvement with illegal drugs. The result of this vicious complex was that Colombian authorities were consistently unable to control much of the national territory and a substantial fraction of the population. Oddly, national political processes, including elections and the conduct of normal government business, go on, in Bogotá and elsewhere, floating like a boat on a lake while vicious struggles for power go on just below the surface. The Colombian military, with a key role in counterinsurgency and counternarcotics strategy, enjoys substantial autonomy from civilian control, and virtual immunity from prosecution, but has not since the 1950s sought to displace the constitutional government (Cepeda Ulloa, 2003; Pizarro Leongómez, 2003).

Peru, like Colombia, confronted prolonged challenges from guerrilla insurgencies, most notably in the 1980s and early 1990s. The Peruvian armed forces, after some initial mistakes, succeeded fairly well in co-opting peasant resistance to the Shining Path (Sendero Luminoso) insurgency, which was dealt a decisive blow by the capture of most of its leadership in the early 1990s. Outside the military, however, the Peruvian state proved extremely weak and unable to formulate and implement key economic and social policies. Thus the government of Alan García left office in 1990 with the economy in freefall and the state in shambles. Alberto Fujimori was able to restore some state capability, but concentrated power so much in his own hands that when he was forced out at the end of the decade his successors had very little to work with. The armed forces have insisted on immunity from prosecution for human rights violations during the war against Shining Path, on the grounds that they were fighting a guerrilla war in which their opponents were notoriously savage. On the other hand, the military has shown no recent inclination to take power (Degregori, 2003).

Ecuador, unlike Peru and Colombia, never confronted a major internal insurgency, but it has suffered chronically weak national governments unable to formulate and carry out consistent economic policies to confront persistently poor economic conditions. An increasingly mobilized populace has posed challenges to a succession of elected governments that they have been unable to meet. The result since the 1990s has been worsening governmental instability, as two recent presidents, Abdalá Bucaram and Jamil Mahuad, have failed to complete their terms. The armed forces have responded to this chronic governmental weakness, not by seizing power but by acting as moderators. One apparent exception was the coup that removed Mahuad in 2000, in which several midranking officers participated, including Colonel Lucio Gutiérrez, who would be elected president in 2002. However, the junta resulting from that coup was dissolved within hours as the high command took control and passed constitutional authority to Mahuad's vice president (Saint-Upéry, 2002; Lucero, 2001).

It is essential to note in this context that an international climate favoring constitutional democracy is now supporting a number of very weak democratic regimes that might otherwise have succumbed to coups. The United States, the European Union, and the international lenders that they control, along with democratically elected governments across Latin America, will work to deter coups or pressure coup-makers to retreat.

■ Party Decay, Delegative Democracy, and Neopopulism

As noted in Chapter 4, political parties are critical to the practice of modern, large-scale liberal democracies. Without them, there is no adequate mechanism to organize the popular will to produce a mandate, nor is there a reliable means to harness those elected into working teams of government and opposition. Parties have been a central feature of Latin American politics since early in the independence period. Yet in the present epoch of widespread liberal democracy, parties have come on hard times. Parties have been widely criticized—with reason—as elitist and exclusionary, keeping the citizenry out of meaningful involvement in governance and excluding counterelites who might challenge the vested interests of those in power. Parties have been frequently portrayed as facilitating the corruption of political elites and the subversion of electoral probity. They have, in short, been portrayed as impediments to the realization of true democracy, rather than as essential means to that end.

Across the region, elites and masses have drawn on the repertoire of their political culture to respond to these perceived shortcomings of parties and party systems. Two sorts of responses are especially worthy of note: delegative democracy and neopopulism. Guillermo O'Donnell's model of delegative democracy has been previously described; here it should be noted that the major cases of delegative democracy have occurred precisely in a context of party decay. Carlos Menem in Argentina took office after the ignominious collapse of the Alfonsín government and the Radical Party, and he presided over the progressive fragmentation of the Peronists. Alberto Fujimori in Peru won his first presidential election after the successive failures of the only two nationally institutionalized parties, Popular Action (AP) and the American Popular Revolutionary Alliance (APRA), in successive presidencies from 1980 to 1990. Carlos Andrés Pérez in Venezuela won the presidency in defiance of his own party leadership and systematically marginalized the party in pursuing his program of neoliberal reforms. Hugo Chávez won the presidency ten years later, walking on the ashes of the party system whose destruction Pérez had initiated. Abdalá Bucaram in Ecuador won election in a chronically inchoate party system and contributed to its further dissolution.

Most of these "delegative democrats" came to office making a populist appeal. That is, they purported to speak for the "common people" and to lead them against the abuses of the powerful, while avoiding systematic Marxist analysis or divisive class appeals. But whereas classic Latin American populists such as Perón and Vargas sought to build an active, clientelistic state capable of channeling resources to their supporters among the urban workers and industrialists, these latter-day neopopulists have used their popular mandates to begin dismantling the very statist apparatus of import substitution and welfare state that resulted from the earlier populism. The neopopulists share with their predecessors a propensity to establish a direct personal link with their supporters, eschewing the mediation of an institutionalized party. Such political organization as they tolerate takes the form of a personalist apparatus dedicated to promoting the leader, though it may often be called a popular movement.

The dynamics of neopopulism and party decay can be illustrated with several cases, and contrasted with other cases wherein party systems have not decayed, or wherein the party system is actually becoming more institutionalized. In Venezuela, the decline of popular confidence in the two main parties, AD and the Independent Committee for Political and Electoral Organization (COPEI), in the course of the long economic decline of the 1980s was not arrested by the adoption of significant state reforms in the late 1980s and early 1990s. President Pérez's unexpected blitzkrieg of neoliberal reforms, after winning the presidency with a populist campaign in 1988, initiated the acute stage of Venezuela's political crisis. Massive popular riots and protests, two unsuccessful military coups, and the president's impeachment preceded the next national elections in 1993. The two major parties lost their electoral dominance as Pérez was succeeded by Rafael Caldera at the head of a weak ad hoc coalition. The emergence of former coup leader Hugo Chávez as a strongly populist critic of the corrupt "partyarchy" sealed the doom of the old system in the elections of 1998. But given the widespread, profound suspicion of parties, Chávez's resistance to institutionalizing his own movement, and the visceral intensity of the opposition to Chávez, it is difficult to discern the shape of a renewed democratic regime in Venezuela (Ellner and Hellinger, 2003).

With the transition to democracy in Peru, there were two established parties (AP and APRA) capable of winning the presidency, and they successively occupied the post from 1980 to 1985 and 1985 to 1990. Faced with the ruthless Shining Path insurgency and increasingly difficult economic conditions, both governments were seen as failures. Thus in the election of 1990, the presidential runoff was between two antiparty candidates, a writer, Mario Vargas Llosa (representing the traditional upper class), and a Japanese-Peruvian agronomist, Alberto Fujimori (appealing to middle-class and poor *cholos,* or people of color). Fujimori, though previously unknown, won easily. Subsequently, in 1992, he short-circuited his problems in Congress and the courts by staging a coup and dissolving these bodies. After a new constitution was drafted that was much more favorable to executive authority, Fujimori subsequently arranged a constitutional amendment to permit his reelection in 1995. He achieved genuine popular support by defeating Shining Path and stabilizing the economy, but by 2000, when he sought another reelection, he relied heavily on fraud. His principal opponent in that election, Alejandro Toledo (also an antiparty candidate), refused to participate in the runoff on grounds of fraud, but did lead massive popular protests after the regime was embarrassed by videotapes of bribery. After Fujimori fled the country and faxed his resignation from Japan, new elections were held that were won by Toledo over former president Alan García of APRA. Toledo, however, proved an ineffective president, and it remains possible that the old parties, APRA and AP, will be able to stage a comeback after more than a decade in the wilderness (Klarén, 2000; Degregori, 2003).

In Argentina, the presidency of Raúl Alfonsín (Radical Civic Union) was brought to an early end by a massive economic crisis in 1989. He was succeeded by the Peronist nominee, Carlos Menem, who had run a classic Peronist populist campaign. Then he quickly implemented massive neoliberal reforms, which were initially quite unpopular, but which did in due course stabilize the economy. Thus Menem was able to get the constitution amended to permit his reelection in 1995. His policies, however, helped to split the Peronists and to give new life to the dispirited Radicals. By 1999, his attempt to gain another reelection was frustrated in a context of renewed economic troubles. The Radical Fernando de la Rua was elected president, but proved remarkably ineffectual. With the economy deteriorating badly, de la Rua was forced to resign in late 2001. After the interim presidency of Peronist Eduardo Duhalde, new elections were held in 2002. A fragmented Peronist movement dominated the polls, as the opposition parties remained discredited and in disarray. Menem qualified for the runoff, but withdrew when it became evident that he would lose to fellow Peronist Nestor Kirchner. Although Kirchner was able to use the widespread sense of crisis to push through a number of important initiatives to stabilize the economy, his organizational base is weak because the Peronists have largely ceased to exist as an organization, while the other major parties are extremely weak. Argentina's party system is thus extremely inchoate, a casualty of chronic economic mismanagement and neopopulist leadership (Corrales, 2002; Weyland, 2002; Levitsky, 2003).

In Ecuador, the party system has never been highly institutionalized, and has become more inchoate. The traditional rivalry between the coastal and Andean regions has been increasingly swamped by the assertiveness of indigenous mobilization and a proclivity on the part of the electorate to turn away from established parties and toward strong individual leaders. The National Indigenous Confederation of Ecuador (CONAIE) used nonviolent popular mobilizations throughout the 1990s to paralyze the country and exact concessions from a succession of governments. In January 2000, such a mobilization was directed at the government of Jamil Mahuad, which was attempting to impose neoliberal reforms and to implement the use of the U.S. dollar as the official currency. Elements of the armed forces charged with controlling the protest in fact collaborated in permitting the protesters to occupy Congress, and to force the removal of Mahuad. A short-lived junta included the leader of CONAIE and one of the collaborating officers, Colonel Lucio Gutiérrez, but the high command of the armed forces, under international pressure, intervened to force the transfer of power to Mahuad's vice president, Gustavo Noboa. In the presidential elections of 2002, however, Gutiérrez was elected after a campaign in which he stressed his opposition to neoliberalism and dollarization. He attracted strong support from CONAIE and from the indigenous-based political party, Pachakutic, but once in office adopted a more moderate line and began to make his peace with the political and economic establishment. In doing so, he secured a happier fate than that of President Abdalá Bucaram, a firebrand populist who was elected in 1996, to the horror of that same establishment. When he reversed course and began to implement sweeping neoliberal reforms, he faced massive popular protests and was impeached and deposed by Congress in 1997. Whereas Bucaram abandoned his former base without building a new one, Gutiérrez proceeded more deliberately and less provocatively, and survived in spite of the disillusionment of his erstwhile supporters (Lucero, 2001; Saint-Upéry, 2002).

In these and other cases, inchoate party systems interacted with neopopulist, antiparty candidates and a proclivity to delegative democracy to produce extreme instability as citizens became disillusioned with their inability to produce governments that would fulfill promises and serve the perceived interests of those who put them in office. In contrast, the polities with the most institutionalized party systems (Costa Rica, Uruguay, and Chile) all maintained political stability in the 1990s even as they confronted serious economic stresses and political tensions. In none of the three was there an important antiparty, neopopulist presidential candidacy, and none witnessed the sweeping policy reversals characteristic of delegative democracy.[16]

In this context, one of the more pleasant surprises has been the progressive institutionalization of an inclusive party system in El Salvador, a country wracked by civil war in the 1980s. Since the peace settlement of 1990 between the government and the Farabundo Martí National Liberation Front (FMLN), the latter has been incorporated as an accepted political party able to compete in local and national elections. The FMLN is well established as the country's second political force, and may soon be able to capture the presidency, as the incumbent party, the National Renewal Alliance (ARENA), shows signs of weakness after over a decade in power. Again, the increasing strength of the party system has anchored the political process, discouraged the emergence of messianic neopopulists, and dampened tendencies to delegative democracy (Zamora, 2003; Call, 2003).

Popular Mobilization, Social Movements, and Insurgencies

An important sign, and at times an important cause of destabilization of any political regime, is the emergence of popular protests or violent outbursts. Many of the fragile democratic regimes emerging in the 1980s have confronted such challenges. When they are relatively well organized but largely nonviolent, we call them "social movements." Well-organized movements committed to violent opposition are called "insurgencies."

Outbursts of popular protests, including spontaneous riots, are a sign that some significant part of the population feels serious grievances toward the government. They are always a challenge to an incumbent government, but rarely suffice to bring it down unless supported by significant elements of the political elite, such as the armed forces or opposition parties. Such relatively spontaneous protests have played a significant role in bringing down elected governments in Ecuador, Guatemala, Venezuela, and Argentina. In Ecuador, massive popular protests against the neoliberal turn of populist president Abdalá Bucaram established a political contest in which he could be impeached and removed by Congress in 1997. In 1993, the attempt of President Jorge Serrano to emulate the successful seizure of dictatorial power by *autogolpe* (self-coup) of Alberto Fujimori in Peru was blocked by popular protests, and the armed forces forced his resignation. In Venezuela, the massive riots called the "Caracazo" in 1989, following the implementation of President Pérez's surprising neoliberal program, started his slide toward impeachment in 1993. And in Argentina, popular protests against the incompetence of Fernando de la Rua's government in the face of a severe economic crisis led to his resignation in 2001.

As we saw in Chapter 4, social movements played an important role in many countries in promoting the transition from military rule. Under democratic regimes, moreover, social movements constitute an important component of the "social capital" that is vital to a healthy democracy, according to the arguments of Robert Putnam and others. Nevertheless, under conditions of state weakness, social movements may pose a serious challenge to the stability of democratic regimes that are incapable of responding adequately to the felt needs of important constituencies. The indigenous social movement CONAIE in Ecuador was the catalyst for the crisis that led to the removal of Jamil Mahuad in 2000. Movements of indigenous and peasants have repeatedly roiled Bolivian politics in the past twenty years, weakening a succession of presidents but not yet bringing any down. The Landless Movement (MST) poses a significant challenge to regional and national authority in Brazil, as it actively promotes land occupations and demands state action to redistribute land, in the face of often violent resistance and repression by the large landowners and their allies in the state governments. The MST cannot bring down a government, but it did help to change the political climate to make possible the election of Lula da Silva in 2002.

In the wake of the successful Cuban Revolution, revolutionary insurgencies were attempted in virtually every Latin American country. In most, they failed during the 1960s. In some (e.g., Argentina, Uruguay, Chile, Brazil, Peru, Bolivia, El Salvador, Guatemala) their existence served to justify military dictatorship and repression. The insurgent Sandinista National Liberation Front (FSLN) actually took power in Nicaragua and held it until 1990 in spite of massive U.S. attempts to bring it down. By the mid-1990s, however, revolutionary insurgencies were no longer significant anywhere except Colombia, Mexico, and Peru.

In Colombia, the long-standing insurgencies mounted by the FARC and the ELN remained active in the early twenty-first century, maintaining control over significant parts of the national territory staging attacks elsewhere, notwithstanding the concerted countinsurgency offensive mounted by President Alvaro Uribe after his election in 2002. Although neither insurgency is positioned to take power, their persistence over decades has chronically distorted Colombian politics (Cepeda Ulloa, 2003; Pizarro Leongómez, 2003). Peru did not have a national insurgency in the 1960s or 1970s, but with the transition to democracy in 1980, the Maoist Shining Path burst onto the scene with a series of bloody attacks in the southern Andes. A smaller guerrilla group, the *fidelista* Tupac Amaru Revolutionary Movement (MRTA) was also active during the period. Over a decade of guerrilla war followed, in which the rebels seemed to be gaining the upper hand until the capture or death of their main leaders in the early 1990s. Shining Path, however, was never totally defeated, and reemerged on a small scale under Alejandro Toledo's inept presidency in the early years of the twenty-first century. As in Colombia, the insurgents are not likely to take power, but their presence has distorted and distracted national politics (Degregori, 2003).

Mexico has not faced a national insurgency since 1920, but has had several organized regional uprisings. The Zapatista Army of National Liberation (EZLN) staged a rebellion in Chiapas in early 1994 to protest the implementation of the North American Free Trade Agreement between Mexico, the United States, and Canada. Based among the Mayan population of rural areas in Chiapas, the EZLN made no attempt to sustain armed resistance after the initial outburst. Rather, it used its newfound notoriety to protect itself from government repression, drew the government into prolonged negotiations, and carried out an extensive information campaign on both the national and international levels. The EZLN steadfastly resisted making any political alliance with the main leftist political party, the PRD, and rejected electoral participation as fraudulent. It preferred to act as a kind of national conscience on the plight of the peasantry and the indigenous minority (Harvey, 1998; Peeler, 2003d; Nash, 2003).

Crisis, Breakdown, and Reequilibration

While no established democracy has broken down completely and been replaced by an authoritarian regime since the second wave began in the late 1970s, there have been several close calls. Moreover, even the democratic regimes that have avoided close calls and acute crises have for the most part existed in a state of chronic crisis. The major cases of acute crisis and near-breakdown in the period were Peru, Ecuador, Venezuela, and Argentina.[17] Among the numerous cases of democracies in chronic crisis, we will here review Bolivia, Guatemala, Nicaragua, and Paraguay.

Peru's democratic regime, reinitiated in 1980, never escaped from crisis and had several brushes with complete breakdown. The challenge of the Shining Path insurgency drained resources and attention from critical social and economic problems. Both the insurgency and socioeconomic conditions had reached acute crisis by 1990, when antiparty candidate Alberto Fujimori was elected. Fujimori chose, in 1992, to checkmate the obstacles to his political dominance by staging a self-coup. Suspending the constitution and closing Congress and the courts, he terminated the democratic regime that had been established in 1980. A new constitutional order, with more power in the hands of the president, was established the next year. That order was twice manipulated to permit Fujimori's reelection, but shortly after the second reelection he was forced to flee the country in the face of a corruption scandal. A caretaker government presided over elections in which Alejandro Toledo defeated former president Alan García. Toledo's government, however, was so inept that popular disillusionment grew rapidly. For over two decades, the country has moved from crisis to crisis, without ever quite losing its formal democracy (Degregori, 2003; Levitsky and Cameron, 2003).

Similarly, Ecuador's democratic regime has never been secure since its reestablishment in 1978. Indeed, the intensity of crises has been worse since 1990. As Terry Karl (1997) argued, the exploitation of significant petroleum deposits in the Amazon Basin failed to solve basic economic and social problems, and a succession of democratic governments of Right and Left came and went, on schedule but without glory. The emergence after 1990 of a major indigenous movement posed an additional challenge to a state that was already just barely coping. The result was increased instability. Firebrand populist Abdalá Bucaram was elected in 1996 and impeached and removed from power in 1997. Former Quito mayor Jamil Mahuad was forced out in 2000 by a CONAIE mobilization that was backed by a military faction. The leader of that military faction, Lucio Gutiérrez, was elected president in 2002, but soon lost the support of the indigenous movement when his economic policies proved too conservative. As with Peru, Ecuador has endured almost constant crisis, but the regime has never quite fallen (Lucero, 2001; Saint-Upéry, 2002; Peeler, 2003a; Gerlach, 2001).

Venezuela at the time of the 1988 elections was regarded as the most consolidated Latin American democracy, after Costa Rica, but since then has witnessed acute crisis and regime transformation. The massive riots in 1989 (the Caracazo) followed President Pérez's surprising turn in a radically neoliberal direction. Two attempted military coups in 1992 and Pérez's impeachment and removal from office in 1993 set the stage for the election of former president Caldera as the formerly dominant party system dissolved. Caldera's failure to right the economy cleared the way for the election of former coup leader Hugo Chávez in 1998. Chávez presided over a major institutional shift to a new constitution that embodied a move from the checks and balances of the previous liberal democracy to a greater emphasis on popular sovereignty as embodied in a very powerful presidency. With a strong base among the poorest part of the population, Chávez has proved a deeply polarizing figure. The days of Venezuela's pacted democracy and partyarchy are over, but what the future holds remains quite unclear (Ramos Rollón, 2002; Ellner and Hellinger, 2003).

Argentina, like Peru, spent much of the 1990s under a dominant, authoritarian, but democratically elected leader, Carlos Menem. Menem came to power on the heels of the disastrous economic failure of the Alfonsín administration in 1989, and remained in power for ten years by arranging to change the constitution to permit his reelection. His early success in stabilizing the economy built strong support for his reelection, but by 1999, with the economy deteriorating, he was forced to retire and was replaced by the Radical candidate, Fernando de la Rua. Disastrous mismanagement of the economy led to de la Rua's resignation in 2001. The new president elected the following year, Nestor Kirchner, had some early success, but a century of economic malpractice in Argentina does not leave much room for optimism (Levitsky, 2003).

Other fragile democracies have not witnessed crises quite so spectacular as those just described, but they have not been far from the ragged edge. Paraguay, after the overthrow of the dictatorship of Alfredo Stroessner in 1989, has struggled over the terms and the depth of democratization. The long-dominant Colorado Party sought to make the transition from being the main support of an authoritarian regime to being a dominant party in a democracy, but in the process developed strong tensions between a faction (led by Luis María Argaña) rooted in the state apparatus and another (led by General Lino Oviedo and Juan Carlos Wasmosy) based on politically connected business. The latter faction got Wasmosy elected president in 1993, but three years later Wasmosy relieved Oviedo of his command. When the general tried to stage a coup and failed, he went into hiding and ultimately exile, but he continued to wield power as a factional leader. In party primaries in 1997, Oviedo was nominated as the party's presidential candidate for the 1998 elections, but was ruled ineligible by the Supreme Court when it upheld his conviction for the 1996 rebellion. His running mate (Raúl Cubas) then became the presidential candidate (with Argaña as vice president) and won against two opposition candidates, with 54 percent of the vote. When President Cubas pardoned Oviedo, his Colorado opponents teamed up with the opposition in Congress to impeach him. With the vote on whether to remove him approaching, Vice President Argaña was assassinated. The Chamber of Deputies then voted (by a two-thirds majority) to remove Cubas. After several days of conflict in the streets, Cubas was finally induced (partly by a call from Brazilian president Fernando Henrique Cardozo) to resign; the president of Congress, Senator Luis González Macchi, was sworn in. González Macchi established a government of national unity, including the two main opposition parties, diluting the Colorado monopoly on power for the first time in decades. Nevertheless, faced with a declining economy and charges of corruption, González Macchi was himself impeached by the Chamber of Deputies in 2002, though the Senate fell short of the two-thirds majority required to remove him from office. In May 2003, another Colorado Party insider, Nicanor Duarte, won the presidency, but with only 37 percent of the vote. There was no indication that Paraguay was emerging from the prolonged period of instability; indeed, the slow erosion of the Colorado dominance might herald even more uncertainty (Abente-Brun, 1999).

Bolivia, although similar in many ways to Peru and Ecuador, has actually enjoyed substantially more political stability than its two Andean neighbors (Toranzo Roca, 2002). Since the first elected government took office in 1982, Bolivia has had an unbroken series of competitive elections in which candidates of three different parties have been victorious. Victory by an opposition candidate is the norm. However, beneath this surprising stability is a persistent pattern of weak presidents with narrow political bases, presiding over a persistently fragile state. Moreover, as in Ecuador, important elements of the indigenous and peasant populations are increasingly organized and assertive. Indeed, in the presidential election of 2002, the second-ranking candidate, Evo Morales, had as his main political base the coca farmers of the southeastern region, a sector subjected to persistent persecution by the government (under strong U.S. pressure to control coca production). Popular mobilizations, riots, and repressive violence by the police are part of everyday life, and in 2003, President Gonzalo Sánchez de Lozada was forced to resign as a result of such an outbreak. Even as the formal institutions of democracy survive, elected leaders are unable to accomplish much to improve the lives of their constituents.

Since the Sandinista victory over Anastasio Somoza Debayle in 1979, Nicaragua has undergone a decade of revolution and U.S.-supported counterrevolution, the establishment under the Sandinistas of a constitutional democracy rejected by most of the opposition, a negotiated peace settlement, and over a decade of turbulent democratic politics after the defeat of the Sandinistas in the elections of 1990 (Ortega Hegg, 2002). The economy has yet to recover from revolution and civil war, and the country is the poorest in Central America. An overwhelming majority of the population are poor, and unemployment or underemployment is widespread. These material conditions have created a difficult environment for political leadership. The Sandinistas retain about 40 percent of the vote and are the largest single party. The Conservatives, after the 1990 election of Violeta de Chamorro, have been gradually eclipsed by the Constitutionalist Liberals of the next two presidents, Arnoldo Alemán and Enrique Bolaños. However, after the 2002 election of Bolaños, he chose to prosecute Alemán for corruption, thus precipitating a split in the governing party. Nicaragua has held its elections on time since 1984, and transitions to opposition candidates took place in 1990 and 1996. Nevertheless, the regime must be considered extremely fragile.

Guatemala, after the establishment of constitutional government in 1985, continued for a decade more to suffer the effects of a prolonged insurgency and a draconian counterinsurgency, which led to thousands of deaths and disappearances, torture on a large scale, and tens of thousands of displaced people, both internally and externally. Since the signing of the peace settlement in 1996, the former guerrillas and other elements of the Left have been haltingly incorporated into the legal democratic political process, even while still suffering repression at the hands of death squads tacitly encouraged by the armed forces (Martínez Cortez, 2003). While the military has shown no inclination to retake power directly, neither has it been tolerant of efforts to call it to account for abuses committed under military rule or later. Indeed, violations of the human rights of dissenters continue at present, including murders of activists such as Guatemalan anthropologist Myrna Mack. A Catholic Church–sponsored study of human rights violations led to the assassination of its principal author, Bishop Juan Gerardi, in 1998, while an official human rights report in 2003 was met with vocal rejection by active and retired military officers. Overall, the Guatemalan democratic regime is more subject to pressure from the armed forces than any other democracy in the region at this time.

■ Conclusion

The many marginal democratic regimes of Latin America have in recent years confronted an array of challenges summarized in this chapter, any one of which might be enough to cause regime breakdown. Yet in point of fact, none have. Even Haiti, which does not count here as an established democratic regime, clung by its fingernails to the semblance of democracy, until the fall of President Aristide in early 2004. Elsewhere, at every potential breaking point, from the fall of de la Rua and Mahuad to the rise of Menem and Fuji-mori, from the dissolution of partyarchy in Venezuela to the election of Lula, events that might have led to breakdown have instead eventuated in regime maintenance. This durability is all the more puzzling because of the low qual-ity of most of these democracies. Without exception they are burdened with extremely inequitable social and economic structures, clientelism and corrup-tion, and persistent militarism. Universally, the states that must deal with these problems are weak. Why have they survived?

Two hypotheses suggest themselves. The first is that Latin Americans (elites and masses) may have actually learned something about how to oper-ate a democratic system, and may have learned that such a system is prefer-able to any alternatives even if it does not solve all problems. There is some evidence for this (McCoy, 2000). El Salvador in the 1990s seems to be a clear case of such political learning, as political violence has been progressively replaced by electoral competition and the day-to-day give-and-take of democ-racy. Brazil may be another example, where elites and masses have learned to manage the incredible complexity and contradiction of the democratic system, even absorbing the election of the socialist Lula da Silva. Lula and his Work-ers Party, in turn, seem to have learned how to operate effectively in the wheeling-and-dealing arena of Brazilian politics. The Dominican Republic, as it moves to the postpatriarchal era with the deaths of Joaquín Balaguer and Juan Bosch, has a good chance of establishing a more deeply rooted democ-racy. Mexico has finally ended the long hegemony of the PRI and entered the era of party competition. Clearly, then, learning has taken place.

However, there are numerous cases wherein political learning is not evi-dent, but the regime has been maintained anyway. The Andean countries of Peru, Ecuador, and Bolivia do not seem to have witnessed the sort of funda-mental changes of behavior that would lead one to hypothesize that political learning has taken place. The Central American countries of Guatemala, Hon-duras, and Nicaragua also display political patterns that are depressingly familiar. For cases like these, we must entertain the alternative hypothesis that the maintenance of democratic regimes owes a great deal to the international conjuncture that favors such regimes. The keystone of this conjuncture is the policy of the United States, the regional hegemon. Since at least the mid-1980s, it has been the clearly articulated policy of the United States to favor and reward the establishment and maintenance of formally constitutional and democratic regimes in Latin America. This policy has been more than rheto-ric, in that substantial aid funds have been devoted to democracy promotion, and the U.S. influence in the World Bank, Inter-American Development Bank, and the International Monetary Fund has been used to commit those institu-tions as well to the promotion of democracy. The European Union, too, has willingly gone along with the new emphasis on democracy. Finally, Latin American democratic regimes themselves have defined the maintenance of democracy as in their collective interest, and have acted diplomatically to protect that interest. Thus the rewards for remaining democratic are tangible, as are penalties for backsliding. The aborting of coups in Ecuador and Venezuela were both substantially attributable to international pressures. The Organization of American States (OAS) and the Carter Center were both very active in brokering negotiations between the Chávez government and the opposition in Venezuela, to keep the democracy from breaking down. The establishment of democracies in Central America in the 1990s was facilitated by the Arias Peace Plan, negotiated among the Central American presidents, and the maintenance of those regimes owes much to U.S. and international pressure, as well as to the continuing presence of the follow-up mechanisms of the Arias Plan. Haiti would surely have slipped into its familiar tyrannical abyss even sooner were it not for continuing involvement by the OAS and the UN. In short, the durability of democracy in Latin America is less due to its quality, or to generalized support for democracy among elites and masses, than to the international forces that, for the moment, insist on its maintenance. The test of this hypothesis will come, perhaps sooner than later, when the hegemon again changes its mind about the virtues of democracy.

▨ Notes

1. In contrast, Allende's 36 percent in 1970 was within the normal range for the Chilean Left.

2. This crisis was caused fundamentally by the sudden rise in world petroleum prices in the late 1970s, covered by extensive Third World borrowing from commercial banks. See Stallings and Kaufman (1989).

3. The principal strategy of Arias aimed for an autonomous Central American peace settlement, which was finally concluded in 1987 after the United States had been diplomatically outmaneuvered (see Rojas and Solís [1988]). The diplomacy of the Arias Peace Plan is an excellent study in how small powers can exercise substantial autonomy relative to great powers.

4. There is no visible reason why Colombia should not have as bad a debt problem as most other Latin American countries, but in fact it does not, and the explanation probably lies at least partially in hidden drug profits that filter into the legal economy. Consult Thoumi (1995).

5. For an overview of the argument and the results in Latin America, see Williamson (1990); Frieden (1991); Borner, Brunetti, and Weder (1995). For critical analyses of prior patterns of economic policy, see de Soto (1989); Dornbusch and Edwards (1991).

6. For a comprehensive comparative analysis of the issue of state promotion of development, see Evans (1995). For analyses of the responses of Latin American governments, see Smith, Acuña, and Gamarra (1994a); Haggard and Kaufman (1995).

7. When finally tried in 1996, he was found guilty on lesser charges, exonerated of the most important, and served only a few more months of house arrest. Subsequently, he has lived in exile.

8. See Haggard and Kaufman (1995); Petras, Leiva, and Veltmeyer (1994); Collins and Lear (1995); Angell and Graham (1995); Kurtz (1995); Boylan (1996).

9. Borner, Brunetti, and Weder (1995) suggested another explanation for Chile's success: the stability of Chilean policies, including the rules about property rights.

10. Those that made the transition in a context of economic crisis were Argentina, Bolivia, Brazil, Peru, Uruguay, and the Philippines. Those making the transition without an economic crisis were Chile, Korea, Thailand, and Turkey.

11. See Halebsky and Harris (1995); Jonas and McCaughan (1994); Morales and McMahon (1993); Smith, Acuña, and Gamarra (1994b); NACLA (1996).

12. See, in particular, Petras, Leiva, and Veltmeyer (1994) and Collins and Lear (1995) on Chile; Pizarro and Bejarano (1994) and Bergquist, Peñaranda, and Sánchez (2001) on Colombia; McCoy et al. (1995) and Goodman et al. (1995) on Venezuela; Espinal (1995) on the Dominican Republic; Malloy (1991) and NACLA (1991) on Bolivia; Sánchez Parga (1993) and Ardaya and Verdesoto (1996) on Ecuador; Acuña (1994) and García Delgado (1994) on Argentina; NACLA (1995), Schneider (1996), and Pereira (2003) on Brazil. For a comparison of Argentina and Uruguay, see Blake (1994). For a comparison of Chile and Venezuela, see Angell and Graham (1995). See Conaghan and Malloy (1994) for a comparative study of democracy and neoliberalism in the Central Andes. For a study of Central America, see Stein and Arias Peñate (1992).

13. See Coraggio and Deere (1987); NACLA (1991); Conaghan and Malloy (1994); Calderón and dos Santos (1995); Collins and Lear (1995).

14. See, for example, Lipset (1959); Lipset, Seong, and Torres (1993); Abootalebi (1995); Vanhanen (1994); Mainwaring and Pérez Liñán (2003).

15. For overviews, see Haggard and Kaufman (1995); Whitehead (1994); Naím (1995); Calderón and dos Santos (1995); Waisman (1992). For critical perspectives on the impact of neoliberal reform, see Chauvin (1995); Halebsky and Harris (1995); Jonas and McCaughan (1994). Relevant case studies are contained in Smith, Acuña, and Gamarra (1994a); Espinal (1995); Blake (1994); Angell and Graham (1995).

16. On recent Chilean party politics, see Agüero (2003). On Costa Rica, see Rovira Mas (2001a). On Uruguay, see Cason (2000).

17. Haiti has been in acute crisis since the overthrow of Jean-Claude Duvalier in 1986, and has undergone at least four regime changes (and many more government changes). However, Haiti is not in any sense an established democratic regime; thus it is not included in this discussion.

6

Democracy at the Dawn of the Twenty-First Century

Based on the cases presented in this book, it is possible at this point to offer some generalizations about the practice of democracy in Latin America and its strengths and weaknesses. I would first reaffirm that liberal democracy is the best system yet invented for protecting people from abuse by their government. It is certainly not perfectly effective in doing this, but no other system does it better over a sustained period. This is the principal basis for the desirability of liberal democracy over other regime types. The institution of individual rights of citizens, not to be violated by rulers, is the major contribution of liberalism to political philosophy. Whether those rights are based in natural law, contract, or utility, their recognition by an increasing number of governments around the world has made people's lives much less "nasty, brutish, and short" (in Hobbes's phrase [1991]) than they used to be. The very newsworthiness at present of egregious violations of human rights by outlaw governments is a sign of how universal the aspiration for inviolable rights has become.

This is what liberal democracy can do well, while also providing mechanisms for pursuit of the common good; this is why Latin Americans increasingly demand it. If liberal democracy is attainable, it no longer appears inevitable that the persons and lives of citizens will be subject to violation at will by rulers. Surely, if the twentieth century—this epoch of global insanity, inhumanity, and carnage—is to have any positive political legacy, the spreading affirmation of human rights and liberal democracy will be a large part of it.

It is now beyond dispute that liberal democracy is attainable in Latin America. The widespread establishment of such regimes, and their persistence through adverse conditions, refutes definitively the arguments of those who said democracy was impossible in the region because of culture, history, or class structure. Given appropriate internal and external structures, it was possible in the most unlikely places to establish and maintain credible liberal democracies. By the late 1990s, liberal democracy was so much the rule in Latin America that countries that did not meet the criteria (Paraguay, Mexico, and Cuba) had to be treated as special cases.

Once these regimes have been established, a key problem is of course to ensure that they fulfill their aspirations with regard to respect for citizen rights. It has not been uncommon for elected presidents to use their popularity as a weapon to intimidate opponents and manipulate elections under cover of a popular mandate. The formal presence of a liberal democracy is no assurance of its vitality. However, the rights of citizens are rarely, if ever, better protected in the formal absence of liberal democracy. In any given setting, some people, both elites and nonelites, may prefer a nondemocratic system if they are unsatisfied with the results of a democracy. It is increasingly true that most Latin Americans state a preference for democracy, at least in the abstract.

Our comparison of many cases over the last generation—and a few earlier cases—makes clear that the establishment of liberal democracy is fundamentally a matter of elite action. This is contrary to the rhetoric of democracy, of course, but everything we know about the practice of liberal democracy, even in advanced industrial countries, confirms that power remains in the hands of elites. In the United States, for example, the argument between pluralists and elitists is over how cohesive the elites are, not over whether elites rule. Joseph Schumpeter's formulation (1950) still captures the essence of liberal democracy: it is a system wherein the people have regular opportunities, through competitive elections, to choose their rulers.

The mass of citizens are important: in the absence of significant mass political mobilization, elites will have no incentive to promote democratization. In democratization, elites compete with each other in mobilizing mass followings and managing them (leading them) to support the establishment of democratic institutions. Spontaneous mass mobilizations can lead to the overthrow of a government, but unless leadership emerges, mass mobilization cannot build anything, including democracy. A liberal democracy is superior to any nondemocracy in that all citizens have the right to choose public officials in periodic, competitive elections. Moreover, the citizen rights that are protected by liberal democracy include freedom of speech and the right to try to influence government actions. But the people do not rule in a liberal democracy. Accountability and responsiveness are legitimate goals for a liberal democracy, but even if they are less than complete, a liberal democracy will still function. In fact, stable liberal democracies are those in which elites have the most control over mass political behavior. That control need not be coercive: it could consist simply in channeling citizen energies into two centrist parties that do not threaten vested elite interests. For forty years, the two great Venezuelan political parties, Democratic Action (AD) and Independent Committee for Political and Electoral Organization (COPEI), so dominated all parts of the political system that all significant political participation was channeled by them. Popular disaffection with the so-called partyarchy grew slowly in the 1980s, and exploded in 1989. That explosion might have come to naught without the emergence of Hugo Chávez as a new popular leader.

Regime changes in general, including transitions to democracy, often involve some kind of mass political breakthrough whereby citizens previously under elite control temporarily break out and act autonomously. Most clearly this was the case in the popular insurrection against Anastasio Somoza Debayle in Nicaragua in 1978–1979; it may also be seen in the Venezuelan uprisings of 1989 that helped to bring down President Carlos Andrés Pérez and put the Venezuelan democratic regime in crisis, and in the Argentine demonstrations of 1982 that protested the defeat in the Malvinas/Falklands War and forced the military to agree to a transition.

Other regime changes may involve successful mobilization of mass publics by opposition elites. The credibility of the opposition elites as potential negotiators with the government depends substantially on their ability to mobilize and guide a mass of their followers. This was most clearly the case in the transitions from military rule in Brazil, Chile, and Uruguay.

Because even in the best of cases individuals and local communities have little impact on national politics and the national government (except in the occasional mass breakthrough as described above), people develop survival strategies that permit them as much as possible to control their own personal and local situations. For individuals, this could be as simple as trying to avoid paying taxes. For local communities, it often takes the form of grassroots organizations and social movements, which often try to do what is in their power to deal with local problems. In the later stages of authoritarian regimes, social movements also briefly took on national significance in many countries as parties were outlawed or harassed. But once parties resumed center stage in national democratic politics, there has been less room for social movements. Much of the energy of political activists in Chile, for example, shifted from social movements to parties after 1988. Another common problem with social movements is a tendency to slide into a clientelistic logic wherein the purpose of the organization ceases to be self-help and instead becomes seeking help from the government. Social movements and community organizations are nevertheless quite significant in showing the potential of a more genuine democracy, where there is little difference between leaders and followers and where participation is needed from most of the members most of the time. Small-scale participatory democracy of this kind must surely be part of any plan for deepening democracy.

Grand structures such as class do matter in setting boundaries: a society with a very weak working class and middle class and very strong landowners is (as suggested by Rueschemeyer, Huber Stephens, and Stephens, 1992) most unlikely to establish a democracy. A shift of the international environment to a pattern less conducive to democracy would surely lead to numerous breakdowns of democratic regimes in the countries least likely to succeed. Nevertheless, in Latin America since the late twentieth century even the least likely countries have been establishing liberal democratic regimes. To some extent this is attributable to international pressures (e.g., in Haiti), but it must also be attributed to a will on the part of competing elites to contain their contestation within the bounds of liberal democracy. Often, this has occurred as a direct reaction to the oppression suffered under the preceding authoritarian regime.

We have observed considerable variation in the kinds of elite action that have led—or not led—to the establishment of liberal democracies. One thing that must happen at the elite level is that groups formerly willing to use any method—force or fraud—to get or keep power must begin to compete for power within the confines of liberal democratic rules. When elites representing all sectors of society with the power to disrupt the political process are committed to competing within liberal democratic rules, a stable liberal democracy becomes possible. Liberal democracies can be established on a narrower elite base, with significant elites left out, but the risks to stability are greater. If the regime is successful, the elites left out may later join (in Burton, Gunther, and Higley's "elite convergence" [1992]). This happened in Costa Rica during the 1950s after the establishment of the regime in 1949 on a relatively narrow base (see Chapter 3).

Left-out elites may also successfully undermine a regime by continuing to use force and to reject the legitimacy of elections and elite pacts within the regime. The clearest example of this came during the 1950s and 1960s in Argentina, when two successive attempts were made to establish liberal democracies that excluded the Peronist elite. Because the Peronist elite was consistently able to mobilize the movement's mass base in the labor unions, both democratic regimes were effectively stillborn and were replaced by military governments. Indeed, in general, a key part of the power of elites is derived from their mass base.

Elites forming a liberal democracy may do so via explicit pacts defining the terms of cooperation and competition or may operate ad hoc, guided in part by constitutional rules and electoral laws. In the latter case, the risk is higher of a degeneration into ungovernability, as each successive government finds itself unable to hold together a legislative coalition because each major leader will be running for president as soon as the last election is over. Bolivia and Ecuador are particularly sharp examples of this latter phenomenon, while El Salvador's transition to democracy under an inclusive pact has, so far, worked reasonably well. On the other hand, the pacted democracy of Venezuela exhausted its popular legitimacy by the early 1990s, and was overwhelmed by Hugo Chávez's populist movement.

Some of the smaller countries of the Caribbean and Central America have made progress toward stable democracy in spite of the absence of pacts because the United States has in recent years played the role of a moderator favoring liberal democracy. This has been most clearly the case in the Dominican Republic, Honduras, and Panama. However, U.S. intervention failed to stabilize a democratic regime in Haiti, in large part because the one leader (Jean-Bertrand Aristide) who could mobilize a mass following was regarded with skepticism or outright hostility by major policymakers in Washington, whereas in the other cases the democratic process produced governments that the United States was comfortable with. Similarly, in Venezuela, the populist democracy of Hugo Chávez failed to achieve stability in part because the Bush administration was deeply suspicious of Chávez but unwilling to move against him and face charges of hypocrisy in its support for democracy.

Where a ruling elite retains overwhelming dominance over the combined opposition, there are no incentives for negotiating a transition from authoritarian rule. The most that can be expected in the short run is a controlled liberalization, with the possibility that liberalization could get out of control and lead to democratization as opposition elites gain more room for maneuver and popular mobilization. In Chile, Brazil, and Uruguay, the military regimes attempted such controlled liberalizations, but unexpectedly lost elections and were compelled to accept a genuine transition to democracy. In Mexico, the ruling Institutional Revolutionary Party (PRI) attempted such a controlled liberalization, but lost the election of 2000 to Vicente Fox of the National Action Party (PAN).

Liberal democracies are neither more nor less capable than authoritarian regimes of dealing successfully with economic stress and adjustment. Substantial investigations concluded that, contrary to many predictions, democratic regimes have at least as good a record on economic policy and performance and are just as capable of carrying out unpopular policies. Political entrepreneurs such as Carlos Menem in Argentina, Alberto Fujimori in Peru, and Gonzalo Sánchez de Lozada in Bolivia were able to push through quite drastic economic reforms while maintaining popular support for sustained periods (though all three were ultimately forced out by popular protests). The stable democracies of Chile and Costa Rica carried out significant, long-term programs of neoliberal reform without endangering democratic stability, again because tangible results were good enough to minimize popular protests. On the other hand, where economic reforms yielded mostly negative results, both authoritarian and democratic regimes were in danger. Most of the military regimes in power in the late 1970s and early 1980s were destabilized by deteriorating economic conditions, as were the weak democracies of Ecuador, Peru, and Bolivia in the 1990s and the early years of the twenty-first century.

The particular shape of political institutions will certainly affect the stability of democratic regimes. Party systems that are institutionalized and characterized by moderate pluralism are most conducive to liberal democratic stability. This pattern is exemplified by the most stable democracies of the region, Costa Rica, Chile, and Uruguay. Costa Rica continues to be dominated by two centrist parties, the National Liberation Party (PLN) and the Social Christian Unity Party (PUSC), while a few minority parties regularly achieve legislative representation. Uruguay is evolving from its traditional two-party system toward three major parties. Chile has moved from its pre-1973 tripolar, multiparty system toward a bipolar, four-party system with two durable blocs, center-left and center-right. Any of these patterns seems to support democratic stability, as long as the party system itself is reasonably stable. The countries with the most success in establishing and maintaining liberal democracies have been those whose party systems show less volatility between elections and have parties with substantial roots in the population. A stable set of two to four major parties suffices to represent major sectors of society in the legislature and the government. Conversely, a party system with a proliferation of short-lived parties representing only ambitious elites and with few popular roots is a recipe for ungovernability, as may be seen in Bolivia and Ecuador.

The debate between presidentialism and parliamentarism poses another institutional issue. Presidentialism may, as its critics argue, be a source of instability, but it is unlikely to be supplanted on a large scale in Latin America. The divided government that is an inherent characteristic of presidential constitutions has probably had negative effects on governability and political stability in Latin America. It is the norm that elected presidents either lack a legislative majority from the beginning or lose their majority in short order after their inauguration. Rival political leaders, rather than supporting the incumbent president, find it more useful to maneuver with a view to winning the next presidential election. The prohibition on immediate reelection, common in Latin America as a means of retarding the concentration of power in the hands of the executive, also works to render an incumbent too weak to govern. Correspondingly, popular presidents, frustrated by congressional intransigence, are tempted to resort to states of emergency or siege, arbitrary actions, plebiscitory appeals to the populace, or constitutional amendments to permit reelection. All of these possibilities tend to weaken the legitimacy and effectiveness of democracy. Notwithstanding these disadvantages, there is little to indicate that either elites or voters are ready to experiment with parliamentarism. The reluctance may be partially due to the widespread contempt in which parliamentarians are held. As previously noted, only in Brazil in the late 1980s was the question of converting to a parliamentary system posed to the electorate; it was soundly defeated. At the same time, it is becoming more common for incumbent presidents to be forced out by popular uprisings, violent or nonviolent. Since the middle of the 1990s, presidents have been forced to leave office before their terms ended, because of popular uprisings, in Argentina, Ecuador, Peru, Bolivia, Paraguay, and Guatemala. Supposedly, the attraction of presidentialism is that it concentrates more effective power in the hands of the chief executive, but as these cases make clear, an unpopular president is quite exposed and vulnerable.

Given conducive structural conditions, liberal democracy can achieve stability in Latin America. Although it is true that at the philosophical level liberal democracy lies uneasily in the procrustean bed of liberal economics, and although it suffers many practical problems such as government inefficiency and elite corruption, these diseases are not necessarily fatal. Whatever practical problems liberal democracies have are no worse than those posed by alternative forms, and liberal democracy has at least an orderly and peaceful mechanism for "throwing the rascals out" periodically. The philosophical difficulty may have limited practical effect, since citizens may in practice have broad tolerance for both economic and political inequality. The occasional adoption of modest reforms will usually suffice to keep popular protest from threatening political stability. People who believe their situation could be worse will be loathe to rock the boat. Within Latin America, Costa Rica provides a particularly good example of a country whose successive political elites, over generations, have been intelligent about ameliorating the worst social and economic injustices and have thereby consolidated the liberal democratic regime. It is no accident that Costa Rica is the senior democracy in the region and still one of the most stable.

Nevertheless, the continuing application of uncompromising neoliberal economic reforms without regard to short- and long-term social costs might well undermine liberal democratic stability, particularly when most of the population come to believe that they have been betrayed by their political leaders. Menem and Fujimori were able to get away with such a reversal of course and consolidated their power at the expense of parliament and opposition parties, but both were finally forced from power after a decade. Pérez did not get away with it, and the Venezuelan democracy has yet to regain its stability.

Low-Quality Democracy

In the last generation, liberal democracy has become the norm in Latin American politics. After a long history of fraud, turmoil, and instability, it is a positive development when almost all Latin American regimes meet minimal criteria for functioning liberal democracies. That is, they have constitutions that actually shape political behavior, elections that are honestly counted and where more than one candidate can win, presidents who leave office when their term ends, competing political parties, and freedom of speech, organization, and press. Each of these features is now present, to some extent, in most countries, most of the time. As a result, the lives of most people are better because they are much less likely to suffer physical repression and because they have some voice in selecting the people and policies that will govern their societies.

Yet for the most part the democracy that prevails in the region is seriously deficient even when judged against the standards of "polyarchy," the term coined by Robert Dahl (1971, chap. 1) to refer to contemporary regimes that are usually called democracies even though they fall short of the ideal. Ideally, in Dahl's view, democracy is completely responsive to all its citizens, which in turn requires that all citizens have unimpaired opportunities (1) to formulate their preferences, (2) to signify their preferences by individual and collective action, and (3) to have their preferences weighed equally in the conduct of government. An ideal democracy, in short, allows unrestricted opportunity for public contestation (i.e., questioning or opposing the government), and allows unrestricted political participation by the whole adult population. While no regime achieves the ideal, polyarchies are those that approach it. They are characterized by universal suffrage through competitive and fairly administered elections in which more than one party normally competes. Opportunities for contestation, through organized interest groups and political parties in particular, are broad. Effective power, rather than being monopolized by a small elite, is more broadly distributed. Citizens, by organizing themselves into parties and interest groups, can participate effectively in political decisionmaking. This alleged pattern of the broad distribution of power is the basis for the concepts of "pluralism," "pluralist democracy," and "polyarchy," each of which depicts a political system with many centers of power and no single ruling class or elite.

As early as 1970, Dahl was thinking of how polyarchy could be improved, and by the 1980s he had developed a pointed critique of the effects of economic inequality on the quality of polyarchy (Dahl, 1970, 1982, 1985). Thus even the principal theorist of liberal democracy came to see that it was being seriously undermined by inequality. One of the major effects of inequality was seen to be a decline in the responsiveness of elected governments to the popular will, as economically privileged sectors are increasingly able to demand special consideration. If this was the case in the most advanced industrial democracies, it is scarcely surprising to find that it is an even bigger problem in Latin American democracies. Indeed, across the region the 1990s were marked by serious disillusionment with democracy. A brief review of some cases discussed earlier will illustrate the point.

Mexico experienced great celebrations in 2000 when Vicente Fox of PAN won the presidency, ending more than seventy years of PRI hegemony. Yet Fox proved largely unable to deliver on his many promises, such as punishing corruption, providing transparency in government, settling the Chiapas insurgency of the Zapatistas, and generating large numbers of new jobs. Most Mexicans three years later perceived that little had really changed. Significant numbers were willing to vote the PRI back in, while the center-left opposition party, the Democratic Revolutionary Party (PRD), was also gaining new support. The viability of Mexico's newly established democracy was not yet in question, partly because voters still had the novel opportunity of choosing an alternative government in the next. Deeper disillusionment may set in if alternative elected governments fail to deliver improvements in people's lives.

Since Chile's transition to democracy in 1988–1989, the country has had three consecutive center-left Concertación governments. The democratic regime inaugurated in 1989 incorporated several elements designed to protect the interests of the former military rulers by restricting democratic decision-making. For example, General Augusto Pinochet became commander in chief of the army when he left the presidency, and under the constitution his elected successors were not permitted to remove him until his term ended in 1996. At that point, as an ex-president, he assumed a lifetime seat in the Senate. The constitution also provided for enough other nonelected senators (appointed by President Pinochet and by other officials loyal to him) to block any constitutional amendment. The courts were packed with Pinochet loyalists prepared to resist attempts to change legal interpretations in order to shift policies, or to hold individuals responsible for human rights violations under the dictatorship.

The Dominican Republic made considerable progress toward democratic stability in the 1990s, but the quality of its democracy must still be considered low. The long preeminence of the post-Trujillo patriarchs, Balaguer, Peña Gómez, and Bosch, is finally over, and the republic has entered an epoch when mere mortals from the three major parties compete for public office, with no party having a clear and durable edge. At the same time, the stresses of economic policy continue to strain the country's political fabric. In late 2003 a nationwide strike severely shook the government of Hipólito Mejía (of the Dominican Revolutionary Party), reflecting protests against poor economic conditions.

Colombia, in spite of the multiple challenges facing it, still has not seen an institutional breakdown of its formally democratic regime. Notwithstanding widespread criminal violence, two surviving forty-year-old revolutionary insurgencies, several right-wing paramilitary organizations, and an illicit drug industry that extends its tentacles into all parts of the society and polity, competitive and reasonably honest elections continue to take place on a regular schedule, opposition candidates and parties still defeat incumbents, and the press is reasonably free. It is as if the formalities of democracy, as a game among political elites, are floating along on the turbulent waters of a society in deepening crisis. Colombia is the quintessential example of a democracy able to persist over a very long time at a remarkably low level of quality.

The cases cited in this section illustrate a broad pattern of democratic regimes that offer little more to their citizens than the formality of periodic competitive elections. Democracies that can do no better than this are unlikely to earn the enduring commitment of their citizens, especially in times of chronic—sometimes acute—economic troubles.

▓ Fragile Democracy

Many of the democratic regimes established in the past quarter century are not only of poor quality, but also fragile and easily destabilized. While the current international climate (U.S. policy and the priorities of the major international lenders) tends to support the maintenance of democratic regimes, many of them have failed to put down deep roots, and are subject to challenge by popular mobilization, by military uprisings, and by elite subversion.

One key reason for this widespread fragility of democracy is the stubborn persistence of high levels of economic inequality, underpinned by the distinctively predatory class relations that continue to characterize the region. That is, to put it bluntly, those who have the most in Latin America, for the most part, do not see any need to sacrifice their own standards of living in order to bring the poor majority up to a minimally humane level. On the contrary, the poor tend to be viewed as, at best, a drag on the development of the country, if not a direct threat that must be suppressed. As we have seen, this attitude is as old as the Conquest; it is one of the most durable features of Latin America's political culture. The contrast with the advanced Western democracies, as well as with such East Asian success stories as South Korea and Taiwan, serves to emphasize that economic development and democracy are best consolidated in a context of much less extreme inequality, and in class relations that acknowledge the human rights of the most poor to share in and contribute to the development of the society.

Paradoxically, the United States, as the hegemonic power of the region, may still be contributing to the fragility of Latin American democracies even as it overtly favors the establishment and maintenance of democratic regimes. For about twenty years the United States has strongly favored transitions from authoritarian to democratic rule, and has publicly worked against attempts to overthrow democratic regimes in such cases as Guatemala and Ecuador. Yet because the United States is also strongly committed to neoliberal economic policies, it tends to be extremely skeptical toward democratic governments like that of Hugo Chávez in Venezuela that pursue heterodox economic policies. Those democratic governments that reject neoliberal orthodoxy may be popular, but without U.S. support will most likely fail. Those that have more orthodox policies, such as the last government of Sánchez de Lozada in Bolivia or that of Jamil Mahuad in Ecuador, will have U.S. support but will probably be unpopular, and thus also will likely fail.

The Central Andean countries (Ecuador, Peru, and Bolivia) are excellent examples of democratic fragility. While each has managed thus far to maintain minimal institutional integrity of its democratic regime (i.e., the regime itself has not collapsed), each has witnessed the forced resignation or removal of at least one constitutionally elected president before the end of his term, due to popular mobilization and resistance. In each case, the president who was ousted was seeking, with external support from the International Monetary Fund, the World Bank, and the United States, to implement neoliberal economic policies that might have helped his country's macroeconomic situation, but that were widely seen as systematically disadvantaging the poor majorities. Under these circumstances, two Ecuadoran presidents (Bucaram and Mahuad), one Peruvian (Fujimori), and one Bolivian (Sánchez de Lozada) were forced from power since the mid-1990s. The political mobilization of the large indigenous populations, as well as other poor peasants and urbanites, is a positive development for the eventual vitality of democracy in these countries, but in the short term clearly poses a challenge to the stability and governability of the existing low-quality democratic regimes.

The continuing travails of Haiti's troubled attempt to make a transition to democracy show many of the same problems as the Andean countries, but more intensely. At the same time, the role of the United States is even more decisive, and even less encouraging. After the overthrow of Jean-Claude Duvalier in 1986, the Haitian political and military elite initially sought to maintain an authoritarian regime without a dominant personal leader. However, rivalries among leaders led to chronic instability, while an authentically popular movement for democracy and social justice arose under the charismatic leadership of Father Jean-Bertrand Aristide. Under pressure from the United States, the provisional government conducted an honest election, which was won by Aristide, in 1990. However, less than a year later, he was overthrown in a military coup. The official opposition of the United States was belied by the refusal of the first Bush administration to put pressure on the military government to restore Aristide. This ambivalence appears to have been related to a lack of confidence in Aristide, muddled by an unwillingness to openly condone the coup. The incoming Clinton administration, after some soul-searching, resolved the ambivalence by firmly advocating the return of Aristide, and backed this up by occupying the country in 1993. Aristide, however, found himself severely constrained by pressures from the United States and international donors, and militantly opposed by elements of the economic elite and middle class. Completing the remainder of his term, he was able to accomplish little. He remained the principal political actor behind the scenes during the presidency of his supporter, René Préval, and returned to the presidency in 2001. Subsequently, the country was paralyzed by opposition demands that Aristide resign. In response, the president showed increasing authoritarian tendencies. Aristide was removed from power with the help of the United States and France, in early 2004. Corruption remains rampant, and the vast majority of Haitians remain miserably poor.

The period since the overthrow of Alfredo Stroessner in Paraguay has not been as futile as the equivalent period in Haiti, but the attempt to move toward a stable democracy must certainly be judged precarious. In the last few years there has been an intense struggle within the governing Colorado Party.

Attempted coups by General Oviedo, the assassination of Vice President Argaña, the impeachment of President González Macchi, all contributed to an atmosphere of chronic instability over several years. As with Haiti, the formal persistence of a democratic regime must be substantially attributed to external pressures, though in this case not so much directly from the United States as from Paraguay's neighbors, Brazil and Argentina.

After its peace accord of 1996, Guatemala seemed poised at long last to construct a stable and inclusive democracy. However, the road has continued to be rocky. In response to efforts to report the truth about human rights violations during the guerrilla wars of the 1980s, the armed forces and their right-wing paramilitary allies have continued to commit assassinations, including that of Bishop Juan Gerardi, the principal coordinator of the Catholic Church's report on human rights violations. The pattern of continuing violence in turn has intimidated potential critics of the regime. Retired general Efraín Ríos Montt, who presided over massive violence during his brief military dictatorship of 1982–1983, persisted in his efforts to run for president, even though the constitution prohibited such a candidacy by anyone who had ruled outside the law. When the Supreme Court finally permitted him to run in 2003, he lost decisively, and perhaps thereby removed a major obstacle to the stabilization of democracy.

Nicaragua has also experienced turbulent times since the overthrow of its dictator, Somoza, in 1979. After over a decade of the Sandinista revolution under implacable siege by the United States, Nicaragua entered the postrevolutionary era in 1990 with the election of Violeta de Chamorro. The reconstituted Constitutionalist Liberal Party won the election of 1996 with Arnoldo Alemán, and repeated in 2002 with Enrique Bolaños. The latter, however, surprised everyone by acting on his campaign pledge to attack corruption, beginning with his predecessor and erstwhile patron, Alemán. In late 2003 the former president was actually found guilty of misappropriation of funds, and sentenced to twenty years of prison. The case profoundly split the ruling party, and touched off violent protests by supporters of Alemán. While the punishment of corruption must be judged a positive development for the eventual stabilization of democracy, taking out Alemán also has obvious political advantages for President Bolaños, as well as obvious risks for the party. What had been shaping up as a bipolar party system dominated by the rivalry between the Sandinistas and the Constitutionalist Liberals now looks much less clear.

All the countries cited in this section have maintained at least the formalities of democracy in spite of severe political crises. In all cases, external pressure greatly affects the survival of democracy: internal forces alone are insufficient to maintain the regime. However, democracies this fragile are scarcely in a position to deliver tangible benefits to their people. They are thus the lowest of low-quality democracies, and their failure to deliver benefits ensures that they will remain exceedingly fragile.

■ Democracy and Neoliberal Globalization

A major cause of the contemporary difficulties of democracy in Latin America is the tension between coming to terms with the global economy and responding to the popular will as expressed in elections, polls, and popular mobilizations. While having an open economy benefits some investors and some workers, few Latin Americans believe the promise that everyone will benefit in the long run. Indeed, most people expect to be harmed by globalization. To this point, the strongest case that can be made for globalization is the highly debatable and speculative affirmation that conditions would have been even worse without it. Under these circumstances, most democratically elected governments won election by promising to resist globalization and attend to pressing social needs. Once elected, however, they confront intense pressure to conform to the standard prescriptions for opening their economy and reducing the social welfare role of the government. Failing to conform will deny them the loans and investment that are needed for economic growth. Conforming will put them in the position of violating their campaign promises and immediately exacerbating economic and social conditions. On the horns of this dilemma, democracies throughout the region have been rendered highly unstable. There have been some temporary success stories wherein globalizing policies were, for a time, associated with economic improvements, but there are many more cases wherein the opposite has been true.

Success Followed by Failure: Argentina and Peru

Both Carlos Menem and Alberto Fujimori won elections based on populist and antiglobalization appeals, then reversed themselves once in office. Their neoliberal, globalizing policies were sufficiently successful in the first few years to earn them substantial popular support in spite of having reversed their campaign promises. Both managed to get inflation under control after severe bouts of hyperinflation, and both presided over significant economic expansion. Yet by the end of the 1990s the seeming magic had worn off, and their economies had returned to crisis conditions. Menem chose not to seek reelection, and Fujimori, having been reelected in a disputed contest, was forced into exile by a corruption scandal. Both countries continued in crisis for several years thereafter, though Argentina seemed to be improving after the election of Nestor Kirchner in 2003.

The Mixed Blessings of Globalization: Mexico and Brazil

Brazil and Mexico are the two most populous countries in Latin America, and are among the leaders in industrialization and economic development. If any Latin American countries should benefit from globalization, they should. And indeed, important sectors of both countries have benefited. The great Brazilian financial and industrial center of São Paulo has gained from trade liberalization (though there are plenty of losers among the winners), as have the highly commercialized producers of such exportable agricultural products as soybeans and citrus. On the other hand, the many industries that are not internationally competitive, as well as more traditional farmers, are worse off. Interests looking to extract wood and minerals from Amazonia are probably better off, as are ecotourism entrepreneurs who look to attract adventurous tourists to the Amazon region. Subsistence farmers and isolated indigenous populations in Amazonia are likely to be big losers, unless they can shift to either extraction or tourism. Brazil has a strong stake in the success of Mercosur, in which it is the dominant player. It is both a key market for the other members, including Argentina, and a key supplier of both manufactured goods and capital. However, Mercosur is being systematically attacked by the United States, which is promoting a Free Trade Area of the Americas in which it would be dominant.

Mexico, like Brazil, is committed to a globalization strategy based strongly on exports. Unlike Brazil, it is also committed to the North American Free Trade Agreement (NAFTA), in which it is a junior partner to the United States. As with Brazil, important financial, industrial, and agricultural sectors have benefited both from NAFTA and from global free trade, while large populations of small farmers, as well as owners and workers in noncompetitive industries, have been severely hurt. An interesting development in Mexico is the decline of *maquiladora* operations along the U.S. border, where manufacturers a couple of decades ago began to locate plants to assemble clothing, electronics, and other goods for export to the United States. The advantage of Mexico lay in its proximity to the United States and its low wages. Now, many of these operations are being moved from Mexico to even lower-wage countries in Southeast Asia or elsewhere. A key component of Mexico's globalization strategy has thus begun to collapse.

In short, globalization as well as regional free trade pacts have had mixed effects, probably exacerbating inequalities as some minorities gain, other minorities lose, and everyone else tries to survive.

The Failure of Globalization: Bolivia and Ecuador

Globalization winners are few and far between in Bolivia and Ecuador. Bolivia's primary engagement with the global economy was traditionally its mining sector, featuring silver in colonial times and tin in the past century. Both those industries had collapsed by the end of the twentieth century. In the 1980s, Bolivia, along with Peru, became a principal supplier of coca for the international drug trade, and the number of Bolivians involved with that crop increased substantially. At the same time, some oil and natural gas deposits were found. However, the vast majority of the population, whether rural or urban, remained miserably poor. This poor majority has become increasingly well organized and mobilized, both around issues of class and economic interest and around indigenous cultural identity. Evo Morales, a leader of the coca growers, finished second in the most recent presidential elections. In 2003, his Movement Toward Socialism and several indigenous movements worked together to protest a plan to license foreign firms to develop a pipeline for the export of natural gas through Chile. While the intensity of the protests was partly explicable by Bolivian hostility to Chile because of the loss of an outlet to the sea in the War of the Pacific over a century ago, the protests also reflected a deeply felt mistrust of the country's economic elites and the global corporations that would carry out the project. Many people seem to have felt, simply, that no benefits from the project would accrue to the vast majority of Bolivians. The protests became so intense that President Gonzalo Sánchez de Losada was compelled to resign and leave the country.

Ecuador's experience with petroleum would tend to reinforce the skepticism of Bolivians. Ecuador has been a significant exporter of petroleum since the 1970s, and oil revenue certainly has been a mainstay of the central government's budget. However, it is highly debatable how much tangible benefit from oil has trickled down to the general population. The widespread perception is that the benefits are scant. When Jamil Mahuad sought to ease Ecuador's integration with the global economy by adopting the U.S. dollar as the official currency, popular protests forced his removal. His vice president and successor did not reverse dollarization, and at the next election was replaced by Lucio Gutiérrez, a former colonel and one of the leaders of the movement that ousted Mahuad. Gutiérrez, in spite of a campaign that criticized neoliberalism and globalization, also refused to reverse dollarization and adopted other neoliberal economic policies. His campaign allies from the country's indigenous movement abandoned him and have returned to street protests. It is not inconceivable that Gutiérrez could be the third Ecuadoran president in a decade to be forced from office by popular protest.

It appears that most Bolivians and Ecuadorians see little or no benefit from globalization; indeed, to many the prospect must be grim indeed as they contemplate a life even less secure than the precarious existence to which they are accustomed. The emerging world order that confronts them, ironically, will appear to them as not unlike the extreme inequality and predatory class relations that have been customary in Latin America since colonial times. That is, a few high rollers will get very rich while the vast majority, if they are lucky, will subsist. The only tool of resistance they have is popular mobilization in a context of liberal democratic liberties, but if democracy cannot deliver real improvements in the lives of the poor majorities, it will be increasingly vulnerable. These people will not wait for the elusive "long run" when everything would work out for the best.

The Success of Globalization: Chile and Costa Rica

Over the past quarter century, Chile and Costa Rica have seen better results from neoliberalism and globalization than any other Latin American country. While each has suffered serious economic downturns and dislocations, their long-term growth rates and per capita income levels have consistently out-performed those of their neighbors. They have reached this level of success by quite different routes, and their current policies are noticeably different in some respects. Each, however, has managed to spread the benefits of global-ization more broadly than is typical in the region, and to mitigate the costs more effectively.

In the late 1970s, the authoritarian government of General Pinochet com-mitted Chile to the most radical program of neoliberal economic transforma-tion ever attempted in Latin America, privatizing state-owned firms, deregu-lating the economy, eliminating subsidies and tariffs, weakening or dismantling labor unions, and reducing the scope of the social safety net. The objective was to make Chile a competitive exporter in the global marketplace. Although there was a significant recession in the early 1980s, the project must be judged a success. Indeed, even as a solid majority of Chilean voters re-jected Pinochet's reelection in 1988, and elected a center-left coalition to replace him in 1989, incoming president Patricio Aylwin and his Concertación coalition were at pains to promise that they would not make fundamental changes in Pinochet's economic policies. And, through three successive Con-certación presidencies, that promise has held. The political sustainability of Chile's option for globalization (in sharp contrast to Bolivia or Ecuador) lies in the perception (and perhaps the reality) that most Chileans are benefiting, even if some benefit much more than others. Those who feel that they are worse off (the indigenous Mapuche, the un- or underemployed urban poor) are a minority incapable of shaking the stability of the system.

There was a theory in the 1980s that neoliberal reforms were so unpopu-lar that they could only be imposed by an authoritarian regime. The Chilean case confirms this, but the Costa Rican case disconfirms it. Costa Rica weath-ered the oil shocks of the 1970s and the debt crisis of the 1980s (not to men-tion the challenges posed by revolution, civil war, and international conflict in Central America in the 1980s) without any threat to the integrity of the dem-ocratic system. Unlike Chile, Costa Rica was not an enthusiastic convert to neoliberalism, but rather a reluctant conscript. Costa Rica has as strong a wel-fare state as any Latin American country save Uruguay, and no government of either major party wanted to risk dismantling it. At the same time, it was fis-cally imperative to control the costs of such programs as the national health service and social security. Costa Rica's economic viability had depended for a century on exports, so the need to adjust to changing world market condi-tions was not controversial. The result, in the course of the 1980s and 1990s, was a cautious, calibrated adoption of neoliberalism so far as was necessary, and an adaptation to globalization so far as was advantageous. The result was that Costa Rica kept its fiscal house in enough order to avoid a crisis, sustained its traditional exports as best it could, developed new exports such as electronics and ecotourism, and managed a slow but steady improvement in the standard of living of the majority of the population. As in Chile, those who felt that they were worse off were a minority.

Chile and Costa Rica are "successful" globalizers only by comparison with the rest of the region. Both still have high levels of inequality, and both are highly vulnerable to the vicissitudes of the increasingly unregulated global economy. Growing portions of their populations are underemployed and working in the informal economy. But they have each managed to do well enough by most of their populations to maintain the stability of their democracies.

■ Consolidation and Deconsolidation

After a generation in which democracy advanced broadly in the region, it is striking that the three countries where democracy is healthiest, closest to consolidation, are drawn from the group of five earlier democratizers discussed in Chapter 3 (i.e., Chile, Uruguay, Costa Rica, Venezuela, and Colombia). While Colombia, as just discussed, remains formally democratic, no one would think of calling it consolidated. Venezuela's democracy may have achieved consolidation in the late 1980s, but as we will see below, it is deeply unstable today. Uruguay and Costa Rica are unquestionably Latin America's strongest democracies today. Chile's democracy, while stable, is seriously limited by the authoritarian structures imposed on it by Pinochet. Finally, El Salvador is the greatest surprise coming out of the great Central American crisis of the 1980s: slowly, but with increasing confidence, this country is building a functioning, inclusive democracy.

Uruguay's quirky but durable democracy emerged from the decade of military dictatorship like an archipelago after a tidal wave (this felicitous image is from Dutrénit Bielous, 1994). The Blancos and Colorados resumed their places as the traditional operators, the Ley de Lemas with its institutionalized factionalism was reinstated, and the Broad Front (FA) resumed its rise as an alternative on the left. On the question of how to deal with the human rights abuses of the military period, the political establishment in Congress opted for an amnesty, and this was confirmed by the voters in a referendum. The country chose, democratically, to turn the page. Uruguay's economy continues its slow decline toward entropy, kept afloat for now by its membership in Mercosur. Uruguayans still have relatively high incomes, and a relatively egalitarian distribution of income, but a low rate of growth. The basic elements of the Uruguayan welfare state are deteriorating but still intact. A population looking for alternatives has increasingly turned to the FA in recent elections. With the replacement of the Ley de Lemas by a conventional runoff system for presidential elections, it appears that the party system is becoming bipolar, with the FA opposed to a traditional bloc composed of the Colorados and Blancos. The biggest threat to democracy in Uruguay is probably a catastrophic economic failure, a danger that is increased by its dependence on the somewhat precarious economies of Brazil and Argentina. Barring that, democracy is well established.

Costa Rica is now by far the most durable democracy in the region, and arguably the most secure. As noted in the previous section, Costa Rica's democracy successfully weathered oil shocks, debt crises, and Central American wars to emerge in the 1990s with the strongest economy in Central America and one of Latin America's higher per capita incomes. There has been an increase in inequality, and some deterioration in healthcare and social security. Unemployment, underemployment, and the informal economy have all tended to increase. Yet all these strains have been handled within the normal channels of democratic politics. The party system remains dominated by PLN and PUSC, as it has been for a generation, although in the most recent elections a split in the PLN allowed the PUSC its second consecutive presidential victory, something that had never happened before. The population continues to support democracy and to express pride in Costa Rica's political system. Costa Rica now displays many of the problems typical of more advanced democracies, such as voter apathy and declining turnout, and the complaint of inadequate choices. But surely, if there is any democratic regime in Latin America that meets Juan Linz and Alfred Stepan's criterion of being "the only game in town" (1997), it must be Costa Rica.

The same cannot yet be said for democracy in Chile, even though the post-Pinochet regime is now on its third elected president. In spite of electoral success and a reasonably strong economy, democracy in Chile continues to be bound by the authoritarian remnants enshrined in the constitution (such as the appointed senators) and the persistence of significant antidemocratic elements on the right, and to a lesser extent on the left. On the right, it is by no means clear that former supporters of the Pinochet regime are unconditional democrats. Should the political center of gravity shift decisively to the left, as it did in 1970 when Allende was elected, it is not hard to imagine important elements on the right (including sectors of the armed forces) becoming disloyal to the regime. At the same time, a key component of Allende's old coalition, the Communist Party, has remained uncommitted to the post-Pinochet order on the not unreasonable grounds that the authoritarian restraints on democracy constitute fatal flaws. Unless these disloyal oppositions come to accept the current regime as legitimate, the continuation of democracy in Chile depends far too much on a continuation of the Concertación coalition in power. Should the Concertación split, or should it lose support to one or both of the disloyal extremes, the outcome could be some form of quasi-democracy. Along with Uruguay, Chile has the region's longest tradition of liberal democracy, but its prognosis at this time is unclear.

If Chile's return to democracy has been, thus far, somewhat disappointing, El Salvador presents us with a pleasant surprise. After fifty years of draconian military rule and more than a decade of guerrilla war and brutal counterinsurgency, after tens of thousands of deaths in a very small country, the 1990s saw the beginnings of what seems to be a genuine transition to democracy. What is more, it is a democracy that is making room in the political arena for the former insurgents of the Farabundo Martí National Liberation Front (FMLN), which is now the second largest party in the National Assembly and could soon win the presidency. The Central American Peace Plan, begun in 1987 under the leadership of President Oscar Arias of Costa Rica, appears to have been a critical turning point, coming at a time when both sides in the armed conflict approached exhaustion. The international conjuncture in the succeeding years continued to promote a settlement, as the external sources of support for each side tended to dry up. Successive elections and successive governments have worked to build mutual confidence enough that a return to violence on a large scale is less and less likely, even in the event of an electoral victory by the FMLN. It is far too soon to talk about democracy being consolidated in El Salvador, but its very persistence for over a decade in such infertile soil is nothing short of remarkable.

Venezuela was widely regarded in the 1980s as a consolidated democracy, but it slid into prolonged instability and regime transformation beginning in 1989, when newly elected president Carlos Andrés Pérez chose to impose a radical program of neoliberal economic reforms that were completely contrary to the approach implied in his campaign. The massive popular riots that ensued—the "Caracazo"—shook the government, but it survived. Two military coup attempts in 1992 further undermined the government, and Pérez was ultimately impeached and removed from office in 1993. The political dominance of the two principal parties—AD and COPEI—came under increasing attack in those years, and the whole democratic regime was increasingly portrayed and perceived as corrupt and fraudulent. The election victory of Hugo Chávez in 1998 led to adoption of a new constitution with strong majoritarian rather than pluralist characteristics, and a prolonged struggle for power ensued between Chávez's predominantly poor supporters and opponents drawn largely from the threatened middle and upper classes. Although the country remains under a democratic regime, it is a different democracy than the regime that held sway from 1958 to 1998. For forty years, Venezuelans repeatedly voted for opposition presidential candidates in hopes of improvement in their prospects; instead, they got a steady decline through the 1980s and 1990s, regardless of the governing party. That democratic regime lost its popular base and was displaced because most citizens came to believe that it was no more than a façade for a greedy oligarchy. The future of democracy in Venezuela is exceedingly cloudy.

The consolidation of a democratic regime is still a rare prize in Latin America, even in these times when the existence of such a regime is almost universal. Even countries with deep democratic traditions and habits can move toward deconsolidation, as in Venezuela, or perch precariously on the edge, as in Chile. These difficulties make the good news from El Salvador all the more welcome, and the solidity of democracy in Costa Rica and Uruguay all the more astonishing.

▓ Conclusion

One hundred years ago there were no democracies of any description in Latin America. Fifty years ago there were three. Today almost all countries in the region have liberal democratic regimes. So why are we not celebrating? It is still true that liberal democracy is a good thing because it protects citizens from authoritarian abuse and allows them substantial rights and freedoms. It is still true that honest and competitive elections are the most effective, least destructive way of selecting and removing governments. Democratically elected governments have proven to be at least as capable of sound economic policymaking, even in crisis conditions, as have authoritarian governments.

Yet this chapter has made clear that liberal democracies in Latin America are predominantly of very low quality. They have largely failed to deal effectively with the region's massive social problems, such as the poverty endured by the majority of the population. They have largely failed to reverse the growing, increasingly visible inequality of Latin American societies. They have largely failed to build strong, institutionalized party systems capable of translating the popular will into stable, effective governments. They have largely failed to build states strong enough to actually carry out a coherent policy agenda. They have largely failed to build a political culture and political habits supportive of democracy. Indeed, the failures are so widespread that what is surprising is the survival of liberal democracy.

A principal reason for that survival is the international climate favoring liberal democracy, a climate fostered by U.S. policy over the last twenty years. The United States now has a clearly stated preference for democratic over nondemocratic regimes in Latin America. That preference does not extend to democratic regimes that do not please the U.S. government (e.g., Haiti or Venezuela), but even then the United States has been reluctant to overtly support their overthrow. The U.S. preference for democracy has helped to head off nondemocratic outcomes in Guatemala, Ecuador, and the Dominican Republic, among other cases. However, this international climate could change very quickly if a U.S. administration should decide that democracy in Latin America is no longer a priority. Without such international support, few of these regimes would have the resources to resist an authoritarian takeover.

The substantive failure of most liberal democracies in Latin America may, in the final analysis, be attributed first to basic flaws in the liberal democratic model itself, and second to the challenges posed by economic globalization to the effective exercise of democracy. Liberal democracy entails a political order that is fundamentally liberal in protecting rights (including especially property rights) and limiting government authority. It is democratic (under conditions of universal suffrage) insofar as the citizens vote to choose their rulers. But the institutional arrangements of liberal democracy are ill-equipped to resolve the basic contradiction cited earlier in this book, between democracy's inherent presumption of equality and capitalism's inevitable production of inequality. Money means power, and money is unequally distributed. Latin America, moreover, remains the most unequal region in the world.

Globalization exacerbates inequality by reinforcing the power of those with money. Under current conditions, capital can move in and out of a country with breathtaking speed, such that governments that want their countries to have access to these capital flows have little alternative but to conform to whatever conventional wisdom prevails in the capital markets of the day, even when such conformity will exact a heavy price from their citizens, and even when they have a clear electoral mandate to the contrary. This was the position of Carlos Andrés Pérez in 1989; the choices he made started Venezuela's long slide from democratic consolidation to chronic instability. Yet had he acted in conformity with his populist promises, Venezuela would have persisted in its long, agonizing economic decline.

The need to deepen democracy is both an ethical imperative and increasingly a practical necessity. Liberal democracies need to be somewhat responsive to the felt needs of the people to maintain the legitimacy of their authority, but they have often been able to maintain stability even with significant unresponsiveness and injustice. With increasing frequency, however, globalizing pressures run counter to clear popular electoral mandates. Governments that defy their mandates run an increasing risk of being forced from power, but the negative power of popular resistance needs to be matched by the positive ability to build a new democracy. A democracy based on a more egalitarian economy and a more participatory polity would have a stronger base of legitimacy—but only if the egalitarian economy were also productive enough to meet expectations. Thus a deeper democracy is in fact a necessity, but it is also an ethical imperative. We ought to favor a deepening of democracy because it is the right thing to do, the just thing to do. Democratic theory (including liberal democracy) assumes the equality of all citizens and the competence of every citizen to judge her or his own interest. Every citizen ought to have equal opportunity to develop her or his potential because if everyone is equal, no one has a right to claim more. Indeed, none of us can achieve our full potential as human beings, and society cannot achieve its full potential without seeing to it that all of us have that opportunity.

Could it be that under present economic and social conditions, internally and globally, liberal democracy is no longer viable in Latin America? The final chapter will explore this possibility.

7

A New Vision of Democracy in a Globalized World

Although liberalism emphasizes citizen rights and limited government, radical approaches to democracy tend to emphasize popular sovereignty and equality. Chantal Mouffe (1992, preface) quite rightly pointed out that liberal democracy involves an articulation of these two currents, which are in conflict on fundamental principles. The principles of equality and liberty do not always fit together easily. She argued that a radical approach to democracy, rather than trying to resolve this tension, should protect and enhance it:

> Between the democratic logic of identity and equivalence and the liberal logic of pluralism and difference, the experience of a radical and plural democracy can only consist in the recognition of the multiplicity of social logics and the necessity of their articulation. But this articulation should always be recreated and renegotiated, and there is no hope of a final reconciliation. This is why radical democracy also means the radical impossibility of a fully achieved democracy. (p. 14)

That is, liberalism promotes a vision of society as composed of unique individuals who should have maximum liberty to develop themselves. Democracy presupposes that fundamentally, all human beings are equal and are equal parts of a community. The two perspectives converge in that liberalism also demands equality, at least in the sense of equal opportunity, whereas democracy demands liberty, at least in the sense that there should be no restrictions imposed by any authority other than the people. Yet the tension remains and must remain: liberalism makes no provision for community except in the narrow sense of temporary and contingent shared interests; democracy vests sovereignty precisely in a community that has a right to restrict the liberties of nonconforming members. If liberty is primary, the people cannot, finally, rule. If popular sovereignty is primary, liberty is contingent on the popular will.

This basic contradiction is rooted in contrasting liberal and radical approaches to truth itself. Liberalism (e.g., John Stuart Mill) promotes pluralism because liberals believe that truth can never be finally known and can best be approached by leaving every person free to express her or his thoughts. Radicalism (e.g., Jean-Jacques Rousseau) affirms that the people, collectively, can know the truth (if they are not poisoned by thoughts of their individual self-interest) and have the right to enforce it on nonconformists. Rousseau's idealization of the whole people is truly sovereign, but they keep their right to rule only so long as they think only of the common good, not of any particular good.

Rousseau resurrects the classical ideal of the citizen as active participant in the affairs of the community, as indeed an integral part of the community. For Rousseau, difference and pluralism are mortal threats to the integrity of the community. However, as we saw in Chapter 1, his vision of how a whole people could rule is so riven by contradictions as to be useless as a guide to practice. It can serve only, as here, as a conceivable but unattainable alternative to liberal democracy.

How can a radical perspective on democracy be reformulated to pose a practical means of enriching and deepening liberal democracy? This is fundamentally a question of coming to terms with the meaning of citizenship in a world in which conventional territorial states—democratic or not—are too small to deal with a globalized economy and too large to be meaningfully governed by the people.

To be a citizen is to be a member, a part, a participant in a political community. In its original classical meaning, the citizens were the demos, the people of a polis. The ancient Greeks certainly assumed that citizenship implied direct and extensive involvement in the collective choices made by the polity. For Plato as well as Aristotle, one could only be fully human as a member of a polis, as a citizen.

Citizenship in this classical sense has been in crisis, not just since the dawn of the modern nation-state but since the advent of the Roman Empire. The old notion of the citizenry collectively ruling themselves simply cannot have the same meaning in polities of tens of millions of people and hundreds of thousands of square miles. Liberal democracy attempts to adapt citizenship by adding the element of representation, but loses the element of direct and intense involvement. Liberalism, moreover, also loses the classical sense of community as prior to the citizen. The liberal political order, instead, is built on a foundation of egoistic individuals pursuing their unique self-interests. Thus liberal democratic citizenship is a poor copy indeed of the classical ideal. Perhaps, though, classical citizenship is not even an ideal worth holding, since modern industrial society is inherently and deeply pluralistic, whereas the classical polis was, in principle, unified. The diversity that liberalism recognizes and encourages would have been highly problematic to the ancient Greeks.

But how is even liberal democratic citizenship possible in a world where economic power is so concentrated—nationally and globally—as to negate the equality of citizens?

Democracy and Capitalism: Not-So-Fraternal Twins

Liberal democracy and capitalism share common roots in liberal thought that sees the world as made up of self-seeking individuals competing with each other. Developed by such economic thinkers as Adam Smith, this perspective was used to justify laissez-faire economics: the best way to serve the common interest is to leave individuals as free as possible to pursue their private interests. Individual enterprise and competition, it was argued, will be far more productive of wealth for the nation as a whole than coordination of the economy by the state.

Liberal political thinkers such as John Stuart Mill developed a parallel argument to the effect that the search for truth is best served by maximizing the liberty of expression, rather than by the use of state authority to impose a version of the truth. Mill, in *Representative Government,* argued for full citizenship, including voting rights, for the working class, and he made the same argument for women in *The Subjection of Women,* on grounds that no authority can be a better judge of people's own interests than they themselves. But he also advocated helping the more affluent, and more educated, minority defend its interests by granting them more than one vote per person. Thus did classical political liberalism try to balance majority rule and minority rights, by setting the rules to make sure that the majority had a voice, but did not truly rule. Although today the idea of one person, one vote is fundamental to democracy, in many other ways liberal democracies are structured to give the majority voice, but not rule.

Notwithstanding their shared roots, liberal economics and liberal politics entailed serious contradictions from the beginning. Most fundamentally, while the emerging liberal democracy was based on the principle of the equality of all citizens, capitalism's free market and competition necessarily produced inequality of economic means, which inevitably translated into inequality of political power. Thus, in practice, one of the most striking features of all modern liberal democracies is the disproportionate influence of those who control capital. The classical Marxist view, of course, was that capitalists are the ruling class and that democracy was no more than a façade. One need not go that far to recognize that minorities with money are everywhere more powerful than their numbers would warrant. Capitalism and liberal democracy are increasingly in tension because the former inevitably generates inequality, while the latter presupposes equality. If they are now in conflict, on what grounds may we give priority to one or the other? Each is founded on the principle that every human being has equal rights, whether to participate in the market or in the political process. Equality is the ethical foundation of liberalism. Capitalism, however, though it begins with the premise of equality, sacrifices it on the altar of the liberty to accumulate wealth and power. In making this sacrifice, capitalism forfeits its own ethical grounding, for liberty without a commitment to equality is merely a recipe for a war of each against all, with victory to the strongest. Capitalism might still be justified on utilitarian grounds: many would argue that it is the most productive economic system the world has ever seen. But it is ethically incoherent.

Democracy, in contrast, is only conceivable in a context of the equality of all citizens, even if that equality has always and everywhere been vitiated by profound economic and social inequalities that create de facto political inequalities. What this means is that, in principle, democracy remains the best political order to serve the human development of all by empowering all. Democracy's ability to fulfill this potential has been and continues to be undermined by the inequalities of capitalism. Perhaps the central challenge in ensuring true majority rule is limiting the power of money to outweigh numbers. This problem is probably most serious among Latin American democracies, where the majority is almost always very poor. However, even in the United States, few effective measures have been taken to counteract the weight of wealth in the political process.

Through most of the twentieth century liberal democracy and capitalism continued to coexist. Liberal democracies continued to produce policies conducive to capitalist interests, and continued to provide enough trappings of popular sovereignty and social welfare to satisfy most citizens. By the end of the century, though, the globalization of capitalism had brought the conflict with liberal democracy to the breaking point.

■ Globalized Capitalism and the Illusion of Democracy

Capitalism has always been global, as Karl Marx and Friedrich Engels pointed out so vividly in this passage from the *Communist Manifesto* of 1848:

> In place of the old local and national seclusion and self-sufficiency, we have intercourse in every direction, universal interdependence of nations. And as in material, so in intellectual production. The intellectual creations of individual nations become common property. National one-sidedness and narrow-mindedness become more and more impossible, and from the numerous national and local literatures there arises a world literature.
>
> The bourgeoisie, by the rapid improvement of all instruments of production, by the immensely facilitated means of communication, draws all, even the most barbarian, nations into civilisation. The cheap prices of its commodities are the heavy artillery with which it batters down all Chinese walls, with which it forces the barbarians' intensely obstinate hatred of foreigners to capitulate. It compels all nations, on pain of extinction, to adopt the bourgeois mode of production; it compels them to introduce what it calls civilisation into

their midst, i.e., to become bourgeois themselves. In one word, it creates a
world after its own image. (Marx and Engels, 1978, pp. 476–477)

Indeed, the ability of capital to transcend national boundaries was a key, in
Marx's analysis, to understanding how capitalists could induce national
authorities to create and protect property rights for them, and protect their
interests. Marx understood that entrepreneurs whose businesses extended
beyond national or state boundaries were to that extent autonomous from state
authorities. The unprecedented power of capitalism derived in part from this
leverage over the state derived from transcending its boundaries.

Clearly, with continuing advances in transportation and communication
technology, the global capitalist economy has become steadily more integrated, more globalized, over the century and a half since the *Manifesto*. Now,
in the early twenty-first century, hundreds of billions of dollars can be moved
from one country to another instantaneously in market waves based on uncon-
firmed rumors or ungrounded fears. Yet these capital movements can have
devastating effects on the national economies involved, closing businesses,
breaking banks, bankrupting governments, and depriving thousands of workers of their jobs. Even countries on the receiving end of such capital movements are not wholly better off, since the economy may be fundamentally distorted by the power of the newly invested capital, and will continue to be
vulnerable to extreme fluctuations in the future. In either case, state authorities are ever more poorly equipped to effectively regulate their own
economies.

Capitalism has always challenged the principle of state sovereignty, the
idea that a government in control of a territorial state has supreme authority
over its territory and population. In the mid–nineteenth century, for example,
the nascent, supposedly sovereign states of Latin America had little choice but
to adopt policies and practices that were attractive to British, German, and
U.S. investors. Otherwise their countries would at best remain stagnant backwaters, or at worst suffer attack by neighboring states acting at the behest of
international capital, as in the case of the Paraguayan War of the 1860s.

Today the imbalance is even more extreme, as even the most powerful
national governments find they have limited control over global capital, and
need to tailor their policies quite carefully to avoid undermining their own
currencies or to keep factories from moving to more attractive venues. The
push toward free trade that began after World War II with the General Agreement on Tariffs and Trade has now culminated in the radical free trade regime
of the World Trade Organization, wherein the vast majority of the world's
states have committed themselves to eliminating, in the relatively short term,
any barriers to the free movement of capital, goods, and services. Such barriers are construed to include environmental or labor regulations that may
unduly burden foreign investors, as well as any attempt to regulate or control

the international flow of capital. The result is an almost complete evisceration of sovereignty, especially for less developed countries.

This loss of sovereignty applies to all states, without regard to their regime type. But the problem is particularly acute for the regime type that concerns us in this book, democracies. This is because democracy vests sovereignty in the people themselves. Whereas with a dictatorship one might argue that sovereignty only benefits the rulers, in a democracy the rulers are, in principle, the people. If their sovereignty is bled of its substance by globalized capitalism, then democracy itself is but a shell.

▓ Deepening Democracy

If we are to take democracy seriously, to take seriously its promise to serve the human development of all by empowering all, we can no longer postpone asserting *democratic control over the economy,* at all levels from the firm to the globe. At the level of the firm, it is necessary to confront the entrenched autocracy of capital at the expense of labor. Such a confrontation could lead in several directions. The least likely, more than a decade after the collapse of the Soviet Union, would be the complete expropriation of capital and the establishment of state ownership of the economy. A very distinct but equally radical approach would turn full ownership and management control over to the employees of each firm, on grounds that it is their labor that has created the capital of the firm.

The full expropriation of capital may prove necessary in order to democratize the firm, but past experience suggests it is likely to be extremely disruptive, as the owners of capital use all means at their disposal to resist. Moreover, expropriation would deprive the firm of the managerial experience and technical expertise possessed by the owners. A more pragmatic approach would be to make the workers joint owners of the firm, giving them an equal voice with the owners of capital in the management of the firm. This would go well beyond most current models of employee ownership, which typically keep the employees at arm's length from actual control of management. Workers with an equal voice in management may be expected to set different priorities on issues like plant relocation: confronting a particular competitive situation, they would likely opt for wage restraint rather than plant closure or layoffs. An equal worker voice in management thus has the potential of taking away one of the principal weapons of capital in escaping the control of the state: the threat to close plants and move elsewhere. That is why democratization of the firm is important to deepening democracy in general.

The economy also must be democratized at the national level. Part of the answer to this lies in democratization of the firm, since capitalist firms band together to exercise overwhelming influence over national economic policy. Democratically controlled firms would still seek to influence policy, but their goals would be quite different, and more compatible with democracy at the national level.

Another element of economic democratization at the national level involves the governance of the economy. The free market may be an efficient allocator of resources when participants are relatively equal, but market transactions between rich and poor will always tend to advantage and further enrich the rich. The market in goods, services, and capital must operate within a planning framework provided by a democratically controlled government that takes into consideration the welfare of the whole society, and that is open to broad participation by all elements of the society.

Finally, and most fundamentally, democratization of the economy requires *taking economic equality seriously*. Democracy is premised on equality, yet economic inequality is deep, and getting deeper, all over the world in this era of free markets and minimal regulation. Democratically controlled governments must make it a priority to substantially reduce income inequality, and further, must mitigate the effects of property inequality by giving workers a voice in economic policymaking equal to that afforded to capital. An important policy to keep economic inequality from feeding on itself would be to impose strict limits on inheritance.

Economic inequality is not the only inequity that must be addressed in the deepening of democracy. A deeper democracy will also provide for much *more genuine equality between the genders, between racial and ethnic groups, and between heterosexuals and those with other sexual preferences.* Taking these kinds of equality seriously involves not only ensuring more equality of power between men and women, or between dominant and subordinate racial, ethnic, or sexual-preference groups, but also ensuring their rights to be different. The right to be different means assuring all persons equal liberty to define themselves, a liberty that must necessarily be limited only by the equivalent rights of others. My right to be different, as John Stuart Mill might have said, does not include a right to oppress or control you.

Taking equality seriously in this way leads directly to the basic democratic principles of *majority rule* and *minority rights*. Classic liberal democracy entails a particular sort of balance between these two principles. Governments are to be elected by the majority of citizens while those who are not part of the majority at any given time are to be ensured the basic rights and freedoms needed to allow them to continue to participate in public life and to seek enough support from fellow citizens to become, in their turn, a majority. However, as was argued earlier in this chapter, in practice liberal democracies give the majority a voice, but do not allow true majority rule.

How can the majority really rule while not tyrannizing over minorities? There are multiple ways to deepen democracy on this front. One option is to make more extensive use of referenda, as a means of posing policy issues directly to the voters, so that a majority vote determines policy. As long as every voter has an equal opportunity to participate in the debate, and as long as the losing side (the minority) can return the issue to the people in a later referendum, then minorities would not have been oppressed by a referendum.

The power of money to distort the democratic debate must obviously be addressed. The doctrine that the right to spend money in a political cause is a matter of free speech must be rejected as undermining the principle of the equality of citizens. The best way of ensuring a democratic balance here is to provide state financing for every candidate or party meeting published criteria (e.g., a minimum percentage of the vote in the most recent election, or a minimum number of petitioners), while prohibiting or very strictly limiting private financing of campaigns. Such an approach still has problems, but it would significantly reduce the power of money in political debates.

Majority rule in the election of governments is at the very core of democracy, yet a variety of electoral systems are used that may distort the popular will. The archaic and arcane system of electing presidents in the United States obviously ought to be changed to a direct popular vote, but even then, there are some choices that are better for majority rule than others. For example, straight plurality election, where citizens vote once and the candidate with the most votes wins, may tend to promote two-party systems wherein the winner gets an absolute majority most of the time, but there are numerous Latin American cases of fragmented party systems yielding winners with less than a third of the vote. Obviously this does not serve majority rule. A better approach, used in France and some Latin American countries, is the runoff between the two leading candidates from the first round. The runoff system allows minorities to seek votes in the first round, but requires that both parties and voters coalesce into a majority in the runoff.

Similarly in parliamentary elections, some electoral systems are better for majority rule than others. The classic winner-take-all electoral system used for legislative elections in the United Kingdom and most of the Commonwealth (as well as in the United States) is perhaps too good for majority rule, since it routinely manufactures legislative majorities for parties that did not in fact win popular majorities. On the other hand, systems of proportional representation widely used in Latin America usually make it extremely difficult for any one party to win a majority of seats. But that is not necessarily bad for majority rule, since a negotiated coalition after an election will in all likelihood represent a majority of the electorate if it has a majority in the parliament. Finally, the French runoff system (also used for parliamentary elections) guarantees that an absolute majority of each constituency will have voted for each deputy elected. Overall, either proportional representation or the runoff system is more likely than the winner-take-all system to accurately reflect popular majorities.

One problem with representative democracy, even when the electoral majority is accurately represented, lies in the relative autonomy of the officials elected: for the duration of their term, they are free to exercise their own judgment, and indeed are expected to do so. In the classic argument of Edmund Burke, the representative ill-serves the constituents if he or she merely reflects their views, for the representative may have information leading to a different view of the true interests of the constituents. (Burke, by the way, lost that election.) On the other hand, there is a very real danger that elected representatives might simply choose to serve other interests once elected, or might prove incapable of defending constituent interests adequately. The Venezuelan constitution of 1999 addresses this issue by providing for the revocation of electoral mandates after half of the term has expired, with a stringent requirement that the number of votes for revocation must equal or exceed those originally received by the official in question.

If we must take majority rule seriously, it is equally important to be serious about minority rights, for two very good reasons. First, majority rule should be seen as a continuing process in which successive decisions are taken by successive majorities that may be differently composed. Any voter may expect to be in a minority on some issue, and thus would rationally want to be assured that those in a minority would retain the freedom to express themselves and try to convince members of the majority to change their minds. The minority should have the right to try to become the majority.

There is, however, a second situation wherein minority rights are even more important: wherein a population constitutes a permanent minority. In societies such as the United States, where racial or ethnic consciousness is pervasive, members of racial or ethnic minorities cannot reasonably hope to be in the majority on issues of central concern to them. They should at least have the right to maintain their difference from the majority without the majority attempting to impose its will upon them. This issue is highly relevant throughout Latin America, where indigenous populations are systematically disadvantaged and their cultural autonomy is severely threatened. In some countries, notably Guatemala and the Central Andean states of Bolivia, Peru, and Ecuador, the indigenous population is actually the majority, or close to a majority, but traditionally subordinate. For these populations, the issue of cultural autonomy is linked to the question of majority rule. The day may not be far off in Bolivia, for example, when the indigenous population elects a president.

Another issue of minority rights arises with regard to property rights. It is well-known that the many protections of minority rights built into the U.S. Constitution were intended by the drafters specifically to protect the propertied interests from the tyranny of the majority. Among those checks was the selection of both the Senate and the president by methods that were intended to be influenced, but not controlled, by the popular vote. In addition, federal judges were to be nominated by the president and confirmed by the Senate, and would hold office for life unless impeached by the House of Representatives and convicted by the Senate. Finally, and most explicitly, the first article in the Bill of Rights provides that no one may be deprived of property without due process of law. In general, all liberal democracies include similar protections, though the precise mechanisms vary.

The question now is, having concluded that capitalism and democracy are fundamentally in conflict, what is the appropriate status of property rights in a deepened democracy? The socialist position is that, in principle, capitalist property (ownership of assets that are expected to produce income) ought not to be a right, since property is derived from exploiting the labor of workers. However, the moral bankruptcy of capitalist property is to some extent mitigated by the absence of any historical example of a wholly socialist economy as productive and self-sustaining as capitalism. This is not to say that such an economy might not develop in the future, and it is certainly not to deny the failings and contradictions of capitalism. But for the moment, it may be prudent to allow the continued existence of capitalist property under the regulation of a legal regime that matches the rights of capital with its obligations. For example, a firm could have its investment in a plant protected by the state, but it would be obliged to consider itself a part of the community from which the plant draws its labor and supplies, and thus obligated to put a very high priority on keeping the plant open. A decision to close the plant and move the business elsewhere would be grounds for expropriation.

Advocates of deepening democracy often call for *decentralization,* or passing real decisionmaking authority to the most local practicable level, on grounds that it is at the local level where it is easiest for the majority of citizens to exercise control. The ancient Athenians understood this principle when they held that democracy could only be possible where the whole body of citizens could gather in an assembly to debate public affairs. Rousseau took a similar stance in *The Social Contract*. Robert Dahl, in *After the Revolution?* (1970), sought to adapt this point to the modern practice of polyarchy in large-scale nation-states. He advocated what he called the "Chinese Box" principle (calling to mind nested boxes from smaller to larger). The idea was that each policy issue ought to be dealt with democratically at the local level, unless its implications were broad enough to require coordination of policy on a larger scale. This approach is now widely accepted in principle, but its practice all too often falls short of democratic ideals. Perhaps the biggest problem is voter apathy and the resultant prevalence of local oligarchies in place of the ideal of direct democracy.

It is possible that voter apathy is a rational response to the correct perception that the most important issues are not decided at the local level, or to the equally correct perception that local affairs are largely controlled by local elites. Either way, measures described earlier to democratize the economy, especially the firm, could begin to teach people to participate more actively at the grassroots level.

Indeed, it is at the grassroots where the immense variety and vitality of civil society operates. Civil society includes all sorts of organized human activity between the family and the state. Civil society organizations may transcend the local, and they may not be democratic. Nevertheless, a deeper democracy will surely have a large part of the population involved in civil society at the local level. Here too, democratization of the economy should be helpful by teaching people that they have a right to participate in matters affecting their daily lives.

■ Globalizing Democracy

Dahl's Chinese Box principle, though primarily used by him to justify decentralization, also supplies a powerful rationale for global democratic governance of what is already a global capitalist economy. Globalized capitalism poses fundamental challenges to sovereignty in general and to democratic sovereignty in particular. Just as at the national level a century ago governments implemented regulatory structures to control the excesses of monopoly capitalism, something similar is needed on the global level today.

Of course, the global capitalist economy is already being governed, through the structures and policies of the International Monetary Fund, the World Bank, and the World Trade Organization, all of which are highly responsive to the interests of the United States, Japan, and the European Union. From the point of view of saving and promoting democracy, this governance system is part of the problem, because it is predicated largely on the disregard of democracy as a value (though the World Bank has recently included the promotion of liberal democracy among its goals). So long as capital and plants are encouraged to move freely in search of the best returns, democratic governments everywhere will be restrained from imposing policies that would improve the lot of their people, but would put their countries at a competitive disadvantage relative to countries that impose fewer costs on businesses.

Theoretically, the most straightforward way to achieve a globalized democracy would be to constitute a global state that would be democratically structured. Such a world state would presumably be federal, allowing broad autonomy to its constituent units and exercising authority only in such areas as basic economic regulations. Such a global state would be able to transcend the difficulties faced by even the largest current states in effectively regulating global capitalism, because its laws would have global reach. Nevertheless, this approach must be regarded as impractical in view of the extreme difficulties experienced in the past century by much more modest integrative schemes. By far the most successful has been the European Union, whose evolution has been painfully slow and which is still very far from being a true "United States of Europe."

An even more sweeping model of change would be some variation on a global revolutionary overthrow of the whole capitalist system. If it could occur, it would assuredly solve the problems posed by capitalism, but there is absolutely no assurance that a postcapitalist global regime might not generate other, even bigger problems. The essence of revolution is the opening of possibilities; only some of those possibilities are actually desirable. Everything would depend on the choices made by the revolutionaries in a position to wield power.

But the model of a global anticapitalist revolution is even further from the realm of possibility at present than a global democratic state. Marx's moral critique of capitalism remains impeccable, and in the same tradition contemporary Marxists continue to make major contributions to our understanding of this constantly evolving beast. Marx and Marxists have been predicting the collapse of capitalism for the last 150 years; if those years have taught us anything, it is that capitalism is far more resourceful and adaptable than Marx ever imagined. It simply strains credulity to think that favorable conditions for revolution could emerge throughout the world at the same time and not be countered by some combination of repression and co-optation.

A world of deepened liberal democracies with elected governments founded on popular organization and mobilization at the grassroots will be better able to balance the global power of contemporary capitalism. David Held (1995) argued that if democracy is to survive globalization, it must be extended to include the economy, and to operate on a global level; it must in short become "cosmopolitan democracy." Proceeding from the principle that every human being has a right to maximum autonomy consistent with the autonomy of others, Held argued:

> In the context of regional and global interconnectedness . . . people's equal interest in autonomy can only be adequately protected by a commitment from all those communities whose actions, policies and laws are interrelated and intertwined. For democratic law to be effective it must be internationalized. Thus, the implementation of a cosmopolitan democratic law and the establishment of a cosmopolitan community—a community of all democratic communities—must become an obligation for democrats, an obligation to build a transnational, common structure of political action which alone, ultimately, can support the politics of self-determination. (p. 231)

Held argued further that a political basis exists for building a more systematic democratic future: "This future has to be conceived in cosmopolitan terms—a new institutional complex with global scope, given shape and form by reference to a basic democratic law, which takes on the character of government to the extent, and only to the extent, that it promulgates, implements and enforces this law" (p. 237). Such a cosmopolitan institutional complex must include the economy, because democracy is challenged . . . by powerful sets of economic relations and organizations which can—by virtue of the bases of their operations—systematically distort democratic processes and outcomes. Accordingly, there is a case that, if democracy is to prevail, the key groups and associations of the economy will have to be rearticulated with political institutions so that they become part of the democratic process—adopting, within their very *modus operandi*, a structure of rules, principles and practices compatible with democracy. (p. 251)

The precise institutional form of cosmopolitan democracy remains to be determined, in Held's view, as does the question of how, in practice, to move the world toward a cosmopolitan democratic order. But he clearly views the establishment of such a new order as essential to the survival of democracy. This approach is probably more feasible than a global state, but still would be extremely difficult to carry out in practice, given all the vested interests in the global status quo. Nevertheless, the concept of cosmopolitan democracy as a goal is an important benchmark to keep in mind. The world may eventually develop to the point where such a move is possible.

For now, we probably must content ourselves with more pragmatic and piecemeal approaches directed toward getting some kind of handle on global capitalism. In the process, we will help to lay the groundwork for more comprehensive approaches such as that of Held. The changes discussed earlier, beginning at the grassroots and including deepening democracy at the national level, hold the key. To the extent that democracy is effectively deepened at local and national levels, national governments will prove more responsive to demands to protect and promote human development, and less responsive to the interests of capital. Since national governments control the great global institutions, when enough countries see the establishment of deepened democracies they will be able to mandate changed priorities. It is by no means implausible to think that deepened democracy is a real possibility in the most advanced capitalist countries, since these are also the most advanced democracies. These are precisely the countries that wield decisive voting power in the great global institutions. Thus a simple takeover of those institutions by deepened democracies is not at all beyond the realm of possibility. We will then be closer than ever to harnessing capitalism to serve the interests of the whole human race.

■ Latin America and the Democratic Vision

This book has shown that something resembling liberal democracy has become almost universal in Latin America in the past twenty-five years, but it is also clear that most of these liberal democracies are little more than empty shells, or at best what Larry Diamond (1999) has called "electoral democracies." They use the formal machinery of competitive elections to select their rulers, but the citizens are powerless to change the pervasive, extreme economic and social inequalities that have long been characteristic of Latin America.

It may be tempting to argue that concerns of deepening democracy are more appropriate to the well-institutionalized liberal democracies of the North Atlantic area. However, the agenda of deepening democracy may lack urgency and broad appeal in those countries precisely because liberal democracy has worked adequately for a long time and has even adapted itself to certain concessions to egalitarianism in the form of social democracy. By contrast, in Latin America, even though liberal democracy is now generally held to be better than the alternatives, few are satisfied with it. It has blatantly failed to address the long-standing problems of social injustice and has failed even to prevent a worsening of social conditions as a result of neoliberal reforms. Moreover, Latin American liberal democracies have done no better than their North Atlantic counterparts in performing their core mission: providing a meaningful link between the popular will expressed in elections and the policies of the government thus elected. Latin American elections, like those in the United States, tend to have a plebiscitory tone, where the issue is the expression of confidence in a ruler, not the communication of a popular will regarding policy. To a great extent, of course, national elections are necessarily blunt instruments that serve better to select rulers than to make policy decisions.

Because problems of social and economic injustice are more acute in Latin America, we may expect more Latin Americans to be receptive to the kind of radical democratic reforms discussed here. At the base, diverse social movements have already shown substantial vitality and have had significant effects on national politics. Such revitalization of popular participation at the community and neighborhood level can make nationally elected governments more responsive. National governments must be induced to open the way, politically and legally, to more worker ownership. Such democratization of the economy is even more critical in Latin America than in the North Atlantic area, because Latin Americans have even less control over decisions about opening and closing plants and are already burdened by wages at or below subsistence level.

Latin American governments also have a key role to play at the global level. Forging the new global economic consensus around minimal levels of human well-being will of course require the agreement of the advanced industrial countries, but it must also have the active commitment of Latin American and other Third World governments. These governments will have good reason to pursue such a new consensus, since it promises to substantially raise the standards of living of their own populations and to help them break out of the old vicious cycle of having to keep wages down in order to compete for investment. In sum, radical democratic reforms at local, national, and global levels would more easily engage elite as well as nonelite interests in Latin

American societies than in advanced liberal democracies such as the United States.

Some radical democratic reforms, however, are particularly important and particularly difficult for Latin America. If it is important that neoliberalism be surmounted, it is equally important to leave behind populism. Populism in Latin America has adapted the state to clientelism in the age of democracy. Throughout the region, politicians appeal for support on the basis of promises of benefits, and this is what the voters have come to expect. A populist state, however, normally has more commitments than resources, so the state satisfies those constituencies with the best connections. Clientelism enshrines private interest as the engine of public policy, and populism democratizes clientelism. The neoliberal political economic offensive proposed precisely to challenge the clientelization of economic policy and to rectify the fiscal penury of the populist state. But neither neoliberalism nor populism is the answer. A strong and responsive state must live within its means if it is to be able to promote the public interest in radical economic reform. Correspondingly, the population, the citizenry, must cease to look to the state for their material salvation. Organization and self-help at the base (especially including worker ownership) are critical to deepening democracy.

Democracy in Venezuela faces precisely this dilemma. As Hugo Chávez said of the long-standing democratic regime of Venezuela, a democracy based on a pact among elites allowing them to share power amounted to nothing more than a screen concealing continued predatory class rule and the de facto exclusion of the poor majority from meaningful participation. It was on the basis of this critique that Chávez was overwhelmingly elected president in 1998. With the old party and interest group elites in disarray and retreat, Chávez pushed through a new, much more participatory constitution, and began to implement a package of policies intended to fundamentally redistribute power in Venezuelan society.

Details of Chávez's struggles with his opponents have been discussed earlier in the book, but here the episode is noteworthy because Chávez raised some of the issues discussed in this chapter, in the context of his proposal for a "Bolivarian democracy." In particular, he proposed to create a democracy rooted in the participation of the whole people, including in particular the poor majority, in place of a regime that worked essentially to the benefit of the economic elite and the middle-class minority. His means for achieving this end were inadequately thought out and incompletely implemented. Moreover, Chávez could not escape from the contradiction between his radically participatory and democratic program and his own role as a caudillo dominating all decisionmaking.

The Chávez episode exemplifies the power of a radically democratic vision in a Latin American society wracked by prolonged economic decline and worsening poverty and inequality. The poor majority in Venezuela were ready to hear what he had to say. At the same time, the episode also shows the difficulties and contradictions of attempting a transition from a seriously defective liberal democracy to a deeper democracy. Particularly in Latin America, with its long tradition of *caudillismo,* one must ask whether such a transition could be brought about by any means other than a caudillo. But to rely on a caudillo to bring about democracy is truly a contradiction in terms, for the caudillo cannot truly empower the people without ceasing to be a caudillo. It is essential to the role that all power lie in his hands.

The changes contemplated by Chávez were not easy, and resistance was to be expected. It is certainly true that his own polarizing rhetoric contributed to conflict and drove away some of his own supporters. Still, he was dismantling the whole structure of the old democracy; it is not surprising, then, that the political and economic elites who ran that democracy should resist, and should try to bring him down. The challenge for Chávez and his opponents was to find a way back to dialogue, to find a way to stabilize a new democracy that would include not only the poor majority but also the wealthy and middle-class minority.

Chávez's rhetoric showed an acute consciousness of the deleterious effects of capitalist globalization, but he was notably cautious in practice, limiting himself to a reaffirmation of Venezuela's ties to the Organization of Petroleum-Exporting Countries, and the successful negotiation of a significant rise in oil prices. Otherwise, his economic policy was remarkably orthodox. Indeed, while he lost few chances to excoriate the Venezuelan bourgeoisie, he avidly courted foreign investment (though without much success). This pattern shows a consciousness of the external limits on his room for maneuver: no single Third World state, even a major oil producer, can break free of the constraints imposed by the globalized capitalist economy.

Chávez would support, and indeed has tried to promote, multilateral efforts to redress the inequities of the global economy. Any successful move toward more democracy on the level of the global economy could only help the effort to establish more equality and deeper democracy in Venezuela. The experience of Venezuela under Hugo Chávez is highly relevant in this context because he represents one of the most explicit and successful attempts to reconstitute and deepen democracy.

Another very important recent example is the election of Lula da Silva as president of Brazil. A key difference from Chávez is that, while Lula captured a majority in the presidential runoff in 2002, his Workers Party did not even come close to controlling a majority in either house of Congress. The Workers Party is already closely associated with the very interesting development of participatory budgeting at the community level in Porto Alegre and other cities. Now it is the leading party in the president's national coalition. Although Lula continues to be a critic of the injustices of the global economic order, and a supporter of Chávez, he has adopted a much more cautious, orthodox approach that has more in common with his centrist predecessor, Fernando Henrique Cardoso, than with Chávez. He has thereby avoided the sort of poisonous relations between his government and the country's economic elites that Chávez has suffered, but Lula has achieved this at the cost of alienating many of his more radical supporters.

In a very different political environment, former colonel Lucio Gutiérrez was elected president of Ecuador in 2002. The most prominent military leader of the coup that ousted Jamil Mahuad two years earlier, Gutiérrez successfully appealed to the same indigenous movement with which he had collaborated in that enterprise. But expectations that he would then pursue a defiant policy toward neoliberalism and globalization were soon dashed as he abandoned the coalition that elected him in favor of an alliance with the country's most conservative elements.

Both Lula and Gutiérrez exemplify the intense pressures on Latin America's democratically elected leaders to conform to capitalist globalization. Hugo Chávez is an example of what happens to those who do not conform. The electoral victories of all three, however, are signs that there is a strong constituency in Latin America for leaders who are willing to challenge the global economic order and to work toward deeper democracy. The forced resignation, in 2003, of Gonzalo Sánchez de Lozada in Bolivia is a sign of increasingly powerful resistance to those leaders who persist in promoting a globalization agenda that appears to offer little benefit to the poor majority. The movements and parties that accomplished these changes are beginning to transform politics at the grassroots as well as at the national level. Their growing strength holds important implications for the global future of democracy. A region that was historically barren ground for democracy could yet prove a nursery of ideas to give it new life.

Latin America thus has an opportunity to make a major contribution to the political theory and practice of democracy by pushing forward with a vision of radical democratic reform at a time when the stable democracies of the north seem unable to move. Such a democracy will include the economic sphere and will provide citizens with greatly expanded opportunities for participating in social decisions. Reduction of economic inequality will permit more citizens to have real access to the benefits of liberty and political participation. Possession of more resources will permit citizens to develop their capacities by acting in the political arena and in civil society. A deeper democracy will thus surpass liberal democracy without negating it. It will still include political liberties, competition for power through elections, and an autonomous civil society—in short, all the democratic achievements of liberal democracy. It will add a commitment to more economic equality and to a pluralism of the whole people rather than only of well-off, well-organized minorities (Dahl, 1982, 1985, 1989; Mouffe, 1992; Munck, 2003).

Conclusion

This chapter has sought to make the case that a substantial deepening of democracy is increasingly necessary to its survival in Latin America and around the world. A deepened democracy is necessary in Latin America, first, because existing liberal democracies are for the most part so deficient in serving the interests of the poor majorities that their legitimacy is being inexorably undermined. The numerous recent cases of presidents being forced from office are the most obvious sign of a deeper malaise.

Second, in Latin America and around the world, deepening democracy and holding national governments truly accountable to their citizens are essential to the larger task of globalizing democracy or achieving democratic control of capitalism on a global scale.

With deepened democracies in power in both First and Third World states, we will then be closer than ever to harnessing capitalism to serve the interests of the whole human race. The road to the globalization of democracy passes through grassroots democracy, and through the deepening of democracy at the level of the state. The revolution that Marx imagined as a proletarian insurrection sweeping away the entire capitalist system at a stroke may occur for the most part peacefully as people all over the world assert their right to more and more self-determination. Rather than being swept away, capitalism may yet be domesticated.

The task is huge, and the prospects, it must be admitted, are not good. But democracy is, at bottom, an ethical commitment that calls upon us always to look to how we can move toward the ideal. As Chantal Mouffe said in the passage previously quoted, "radical democracy also means the radical impossibility of a fully achieved democracy." Meaning lies in moving toward the goal, not only in getting there. Liberal democracies in Latin America probably can, with international support, persist without radical reform, even though they rest upon deeply unjust societies. But the democratic ideal they ambivalently embody clamors for realization, for those who have ears to hear.

Note

An earlier version of this chapter was presented at the Congress of the International Political Science Association, Durban, South Africa, 29 June–4 July 2003.

Acronyms

AD	Democratic Action (Venezuela)
ADN	National Democratic Alliance (Bolivia)
AP	Popular Action (Peru)
APRA	American Popular Revolutionary Alliance (Peru)
ARENA	National Renewal Alliance (El Salvador)
CIA	Central Intelligence Agency
CIERA	Research Center on Agrarian Reform (Nicaragua)
COB	Bolivian Workers Central
CONAIE	National Indigenous Confederation of Ecuador
COPEI	Independent Committee for Political and Electoral Organization (Venezuela)
DC	Christian Democratic Party (Chile)
ELN	National Liberation Army (Colombia)
EZLN	Zapatista Army of National Liberation (Mexico)
FA	Broad Front (Uruguay)
FARC	Revolutionary Armed Forces of Colombia
FDN	National Democratic Front (Mexico)
FMLN	Farabundo Martí National Liberation Front (El Salvador)
FREPASO	National Solidarity Front (Argentina)
FRG	Guatemalan Republican Front
FSLN	Sandinista National Liberation Front (Nicaragua)
GDP	gross domestic product
IMF	International Monetary Fund
M-19	April 19 Movement (Colombia)
MAS	Movement Toward Socialism (Bolivia, Venezuela)
MBL	Free Bolivia Movement
MIR	Revolutionary Left Movement (Bolivia, Chile, Venezuela)

MNR	National Revolutionary Movement (Bolivia)
MRTA	Tupac Amaru Revolutionary Movement
MST	Landless Movement (Brazil)
MVR	Fifth Republic Movement (Venezuela)
NACLA	North American Congress on Latin America
NAFTA	North American Free Trade Agreement
NE	New Space (Uruguay)
OAS	Organization of American States
OPEC	Organization of Petroleum-Exporting Countries
PAN	National Action Party (Mexico)
PCV	Communist Party of Venezuela
PLC	Constitutionalist Liberal Party (Nicaragua)
PLD	Dominican Liberation Party (Dominican Republic)
PLN	National Liberation Party (Costa Rica)
PMDB	Party of the Brazilian Democratic Movement
PPD	Party for Democracy (Chile)
PR	proportional representation
PR	Reformist Party (Dominican Republic)
PRD	Democratic Revolutionary Party (Mexico)
PRD	Dominican Revolutionary Party (Dominican Republic)
PRI	Institutional Revolutionary Party (Mexico)
PRONASOL	National Solidarity Program (Mexico)
PS	Socialist Party (Chile)
PT	Workers Party (Brazil)
PUSC	Social Christian Unity Party (Costa Rica)
RN	National Renewal (Chile)
UN	United Nations
UNO	National Opposition Union (Nicaragua)
UP	Popular Unity (Chile)
URD	Republican Democratic Union (Venezuela)
URNG	National Revolutionary Union of Guatemala

References

Abente, Diego. 1995. "A Party System in Transition: The Case of Paraguay." In Scott Mainwaring and Timothy Scully, eds., *Building Democratic Institutions: Party Systems in Latin America*. Stanford: Stanford University Press, pp. 298–320.

Abente-Brun, Diego. 1999. "'People Power' in Paraguay." *Journal of Democracy* 10 (3): 93–100.

Abootalebi, Ali R. 1995. "Democratization in Developing Countries, 1980–1989." *Journal of Developing Areas* 29:507–530.

Acosta Silva, Adrián, et al. 1995. "El fin del sistema político mexicano." *Nexos* 18 (208) (April): 40–53.

Acuña, Carlos H. 1994. "Politics and Economics in the Argentina of the Nineties (Or, Why the Future No Longer Is What It Used to Be)." In William C. Smith, Carlos H. Acuña, and Eduardo A. Gamarra, eds., *Democracy, Markets, and Structural Reform in Latin America*. New Brunswick, N.J.: Transaction, pp. 30–73.

Adrianzén, Alberto. 1998. "Perú: Adiós a la izquierda." *Nueva Sociedad* 157:75–86.

Agüero, Felipe. 2003. "Chile: Unfinished Transition and Increased Political Competition." In Jorge Domínguez and Michael Shifter, eds., *Constructing Democratic Governance in Latin America*. Baltimore: Johns Hopkins University Press, pp. 292–320.

Aguilar Bulgarelli, Oscar. 1980. *Costa Rica y sus hechos políticos de 1948*. San José: EDUCA.

Albala-Bertrand, Luis, coord. 1992. *Democratic Culture and Governance*. New York: UNESCO.

Allison, Graham T., and Robert P. Beschel. 1992. "Can the United States Promote Democracy?" *Political Science Quarterly* 107:81–98.

Almond, Gabriel. 1973. "Approaches to Developmental Causation." In Gabriel Almond, Scott Flanagan, and Robert Mundt, eds., *Crisis, Choice, and Change: Historical Studies of Political Development*. Boston: Little, Brown, pp. 1–42.

Almond, Gabriel, and James Coleman, eds. 1960. *The Politics of the Developing Areas*. Princeton: Princeton University Press.

Almond, Gabriel, Scott Flanagan, and Robert Mundt, eds. 1973. *Crisis, Choice, and Change: Historical Studies of Political Development*. Boston: Little, Brown.

Almond, Gabriel, and G. Bingham Powell. 1966. *Comparative Politics: A Developmental Approach*. Boston: Little, Brown.

Ameringer, Charles. 1982. *Democracy in Costa Rica*. New York: Praeger.

Ames, Barry, 2001. *The Deadlock of Democracy in Brazil*. Ann Arbor: University of Michigan Press.

Anderson, Leslie. 1995. "Elections and Public Opinion in the Development of Nicaraguan Democracy." In Mitchell A. Seligson and John A. Booth, eds., *Elections and Democracy in Central America Revisited*. Chapel Hill: University of North Carolina Press, pp. 84–102.

Anderson, Terry. 1995. *The Movement and the Sixties*. New York: Oxford University Press.

Andrade, Régis de Castro. 1992. "Presidencialismo e reforma eleitoral no Brasil." In Hélgio Trindade, org., *Reforma eleitoral e representação política*. Porto Alegre: Ed. da Universidade, pp. 74–88.

Angell, Alan. 1993. "The Transition to Democracy in Chile: A Model or an Exceptional Case?" *Parliamentary Affairs* 46:563–578.

Angell, Alan, and Carol Graham. 1995. "Can Social Sector Reform Make Adjustment Sustainable and Equitable? Lessons from Chile and Venezuela." *Journal of Latin American Studies* 27:189–219.

Angell, Alan, and Benny Pollack. 2000. "The Chilean Presidential Elections of 1999–2000 and Democratic Consolidation." *Bulletin of Latin American Research* 19:357–378.

Aquinas, Thomas. 1952. *The Summa Theologica*. Chicago: Encyclopaedia Britannica.

Archer, Ronald. 1995. "Party Strength and Weakness in Colombia's Besieged Democracy." In Scott Mainwaring and Timothy Scully, eds., *Building Democratic Institutions: Party Systems in Latin America*. Stanford: Stanford University Press, pp. 164–199.

Archer, Ronald, and Matthew Soberg Shugart. 1997. "The Unrealized Potential of Presidential Dominance in Colombia." In Scott Mainwaring and Matthew Soberg Shugart, eds., *Presidentialism and Democracy in Latin America*. Cambridge: Cambridge University Press, pp. 110–159.

Archondo, Rafael. 1999. "Bolivia: El auge del multipartidismo." *Nueva Sociedad* 164:19–25.

Ardaya, Gloria, and Luis Verdesoto. 1996. "Ecuador: De la expectativa por la nación a una sociedad sin expectativas." *Nueva Sociedad* 142 (March–April): 16–21.

Arendt, Hannah. 1951. *The Origins of Totalitarianism*. New York: Harcourt, Brace.

Aristide, Jean-Bertrand. 1997. "Democratize Democracy." *Latinamerica Press,* 23 January, p. 3.

Aristotle. 1892. *Aristotle on the Constitution of Athens*. Ed. F. G. Kenyon. London: Museum and Longmans.

———. 1960. *Politics*. Trans. Ernest Barker. Oxford: Oxford University Press.

Arriagada, Genaro. 1988. *Pinochet: The Politics of Power*. Boston: Unwin Hyman.

Arroyo Talavera, Eduardo. 1988. *Elecciones y negociaciones: Los límites de la democracia en Venezuela*. Caracas: Fondo Editorial CONICIT.

Augustine. 1948. *The City of God*. Trans. Marcus Dods. New York: Hafner.

Avritzer, Leonardo. 1995. "Transition to Democracy and Political Culture: An Analysis of the Conflict Between Civil and Political Society in Post-Authoritarian Brazil." *Constellations* 2 (2): 242–267.

Bachrach, Peter. 1967. *The Theory of Democratic Elitism*. Boston: Little, Brown.

Balladares, José Emilio, ed. 1987. *Sobre el contrato social*. San José: Libro Libre.

Baloyra, Enrique, ed. 1987. *Comparing New Democracies: Transition and Consolidation in Mediterranean Europe and the Southern Cone.* Boulder: Westview.

Baloyra-Herp, Enrique. 1995. "Elections, Civil War, and Transition in El Salvador, 1982–1994." In Mitchell A. Seligson and John A. Booth, eds., *Elections and Democracy in Central America Revisited.* Chapel Hill: University of North Carolina Press, pp. 45–65.

Baño, Rodrigo. 1995. "Coaliciones políticas y representación en Chile." In Manuel Antonio Garretón, ed., *Los partidos y la transformación política de América Latina.* Santiago: FLACSO, pp. 87–94.

Baracho, José Alfredo de Oliveira. 1985. "Teoria geral das constituções escritas." *Revista Brasileira de Estudos Politicos* 60–61 (January–July): 25–98.

Barber, Benjamin. 1984. *Strong Democracy: Participatory Politics for a New Age.* Berkeley: University of California Press.

Barker, Ernest. 1947. *Social Contract: Essays by Locke, Hume, and Rousseau.* Oxford: Oxford University Press.

Barrett, Patrick. 1999. "The Limits of Democracy: Socio-Political Compromise and Regime Change in Post-Pinochet Chile." *Studies in Comparative International Development* 34 (3): 3–36.

———. 2000. "Chile's Transformed Party System and the Future of Democratic Stability." *Journal of Inter-American Studies and World Affairs* 42 (3): 1–32.

Basañez, Miguel. 1994. "Encuestas y resultados de la elección de 1994." *Este País,* October, pp. 13–21.

Bates, Robert H. 2001. *Prosperity and Violence: The Political Economy of Development.* New York: Norton.

Beiner, Ronald, ed. 1995. *Theorizing Citizenship.* Albany: State University of New York Press.

Bentham, Jeremy. 1988. *The Principles of Morals and Legislation.* Buffalo, N.Y.: Prometheus.

Bergquist, Charles, Ricardo Peñaranda, and Gonzalo Sánchez, eds. 2001. *Violence in Colombia, 1990–2000.* Wilmington: Scholarly Resources.

Bernhard, Michael. 1996. "Civil Society After the First Transition." *Communist and Post-Communist Studies* 29 (September): 309–330.

Bernstein, Eduard. 1961. *Evolutionary Socialism.* New York: Schocken.

Berryman, Phillip. 1987. *Liberation Theology.* New York: Pantheon.

Bethell, Leslie, ed. 1987a. *Colonial Brazil.* Cambridge: Cambridge University Press.

———. 1987b. *Colonial Spanish America.* Cambridge: Cambridge University Press.

———. 1987c. *The Independence of Latin America.* Cambridge: Cambridge University Press.

———. 1987d. *Spanish America After Independence.* Cambridge: Cambridge University Press.

———. 1993. *Chile Since Independence.* Cambridge: Cambridge University Press.

Black, Jan Knippers. 1986. *The Dominican Republic: Politics and Development in an Unsovereign State.* Winchester, Mass.: Allen and Unwin.

Blake, Charles. 1994. "Social Pacts and Inflation Control in New Democracies: The Impact of 'Wildcat Cooperation' in Argentina and Uruguay." *Comparative Political Studies* 27:381–401.

Blakemore, Harold. 1993. "From the War of the Pacific to 1930." In Leslie Bethell, ed., *Chile Since Independence.* Cambridge: Cambridge University Press.

Blank, David Eugene. 1984. *Venezuela: Politics in a Petroleum Republic.* New York: Praeger.

Booth, John A. 1985. *The End and the Beginning,* 2nd ed. Boulder: Westview.
———. 1998. *Costa Rica: Quest for Democracy.* Boulder: Westview.
Booth, John A., and Patricia Bayer Richard. 1996. "Repression, Participation, and Democratic Norms in Urban Central America." *American Journal of Political Science* 40:1205–1232.
Borner, Silvio, Aymo Brunetti, and Beatrice Weder. 1995. *Political Credibility and Economic Development.* New York: St. Martin's.
Borón, Atilio, et al. 1995. *Peronismo y Menemismo: Avatares del populism en la Argentina.* Buenos Aires: Ed. El Cielo por Asalto.
Boudon, Lawrence. 2001. "Colombia's M-19 Democratic Alliance: A Case Study in New-Party Self-Destruction." *Latin American Perspectives* 28 (1): 73–92.
Bowman, Kirk. 2002. *Militarization, Democracy, and Development: The Perils of Praetorianism in Latin America.* University Park: Pennsylvania State University Press.
Boylan, Delia. 1996. "Taxation and Transition: The Politics of the 1990 Chilean Tax Reform." *Latin American Research Review* 31:7–32.
Bracey, John, August Meier, and Elliott Rudwick, eds. 1970. *Black Nationalism in America.* Indianapolis: Bobbs Merrill.
Bradford, James, ed. 1993. *Crucible of Empire: The Spanish American War and Its Aftermath.* Annapolis: Naval Institute Press.
Brading, D. A. 1987. "Bourbon Spain and Its American Empire." In Leslie Bethell, ed., *Colonial Spanish America.* Cambridge: Cambridge University Press.
Bresser Pereira, Luiz Carlos, José María Maravall, and Adam Przeworski. 1993. *Economic Reforms in New Democracies: A Social Democratic Approach.* New York: Cambridge University Press.
Brewer-Carías, Allan R. 1988. *Problemas del estado de partidos.* Caracas: Editorial Jurídica Venezolana.
Bruhn, Kathleen. 1997. *Taking on Goliath: The Emergence of a New Left Party and the Struggle for Democracy in Mexico.* University Park: Pennsylvania State University Press.
Bruneau, Thomas. 1992. "Brazil's Political Transition." In John Higley and Richard Gunther, eds., *Elites and Democratic Consolidation in Latin America and Southern Europe.* Cambridge: Cambridge University Press, pp. 257–281.
Burns, E. Bradford. 1980. *The Poverty of Progress: Latin America in the Nineteenth Century.* Berkeley: University of California Press.
———. 1986. *Latin America: A Concise Interpretive History.* 4th ed. Englewood Cliffs, N.J.: Prentice-Hall.
———. 1993. *A History of Brazil.* 3rd ed. New York: Columbia University Press.
Burton, Michael, Richard Gunther, and John Higley. 1992. "Introduction: Elite Transformations and Democratic Regimes." In John Higley and Richard Gunther, eds., *Elites and Democratic Consolidation in Latin America and Southern Europe.* Cambridge: Cambridge University Press, pp. 1–37.
Bushnell, David. 1993. *The Making of Modern Colombia: A Nation in Spite of Itself.* Berkeley: University of California Press.
Bushnell, David, and Neill Macaulay. 1994. *The Emergence of Latin America in the Nineteenth Century.* 2nd ed. New York: Oxford University Press.
Cabezas Castillo, Tito. 1995. "Partidos y organismos electorales, una relación que debe mejorarse: El caso de Ecuador." In Carina Perelli et al., eds., *Partidos y clase política en América Latina en los 90.* San José: IIDH/CAPEL, pp. 455–473.
Caetano, Gerardo. 1995. "Uruguay: La encrucijada política del fin de siglo." *Nueva Sociedad* 138:6–16.

Caetano, Gerardo, and José Rilla. 1995. *Historia contemporánea del Uruguay.* Montevideo: Colección CLAEH.

Caetano, Gerardo, José Rilla, and Romeo Pérez. 1987. "La partidocracia uruguaya." *Cuadernos del CLAEH* 44:37–62.

Calderón, Fernando, and Mario R. dos Santos. 1995. *Sociedades sin atajos: Cultura, política y reestructuración en América Latina.* Buenos Aires: Paidós.

Call, Charles. 2003. "Democratization, War, and State-Building: Constructing the Rule of Law in El Salvador," *Journal of Latin American Studies* 35:827–862.

Calvert, Peter. 1985. *Guatemala: A Nation in Turmoil.* Boulder: Westview.

Camp, Roderic Ai, ed. 1996. *Democracy in Latin America: Patterns and Cycles.* Wilmington, Del.: Scholarly Resources.

———. 2003. *Politics in Mexico.* 4th ed. New York: Oxford University Press.

Cansino, César. 1995. "Mexico: The Challenge of Democracy." *Government and Opposition* 30 (1): 60–73.

Carey, John. 2003. "Presidentialism and Representative Institutions." In Jorge Domínguez and Michael Shifter, eds., *Constructing Democratic Governance in Latin America.* Baltimore: Johns Hopkins University Press, pp. 11–42.

Carrigan, Ana. 1993. *The Palace of Justice.* New York: Four Walls, Eight Windows.

———. 1995. "Chiapas: The First Post-Modern Revolution." *Fletcher Forum of World Affairs* 19 (Winter–Spring): 71–98.

Cason, Jeffrey. 2000. "Electoral Reform and Stability in Uruguay." *Journal of Democracy* 11 (2): 85–98.

———. 2002. "Electoral Reform, Institutional Change, and Party Adaptation in Uruguay." *Latin American Politics and Society* 44 (3): 89–109.

Casper, Gretchen, and Michelle Taylor. 1996. *Negotiating Democracy: Transitions from Authoritarian Rule.* Pittsburgh: University of Pittsburgh Press.

Castillo Ochoa, Manuel. 1996. "Fujimori and the Business Class: A Prickly Partnership." *NACLA Report on the Americas* 30 (1): 25–30.

Cavarozzi, Marcelo. 1983. *Autoritarismo y democracia (1955–1983).* Buenos Aires: Centro Editor de America Latina.

———. 1986. "Political Cycles in Argentina Since 1955." In Guillermo O'Donnell, Philippe Schmitter, and Laurence Whitehead, eds., *Transitions from Authoritarian Rule: Latin America.* Baltimore: Johns Hopkins University Press, pp. 19–48.

———. 1992. "Patterns of Elite Negotiation and Confrontation in Argentina and Chile." In John Higley and Richard Gunther, eds., *Elites and Democratic Consolidation in Latin America and Southern Europe.* Cambridge: Cambridge University Press, pp. 208–236.

Caviedes, César N. 1991. *Elections in Chile.* Boulder: Lynne Rienner.

Cepeda Ulloa, Fernando. 2003. "Colombia: The Governability Crisis." In Jorge Domínguez and Michael Shifter, eds., *Constructing Democratic Governance in Latin America.* Baltimore: Johns Hopkins University Press, pp. 193–219.

Cerdas Cruz, Rodolfo. 1985. *Formación del estado en Costa Rica (1821–1842).* San José: Ed. Universidad de Costa Rica.

———. 1992. "Colonial Heritage, External Domination, and Political Systems in Central America." In Louis W. Goodman, William Leo Grande, and Johanna Mendelson Forman, eds., *Political Parties and Democracy in Central America.* Boulder: Westview, pp. 17–32.

Chalker, Cynthia. 1995. "Elections and Democracy in Costa Rica." In Mitchell A. Seligson and John A. Booth, eds., *Elections and Democracy in Central America Revisited.* Chapel Hill: University of North Carolina Press, pp. 103–122.

Chalmers, Douglas, Maria do Carmo Campello de Souza, and Atilio Borón, eds. 1992. *The Right and Democracy in Latin America.* New York: Praeger.

CIERA (Centro de Investigaciones y Estudios de la Reforma Agraria). 1984. *La democracia participativa en Nicaragua.* Managua: CIERA.

Cintra, António Octávio. 1992. "Reforma eleitoral, representação e política." In Hélgio Trindade, org., *Reforma eleitoral e representação política.* Porto Alegre: Ed. da Universidade, pp. 96–105.

Cleary, Edward, and Hannah Stewart-Gambino, eds. 1992. *Conflict and Competition: The Latin American Church in a Changing Environment.* Boulder: Lynne Rienner.

Cnudde, Charles, and Deane Neubauer, eds. 1969. *Empirical Democratic Theory.* Chicago: Markham.

Cohen, Jean, and Andrew Arato. 1992. *Civil Society and Political Theory.* Cambridge: Massachusetts Institute of Technology Press.

Collier, David, ed. 1979. *The New Authoritarianism in Latin America.* Princeton: Princeton University Press.

Collier, Ruth Berins, and David Collier. 1991. *Shaping the Political Arena.* Princeton: Princeton University Press.

Collier, Simon. 1993. "From Independence to the War of the Pacific." In Leslie Bethell, ed., *Chile Since Independence.* Cambridge: Cambridge University Press.

Collins, Joseph, and John Lear. 1995. *Chile's Free-Market Miracle: A Second Look.* San Francisco: Institute for Food and Development Policy.

Conaghan, Catherine M. 1995. "Politicians Against Parties: Discord and Disconnection in Ecuador's Party System." In Scott Mainwaring and Timothy Scully, eds., *Building Democratic Institutions: Party Systems in Latin America.* Stanford: Stanford University Press, pp. 434–458.

Conaghan, Catherine M., and Rosario Espinal. 1990. "Unlikely Transitions to Uncertain Regimes? Democracy Without Compromise in the Dominican Republic and Ecuador." *Journal of Latin American Studies* 22:553–574.

Conaghan, Catherine M., and James M. Malloy. 1994. *Unsettling Statecraft: Democracy and Neoliberalism in the Central Andes.* Pittsburgh: University of Pittsburgh Press.

Cooper, Frederick, et al. 1993. *Confronting Historical Paradigms.* Madison: University of Wisconsin Press.

Coppedge, Michael. 1993. "Parties and Society in Mexico and Venezuela: Why Competition Matters." *Comparative Politics* 25:253–274.

———. 1994a. "Prospects for Democratic Governability in Venezuela." *Journal of Inter-American Studies and World Affairs* 36 (2): 39–65.

———. 1994b. *Strong Parties and Lame Ducks: Presidential Partyarchy and Factionalism in Venezuela.* Stanford: Stanford University Press.

———. 2003. "Venezuela: Popular Sovereignty Versus Liberal Democracy." In Jorge Domínguez and Michael Shifter, eds., *Constructing Democratic Governance in Latin America.* Baltimore: Johns Hopkins University Press, pp. 165–192.

Coraggio, José Luis. 1986. *Nicaragua: Revolution and Democracy.* Winchester, Mass.: Allen and Unwin.

Coraggio, José Luis, and Carmen Diana Deere, coords. 1987. *La transición difícil: La autodeterminación de los pequeños países periféricos.* Managua: Vanguardia.

Cordera, Rolando, and Adolfo Sánchez Rebolledo. 1995. "La transición mexicana: La política y la reforma social." In Carina Perelli et al., eds., *Partidos y clase política en América Latina en los 90.* San José: IIDH/CAPEL, pp. 437–454.

Cornelius, Wayne A. 1996. *Mexican Politics in Transition: The Breakdown of a One-Party-Dominant Regime*. San Diego: Center for U.S.-Mexican Studies, University of California.

Corradi, Juan E., Patricia Weiss Fagen, and Manuel Antonio Garretón, eds. 1992. *Fear at the Edge: State Terror and Resistance in Latin America*. Berkeley: University of California Press.

Corrales, Javier. 2002. *Presidents Without Parties: The Politics of Economic Reform in Argentina and Venezuela in the 1990s*. University Park: Pennsylvania State University Press.

———. 2003. "Market Reforms." In Jorge Domínguez and Michael Shifter, eds., *Constructing Democratic Governance*. Baltimore: Johns Hopkins University Press, pp. 74–99.

Cortés Ramos, Alberto. 2001. "Cultura política y sistema de partidos en Costa Rica: ¿Nuevas tendencies en el 2002?" in Jorge Rovira Mas, ed., *La democracia de Costa Rica ante el siglo XXI*. San José: Editorial de la Universidad de Costa Rica, pp. 233–254.

Cotler, Julio. 1995a. "Crisis política, outsiders y democraduras: El 'Fujimorismo.'" In Carina Perelli et al., eds., *Partidos y clase política en América Latina en los 90*. San José: IIDH/CAPEL, pp. 117–141.

———. 1995b. "Political Parties and the Problems of Democratic Consolidation in Peru." In Scott Mainwaring and Timothy Scully, eds., *Building Democratic Institutions: Party Systems in Latin America*. Stanford: Stanford University Press, pp. 323–353.

Craig, Ann L., and Wayne A. Cornelius. 1995. "Houses Divided: Parties and Political Reform in Mexico." In Scott Mainwaring and Timothy Scully, eds., *Building Democratic Institutions*. Stanford: Stanford University Press, pp. 249–299.

Crespo Martínez, Ismael. 1991. "Brasil: El debate sobre la reforma constitucional." *Cuadernos del CLAEH* 57 (September): 19–36.

Crisp, Brian. 1994. "Limitations to Democracy in Developing Capitalist Societies: The Case of Venezuela." *World Development* 22:1491–1509.

———. 2000. *Democratic Institutional Design: The Powers and Incentives of Venezuelan Politicians and Interest Groups*. Stanford: Stanford University Press.

Cross, Peter. 1995. "Cuba's Socialist Revolution: Last Rites or Rejuvenation?" in Barry Gills and Shahid Qadir, eds., *Regimes in Crisis: The Post-Soviet Era and the Implications for Development*. London: Zed, pp. 243–285.

Dahl, Robert. 1956. *A Preface to Democratic Theory*. Chicago: University of Chicago Press.

———. 1961. *Who Governs?* New Haven: Yale University Press.

———. 1970. *After the Revolution?* New Haven: Yale University Press.

———. 1971. *Polyarchy: Participation and Opposition*. New Haven: Yale University Press.

———. 1982. *Dilemmas of Pluralist Democracy*. New Haven: Yale University Press.

———. 1985. *A Preface to Economic Democracy*. Berkeley: University of California Press.

———. 1989. *Democracy and Its Critics*. New Haven: Yale University Press.

Davis, Harold Eugene. 1972. *Latin American Thought: A Historical Introduction*. Baton Rouge: Louisiana State University Press.

De Riz, Liliana, and Catalina Smulovitz. 1992. "Instauración democrática y reforma política en Argentina y Uruguay: Un análisis comparado." *Ibero-Amerikanisches Archiv* 18:181–224.

De Soto, Hernando. 1989. *The Other Path: The Invisible Revolution in the Third World.* New York: Harper and Row.

Dealy, Glen Candill. 1992. *The Latin Americans: Spirit and Ethos.* Boulder: Westview.

Degregori, Carlos Iván. 2003. "Peru: The Vanishing of a Regime and the Challenge of Democratic Rebuilding." In Jorge Domínguez and Michael Shifter, eds., *Constructing Democratic Governance in Latin America.* Baltimore: Johns Hopkins University Press, pp. 220–243.

del Aguila, Juan M. 1994. *Cuba: Dilemmas of a Revolution.* 3rd ed. Boulder: Westview.

Diamint, Rut. 2003. "The Military." In Jorge Domínguez and Michael Shifter, eds., *Constructing Democratic Governance in Latin America,* 2nd ed. Baltimore: Johns Hopkins University Press, pp. 43–73.

Diamond, Larry. 1994. "Rethinking Civil Society: Toward Democratic Consolidation." *Journal of Democracy* 5 (3): 4–17.

———. 1999. *Developing Democracy: Toward Consolidation.* Baltimore: Johns Hopkins University Press.

Diamond, Larry, Juan J. Linz, and Seymour Martin Lipset, eds. 1989. *Democracy in Developing Countries.* Vol. 4, *Latin America.* Boulder: Lynne Rienner.

———. 1995. *Politics in Developing Countries.* 2nd ed. Boulder: Lynne Rienner.

Dietz, Gunther. 1995. "Zapatismo y movimientos étnico-regionales en México." *Nueva Sociedad* 140 (November–December): 33–50.

Dix, Robert H. 1987. *The Politics of Colombia.* New York: Praeger.

Domínguez, Jorge. 1997. "Latin America's Crisis of Representation." *Foreign Affairs* 76 (1): 100–113.

———. 1998. *Democratic Politics in Latin America and the Caribbean.* Baltimore: Johns Hopkins University Press.

Domínguez, Jorge, and Marc Lindenberg, eds. 1997. *Democratic Transitions in Central America.* Gainesville: University Press of Florida.

Domínguez, Jorge, and Michael Shifter, eds. 2003. *Constructing Democratic Governance in Latin America.* 2nd ed. Baltimore: Johns Hopkins University Press.

Dornbusch, Rudiger, and Sebastian Edwards, eds. 1991. *The Macroeconomics of Populism in Latin America.* Chicago: University of Chicago Press.

dos Santos, Wanderley Guilherme. 1992. "Reforma eleitoral, cidadania e cultura cívica." In Hélgio Trindade, org., *Reforma eleitoral e representação política.* Porto Alegre: Ed. da Universidade, pp. 89–95.

Downs, Anthony. 1957. *An Economic Theory of Democracy.* New York: Harper.

Drake, Paul. 1993. "Chile, 1930–1958." In Leslie Bethell, ed., *Chile Since Independence.* Cambridge: Cambridge University Press.

———. 1996. *Labor Movements and Dictatorships: The Southern Cone in Comparative Perspective.* Baltimore: Johns Hopkins University Press.

Drake, Paul, and Eduardo Silva, eds. 1986. *Elections and Democratization in Latin America, 1980–1985.* San Diego: Center for Iberian and Latin American Studies.

Dresser, Denise. 1997. "Mexico: Uneasy, Uncertain, Unpredictable." *Current History* 96 (607): 49–54.

———. 2003. "Mexico: From PRI Predominance to Divided Democracy." In Jorge Domínguez and Michael Shifter, eds., *Constructing Democratic Governance in Latin America.* Baltimore: Johns Hopkins University Press, pp. 321–347.

Dunkerley, James. 1984. *Rebellion in the Veins: Political Struggle in Bolivia, 1952–1982.* London: Verso.

Durkheim, Emile. 1986. *Durkheim on Politics and the State.* Ed. Anthony Giddens. Stanford: Stanford University Press.

Dutrénit Bielous, Silvia. 1994. *El maremoto militar y el arquipiélago partidario: Testimonios para la historia reciente de los partidos políticos uruguayos.* Montevideo: Instituto Mora.

Duverger, Maurice. 1962. *Political Parties: Their Organization and Activity in the Modern State.* New York: Wiley.

Easton, David. 1953. *The Political System.* New York: Knopf.

———. 1965. *A Systems Analysis of Political Life.* New York: Wiley.

———. 1990. *The Analysis of Political Structure.* New York: Routledge.

Eckstein, Susan. 1994. *Back from the Future: Cuba Under Castro.* Princeton: Princeton University Press.

———, ed. 1989. *Power and Popular Protest: Latin American Social Movements.* Berkeley: University of California Press.

Eckstein, Susan Eva, and Timothy Wickham-Crowley, eds. 2003. *What Justice? Whose Justice? Fighting for Fairness in Latin America.* Berkeley: University of California Press.

Edelman, Marc. 1999. *Peasants Against Globalization: Rural Social Movements in Costa Rica.* Stanford: Stanford University Press.

Eguizábal, Cristina. 1992. "Parties, Programs, and Politics in El Salvador." In Louis W. Goodman, William LeoGrande, and Johanna Mendelson Forman, eds., *Political Parties and Democracy in Central America.* Boulder: Westview, pp. 135–160.

Ellison, Katherine. 1997. "Congress Clears Cardoso's Path." *Miami Herald,* Internet edition, 29 January.

Ellner, Steve. 2003. "Venezuela imprevisible: Populismo radical y globalización." *Nueva Sociedad* 183:11–26.

Ellner, Steve, and Daniel Hellinger, eds. 2003. *Venezuelan Politics in the Chávez Era: Class, Polarization, and Conflict.* Boulder: Lynne Rienner.

Ensalaco, Mark. 1994. "In with the New, Out with the Old? The Democratising Impact of Constitutional Reform in Chile." *Journal of Latin American Studies* 26:409–429.

Escobar, Arturo, and Sonia Alvarez, eds. 1992. *The Making of Social Movements in Latin America.* Boulder: Westview.

Espinal, Rosario. 1987. *Autoritarismo y democracia en la política dominicana.* San José: Centro Interamericano de Asesoría y Promoción Electoral/Instituto Interamericano de Derechos Humanos.

———. 1995. "Economic Restructuring, Social Protest, and Democratization in the Dominican Republic." *Latin American Perspectives* 22 (3): 63–79.

Etzioni, Amitai, ed. 1995. *New Communitarian Thinking: Persons, Virtues, Institutions, and Communities.* Charlottesville: University Press of Virginia.

Evans, Peter. 1979. *Dependent Development: The Alliance of Multinational, State, and Local Capital in Brazil.* Princeton: Princeton University Press.

———. 1995. *Embedded Autonomy: States and Industrial Transformations.* Princeton: Princeton University Press.

Evans, Peter, Dietrich Rueschemeyer, and Theda Skocpol, eds. 1987. *Bringing the State Back In.* New York: Cambridge University Press.

Fatton, Robert, Jr. 2002. *Haiti's Predatory Republic: The Unending Transition to Democracy.* Boulder: Lynne Rienner.

Ferguson, Ann. 1991. *Sexual Democracy: Women, Oppression, and Revolution.* Boulder: Westview.

Fernández, Oscar. 1994. "Costa Rica: La reafirmación del bipartidismo." *Nueva Sociedad* 131 (May–June): 4–10.

Finch, M. H. J. 1981. *A Political Economy of Uruguay Since 1870.* London: Macmillan.

Finley, M. I. 1980. *Ancient Slavery and Modern Ideology.* New York: Viking.

———. 1983. *Politics in the Ancient World.* Cambridge: Cambridge University Press.

———. 1985. *Democracy Ancient and Modern.* New Brunswick: Rutgers University Press.

Fisher, Lillian. 1966. *The Last Inca Revolt, 1780–1783.* Norman: University of Oklahoma Press.

Fitch, John Samuel 1998. *The Armed Forces and Democracy in Latin America.* Baltimore: Johns Hopkins University Press.

Fleischer, David. 1986. "Brazil at the Crossroads: The Elections of 1982 and 1985." In Paul Drake and Eduardo Silva, eds., *Elections and Democratization in Latin America, 1980–1985.* San Diego: Center for Iberian and Latin American Studies, pp. 299–328.

Fournier, Dominique, and Sean Burges. 2000. "Form Before Function: Democratization in Paraguay." *Canadian Journal of Latin American and Caribbean Studies* 25 (49): 5–32.

Fox, Jonathan. 1994. "The Difficult Transition from Clientelism to Citizenship: Lessons from Mexico." *World Politics* 46 (2): 151–184.

Fraga, Rosendo. 1995. *Argentina en las urnas, 1916–1994.* Buenos Aires: Centro de Estudios Unión para la Nueva Mayoría.

Frieden, Jeffrey. 1991. *Debt, Development, and Democracy: Modern Political Economy and Latin America, 1965–1985.* Princeton: Princeton University Press.

Friedrich, Carl, and Zbigniew Brzezinski. 1965. *Totalitarian Dictatorship and Autocracy.* 2nd ed. Cambridge: Harvard University Press.

Gager, John. 1975. *Kingdom and Community: The Social World of Early Christianity.* Englewood Cliffs, N.J.: Prentice-Hall.

Gamarra, Eduardo A. 1992. "Presidencialismo híbrido y democratización." In René Antonio Mayorga, coord., *Democracia y gobernabilidad: América Latina.* Caracas: Nueva Sociedad, pp. 21–40.

———. 1994. "Crafting Political Support for Stabilization: Political Pacts and the New Economic Policy in Bolivia." In William C. Smith, Carlos H. Acuña, and Eduardo A. Gamarra, eds., *Democracy, Markets, and Structural Reform in Latin America: Argentina, Bolivia, Brazil, Chile, and Mexico.* New Brunswick, N.J.: Transaction, pp. 105–127.

———. 1997. "Hybrid Presidentialism and Democratization: The Case of Bolivia." In Scott Mainwaring and Matthew Soberg Shugart, eds., *Presidentialism and Democracy in Latin America.* Cambridge: Cambridge University Press, pp. 363–393.

Gamarra, Eduardo A., and James M. Malloy. 1995. "The Patrimonial Dynamics of Party Politics in Bolivia." In Scott Mainwaring and Timothy Scully, eds., *Building Democratic Institutions: Party Systems in Latin America.* Stanford: Stanford University Press, pp. 399–433.

García Delgado, Daniel. 1994. *Estado y sociedad: La nueva relación a partir del cambio estructural.* Santiago: FLACSO.

García Márquez, Gabriel. 1976. *The Autumn of the Patriarch.* New York: Harper and Row.

Garretón, Manuel Antonio. 1989. *The Chilean Political Process.* Boston: Unwin Hyman.

———. 1993a. "Coaliciones políticas y procesos de democratización: El caso chileno." In Manuel Antonio Garretón, ed., *Los partidos y la transformación política de América Latina.* Santiago: FLACSO, pp. 95–103.

————, ed. 1993b. *Los partidos y la transformación política de América Latina.* Santiago: FLACSO.

————. 1995. *Hacia una nueva era política: Estudio sobre las democratizaciones.* Santiago: Fondo de Cultura Económica.

Gay, Robert. 1998. "Rethinking Clientelism: Demands, Discourses and Practices in Contemporary Brazil." *European Review of Latin American and Caribbean Studies* 65:7–24.

Gerlach, Allen. 2003. *Indians, Oil, and Politics: A Recent History of Ecuador.* Wilmington: Scholarly Resources.

Germani, Gino. 1968. *Política y sociedad en una época de transición.* Buenos Aires: Paidós.

Gil, Federico. 1966. *The Political System of Chile.* Boston: Houghton Mifflin.

Gil Yepes, José Antonio. 1981. *The Challenge of Venezuelan Democracy.* New Brunswick, N.J.: Transaction.

Gillespie, Charles. 1986. "Uruguay's Transition from Collegial Military-Technocratic Rule." In Guillermo O'Donnell, Philippe Schmitter, and Laurence Whitehead, eds., *Transitions from Authoritarian Rule: Latin America.* Baltimore: Johns Hopkins University Press, pp. 173–195.

————. 1991. *Negotiating Democracy: Politicians and Generals in Uruguay.* Cambridge: Cambridge University Press.

————. 1992. "The Role of Civil-Military Pacts in Elite Settlements and Elite Convergence: Democratic Consolidation in Uruguay." In John Higley and Richard Gunther, eds., *Elites and Democratic Consolidation in Latin America and Southern Europe.* Cambridge: Cambridge University Press, pp. 178–207.

Gillespie, Charles, and Luis Eduardo González. 1989. "Uruguay: The Survival of Old and Autonomous Institutions." In Larry Diamond, Juan J. Linz, and Seymour Martin Lipset, eds., *Democracy in Developing Countries,* vol. 4, *Latin America.* Boulder: Lynne Rienner, pp. 207–246.

Gilmore, Robert L. 1965. *Caudillism and Militarism in Venezuela, 1830–1910.* Athens: Ohio University Press.

Godoy Reyes, Virgilio. 1992. "Nicaragua 1944–84: Political Parties and Electoral Processes." In Louis W. Goodman, William LeoGrande, and Johanna Mendelson Forman, eds., *Political Parties and Democracy in Central America.* Boulder: Westview, pp. 175–186.

González, Luis Eduardo. 1991. *Political Structures and Democracy in Uruguay.* Notre Dame: University of Notre Dame Press.

————. 1995. "Continuity and Change in the Uruguayan Party System." In Scott Mainwaring and Timothy Scully, eds., *Building Democratic Institutions: Party Systems in Latin America.* Stanford: Stanford University Press, pp. 138–163.

González Casanova, Pablo. 1970. *Democracy in Mexico.* New York: Oxford University Press.

Goodin, Robert. 1995. *Utilitarianism as a Public Philosophy.* Cambridge: Cambridge University Press.

Goodman, Louis W., William LeoGrande, and Johanna Mendelson Forman, eds. 1992. *Political Parties and Democracy in Central America.* Boulder: Westview.

Goodman, Louis W., Johanna Mendelson Forman, Moisés Naím, Joseph Tulchin, and Gary Bland. 1995. *Lessons of the Venezuelan Experience.* Baltimore: Johns Hopkins University Press.

Gould, Carol. 1988. *Rethinking Democracy: Freedom and Social Cooperation in Politics, Economy, and Society.* Cambridge: Cambridge University Press.

Gramsci, Antonio. 1971. *Selections from the Prison Notebooks.* New York: International.

Grinspun, Ricardo, and Maxwell Cameron, eds. 1993. *The Political Economy of North American Free Trade.* New York: St. Martin's.

Gudmundson, Lowell, and Héctor Lindo-Fuentes. 1995. *Central America, 1821–1871: Liberalism Before Liberal Reform.* Tuscaloosa: University of Alabama Press.

Guillén, Abraham. 1973. *Philosophy of the Urban Guerrilla: The Revolutionary Writings of Abraham Guillén.* New York: William Morrow.

Guillén Martínez, Fernando. 1979. *El poder político en Colombia.* Bogotá: Ponta de Lanza.

Gutmann, Matthew. 2002. *The Romance of Democracy: Compliant Defiance in Contemporary Mexico.* Berkeley: University of California Press.

Guzmán Bouvard, Marguerite. 1994. *Revolutionizing Motherhood: The Mothers of the Plaza de Mayo.* Wilmington, Del.: Scholarly Resources.

Haggard, Stephan, and Robert R. Kaufman. 1995. *The Political Economy of Democratic Transitions.* Princeton: Princeton University Press.

Hagopian, Frances. 1996. *Traditional Politics and Regime Change in Brazil.* New York: Cambridge University Press.

Halebsky, Sandor, and Richard Harris, eds. 1995. *Capital, Power, and Inequality in Latin America.* Boulder: Westview.

Halebsky, Sandor, and John Kirk, eds. 1992. *Cuba in Transition: Crisis and Transformation.* Boulder: Westview.

Hall, John A., ed. 1995. *Civil Society: Theory, History, Comparison.* Cambridge: Polity Press.

Halperín Donghi, Tulio. 1993. *The Contemporary History of Latin America.* Durham, N.C.: Duke University Press.

————. 1994. *La larga agonía de la Argentina peronista.* Buenos Aires: Ariel.

Handy, Jim. 1984. *Gift of the Devil: A History of Guatemala.* Boston: South End Press.

Hartlyn, Jonathan. 1988. *The Politics of Coalition Rule in Colombia.* Cambridge: Cambridge University Press.

————. 1994. "Presidentialism and Colombian Politics." In Juan Linz and Arturo Valenzuela, eds., *The Failure of Presidential Democracy.* Baltimore: Johns Hopkins University Press, pp. 294–327.

————. 1998. *The Struggle for Democratic Politics in the Dominican Republic.* Chapel Hill: University of North Carolina Press.

Hartlyn, Jonathan, Lars Schoultz, and Augusto Varas, eds. 1992. *The United States and Latin America in the 1990s: Beyond the Cold War.* Chapel Hill: University of North Carolina Press.

Harvey, Neil. 1998. *The Chiapas Rebellion: The Struggle for Land and Democracy.* Durham, N.C.: Duke University Press.

Held, David. 1995. *Democracy and the Global Order.* Stanford: Stanford University Press.

Hellinger, Daniel. 2003. "Political Overview: The Breakdown of *Puntofijismo* and the Rise of *Chavismo.*" In Steve Ellner and Daniel Hellinger, eds., *Venezuelan Politics in the Chávez Era: Class, Polarization, and Conflict.* Boulder: Lynne Rienner, pp. 27–54.

Hellman, Judith Adler. 1983. *Mexico in Crisis.* 2nd ed. New York: Holmes and Meier.

————. 1994. "Mexican Popular Movements, Clientelism, and the Process of Democratization." *Latin American Perspectives* 21 (2) (Spring): 124–142.

Hengel, Martin. 1974. *Property and Riches in the Early Church: Aspects of a Social History of Early Christianity.* Philadelphia: Fortress.

Hernández Naranjo, Gerardo. 2001. "Tendencias electorales en Costa Rica, 1986–1998." In Jorge Rovira Mas, ed., *La democracia de Costa Rica ante el siglo XXI*. San José: Editorial de la Universidad de Costa Rica, pp. 255–276.

Higley, John, and Michael Burton. 1989. "The Elite Variable in Democratic Transitions and Breakdowns." *American Sociological Review* 54:17–32.

Higley, John, and Richard Gunther, eds. 1992. *Elites and Democratic Consolidation in Latin America and Southern Europe*. Cambridge: Cambridge University Press.

Hill, Bennett, ed. 1970. *Church and State in the Middle Ages*. New York: Wiley.

Hill, Christopher. 1965. *The Intellectual Origins of the English Revolution*. Oxford: Clarendon.

———. 1972. *The World Turned Upside Down: Radical Ideas During the English Revolution*. New York: Viking.

———. 1980. *The Century of Revolution, 1603–1714*. New York: Norton.

Hillman, Richard. 1994. *Democracy for the Privileged: Crisis and Transition in Venezuela*. Boulder: Lynne Rienner.

Hipsher, Patricia. 1996. "Democratization and the Decline of Urban Social Movements in Chile and Spain." *Comparative Politics* 28 (April): 273–298.

Hirschman, Albert O. 1970. *Exit, Voice, and Loyalty: Responses to Decline in Firms, Organizations, and States*. Cambridge: Harvard University Press.

Hobbes, Thomas. 1991. *Leviathan*. Cambridge: Cambridge University Press.

Holmes, Stephen. 1995. *Passions and Constraint: On the Theory of Liberal Democracy*. Chicago: University of Chicago Press.

Horowitz, Donald L. 1990. "Presidents vs. Parliaments: Comparing Democratic Systems." *Journal of Democracy* 1 (4): 74–79.

Huber, Evelyne, and Michelle Dion. 2001. "Revolution or Contribution? Rational Choice Approaches in the Study of Latin American Politics." *Journal of Inter-American Studies and World Affairs* 44 (3): 2–28.

Hunter, Floyd. 1953. *Community Power Structure: A Study of Decision-Makers*. Chapel Hill: University of North Carolina Press.

Huntington, Samuel. 1968. *Political Order in Changing Societies*. New Haven: Yale University Press.

———. 1991. *The Third Wave: Democratization in the Late Twentieth Century*. Norman: University of Oklahoma Press.

———. 1996. "Democracy for the Long Haul." *Journal of Democracy* 7 (2): 3–13.

Immerman, Richard. 1982. *The CIA in Guatemala*. Austin: University of Texas Press.

Isaacs, Anita. 1993. *Military Rule and Transition in Ecuador, 1972–92*. Pittsburgh: University of Pittsburgh Press.

Jaquette, Jane S. 1994. *The Women's Movement in Latin America*. 2nd ed. Boulder: Westview.

Jefferson, Thomas. 1974. *The Portable Thomas Jefferson*. Ed. Merrill Peterson. New York: Viking.

Jelin, Elizabeth. 1994. "The Politics of Memory: The Human Rights Movement and the Construction of Democracy in Argentina." *Latin American Perspectives* 21 (2): 38–58.

Jonas, Susanne. 1989. "Elections and Transitions: The Guatemalan and Nicaraguan Cases." In John A. Booth and Mitchell A. Seligson, eds., *Elections and Democracy in Central America*. Chapel Hill: University of North Carolina Press, pp. 126–157.

———. 1991. *The Battle for Guatemala: Rebels, Death Squads, and U.S. Power*. Boulder: Westview.

———. 1995. "Electoral Problems and the Democratic Project in Guatemala." In Mitchell A. Seligson and John A. Booth, eds., *Elections and Democracy in Central America Revisited*. Chapel Hill: University of North Carolina Press, pp. 25–44.

Jonas, Susanne, and Edward McCaughan, eds. 1994. *Latin America Faces the Twenty-First Century: Reconstructing a Social Justice Agenda*. Boulder: Westview.

Jonas, Susanne, and Nancy Stein, eds. 1990. *Democracy in Latin America: Visions and Realities*. New York: Bergin and Garvey.

Jones, Mark P. 1995. *Electoral Laws and the Survival of Presidential Democracies*. Notre Dame, Ind.: University of Notre Dame Press.

Jorrín, Miguel, and John Martz. 1970. *Latin American Political Thought and Ideology*. Chapel Hill: University of North Carolina Press.

Karl, Terry. 1987. "Petroleum and Political Pacts: The Transition to Democracy in Venezuela." *Latin American Research Review* 22:63–94.

———. 1997. *The Paradox of Plenty: Oil Booms and Petro-States*. Berkeley: University of California Press.

Kaufman, Edy. 1979. *Uruguay in Transition*. New Brunswick, N.J.: Transaction.

Keane, John. 1988. *Democracy and Civil Society*. London: Verso.

Keck, Margaret E. 1992. *The Workers' Party and Democratization in Brazil*. New Haven: Yale University Press.

———. 1995. "Social Equity and Environmental Politics in Brazil: Lessons from the Rubber Tappers of Acre." *Comparative Politics* 27:409–424.

Keen, Benjamin, and Mark Wasserman. 1988. *A History of Latin America*. 3rd ed. Boston: Houghton Mifflin.

Kelley, Jonathan, and Herbert S. Klein. 1981. *Revolution and the Rebirth of Inequality: A Theory Applied to the National Revolution in Bolivia*. Berkeley: University of California Press.

Kinsbruner, Jay. 1973. *Chile: A Historical Interpretation*. New York: Harper and Row.

Kirkpatrick, Jeane. 1982. *Dictatorships and Double Standards*. New York: Simon and Schuster.

———. 1990. *The Withering Away of the Totalitarian State . . . and Other Surprises*. Washington, D.C.: American Enterprise Institute Press.

Klarén, Peter. 2000. *Peru: Society and Nationhood in the Andes*. New York: Oxford University Press.

Klein, Herbert S. 1992. *Bolivia: The Evolution of a Multi-Ethnic Society*. 2nd ed. New York: Oxford University Press.

Klesner, Joseph L. 1995. "The 1994 Mexican Elections: Manifestation of a Divided Society?" *Mexican Studies/Estudios Mexicanos* 11 (1) (Winter): 137–149.

Knight, Alan. 1986. *The Mexican Revolution*. Cambridge: Cambridge University Press.

———. 1992. "Mexico's Elite Settlement: Conjuncture and Consequences." In John Higley and Richard Gunther, eds., *Elites and Democratic Consolidation in Latin America and Southern Europe*. Cambridge: Cambridge University Press, pp. 113–145.

———. 1994. "Cardenismo: Juggernaut or Jalopy?" *Journal of Latin American Studies* 26 (1): 73–107.

———. 2001. "Democratic and Revolutionary Traditions in Latin America." *Bulletin of Latin American Research* 20 (2): 147–186.

Kornblith, Miriam. 1995. "Public Sector and Private Sector: New Rules of the Game." In Jennifer McCoy, Andrés Serbin, William C. Smith, and Andrés Stambouli, eds., *Venezuelan Democracy Under Stress*. New Brunswick, N.J.: Transaction, pp. 77–105.

Kornblith, Miriam, and Daniel Levine. 1995. "Venezuela: The Life and Times of the Party System." In Scott Mainwaring and Timothy Scully, eds., *Building Democratic Institutions: Party Systems in Latin America*. Stanford: Stanford University Press, pp. 37–71.

Korzeniewicz, Roberto Patricio. 2000. "Democracy and Dictatorship in Continental Latin America During the Interwar Period." *Studies in Comparative International Development* 35 (1): 41–72.

Kristeller, Paul. 1961. *Renaissance Thought: The Classic, Scholastic, and Humanistic Strains*. New York: Harper.

Kryzanek, Michael J. 1996. "The Dominican Republic: The Challenge of Preserving a Fragile Democracy." In Howard Wiarda and Harvey Kline, eds., *Latin American Politics and Development*. 4th ed. Boulder: Westview, pp. 490–505.

Kurtz, Marcus. 1995. "Urban Participation and Rural Exclusion: Neo-Liberal Transformation and Democratic Transition in Chile." Paper presented at the American Political Science Association meeting, Chicago.

LaBotz, Dan. 1995. *Democracy in Mexico: Peasant Rebellion and Political Reform*. Boston: South End Press.

Ladman, Jerry R., ed. 1982. *Bolivia: Legacy of the Revolution and Prospects for the Future*. Tempe: Center for Latin American Studies, Arizona State University.

Lambert, Peter. 2000. "A Decade of Electoral Democracy: Continuity, Change, and Crisis in Paraguay." *Bulletin of Latin American Research* 19 (3): 379–396.

Lamounier, Bolívar. 1994a. "Brazil at an Impasse." *Journal of Democracy* 5 (3): 72–87.

———. 1994b. "Brazil: Toward Parliamentarism?" In Juan Linz and Arturo Valenzuela, eds., *The Failure of Presidential Democracy*. Baltimore: Johns Hopkins University Press, pp. 253–293.

———. 2003. "Brazil: An Assessment of the Cardoso Administration." In Jorge Domínguez and Michael Shifter, eds., *Constructing Democratic Governance in Latin America*. Baltimore: Johns Hopkins University Press, pp. 269–291.

Langston, Joy. 2002. "Breaking Out Is Hard to Do: Exit, Voice, and Loyalty in Mexico's One-Party Hegemonic Regime." *Latin American Politics and Society* 44 (3): 61–88.

LaRamée, Pierre. 1995. "Differences of Opinion: Interviews with Sandinistas." *NACLA Report on the Americas* 27 (5): 11–14.

Las Casas, Bartolomé de. 1992. *The Devastation of the Indies*. Trans. Erma Briffault. Baltimore: Johns Hopkins University Press.

Lehoucq, Fabrice Edouard. 1996. "The Institutional Foundations of Democratic Cooperation in Costa Rica." *Journal of Latin American Studies* 28 (2): 329–356.

Lehoucq, Fabrice Edouard, and Iván Molina. 2002. *Stuffing the Ballot Box: Fraud, Electoral Reform, and Democratization in Costa Rica*. New York: Cambridge University Press.

Lenin, Vladimir. 1963. *What Is to Be Done?* London: Clarendon.

LeoGrande, William. 1992. "Political Parties and Postrevolutionary Politics in Nicaragua." In Louis W. Goodman, William LeoGrande, and Johanna Mendelson Forman, eds., *Political Parties and Democracy in Central America*. Boulder: Westview, pp. 187–202.

Levine, Daniel H. 1989. "Venezuela: The Nature, Sources, and Future Prospects of Democracy." In Larry Diamond, Juan J. Linz, and Seymour Martin Lipset, eds.,

Democracy in Developing Countries, vol. 4, *Latin America.* Boulder: Lynne Rienner, pp. 247–290.

———, ed. 1993. *Constructing Culture and Power in Latin America.* Ann Arbor: University of Michigan Press.

Levitsky, Steven. 2003. "Argentina: From Crisis to Consolidation (and Back)." In Jorge Domínguez and Michael Shifter, eds., *Constructing Democratic Governance in Latin America.* Baltimore: Johns Hopkins University Press, pp. 244–268.

Levitsky, Steven, and Maxwell Cameron. 2003. "Democracy Without Parties: Political Parties and Regime Change in Fujimori's Peru." *Latin American Politics and Society* 45 (3): 1–33.

Levy, Daniel. 2001. *Mexico: The Struggle for Democratic Development.* Berkeley: University of California Press.

Lewis, Paul. 1982. *Socialism, Liberalism, and Dictatorship in Paraguay.* New York: Praeger.

———, ed. 1992. *Parliamentary Versus Presidential Government.* Oxford: Oxford University Press.

———. 1993a. *Paraguay Under Stroessner.* Chapel Hill: University of North Carolina Press.

———. 1993b. *Political Parties and Generations in Paraguay's Liberal Era.* Chapel Hill: University of North Carolina Press.

Lijphart, Arend. 1994. *Electoral Systems and Party Systems.* Oxford: Oxford University Press.

———. 1999. *Patterns of Democracy.* New Haven: Yale University Press.

Lijphart, Arend, and Carlos Waisman, eds. 1996. *Institutional Design in New Democracies: Eastern Europe and Latin America.* Boulder: Westview.

Linz, Juan. 1975. "Totalitarian and Authoritarian Regimes." In Fred Greenstein, ed., *Handbook of Political Science,* vol. 3. Reading, Mass.: Addison-Wesley, pp. 175ff.

———. 1978. *Crisis, Breakdown, and Equilibrium.* Vol. 1 of Juan Linz and Alfred Stepan, eds., *The Breakdown of Democratic Regimes.* Baltimore: Johns Hopkins University Press.

Linz, Juan, and Alfred Stepan, eds. 1978. *The Breakdown of Democratic Regimes.* Baltimore: Johns Hopkins University Press.

———. 1996a. *Problems of Democratic Transition and Consolidation.* Baltimore: Johns Hopkins University Press.

———. 1996b. "Toward Consolidated Democracies." *Journal of Democracy* 7 (2): 14–33.

Linz, Juan, and Arturo Valenzuela, eds. 1994. *The Failure of Presidential Democracy.* Baltimore: Johns Hopkins University Press.

Lipset, Seymour Martin. 1959. "Some Social Requisites of Democracy: Economic Development and Political Legitimacy." *American Political Science Review* 53:69–105.

———. 1990. "Presidents vs. Parliaments: The Centrality of Political Culture." *Journal of Democracy* 1 (4): 80–83.

Lipset, Seymour Martin, Kyoung-Ryung Seong, and John Charles Torres. 1993. "A Comparative Analysis of the Social Requisites of Democracy." *International Social Science Journal* 136:155–175.

Lockhart, James, and Stuart Schwartz. 1983. *Early Latin America: A History of Colonial Spanish America and Brazil.* Cambridge: Cambridge University Press.

Lombardi, John V. 1982. *Venezuela: The Search for Order, the Dream of Progress.* New York: Oxford University Press.

Longley, Kyle. 1997. *The Sparrow and the Hawk: Costa Rica and the United States During the Rise of José Figueres.* Tuscaloosa: University of Alabama Press.

López Maya, Margarita. 1994. "The Rise of Causa R: A Workers' Party Shakes Up the Old Politics." *NACLA* 27 (5) (March–April): 29–34.

López Maya, Margarita, and Luis Gómez Calcaño. 1989. "Desarrollo y hegemonía en la sociedad venezolana: 1958 a 1985." In Margarita López Maya et al., *De Punto Fijo al Pacto Social.* Caracas: Fondo Editorial Acta Científica Venezolana, pp. 15–125.

López Maya, Margarita, Luis Gómez Calcaño, and Thaís Maingón. 1989. *De punto fijo al Pacto Social: Desarrollo y hegemonía en Venezuela (1958–1985).* Caracas: Fondo Editorial Acta Científica Venezolana.

Loveman, Brian. 1988. *Chile: The Legacy of Hispanic Capitalism.* 2nd ed. New York: Oxford University Press.

———. 1993. *The Constitution of Tyranny: Regimes of Exception in Spanish America.* Pittsburgh: University of Pittsburgh Press.

Lucero, José Antonio. 2001. "Crisis and Contention in Ecuador." *Journal of Democracy* 12 (2): 59–73.

Machiavelli, Niccolo. 1995. *The Prince.* New York: Humanities.

Macpherson, C. B. 1972. *The Real World of Democracy.* Oxford: Oxford University Press.

———. 1973. *Democratic Theory: Essays in Retrieval.* Oxford: Oxford University Press.

———. 1977. *The Life and Times of Liberal Democracy.* Oxford: Oxford University Press.

———. 1985. *The Rise and Fall of Economic Justice.* Oxford: Oxford University Press.

Madison, James, Alexander Hamilton, and John Jay. 1987. *The Federalist Papers.* New York: Viking Penguin.

Mahoney, James. 2001. *The Legacies of Liberalism: Path Dependence and Political Regimes in Central America.* Baltimore: Johns Hopkins University Press.

Mainwaring, Scott. 1993. "Presidentialism, Multipartism, and Democracy: The Difficult Combination." *Comparative Political Studies* 26 (July): 198–228.

———. 1995. "Brazil: Weak Parties, Feckless Democracy." In Scott Mainwaring and Timothy Scully, eds., *Building Democratic Institutions: Party Systems in Latin America.* Stanford: Stanford University Press, pp. 354–398.

———. 1999. *Rethinking Party Systems in the Third Wave of Democratization: The Case of Brazil.* Stanford: Stanford University Press.

Mainwaring, Scott, and Aníbal Pérez Liñán. 2003. "Level of Development and Democracy: Latin American Exceptionalism, 1945–1996." *Comparative Political Studies* 36 (9) (November): 1031–1067.

Mainwaring, Scott, and Timothy Scully, eds. 1995. *Building Democratic Institutions: Party Systems in Latin America.* Stanford: Stanford University Press.

Mainwaring, Scott, and Matthew Shugart. 1994. "Juan J. Linz: Presidencialismo y democracia: Una revisión crítica." *Desarrollo Económico* 34 (135) (October–December): 397–418.

———, eds. 1997. *Presidentialism and Democracy in Latin America.* Cambridge: Cambridge University Press.

Mainwaring, Scott, and Alexander Wilde, eds. 1989. *The Progressive Church in Latin America.* Notre Dame: University of Notre Dame Press.

Malloy, James M. 1991. "Democracy, Economic Crisis, and the Problem of Governance: The Case of Bolivia." *Studies in Comparative International Development* 26 (2): 37–57.

Malloy, James M., and Eduardo Gamarra. 1987. "The Transition to Democracy in Bolivia." In James M. Malloy and Mitchell Seligson, eds., *Authoritarians and Democrats: Regime Transition in Latin America.* Pittsburgh: University of Pittsburgh Press, pp. 93–120.

———. 1988. *Revolution and Reaction: Bolivia, 1964–1985.* New Brunswick: Transaction.

Malloy, James M., and Mitchell Seligson, eds. 1977. *Authoritarianism and Corporatism in Latin America.* Pittsburgh: University of Pittsburgh Press.

———. 1987. *Authoritarians and Democrats: Regime Transition in Latin America.* Pittsburgh: University of Pittsburgh Press.

Markoff, John. 1996. *Waves of Democracy: Social Movements and Political Change.* Thousand Oaks, Calif.: Pine Forge Press.

Marta Sosa, Joaquín. 2002. "Dos constituciones cara a cara." In Marisa Ramos Rollón, ed., *Venezuela: Rupturas y continuidades del sistema político (1999–2004).* alamanca: Ediciones Universidad de Salamanca, pp. 19–36.

Martínez Barahona, Elena. 2002. "¿Ante un nuevo parlamento en la V República venezolana?" In Marysa Ramos Rollón, ed., *Venezuela: Rupturas y continuidades del sistema politico (1999–2001).* Salamanca: Ediciones Universidad de Salamanca, pp. 217–246.

Martínez Cortez, Carlos Aníbal. 2003. "Guatemala: Los retos de la democracia." *Nueva Sociedad* 185:23–32.

Martins, Luciano. 1986. "The 'Liberalization' of Authoritarian Rule in Brazil." In Guillermo O'Donnell, Philippe Schmitter, and Laurence Whitehead, eds., *Transitions from Authoritarian Rule: Latin America.* Baltimore: Johns Hopkins University Press, pp. 72–94.

Martz, John D. 1987. *Politics and Petroleum in Ecuador.* New Brunswick: Transaction.

———. 1992. "Party Elites and Leadership in Colombia and Venezuela." *Journal of Latin American Studies* 24:87–121.

———. 1994. "Technological Elites and Political Parties: The Venezuelan Professional Community." *Latin American Research Review* 29 (1): 7–27.

———. 1997. *The Politics of Clientelism: Democracy and the State in Colombia.* New Brunswick, N.J.: Transaction.

Marx, Karl, and Friedrich Engels. 1978. *The Marx-Engels Reader.* 2nd ed. Ed. Robert C. Tucker. New York: Norton.

Mauceri, Philip. 1995. "State Reform, Coalitions, and the Neoliberal *Autogolpe* in Peru." *Latin American Research Review* 30 (1): 7–38.

Mayorga, René Antonio. 1991. *¿De la autonomía política al orden democrático?* La Paz: CEBEM.

———, coord. 1992a. *Democracia y gobernabilidad: América Latina.* Caracas: Nueva Sociedad.

———. 1992b. "Gobernabilidad en entredicho: Conflictos institucionales y sistema presidencialista." In René Antonio Mayorga, coord., *Democracia y gobernabilidad: América Latina.* Caracas: Nueva Sociedad, pp. 41–62.

———. 1994a. "Gobernabilidad y reforma política: La experiencia de Bolivia." *América Latina Hoy: Revista de Ciencias Sociales,* no. 8. Universidad Complutense de Madrid, pp. 35–60.

————. 1994b. "Neopopulist Actors and Democracy in Latin America: A Comparative Analysis of Peru, Brazil, and Bolivia." Paper presented at the Vienna Dialogue on Democracy.

————. 1995a. "Outsiders y Kataristas en el sistema de partidos, la política de pactos y la gobernabilidad en Bolivia." In Carina Perelli et al., eds., *Partidos y clase política en América Latina en los 90.* San José: IIDH/CAPEL, pp. 219–264.

————. 1995b. "Parliamentarized Presidentialism, Moderate Multiparty System, and State Transformation: The Case of Bolivia." Paper presented at the seminar "L'état en Amérique Latine: Privatisation ou redéfinition?" Institut des Hautes Études de l'Amérique Latine, Paris.

McClintock, Cynthia, and Abraham Lowenthal, eds. 1983. *The Peruvian Experiment Reconsidered.* Princeton: Princeton University Press.

McCoy, Jennifer. 1999. "Chávez and the End of 'Partyarchy' in Venezuela."*Journal of Democracy* 10 (3): 64–77.

————, ed. 2000. *Political Learning and Redemocratization in Latin America.* Miami: North-South Center Press.

McCoy, Jennifer, and Shelley McConnell. 1997. "Nicaragua: Beyond the Revolution." *Current History* 96 (607): 75–80.

McCoy, Jennifer, Andrés Serbin, William C. Smith, and Andrés Stambouli, eds. 1995. *Venezuelan Democracy Under Stress.* New Brunswick, N.J.: Transaction.

McDonald, Ronald H., and J. Mark Ruhl. 1989. *Party Politics and Elections in Latin America.* Boulder: Westview.

McGuire, James W. 1995. "Political Parties and Democracy in Argentina." In Scott Mainwaring and Timothy Scully, eds., *Building Democratic Institutions: Party Systems in Latin America.* Stanford: Stanford University Press, pp. 200–246.

McManus, Philip, and Gerald Schlabach, eds. 1991. *Relentless Persistence: Nonviolent Action in Latin America.* Philadelphia: New Society.

Meyer, Michael, and William Sherman. 1991. *The Course of Mexican History.* 4th ed. New York: Oxford University Press.

Michels, Robert. 1949. *Political Parties: A Sociological Study of the Oligarchical Tendencies of Modern Democracy.* Glencoe: Free Press.

Mieres, Pablo. 1994a. *Desobediencia y lealtad: El voto en el Uruguay de fin de siglo.* Montevideo: CLAEH.

————. 1994b. "Uruguay: Un escenario competitivo." *Nueva Sociedad* 133 (September–October): 4–12.

Mill, James. 1992. *Political Writings.* Cambridge: Cambridge University Press.

Mill, John Stuart. 1975. *Three Essays: On Liberty, Representative Government, The Subjection of Women.* London: Oxford University Press.

————. 1994. *Principles of Political Economy.* Oxford: Oxford University Press.

Miller, John. 1990. *Absolutism in Seventeenth Century Europe.* New York: St. Martin's.

Mills, C. Wright. 1956. *The Power Elite.* New York: Oxford University Press.

Mintz, Sidney W. 1995. "Can Haiti Change?" *Foreign Affairs* 74 (1): 73–86.

Miranda, Carlos R. 1990. *The Stroessner Era: Authoritarian Rule in Paraguay.* Boulder: Westview.

Monge Alfaro, Carlos. 1980. *Historia de Costa Rica.* 16th ed. San José: Trejos.

Montesquieu, Charles Louis de Secondat, Baron. 1952. *The Spirit of the Laws.* Chicago: Encyclopaedia Britannica.

Montgomery, Tommie Sue. 1995. *Revolution in El Salvador: From Civil Strife to Civil Peace.* 2nd ed. Boulder: Westview.

————. 1997. "Constructing Democracy in El Salvador." *Current History* 96 (607): 61–67.

Moore, Barrington. 1966. *Social Origins of Dictatorship and Democracy.* Boston: Beacon.

Mora Mérida, José Luis. 1981. *Paraguay y Uruguay contemporáneos.* Sevilla: Escuela de Estudios Hispano-Americanos.

Morales, Juan Antonio, and Gary McMahon, eds. 1993. *La política económica en la transición a la democracia.* Santiago: CIEPLAN.

Morris, James A. 1984. *Honduras: Caudillo Politics and Military Rulers.* Boulder: Westview.

Morris, Stephen D. 1995. *Political Reformism in Mexico: An Overview of Contemporary Mexican Politics.* Boulder: Lynne Rienner.

Mosca, Gaetano. 1939. *The Ruling Class.* New York: McGraw-Hill.

Mouffe, Chantal, ed. 1992. *Dimensions of Radical Democracy.* London: Verso.

Munck, Gerardo. 1994. "Democratic Stability and Its Limits: An Analysis of Chile's 1993 Elections." *Journal of Inter-American Studies and World Affairs* 36 (2): 1–37.

————. 2003. "Gobernabilidad democrática a comienzos del siglo XXI: una perspectiva latinoamericana." *Revista Mexicana de Sociología* 65 (3): 565–588.

Munck, Ronaldo. 1989. *Latin America: The Transition to Democracy.* London: Zed.

Muñoz Guillén, Mercedes. 1990. *El estado y la abolición del ejército, 1914–1949.* San José: Ed. Porvenir.

Muñoz Patraca, Víctor Manuel. 1994. "Transición a la democracia en México." *Revista Mexicana de Ciencias Políticas y Sociales* 39 (157) (July–September): 9–23.

Murillo, M. Victoria. 2003. "Latin American Labor." In Jorge Domínguez and Michael Shifter, eds., *Constructing Democratic Governance in Latin America.* Baltimore: Johns Hopkins University Press, pp. 100–117.

Murillo Castaño, Gabriel. 1999. "Representación, ciudadanía y nueva constitución en Colombia." *Nueva Sociedad* 160:47–55.

Myers, David J. 1986. "The Venezuelan Party System: Regime Maintenance Under Stress." In John D. Martz and David J. Myers, eds., *Venezuela: The Democratic Experience,* rev. ed. New York: Praeger, pp. 109–147.

————. 1995. "Perceptions of a Stressed Democracy: Inevitable Decay or Foundation for Rebirth?" In Jennifer McCoy, Andrés Serbin, William C. Smith, and Andrés Stambouli, eds., *Venezuelan Democracy Under Stress.* New Brunswick, N.J.: Transaction, pp. 107–138.

NACLA (North American Congress on Latin America). 1982. "Dominican Republic: The Launching of Democracy?" *Report on the Americas* 16 (6) (November–December): 2–35.

————. 1987. "Haiti: Plus ça change . . ." *Report on the Americas* 21 (3) (May–June): 14–39.

————. 1991. "Bolivia: The Poverty of Progress." *Report on the Americas* 25 (1) (July): 10–38.

————. 1994. "Haiti: Dangerous Crossroads." *Report on the Americas* 27 (4) (January–February): 15–53.

————. 1995. "Brazil: The Persistence of Inequality." *Report on the Americas* 28 (6) (May–June): 16–45.

————. 1996. "Rhetoric and Reality: The World Bank's New Concern for the Poor." *Report on the Americas* 29 (6) (May–June): 15–43.

———. 1997. "Contesting Mexico." *Report on the Americas* 30 (4) (January–February): 13–40.

Naím, Moisés. 1995. "Latin America the Morning After." *Foreign Affairs* 74 (4): 45–61.

Naím, Moisés, and Antonio Francés. 1995. "The Venezuelan Private Sector: From Courting the State to Courting the Market." In Louis W. Goodman, Johanna Mendelson Forman, Moisés Naím, Joseph Tulchin, and Gary Bland, eds., *Lessons of the Venezuelan Experience*. Baltimore: Johns Hopkins University Press.

Nash, June. 1995. "The Reassertion of Indigenous Identity: Mayan Responses to State Intervention in Chiapas." *Latin American Research Review* 30 (3): 7–42.

———. 2003. "The War of the Peace: Indigenous Women's Struggle for Social Justice in Chiapas, Mexico." In Susan Eva Eckstein and Timothy Wickham-Crowley, eds., *What Justice? Whose Justice?* Berkeley: University of California Press, pp. 285–312.

Needler, Martin C. 1987. *The Problem of Democracy in Latin America*. Lexington, Mass.: Heath.

Nef, Jorge, and Nibaldo Galleguillos. 1995. "Legislatures and Democratic Transitions in Latin America: The Chilean Case." In David Close, ed., *Legislatures and the New Democracies in Latin America*. Boulder: Lynne Rienner, pp. 113–136.

Nunn, Frederick. 1976. *The Military in Chilean History*. Albuquerque: University of New Mexico Press.

Oconitrillo, Eduardo. 1982. *Un siglo de política costarricense*. San José: Ed. Universidad Estatal a Distancia.

O'Donnell, Guillermo. 1979. *Modernization and Bureaucratic-Authoritarianism*. 2nd ed. Berkeley: Institute of International Studies, University of California.

———. 1994. "Delegative Democracy." *Journal of Democracy* 5:55–69.

———. 1996. "Illusions About Consolidation." *Journal of Democracy* 7 (2): 34–51. See also related debate in *Journal of Democracy* 7 (4): 151–168.

O'Donnell, Guillermo, and Philippe Schmitter. 1986. *Tentative Conclusions About Uncertain Democracies*. Vol. 4 of Guillermo O'Donnell, Philippe Schmitter, and Laurence Whitehead, eds., *Transitions from Authoritarian Rule*. Baltimore: Johns Hopkins University Press.

O'Donnell, Guillermo, Philippe Schmitter, and Laurence Whitehead, eds. 1986. *Transitions from Authoritarian Rule*. Baltimore: Johns Hopkins University Press.

Oppenheim, Lois Hecht. 1993. *Politics in Chile: Democracy, Authoritarianism, and the Search for Development*. Boulder: Westview.

Ortega Hegg, Manuel. 2002. "Nicaragua 2001: Un gobierno sin partido." *Nueva Sociedad* 178:4–14.

O'Shaughnessy, Laura Nuzzi, and Michael Dodson. 1999. "Political Bargaining and Democratic Transitions: A Comparison of Nicaragua and El Salvador." *Journal of Latin American Studies* 31:99–127.

Osorio, Jaime. 1990. *Raíces de la democracia en Chile, 1850–1970*. Mexico: Ediciones Era.

Ostrogorski, M. 1974. *Democracy and the Organization of Political Parties*. New York: Ayer.

Oxhorn, Philip. 1995. *Organizing Civil Society: The Popular Sectors and the Struggle for Democracy in Chile*. University Park: Pennsylvania State University Press.

Paine, Thomas. 1995. *Collected Writings*. New York: Library of America.

Palmer, David Scott. 1980. *Peru: The Authoritarian Tradition*. New York: Praeger.

Pangle, Thomas. 1992. *The Ennobling of Democracy: The Challenge of the Postmodern Era*. Baltimore: Johns Hopkins University Press.

Panizza, Francisco. 1990. *Uruguay: Batllismo y después.* Montevideo: Ediciones de la Banda Oriental.

Pareto, Vilfredo. 1984. *The Transformation of Democracy.* Ed. Charles Powers. New Brunswick, N.J.: Transaction.

Pastor, Robert, ed. 1989. *Democracy in the Americas: Stopping the Pendulum.* New York: Holmes and Meier.

———. 1992. *Whirlpool: U.S. Foreign Policy Toward Latin America and the Caribbean.* Princeton: Princeton University Press.

Paternostro, Silvana. 1995. "Mexico as a Narco-Democracy." *World Policy Journal* 12 (1) (Spring): 41–48.

Payne, Stanley. 1973. *A History of Spain and Portugal.* 2 vols. Madison: University of Wisconsin Press.

Paz Aguilar, Ernesto. 1992. "The Origin and Development of Political Parties in Honduras." In Louis W. Goodman, William LeoGrande, and Johanna Mendelson Forman, eds., *Political Parties and Democracy in Central America.* Boulder: Westview, pp. 161–174.

Peckenham, Nancy, and Annie Street, eds. 1985. *Honduras: Portrait of a Captive Nation.* New York: Praeger.

Peeler, John A. 1976. "Colombian Parties and Political Development." *Journal of Interamerican Studies and World Affairs* 18:203–224.

———. 1985. *Latin American Democracies: Colombia, Costa Rica, Venezuela.* Chapel Hill: University of North Carolina Press.

———. 1992. "Elite Settlements and Democratic Consolidation: Colombia, Costa Rica, and Venezuela." In John Higley and Richard Gunther, eds., *Elites and Democratic Consolidation in Latin America and Southern Europe.* Cambridge: Cambridge University Press, pp. 81–112.

———. 1999. "La política de élites y la política económica: La democrácia en Costa Rica y Venezuela." *América Latina* 21 (April 1999): 113–126.

———. 2001. "Elites, Structures, and Political Action in Latin America." *International Review of Sociology* 11 (2): 233–248.

———. 2003a. "Citizenship and Difference in Latin American Indigenous Politics: Democratic Theory and Comparative Politics." In Jennifer Holmes, ed., *New Approaches to Comparative Politics: Insights from Political Theory.* Lanham, Md.: Lexington Books, pp. 65–82.

———. 2003b. "Costa Rica: Neither Client nor Defiant." In Frank Mora and Jeanne Hey, eds., *Latin American and Caribbean Foreign Policy.* Lanham, Md.: Rowman and Littlefield.

———. 2003c. "Elementos estructurales de la desestabilización de una democracia consolidada: La desconsolidación en Venezuela." Paper presented at the symposium "Venezuela en la Encrucijada," Instituto Ibero-Americano, Berlin, 2003.

———. 2003d. "Social Justice and the New Indigenous Politics: An Analysis of Guatemala, the Central Andes, and Chiapas." In Susan Eva Eckstein and Timothy Wickham-Crowley, eds., *What Justice? Whose Justice?* Berkeley: University of California Press, pp. 257–284.

Pereira, Anthony. 2003. "Brazil's Agrarian Reform: Democratic Innovation or Oligarchic Exclusion Redux?" *Latin American Politics and Society* 45 (2) (Summer): 41–65.

Perelli, Carina, Sonia Picado, and Daniel Zovatto, eds. 1995. *Partidos y clase política en América Latina en los 90.* San José: IIDH/CAPEL.

Pérez, Louis. 1995. *Cuba: Between Reform and Revolution.* 2nd ed. New York: Oxford University Press.

Pérez, Orlando. 1995. "Elections Under Crisis: Background to Panama in the 1980s." In Mitchell A. Seligson and John A. Booth, eds., *Elections and Democracy in Central America Revisited*. Chapel Hill: University of North Carolina Press, pp. 123–147.

Pérez Brignoli, Héctor. 1987. *Breve historia de Centroamérica*. Madrid: Alianza.

Pérez Herrero, Pedro. 2001. "Mexico After the Elections of July 2, 2000." *Mexican Studies/Estudios Mexicanos* 17 (2): 283–297.

Pérez-Stable, Marifeli. 1999. *The Cuban Revolution: Origins, Course, and Legacy,* 2nd ed. New York: Oxford University Press.

Peruzzotti, Enrique. 2001. "The Nature of the New Argentine Democracy: The Delegative Democracy Argument Revisited." *Journal of Latin American Studies* 33: 133–155.

Petras, James. 1969. *Politics and Social Forces in Chilean Development*. Berkeley: University of California Press.

Petras, James, and Fernando Ignacio Leiva, with Henry Veltmeyer. 1994. *Democracy and Poverty in Chile: The Limits to Electoral Politics*. Boulder: Westview.

Phelan, John. 1978. *The People and the King: The Comunero Revolt in Colombia, 1781*. Madison: University of Wisconsin Press.

Pimenta, Cornelio Octavio Pinheiro. 1989–1990. "Estudo comparativo da Constituição de 1988." *Revista de Ciencia Politica*, pt. 1, 32 (3) (May–July 1989): 67–93; pt. 2, 32 (4) (August–October 1989): 123–169; pt. 3, 33 (1) (November 1989–January 1990): 102–152.

Pizarro, Eduardo, and Ana María Bejarano. 1994. "Colombia: Neoliberalismo moderado y liberalismo socialdemócratica." *Nueva Sociedad* 133 (September–October): 12–19.

Pizarro Leongómez, Eduardo. 2003. "Colombia: El proyecto de seguridad democrática de Alvaro Uribe." *Nueva Sociedad* 186 (July–August): 4–17.

Plato. 1983. *The Republic*. Trans. Benjamin Jowett. New York: Random House.

Pole, J. R., ed. 1987. *The American Constitution, For and Against: The Federalist and Anti-Federalist Papers*. New York: Hill and Wang.

Polity Forum. 1995. "Institutions and Institutionalism." *Polity* 28:81–140.

Pottenger, John. 1989. *The Political Theory of Liberation Theology*. Albany: State University of New York Press.

Prevost, Gary. 1991. "The FSLN as Ruling Party." In Thomas W. Walker, ed., *Revolution and Counterrevolution in Nicaragua*. Boulder: Westview, pp. 101–116.

Priestley, George. 1986. *Military Government and Popular Participation in Panama: The Torrijos Regime, 1968–1975*. Boulder: Westview.

Przeworski, Adam. 1991. *Democracy and the Market: Political and Economic Reforms in Eastern Europe and Latin America*. Cambridge: Cambridge University Press.

Przeworski, Adam, et al. 1996. "What Makes Democracies Endure?" *Journal of Democracy* 7 (1): 39–55.

Puryear, Jeffrey. 1994. *Thinking Politics: Intellectuals and Democracy in Chile, 1973–1988*. Baltimore: Johns Hopkins University Press.

Putnam, Robert. 1993. *Making Democracy Work: Civic Traditions in Modern Italy*. Princeton: Princeton University Press.

Quiroga, Hugo. 1993. "Los derechos humanos en la Argentina: Entre el realismo politico y la ética." *Cuadernos Hispanoamericanos* 517–519 (July–September): 123–130.

Ramírez Necochea, Hernán. 1985. *Fuerzas armadas y política en Chile*. Havana: Casa de las Américas.

Ramos, Carlos Guillermo. 1998. "El Salvador: Transición y procesos electorales a fines de los 90." *Nueva Sociedad* 158:28–39.

Ramos Jiménez, Alfredo. 2001. "Viejo y nuevo: Partidos y sistemas de partidos en las democracies andinas." *Nueva Sociedad* 173:65–75.

Ramos Rollón, Marisa, ed. 2002. *Venezuela: Rupturas y continuidades del sistema politico (1999–2001)*. Salamanca: Ediciones Universidad de Salamanca.

Reiter, Frederick. 1995. *They Built Utopia: The Jesuit Missions in Paraguay, 1610–1768*. Potomac, Md.: Scripta Humanistica.

Remmer, Karen. 1984. *Party Competition in Argentina and Chile*. Lincoln: University of Nebraska Press.

———. 1990. "Democracy and Economic Crisis: The Latin American Experience." *World Politics* 42:315–335.

———. 1991a. "New Wine or Old Bottlenecks? The Study of Latin American Democracy." *Comparative Politics* 23:479–495.

———. 1991b. "The Political Impact of Economic Crisis in Latin America in the 1980s." *American Political Science Review* 85:777–800.

———. 1993. "The Political Economy of Elections in Latin America, 1980–1991." *American Political Science Review* 87:393–407.

Restrepo, Darío. 1992. "El trasfondo político de la constitución política de Colombia." *Revista Interamericana de Planificación* 25 (99–100) (July–December): 17–43.

Rial, Juan. 1986. "The Uruguayan Elections of 1984: A Triumph of the Center." In Paul Drake and Eduardo Silva, eds., *Elections and Democratization in Latin America, 1980–1985*. San Diego: Center for Iberian and Latin American Studies, pp. 245–272.

Richard, Patricia Bayer, and John A. Booth. 1995. "Election Observation and Democratization: Reflections on the Nicaraguan Case." In Mitchell A. Seligson and John A. Booth, eds., *Elections and Democracy in Central America Revisited*. Chapel Hill: University of North Carolina Press, pp. 202–223.

Rizzo de Oliveira, Eliézer. 1988. "O papel das forças armadas na nova constituição e no futuro da democracia no Brasil." *Vozes* 82 (2) (July–December): 21–27.

Roberts, Kenneth. 2002. "Party-Society Linkages and Democratic Representation in Latin America." *Canadian Journal of Latin American and Caribbean Studies* 27 (53): 9–34.

Rock, David. 1987. *Argentina, 1516–1987*. Berkeley: University of California Press.

Roett, Riordan. 1992. *Brazil: Politics in a Patrimonial Society*. 4th ed. New York: Praeger.

———, ed. 1995. *The Challenge of Institutional Reform in Mexico*. Boulder: Lynne Rienner.

———. 1997. "Brazilian Politics at Century's End." In Susan Kaufman Purcell and Riordan Roett, eds., *Brazil Under Cardoso*. Boulder: Lynne Rienner, pp. 19–42.

Roett, Riordan, and Richard Scott Sacks. 1991. *Paraguay: The Personalist Legacy*. Boulder: Westview.

Rojas Aravena, Francisco, and Luis Guillermo Solís. 1988. *¿Súbditos o aliados? La política exterior de Estados Unidos y Centroamérica*. San José: FLACSO.

Rojas Bolaños, Manuel, and Carlos Sojo. 1995. *El malestar con la política*. San José: FLACSO.

Ropp, Steve C. 1982. *Panamanian Politics*. New York: Praeger.

———. 1996. "Panama: Cycles of Elitist Democracy and Authoritarian Populism." In Howard Wiarda and Harvey Kline, eds., *Latin American Politics and Development*, 4th ed. Boulder: Westview, pp. 507–517.

―――. 1997. "Panama: Tailoring a New Image." *Current History* 96 (607) (February): 55–60.

Rosada Granados, Héctor. 1992. "Parties, Transitions, and the Political System in Guatemala." In Louis W. Goodman, William LeoGrande, and Johanna Mendelson Forman, eds., *Political Parties and Democracy in Central America*. Boulder: Westview, pp. 89–110.

Rosenberg, Mark. 1989. "Can Democracy Survive the Democrats? From Transition to Consolidation in Honduras." In John A. Booth and Mitchell A. Seligson, eds., *Elections and Democracy in Central America*. Chapel Hill: University of North Carolina Press, pp. 40–59.

―――. 1995. "Democracy in Honduras: The Electoral and the Political Reality." In Mitchell A. Seligson and John A. Booth, eds., *Elections and Democracy in Central America Revisited*. Chapel Hill: University of North Carolina Press, pp. 66–83.

Rottenberg, Simon, ed. 1993. *Costa Rica and Uruguay*. New York: World Bank.

Rouquié, Alain. 1990. *Extremo occidente: Introducción a América Latina*. Buenos Aires: Emecé.

―――. 1994. *Autoritarismos y democracia: Estudios de política argentina*. Buenos Aires: Edicial.

Rovira Mas, Jorge. 1988. *Estado y política económica en Costa Rica, 1948–1970*. San José: Ed. Porvenir.

―――. 1992. "Elecciones y democracia en Centroamérica y República Dominicana: Un análisis introductorio." In Rodolfo Cerdas Cruz, Juan Rial, and Daniel Zovatto, eds., *Una tarea inconclusa: Elecciones y democracia en América Latina, 1988–1991*. San José: Instituto Interamericano de Derechos Humanos/Centro de Asesoría y Promoción Electoral.

―――. 1994. "Costa Rica 1994: ¿Hacia la consolidación del bipartidismo?" *Espacios: Revista Centroamericana de Cultura Política* 7 (July–September): 38–47.

―――, ed. 2001a. *La democracia de Costa Rica ante el siglo XXI*. San José: Editorial de la Universidad de Costa Rica.

―――. 2001b. "¿Se debilita el bipartidismo?" In Jorge Rovira Mas, ed., *La democracia de Costa Rica ante el siglo XXI*. San José: Editorial de la Universidad de Costa Rica, pp. 195–232.

Ruchwarger, Gary. 1987. *People in Power: Forging a Grassroots Democracy in Nicaragua*. South Hadley, Mass.: Bergin and Garvey.

Rudolph, James D. 1992. *Peru: The Evolution of a Crisis*. Westport, Conn.: Praeger.

Rueschemeyer, Dietrich, Evelyne Huber Stephens, and John Stephens. 1992. *Capitalist Development and Democracy*. Chicago: University of Chicago Press.

Ruhl, J. Mark. 1997. "Doubting Democracy in Honduras." *Current History* 96 (607) (February): 81–86.

Sabatini, Christopher. 2003. "Decentralization and Political Parties." *Journal of Democracy* 14 (2) (April): 138–150.

Saffirio S., Eduardo. 1994. "El sistema de partidos y la sociedad civil en la redemocratización chilena." *Estudios Sociales* 82 (October–December): 63–113.

Saint-Upéry, Marc. 2002. "Ecuador: El coronel tiene quien le escuche." *Nueva Sociedad* 182 (November–December): 4–11.

Salcedo-Bastardo, J. L. 1979. *Historia fundamental de Venezuela*. Caracas: Fundación Gran Mariscal de Ayacucho.

Salom, Roberto. 1987. *La crisis de la izquierda en Costa Rica*. San José: Ed. Porvenir.

Sánchez Parga, José. 1993. "Ecuador en el engranaje neoliberal." *Nueva Sociedad* 123 (January–February): 12–17.

Schemo, Diana Jean. 1997. "Ecuadorian Crisis over Presidency Ends Peacefully." *New York Times,* Internet edition, 10 February.

Schifter, Jacobo. 1979. *La fase oculta de la guerra civil en Costa Rica.* San José: EDUCA.

———. 1986. *Las alianzas conflictivas.* San José: Libro Libre.

Schlesinger, Stephen, and Stephen Kinzer. 1982. *Bitter Fruit: The Untold Story of the American Coup in Guatemala.* Garden City, N.Y.: Anchor.

Schmidt, Gregory. 1996. "Fujimori's 1990 Upset Victory in Peru: Electoral Rules, Contingencies, and Adaptive Strategies." *Comparative Politics* 28 (April): 321–354.

Schmidt, Samuel. 1986. *El deterioro del presidencialismo mexicano: Los años de Luis Echeverría.* México: Edamex.

Schneider, Ronald. 1996. *Brazil: Culture and Politics in a New Industrial Powerhouse.* Boulder: Westview.

Schoultz, Lars. 1981. *Human Rights and United States Policy Toward Latin America.* Princeton: Princeton University Press.

———. 1987. *National Security and United States Policy Toward Latin America.* Princeton: Princeton University Press.

———. 1998. *Beneath the United States: A History of U.S. Policy Toward Latin America.* Cambridge: Harvard University Press.

Schumpeter, Joseph. 1950. *Capitalism, Socialism, and Democracy.* 3rd ed. New York: Harper.

Scully, Timothy R. 1992. *Rethinking the Center: Party Politics in Nineteenth- and Twentieth-Century Chile.* Stanford: Stanford University Press.

———. 1995. "Reconstituting Party Politics in Chile." In Scott Mainwaring and Timothy Scully, eds., *Building Democratic Institutions: Party Systems in Latin America.* Stanford: Stanford University Press, pp. 100–137.

Seligson, Mitchell. 2000. "Toward a Model of Democratic Stability: Political Culture in Central America." *Estudios Interdisciplinarios de América Latina y el Caribe* 11 (2): 5–29.

———. 2002. *Auditoría de la democracia: Ecuador.* Pittsburgh: University of Pittsburgh.

———. 2003. *Auditoría de la democracia: Bolivia.* Pittsburgh: University of Pittsburgh.

Seligson, Mitchell A., and John A. Booth, eds. 1995. *Elections and Democracy in Central America Revisited.* Chapel Hill: University of North Carolina Press.

Selverston-Scher, Melina. 2001. *Ethnopolitics in Ecuador: Indigenous Rights and the Strengthening of Democracy.* Miami: North-South Center Press.

Sharpless, Richard. 1978. *Gaitán of Colombia: A Political Biography.* Pittsburgh: University of Pittsburgh Press.

Silva Michelena, José A. 1971. *The Illusion of Democracy in Dependent Nations.* Vol. 3 of Frank Bonilla and Silva Michelena, eds., *The Politics of Change in Venezuela.* Cambridge: Massachusetts Institute of Technology Press.

Simons, Geoff. 1996. *Cuba: From Conquistadors to Castro.* New York: St. Martin's.

Skocpol, Theda. 1994. *Social Revolutions in the Modern World.* Cambridge: Cambridge University Press.

Small, Melvin, and William Hoover, eds. 1992. *Give Peace a Chance: Exploring the Vietnam Antiwar Movement.* Syracuse: Syracuse University Press.

Smith, Adam. 1952. *An Inquiry into the Nature and Causes of the Wealth of Nations.* Chicago: Encyclopaedia Britannica.

Smith, David. 1992. "Panama: Political Parties, Social Crisis, and Democracy in the 1980s." In Louis W. Goodman, William LeoGrande, and Johanna Mendelson Forman, eds., *Political Parties and Democracy in Central America*. Boulder: Westview, pp. 213–233.

Smith, William C., Carlos H. Acuña, and Eduardo A. Gamarra, eds. 1994a. *Democracy, Markets, and Structural Reform in Latin America: Argentina, Bolivia, Brazil, Chile, and Mexico*. New Brunswick, N.J.: Transaction.

———. 1994b. *Latin American Political Economy in the Age of Neoliberal Reform*. New Brunswick, N.J.: Transaction.

Soares, Glaucio Ary Dillon. 1986. "Elections and the Redemocratization of Brazil." In Paul Drake and Eduardo Silva, eds., *Elections and Democratization in Latin America, 1980–1985*. San Diego: Center for Iberian and Latin American Studies, pp. 273–298.

Spinoza, Benedict de. 1951. *Chief Works*. 2 vols. New York: Dover.

Stallings, Barbara, and Robert Kaufman, eds. 1989. *Debt and Democracy in Latin America*. Boulder: Westview.

Stein, Eduardo, and Salvador Arias Peñate, coords. 1992. *Democracia sin pobreza: Alternativa de desarrollo para el istmo centroamericano*. San José: DEI.

Stepan, Alfred. 1978. *The State and Society: Peru in Comparative Perspective*. Princeton: Princeton University Press.

———. 1988. *Rethinking Military Politics: Brazil and the Southern Cone*. Princeton University Press.

———, ed. 1989. *Democratizing Brazil: Problems of Transition and Consolidation*. New York: Oxford University Press.

Stepan, Alfred, and Cindy Skach. 1993. "Constitutional Frameworks and Democratic Consolidation: Parliamentarism Versus Presidentialism." *World Politics* 46:1–22.

Stephen, Lynn. 1995. "The Zapatista Army of National Liberation and the National Democratic Convention." *Latin American Perspectives* 22 (4): 88–100.

Stokes, Susan. 1997. "Democratic Accountability and Policy Change: Economic Policy in Fujimori's Peru." *Comparative Politics* 29:209–228.

Stone, Samuel. 1975. *La dinastía de los conquistadores: La crisis de poder en la Costa Rica contemporánea*. San José: Ed. Universidad de Costa Rica.

Tarrow, Sidney. 1994. *Power in Movement: Social Movements, Collective Action, and Politics*. Cambridge: Cambridge University Press.

Thibaut, Bernard. 1993. "Presidencialismo, parlamentarismo y el problema de la consolidación democrática en América Latina." *Estudios Internacionales* 26 (102) (April–June): 216–252.

Thoumi, Francisco. 1995. *Political Economy and Illegal Drugs in Colombia*. Boulder: Lynne Rienner.

Tirado López, Victor. 1986. *Nicaragua: Una nueva democracia en el tercer mundo*. Managua: Vanguardia.

Tocqueville, Alexis de. 1980. *Alexis de Tocqueville on Democracy, Revolution, and Society: Selected Writings*. Eds. John Stone and Stephen Mennell. Chicago: University of Chicago Press.

———. 1988. *Democracy in America*. New York: Harper and Row.

Tonkin, John. 1971. *The Church and the Secular Order in Reformation Thought*. New York: Columbia University Press.

Tönnies, Ferdinand. 1971. *Ferdinand Tönnies on Sociology*. Chicago: University of Chicago Press.

Toranzo Roca, Carlos. 2002. "Bolivia: Nuevo escenario politico." *Nueva Sociedad* 182:12–20.

Torres, Rosa María, and José Luis Coraggio. 1987. *Transición y crisis en Nicaragua*. San José: DEI.

Torres Calderón, Manuel. 2003. "Honduras ¿Transición hacia dónde?" *Nueva Sociedad* 185:15–22.

Torres Rivas, Edelberto. 1993. *History and Society in Central America*. Austin: University of Texas Press.

Truman, David. 1951. *The Governmental Process: Political Interests and Public Opinion*. New York: Knopf.

Tucker, Robert C., ed. 1978. *The Marx-Engels Reader*. 2nd ed. New York: Norton.

Tulchin, Joseph, ed. 1995. *The Consolidation of Democracy in Latin America*. Boulder: Lynne Rienner.

United Nations Development Programme. 1991. *Human Development Report*. New York: Oxford University Press.

———. 1996. *Human Development Report*. New York: Oxford University Press.

———. 2002. *Human Development Report*. New York: Oxford University Press.

Vacs, Aldo C. 1987. "Authoritarian Breakdown and Redemocratization in Argentina." In James Malloy and Mitchell Seligson, eds., *Authoritarians and Democrats: Regime Transition in Latin America*. Pittsburgh: University of Pittsburgh Press, pp. 15–42.

Valenzuela, Arturo. 1978. *The Breakdown of Democratic Regimes: Chile*. Baltimore: Johns Hopkins University Press.

———. 1989. "Chile: Origins, Consolidation, and Breakdown of a Democratic Regime." In Larry Diamond, Juan J. Linz, and Seymour Martin Lipset, eds., *Democracy in Developing Countries*. Boulder: Lynne Rienner, pp. 159–206.

Valenzuela, Arturo, and J. Samuel Valenzuela, eds. 1986. *Military Rule in Chile: Dictatorship and Oppositions*. Baltimore: Johns Hopkins University Press.

Van Parijs, Philippe. 1995. *Real Freedom for All: What (If Anything) Can Justify Capitalism?* Oxford: Clarendon.

Vanger, Milton. 1980. *The Model Country: José Batlle y Ordóñez of Uruguay, 1907–1915*. Hanover, N.H.: University Press of New England.

Vanhanen, Tatu. 1994. "Global Trends of Democratization in the 1990s: A Statistical Analysis." Paper presented at the International Political Science Association meeting, Berlin.

Vargas, Oscar René. 1995. "Nicaragua: Peligra la consolidación democrática." *Nueva Sociedad* 137:10–16.

Veblen, Thorstein. 1934. *The Theory of the Leisure Class*. New York: Modern Library.

Vega Carballo, José Luis. 1982. *Poder político y democracia en Costa Rica*. San José: Ed. Porvenir.

———. 1992. "Party Systems and Democracy in Costa Rica." In Louis W. Goodman, William LeoGrande, and Johanna Mendelson Forman, eds., *Political Parties and Democracy in Central America*. Boulder: Westview, pp. 203–212.

Vélez Rodríguez, Ricardo. 1987. "Constituinte e Tradições Politicas Brasileiras." *Convivium* 30 (2) (March–April): 150–161.

Véliz, Claudio. 1980. *The Centralist Tradition of Latin America*. Princeton: Princeton University Press.

Vilas, Carlos. 1995a. "Economic Restructuring, Neoliberal Reforms, and the Working Class in Latin America." In Sandor Halebsky and Richard Harris, eds., *Capital, Power, and Inequality in Latin America*. Boulder: Westview, pp. 137–164.

———, coord. 1995b. *Estado y políticas sociales después del ajuste*. Caracas: Nueva Sociedad.

von Mettenheim, Kurt, ed. 1997. *Presidential Institutions and Democratic Politics: Comparing Regional and National Contexts*. Baltimore: Johns Hopkins University Press.

Vunderink, Gregg. 1991. "Peasant Participation and Mobilization During Economic Crisis: The Case of Costa Rica." *Studies in Comparative International Development* 25 (4): 3–34.

Wahl, Rainer. 1986. "A primazia da constituição." *Revista de Ciencia Politica* 29 (3) (July–September): 9–34.

Waisman, Carlos. 1992. "Capitalism, the Market, and Democracy." In Gary Marks and Larry Diamond, eds., *Reexamining Democracy*. Newbury Park, Calif.: Sage, pp. 140–155.

Walker, Thomas W., ed. 1986. *Nicaragua: The First Five Years*. New York: Praeger.

———. 1991. *Revolution and Counterrevolution in Nicaragua*. Boulder: Westview.

———. 1997. *Nicaragua Without Illusions*. Wilmington, Del.: Scholarly Resources.

———. 2003. *Nicaragua: Living in the Shadow of the Eagle*. Boulder: Westview.

Walton, John. 1984. *Reluctant Rebels: Comparative Studies of Revolution and Underdevelopment*. New York: Columbia University Press.

Walzer, Michael. 1965. *The Revolution of the Saints: A Study in the Evolution of Radical Politics*. Cambridge: Harvard University Press.

Warren, Kay. 1998. *Indigenous Movements and Their Critics*. Princeton: Princeton University Press.

Weaver, Eric, and William Barnes. 1991. "Opposition Parties and Coalitions." In Thomas W. Walker, ed., *Revolution and Counterrevolution in Nicaragua*. Boulder: Westview, pp. 117–142.

Weaver, Frederick Stirton. 1994. *Inside the Volcano: The History and Political Economy of Central America*. Boulder: Westview.

Weber, Max. 1983. *Max Weber on Capitalism, Bureaucracy, and Religion*. Ed. Stanislav Andreski. London: Allen and Unwin.

Weeks, John. 1995. "The Contemporary Latin American Economies: Neoliberal Reconstruction." In Sandor Halebsky and Richard Harris, eds., *Capital, Power, and Inequality in Latin America*. Boulder: Westview, pp. 109–136.

Weinstein, Martin. 1988. *Uruguay: Democracy at the Crossroads*. Boulder: Westview.

———. 1995. "Uruguay: The Legislature and the Reconstitution of Democracy." In David Close, ed., *Legislatures and the New Democracies in Latin America*. Boulder: Lynne Rienner, pp. 137–150.

Weyland, Kurt. 2001. "Limitations of Rational-Choice Institutionalism for the Study of Latin American Politics." *Studies in Comparative International Development* 37 (1): 57–85.

———. 2002. *The Politics of Market Reform in Fragile Democracies*. Princeton: Princeton University Press.

Whitehead, Laurence. 1994. "Liberalización económica y consolidación de la democracia." In Georges Couffignal, comp., *Democracias posibles: El desafío latinoamericano*. Buenos Aires: Fondo de Cultura Económica, pp. 129–148.

———, ed. 1996. *The International Dimensions of Democratization: Europe and the Americas*. Oxford: Oxford University Press.

Wiarda, Howard. 1990. *The Democratic Revolution in Latin America: History, Politics, and U.S. Policy*. New York: Holmes and Meier.

———, ed. 1992. *Politics and Social Change in Latin America: Still a Distinct Tradition?* Boulder: Westview.

Wickham-Crowley, Timothy. 1991. *Exploring Revolution: Essays on Latin American Insurgency and Revolutionary Theory*. Armonk, N.Y.: M. E. Sharpe.

———. 1992. *Guerrillas and Revolution in Latin America: A Comparative Study of Insurgents and Regimes Since 1956.* Princeton: Princeton University Press.

Wilkinson, Bertie, ed. 1972. *The Creation of Medieval Parliaments.* New York: Wiley.

Williams, Eric. 1984. *From Columbus to Castro: The History of the Caribbean.* New York: Vintage.

Williams, Philip J. 1994. "Dual Transitions from Authoritarian Rule: Popular and Electoral Democracy in Nicaragua." *Comparative Politics* 26:169–185.

Williamson, Edwin. 1992. *The Penguin History of Latin America.* London: Penguin.

Williamson, John, ed. 1990. *Latin American Adjustment: How Much Has Happened?* Washington: Institute for International Economics.

Wilson, Bruce. 1998. *Costa Rica: Politics, Economics, and Democracy.* Boulder: Lynne Rienner.

Wilson, Woodrow. 1885. *Congressional Government.* Boston: Houghton Mifflin.

Winson, Anthony. 1989. *Coffee and Democracy in Modern Costa Rica.* New York: St. Martin's.

Woldenburg, José. 1995. "México: Los partidos en un momento de transición política." In Carina Perelli et al., eds., *Partidos y clase política en América Latina en los 90.* San José: IIDH/CAPEL, pp. 415–436.

Wollstonecraft, Mary. 1929. *A Vindication of the Rights of Woman.* New York: Dutton.

Womack, John, ed. 1999. *Rebellion in Chiapas: An Historical Reader.* New York: New Press.

Woodward, Ralph Lee. 1993. *Rafael Carrera and the Emergence of the Republic of Guatemala.* Athens: University of Georgia Press.

World Bank. 1991. *World Development Report: The Challenge of Development.* New York: Oxford University Press.

Wynia, Gary W. 1986. *Argentina: Illusions and Realities.* New York: Holmes and Meier.

———. 1995. "Argentina's New Democracy: Presidential Power and Legislative Limits." In David Close, ed., *Legislatures and the New Democracies in Latin America.* Boulder: Lynne Rienner, pp. 71–88.

Yashar, Deborah. 1995. "Civil War and Social Welfare: The Origins of Costa Rica's Competitive Party System." In Scott Mainwaring and Timothy Scully, eds., *Building Democratic Institutions: Party Systems in Latin America.* Stanford: Stanford University Press, pp. 72–99.

———. 1997. *Demanding Democracy: Reform and Reaction in Costa Rica and Guatemala, 1870s–1950s.* Stanford: Stanford University Press.

———. 1998. "Contesting Citizenship: Indigenous Movements and Democracy in Latin America." *Comparative Politics* 31:23–42.

Zamora, Rubén. 2003. "El Salvador en la encrucijada: ¿Alternabilidad o continuidad?" *Nueva Sociedad* 186 (July–August): 18–27.

Zeitlin, Maurice. 1984. *The Civil Wars in Chile.* Princeton: Princeton University Press.

Zeitlin, Maurice, and Richard Ratcliff. 1988. *Landlords and Capitalists: The Dominant Class of Chile.* Princeton: Princeton University Press.

Zermeño, Sergio. 1995. "Zapatismo: Región y nación." *Nueva Sociedad* 140 (November–December): 51–57.

Index

About the Book

Providing a comprehensive, comparative analysis of the democratic experience in Latin America, the second edition of this widely acclaimed book reflects important new developments both in the region and in the literature on democracy.

John Peeler is professor of political science at Bucknell University. His publications include *Latin American Democracies: Colombia, Costa Rica, and Venezuela.*